télescope

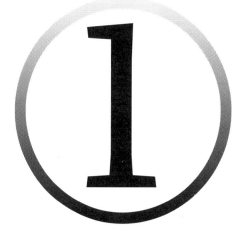

Ian Maun
Richard Marsden

Consultants:
Ian Bauckham
Iain Mitchell
Maureen Raud

ICT consultant:
Anne Looney

teacher's guide

JOHN MURRAY

Acknowledgements

The authors and publishers would like to thank the following for their contributions to the recording:

Patricia Benadiba, Bipin, Jean-Pierre Blanchard, Evelyne Celerien, Philippe Cruard, Rupert Degas, Webber Emile, Nicolas Fournier, Pauline Lockwood, Catherine Lecavalier, Joachim Marcerno, Wilford Marous, Marie-Laure Moisset, Francilien Paul, Jean-Luc Rebaldi, Tangui Rohan, Carole Rousseau, Vanessa Seydoux, Philippe Smolokowski, Jean Tox, Jeanne Weber.

Audio material recorded and produced by John Green/TEFL tapes

First published 2001
by John Murray (Publishers) Ltd
50 Albemarle Street
London W1S 4BD

Reprinted 2005

Layouts by Jenny Fleet
Typeset in Great Britain by Wearset, Boldon, Tyne and Wear
Printed and bound in Great Britain by Athenaeum Press Ltd., Gateshead, Tyne & Wear
A CIP catalogue record for this book is available from the British Library

ISBN 0 7195 7827 2
Student's Book 0 7195 7826 4
Teacher's Repromaster Book 0 7195 7828 0
Audio on cassette 0 7195 7847 7
Audio on CD 0 7195 7848 5

Contents

Unité 1   **Je m'amuse**   *1*

Language skills
- using the present tense of regular *-er* verbs
- using the present tense of reflexive verbs
- using *avoir* and *être* (present tense)
- saying when and how often you do something
- using adjectives to describe people and things
- using imperatives

Finding out about . . .
- leisure time in France
- music celebrities and their
  leisure interests

Unité 2   **En forme!**   **10**

Language skills
- using high numbers
- making comparisons
- recognising masculine and feminine nouns
- using the perfect tense with *avoir*
- using the verb *passer* with *à* to say how much time
  you spend on something
- using *on*
- using *il faut* and *devoir*

Finding out about . . .
- popular sports in France
- sports personalities
- record holders
- fitness and exercise
- healthy lifestyles

Unité 3   **Boulot**   **21**

Language skills
- using *pouvoir* and *savoir*
- using *aller*, *vouloir* and *espérer* to say what you
  intend to do
- using the perfect tense with *être*
- making comparisons using adverbs
- using possessive adjectives: *mon*, *ton*, *son*

Finding out about . . .
- the school system in France
- jobs in France
- a French CV
- French business letters and
  job applications
- voluntary work and organisations

Unité 4   **Communications**   **34**

Language skills
- using direct object pronouns
- using the present tense of *finir* and *dire*
- using the perfect tense with *être*
- using indirect object pronouns: *lui* and *leur*
- using negatives: *ne . . . jamais* and *ne . . . plus*

Finding out about . . .
- TV in France
- radio in France
- using the Internet
- multimedia
- French newspapers and magazines

Unité 5   **Allons-y! Le Québec**   **47**

This unit uses the language skills practised so far to explore
the French-speaking Canadian province, Quebec.

Unité 6   **Le grand départ**   **51**

Language skills
- using *à* and *en* to talk about places
- using *du . . . au . . .* to talk about dates
- using *-re* verbs in the present tense
- using the verbs *prendre* and *mettre*
- using *qui* and *que* to say 'the x which/who/that'
- asking questions using *quel* and *lequel*
- using *celui*, *celle*, *ceux*, *celles* to say 'this one, that one'

Finding out about . . .
- French holiday
  destinations
- hotels and camping in France
- holiday activities
- safety advice on a French beach
- giving/accepting/
  rejecting invitations

Unité 7   **La France en huit jours**   **66**

Language skills
- using prepositions: *de, à, en, entre, dans* to talk about time
- using the verb *venir* and others like it
- using the perfect tense with pronouns
- using the pronoun *y*
- using strong pronouns *moi, toi*, etc.

Finding out about . . .
- the Channel Tunnel,
  Eurostar, Le Shuttle
- travelling by French train and Métro
- car hire and driving on French roads
- cycle hire in France and
  the *Tour de France*
- air travel in France
- regions of France

Contents

Introduction

Aims and approaches of Télescope

AIMS

The aim of *Télescope* is to make the study of French:

- interesting at a level that suits the maturity of the students;
- a progressive learning experience, so that students really feel that their understanding and skills are increasing as they progress through the course.

An **understanding of the structures** of the language and **the ability to apply them** in different contexts are the main objectives of the course as a whole. The **contexts** in which this is done have been chosen on the basis of two simple criteria:

- will this context interest and motivate the students?
- will this context provide a memorable setting for the learning of a new structure?

APPROACHES

The approaches we have used are as follows.

1 **Grammar is explained in English** on the pages of the units, making comparisons, where useful, with English structures and drawing on literacy studies.
2 **Understanding, not just practice,** is integral to all the tasks.
3 To **sustain students' interest** we've used among other things:
   - an experience of discovery – learning facts through the medium of French;
   - 'Recreational Units' (see below);
   - a Quiz and a Test at the end of each unit;
   - a strong ICT strand, with frequent use of website sources and e-mail for reading/writing (plus specific, practical ICT ideas in the Teaching Notes).
4 With an awareness of the need to **motivate boys** learning French (and suspecting that if this is successfully achieved, girls will benefit too), we've gone for:
   - a 'factual' topic focus, limiting the space given to 'feminine' topics such as shopping or relationships;
   - less emphasis on talking about one's own feelings, and more on the expression of opinions about more objective matters.

Structure of the Student's Book

There are 14 units in total. Eleven of these are Teaching Units, through which:

- new language is introduced;
- new information and contexts are presented;
- previously learned language is revisited.

These units all work in double-page spreads.

The other three units (5, 10 and 14) are intended as Recreational Units; in other words, they are designed to be as enjoyable as possible, with the tasks having a game-like format and no new language points being introduced. These units are four pages each.

At the end of the Student's Book is a **Grammar Reference section**, and a two-way **vocabulary list**.

WHAT'S IN A TEACHING UNIT?

Each unit starts with two sets of goals: the **language skills** and the **areas of knowledge** that will be developed. At the end of each unit, the final pages recap and check achievement of these goals by means of a **Test** and a **Quiz**, respectively.

Within the units, the following are regular feature headings:

- **Point grammaire** – always in a green box, these are where new language structures are presented and explained and they are the core focal point of most spreads, being used together with the text as the point of reference for all the surrounding tasks.
- **Tips** – these are reminders about language pitfalls, French usage, and sometimes cultural points
- **Ça se dit comment?** – pronunciation tips.

Texts are presented in a range of formats but some appear on a regular basis: *Le Quotidien* is the vehicle for newspaper items such as reports, classified ads, and some advice letters; *Radio Corsaire* is the means of including some journalistic listening items. **Alain Chasseur** is a journalist who is often the 'author' of texts presented in one of these ways. A cartoon family called **the Fériens** make regular appearances to provide a narrative setting and some humour.

WHAT'S IN A RECREATIONAL UNIT?

As stated, Recreational Units include **no new grammar** but some new vocabulary and some new information, since each of the three units focuses on one francophone region. The main purpose of the units is to prove to students that they have made progress, and to enable them to enjoy their increased skills in French through some games, while finding out a bit more about Quebec, Mauritius and Haiti. Each of the units revisits the broad topic areas and major language points of the preceding units.

Differentiation

IN THE STUDENT'S BOOK

Some tasks in the Student's Book are numbered or headed in a different colour. These are questions within a task, or whole tasks, that in our view are better suited to higher-ability students – usually because they require more deductive work, or the production of more language; occasionally because they are testing a more challenging language point.

IN THE TEACHING NOTES

There are frequent **Differentiation opportunity** headings, each signalling an idea for support ⬇ or extension ⬆.

The support could be in the form of ideas for:

- preliminary activities to do before tackling the material on the page;
- easier ways into a particular text;
- extra reference support that could be provided for less able students for their use as they work on a task.

The **extension** could be in the form of ideas for:

- broadening a task into more productive work;
- increasing students' range in speaking or writing tasks;
- extending the range of opinions expressed;
- combining practice of a wider range of points within a task.

IN THE TEACHER'S REPROMASTER BOOK

There are five **Differentiated Worksheets** for each unit: two pairs (e.g. DW1.1A and DW1.1B, and DW1.2A and DW1.2B) in which **sheet A** is always designed to support lower-ability students, while **sheet B** extends the more able.

The fifth DW, e.g. DW1.3, is always a lower-ability sheet.

What's in the Teacher's Guide?

The unit-by-unit Teaching Notes are unusually practical and extensive. As well as clear teaching guidance, transcripts* and answers for the material on the Student's Book pages, the Teaching Notes include the following regular features:

- **Differentiation opportunity** (see Differentiation above)
- **Extra idea(s):** ideas for broadening the context and/or the practice on the page, and for class activities, team games, bringing in a competitive or beat-the-clock element, and generally livening things up. (See also the list of suggestions on page vii of this Teacher's Guide for ways in which more use can be made of any text.)
- **Preliminary work**
- **ICT activity** and **ICT opportunity** (see ICT Introduction on page vii of this guide)

*Most of the texts are also on the cassette or CD so that students can listen while they read if you wish, to increase their association of the sounds of French with what they see.

What's in the Teacher's Repromaster Book?

Photocopiable material, as follows:

- **Vocabulary sheets:** One 'core' and one 'extension' sheet for each unit.
- **DWs: Differentiation Worksheets** (see Differentiation above).
- **CMs: Copymasters,** for use in various ways from OHTs to game cards.

- **EGWs: Extra Grammar Worksheets:** ideal for **homework** use, these provide extra practice of two or three major grammar points in the unit, always in a familiar topic context but not necessarily in exactly the same context as in the unit.
- **Assessment Tasks:** Designed to be used at the end of each term, three groups of assessment tasks (units 1–4, 6–9 and 11–13) provide practice of all four skills, at levels A (core/foundation) and B (extension/higher) assessing the content of the previous units (see scheme of work notes below).
- **Synoptic course assessment:** This final group of tasks assesses language from the whole book.

Scheme of work

The teaching units are in three groups, intended to be one group per term, each concluding with a reward unit, as shown below (bold unit numbers represent the Reward Units). The assessment material is also grouped to fit in with this pattern.

1	2	3	4	**5**	6	7	8	9	**10**	11	12	13	**14**

AN ALTERNATIVE APPROACH

Télescope 1 has more substance than many books for this year-group, in terms of grammar coverage, range of contexts and volume of language practice. *Télescope 2* is also unusual in that it concentrates on revisiting and consolidation, followed by tightly designed practice of exam-style tasks – rather than introducing new grammar.

Because of this and because of the relatively ambitious content of the last two teaching units of *Télescope 1*, you may prefer to run the course on a different pattern. Instead of covering the whole of *Télescope 1* in Year 10, you could take over the last two units into the first term of Year 11, moving on to *Télescope 2* for the second and third terms of Year 11.

Term 1 of Y10				Term 2 of Y10				Term 3 of Y10			Term 1 of Y11		
1	2	3	4	**5**	6	7	8	9	**10**	11	12	13	**14**

The audio element

As well as the recordings for the listening exercises, the audio component also includes the following.

- A **recording of the reading texts** (omitting only those which we felt would be inappropriate in aural form); this is to reinforce the association between the sound and appearance of French words. It also means that you can get double use from any such passage (see the following for ideas on how to make extra use of the recorded reading texts).
- A **recording of the prompts** for structured role-plays.

- A recording of the model words and tongue-twisters in the **'Ça se dit comment?'** pronunciation tips.

Task types for extra exploitation of texts

BEFORE LISTENING/READING

- Jumble 10–12 key French words and their English translations on the board. Divide the class into two teams, and ask members of alternate teams to come up to the board and draw a line joining any French/English pair. If they fail to do so within the time limit you set, it's the next team's turn.
- In a text which involves, e.g. key opinion phrases, run through a few of these beforehand so that students are primed to recognise them when they listen. The same applies to any other key structures which have already been encountered and which crop up in the text.
- Before moving on to the printed exploitations on a text, have a class Question/Answer session with closed questions requiring only *oui/non* or *vrai/faux* responses, to tune into the topic.
- Where the text lends itself to predictions, ask students to predict words or phrases they are likely to hear, given the topic.

BEFORE AND DURING LISTENING, BUT BEFORE READING

- Write the opposites of key words in the text on the board and ask students to spot the key words and scribble them down as they listen. Some will be predictable, others less so.
- Write words which are key to the topic on the board – include those which are in the text but also some others. Put them in the order in which they appear in the text, mixing in at intervals those which don't appear. Students listen and write down the words they hear. Alternatively, hand out a copy of the list of words and get students to tick the words they hear.
- Ask students to write down words within a particular category that they hear or see in the listening/reading text (for example, you could pick on certain parts of speech, certain categories of noun, ✦ positive or negative words, who expresses positive/negative opinions, etc.

- Where listening texts consist of a series of people voicing their views, write a few adjectives on the board, e.g. *heureux, malheureuse, arrogant, frustrée, ennuyé, aimable,* etc. During or after listening, ask students to match the speakers with the adjectives. Make the most of the fact that the gender of the adjective gives a clue! To make it accessible to more students, pause the tape after each speaker and identify his/her adjectives.

The ICT strand in Télescope 1

BUILDING ICT INTO FRENCH TEACHING

As is made explicit in *The Use of Information and Communications Technology in Subject Teaching – Identification of Training Needs (TTA 1999)* there are three key principles which should underpin the use of ICT in Modern Languages.

They are that:

- any decision about when, when not and how to use ICT should be based on whether the use of ICT supports good practice in the teaching of Modern Languages;
- decisions about the use of ICT should be linked directly to the learning objectives for the lesson, or series of lessons;
- ICT should either allow the teacher or student to achieve something which could not be achieved without the use of ICT, or allow the teacher to teach or the student to learn more effectively and efficiently than they could otherwise.

When planning for the use of ICT, therefore, the teacher should ask a series of questions:

- What are the linguistic objectives for the lesson?
- Will ICT help my students reach those objectives?
- Will I need to differentiate my objectives and the activity?
- What ICT skills must my students have to be able to benefit linguistically?
- What preparation do I need to do, e.g. in terms of identifying and book-marking websites?
- How do I need to prepare my students?

The Programme of Study for Modern Foreign Languages (QCA 1999) makes clear links to ICT. The table on page viii lists the statements from the Programme of Study and suggests ways in which ICT might be used to support language learning skills.

Statement from Programme of Study	Possible ICT activity – What students might be asked to do
2h . . . *techniques for skimming and scanning written texts, including those from ICT-based sources*	• Search the internet or a CD ROM for a specific purpose, e.g. selected texts on a range of holiday destinations • Use an on-line data base
2j . . . *how to redraft their writing to improve its accuracy and presentation, including the use of ICT* Link to ICT/3b	• Use a word processor to enable redrafting to be done quickly and efficiently • Use multimedia software to support an oral presentation, e.g. integrating texts, images, tables and sound
4a . . . *working with authentic materials in the target language, including some from ICT-based sources*	• Use an on-line database, e.g. restaurant booking as a stimulus for oral work • Work on up-to-date materials, e.g. newspaper articles downloaded by the teacher • Work on-line researching a specific topic • Work on the audio aspect of a satellite broadcast
5d . . . *producing and responding to different types of written language, including texts produced using ICT* Link to ICT/3b	• Use a range of software to create a piece of writing for a specific purpose, e.g. a presentation or magazine article
5e . . . *using a range of resources, including ICT, for accessing and communicating information* Link to ICT/3c	• Use e-mail, audio- and video-conferencing to correspond with native speakers on a particular topic • Create/contribute to a web page

In addition to the students' use, ICT has the potential to be a support to the teacher both in preparation and marking.

ICT can:

- extend the range of authentic materials the teacher can access for all levels of language learner;
- allow the teacher to intervene at different stages of a student's writing to correct and make suggestions on style and content;
- allow the teacher to adapt a text to meet the needs of a range of students by, for example, offering increased support in gapped texts for lower attaining students or by highlighting key words in a reading text for those students who find longer texts too 'dense'.

HARDWARE

It is particularly helpful when presenting material on-line if the teacher either has access to a data (LCD) projector or to an interactive whiteboard. These make it easier to model an activity to a whole class or to show exactly how to access a site.

ICT OPPORTUNITIES AND ACTIVITIES IN *TÉLESCOPE 1*

ICT opportunities. These are suggestions of how ICT might be used to support or extend the work of the unit. These mostly take the form of suggestions for using the Internet. For these opportunities to

lead to effective learning, students need to be given guidance on search strategies so that they are, in effect, 'asking the right questions'. Alternatively, students might be directed towards **yahoo.fr** which has clearly defined categories as a basis for a search.

ICT activities. These are more detailed and include:

- **learning objectives**;
- **detailed guidance** on how to prepare for and carry out the activity;
- **differentiated tasks** where practical and appropriate.

Both the opportunities and the more detailed activities are integral to the work of the unit.

Where a suitable website is available the URL of that website has been identified. As the Internet is a dynamic medium it is not possible to guarantee that the website will still be there when visited a month or two later. It is crucial, therefore, that each suggested website is visited by the teacher and evaluated for its usefulness at the time they want their students to use it.

Two good starting points, however, for guidance on the use of ICT in Modern Languages teaching are:

- the Virtual Teachers' Centre: **http://vtc.ngfl.gov.uk/resource/cits/mfl/index.html** (home page for MFL);
- and **Lingu@net** at which you can find a directory of websites: **http://www.linguanet.org.uk/websites/websites.htm**

Matrices for curriculum mapping

French GCSE grammar requirements

Points for Higher tier only are in shaded rows.

The listings in this matrix refer to the Student's Book pages on which **explanations** of the given grammar points occur. **Practice** of each point may occur in any of the subsequent units.

   Units 5, 10 and 14 introduce no new grammar points but revisit those previously covered.

   (R) = receptive only

Grammar point	Points grammaire in *Télescope 1*
Nouns	
gender	U2 pp.13, 15
Adjectives	
agreement	U1 pp.7, 8; U12 p.115
comparative and superlative: regular	U2 pp.13, 14; U11 p.104; U12 p.120
demonstrative (*ce, cet, cette, ces*)	U6 p.57
indefinite (*chaque, quelque*)	U13 p.126
possessive	U3 p.29
interrogative (*quel, quelle*)	U6 p.57
Adverbs	
comparative and superlative: regular	U3 p.27
mieux, le mieux	U3 p.27
interrogative (*comment, quand*)	U12 p.122
adverbs of time and place (*aujourd'hui, demain, ici, là-bas*)	U1 pp.4–5; U6 p.52; U9 p.86
common adverbial phrases	U8 p.80; U9 p.92
position	U9 p.92
Pronouns	
personal: all subject, including *on*	U2 p.17
reflexive	U1 p.5
relative: *qui*	U6 p.55
relative: *que* (R)	U6 p.55
relative: *que*	U6 p.55
relative: *lequel, auquel, dont* (R)	U8 pp.76, 81
object: direct (R) and indirect (R)	U4 pp.35, 37, 39
object, direct and indirect	U4 pp.35, 37, 39
position and order of object pronouns (R)	U4 pp.35, 37, 39, 43
position and order of object pronouns	U4 pp.35, 37, 39, 43; U7 p.66
disjunctive/emphatic	U7 p.69
demonstrative (*ça, cela*)	U9 p.92
demonstrative (*celui*)	U6 p.59
indefinite (*chacun, quelqu'un*)	U13 p.126
interrogative (*qui, que*)	U6 p.57
use of *y, en* (R)	U7 p.65; U8 p.80
use of *y, en*	U7 p.65; U8 p.80
possessive (*le mien*)	U8 p.75

Verbs	
regular and irregular forms of verbs, including reflexive verbs	U1 pp.3, 5, 6, 8; all units
negative forms	U4 pp.38, 41; U9 p.94; U12 p.117
interrogative forms	U3 p.29; U7 p.71
modes of address: *tu, vous*	U1 p.9; U3 pp.23, 28
impersonal verbs (*il faut*)	U2 p.18
verbs followed by an infinitive, with or without a preposition	U1 pp.18–19; U3 pp.25–27; U6 p.59; U8 p.82
present tense	U1 p.3 (*-er*); U4 pp.36, 39 (*dire, finir*); U6 pp.53, 56, 58 (*-re, mettre, prendre*); U7 p. 64 (*venir*, etc.)
perfect tense	U2 p.16 (*avoir*); U3 p.30 (*être*); U3 p.31 (reflexives); U11 pp.105, 109
perfect infinitive	U11 p.107
imperfect tense	U9 pp.91, 93, 95; U11 pp.105, 106, 109
imperfect	U9 pp.91, 93, 95; U11 pp.105, 106, 109; U13 p.129
immediate future	U7 p.62
future (R)	U8 pp.78, 79; U9 pp.87, 88, 90, 92; U12 p.119
future	U8 pp.78, 79; U9 pp.87, 88, 90, 92; U12 p.119
conditional: *vouloir* and *aimer*	U11 p.102
conditional	U13 pp.128, 129
pluperfect (R)	U11 p.111; U13 p.135
pluperfect	U11 p.111; U13 p.135
past historic	U12 p.121
passive voice: present tense (R)	U13 p.130
passive voice: future, imperfect and perfect tenses (R)	U13 p.131
imperative	U1 p.9
present participle (R)	U12 pp.122, 123
present participle, including use after *en*	U12 pp.122, 123
past participle agreement	U7 p.66
subjunctive mood: present, in commonly used expressions (R)	U13 p.134
Prepositions	U6 p.51; U7 pp.63, 68, 69; U13 p.127
Number, quantity, dates and time	U2 p.12; U6 p.52; U7 p.68; U9 p.87
use of *depuis* with present tense	U6 p.53

French GCSE context coverage requirements

The listings in this matrix refer to the pages on which the **focus** is on the listed context. However, it is a feature of *Télescope* that contexts are revisited systematically across different units, so that any one grammar point is clearly seen to be relevant in different contexts.

Context					Main location of coverage in *Télescope 1*
daily routine, home life	A	E	O	W	U1 pp.2, 8; U4 pp.34, 40, 43; U4 p.139
self/family/friends, personal relationships	A	E	O	W	U1 pp.2, 7, 8; U4 p.38
school, education	A	E	O	W	U3 pp.22, 23; U8 pp.74–83, U9 p.95; U14 p.139
home, local area	A	E	O	W	Units 5, 6, 7, 8, 10, 11, 14
interests, hobbies, leisure	A	E	O	W	U1 pp.2–9; U2 pp.12–20; U4 pp.34–43; U5 pp.46–49; U6 p.56; U7 p.67; U9 p.88; U10 pp.98–100
social activities			O		U1 pp. 2–9; U2 pp.12–20; U5 p.57; U6 p.68; U8 pp.82–83
media		E	O	W	U4 pp.34–44; U9 pp. 89–90
famous personalities		E	O		U1 pp.3, 6, 7, 8; U2 p.13, 16, 17
travel, transport	A	E	O	W	U7 pp. 62–71, U9 pp.90–91; U10 p.98; U11 p.109; U12 p.119
directions, finding the way	A	E	O		U11 p.108
tourism, holidays	A	E	O	W	U5 pp.46–49; U6 pp.50–59; U7 pp.62–71; U10 pp.98–101; U11 pp.102–111; U12 pp.114–122
shopping, fashion	A	E	O	W	U4 p.38; U9 p.92; U11 pp.104–105
accommodation	A	E	O		U6 pp.52–55
services	A	E	O		U7 pp. 65–67
part-time jobs, work experience	A	E	O	W	U3 pp.24–25
careers, future plans	A	E	O	W	U3 pp. 26–27
job adverts, applications		E			U3 pp. 28–29
exercise, fitness	A	E		W	U2 pp.12–20
food and drink		E	O	W	U2 pp.19–20; U9 pp.92–93; U10 p.101; U11 p.111; U12 pp.115–116; U13 p.127; U14 pp.139–140
healthy eating	A	E	O	W	U2 pp. 19–20; U9 pp.92–93
health problems, ailments	A	E	O	W	U6 p.58; U8 pp.80–81
accidents, crime, disasters			O	W	U6 p.58; U11 p.189; U13 pp.129–132
weather and climate		E	O	W	U6 p.58; U8 p.79; U9 p.93; U10 p.98; U12 p.114; U13 pp.130–132
environment	A	E	O	W	U10 p.100; U13 pp.126–135; U14 pp. 138–141
social issues and responsibilities	A	E		W	U3 pp.26–27; U12 pp.114–123; U13 pp. 126–135; U14 pp.138–141
culture and traditions		E			U5 pp.46–49; U7 pp.64, 67–71; U10 pp.98–101; U11 pp.105, 107, 108; U12 pp.116, 117; U14 pp.138–141

A = AQA
E = Edexcel
O = OCR
W = WJEC

    Teacher's Guide 1 © John Murray

unité 1
Je m'amuse

Contexts
- leisure time in France
- music celebrities and their leisure interests

Grammar
- using the present tense of regular -er verbs
- using the present tense of reflexive verbs (e.g. s'habiller)
- using avoir and être in the present tense
- saying when and how often you do something
- using adjectives to describe people and things
- using imperatives to give instructions

Pronunciation
- -an-, -en-, -am-, -em- and -ent (when pronounced, when silent)

Unité 1 Pages 2–3

The opening two pages focus on revision of regular -er present tense forms and present/practise a range of these along with some common time expressions. The article Le week-end – like other main reading items in the course – is also provided on audio so that the sound and the appearance of the words can be experienced in parallel.

Presentation idea

Preliminary work could include looking at an OHT of weekend activities and identifying as many as possible (CM1). Using the numbers, you could ask students to name the activities (e.g. surfer sur Internet = Deux!). Then ask students to give verbs in the infinitive (e.g. jouer au tennis), prompting them with a number.

1 📖 [CD 1 track 2]

Students find French expressions in the text and go on to work out related expressions.

Transcript

Le week-end

En France, le week-end n'est pas long. D'habitude les enfants travaillent au collège le samedi matin. Alors, le samedi après-midi et le dimanche, on s'amuse! Les parents bricolent ou jardinent, ou comme leurs enfants, ils regardent la télévision ou écoutent de la musique. Les adolescents parlent avec leurs copains au téléphone et ils surfent sur Internet. Certains

aiment lire ou tchatcher sur Internet, d'autres aiment faire du sport ou de la musique. Les Français aiment passer le dimanche en famille. Quelquefois on déjeune chez les grands-parents. On passe beaucoup de temps à table, on parle, on mange. . . et puis, on se relaxe!

Solution

1 en France
2 d'habitude
3 le samedi matin
4 le samedi après-midi
5 comme leurs enfants
6 en famille
⬆ 7 on surfe sur Internet
⬆ 8 en Écosse
⬆ 9 le dimanche matin
⬆10 le dimanche après-midi
⬆11 comme leurs parents
⬆12 on travaille

Differentiation opportunities ⬇

Students of lower ability may concentrate firstly on je and tu, e.g. Moi, je tchatche sur Internet. Et toi, tu tchatches sur Internet aussi, Sam? Follow this with 3rd person singular forms, getting students to report what they have just heard (Susie tchatche sur Internet) followed by 3rd person plural forms (Susie, Daniel et Sam tchatchent sur Internet), stressing that all these endings sound the same. 3rd person forms, vous and nous may all be practised by using the activity symbols from CM1 and CM2, e.g.

– Vous écoutez de la musique, Darren et Emma?
– Oui, nous écoutons de la musique.

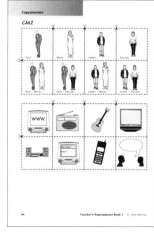

Once this is established, try Qu'est-ce que vous faites, Sam et Linda?, eliciting Nous écoutons la radio, etc. Ask students to make up other activities beginning Nous . . .

Point grammaire: Revision of the present tense of *-er* verbs

 More able classes may revise the whole paradigm of *-er* verbs (see Grammar, page 146).

CM3 presents for revision the verb endings for the present tense of *-er* verbs. This may be made into an OHT, issued as a reference tool to each student or enlarged and used as a classroom poster. Remind students that most of the verb sounds the same, except for the *nous* and *vous* forms. Attention is drawn on the Copymaster to the use of *ils* for subjects of mixed gender.

2

Students match verb endings to verbs in order to compose complete sentences.

Solution
1 Tu pratiques le skate, Alain?
2 Marc déjeune dans un petit restaurant le samedi.
3 Tu surfes sur Internet, Philippe?
4 Vous aussi, vous surfez sur Internet, monsieur?
5 La copine de Marc aime danser dans le club ou la disco.
6 Mes grands-parents invitent la famille à déjeuner.
7 Nous jouons de la musique.
8 On parle avec ses amis.

Ça se dit comment? p.3 🎧 [CD 1 track 3]

Explains when *-ent* is pronounced/not pronounced.

Transcript
– par**ent**, d**ent**, présid**ent**, régulièrem**ent**, lentem**ent**, évidemm**ent**
– ils travaill**ent**, elles regard**ent**, ils jou**ent**, elles surf**ent**
– les par**ent**s bricol**ent**, les grands-par**ent**s mang**ent**, les adolesc**ent**s écout**ent** la radio

Extra ideas

To reinforce the pronunciation point, using cut-outs from **CM1** and **CM2** as an OHT (people and activities) as overlays on **CM4** as an OHT (house and garden), suggest some sentences and ask if they are true or false.

Firstly, single people are used, e.g. *Paul téléphone à un ami, Pascale écoute des disques.* This establishes the pronunciation of the verb. Then, pairs of people are used, e.g. *Paul et Pascale surfent sur Internet; André et Marie regardent la télé.* The comparison should be made between *Paul surfe sur Internet* and *Paul et Pascale surfent sur Internet* (i.e. the verbs sound the same). Move the people overlays and ask students to produce sentences such as: *Paul et*

Marie regardent la télé; André et Pascale surfent sur Internet. Other students say if these are true or false and correct those which are wrong. Write the different forms on the whiteboard. Concentrate on the pronunciation of the (silent) ending of the verb.

Students could practise this using **CM1**, **CM2** and **CM3** in photocopied form.

Extension activity

Place a mixture of single people and pairs of people in the rooms/garden with their accompanying activities and ask students to write down the corresponding sentences, concentrating on the verb ending in each case.

3 🎧

Students use the table to produce sentences using regular *-er* verbs. Answers will depend on students' choices of elements, but the correct form of the verb should be present in each example.

Unité 1 Pages 4–5

Presentation ideas

Revise expressions of frequency, e.g *une fois par semaine, deux fois par semaine, tous les jours* using **CM5** as an OHT, which may subsequently be distributed as a photocopy for reference. It is useful to start with *une fois par semaine,* and to work up to *six fois par semaine.*

This can be done by saying a number of days aloud (e.g. *lundi, jeudi et samedi*), to which the students reply with the appropriate expression of frequency (i.e. *trois fois par semaine*). *Plusieurs fois* could be three or more times per week.

When the total is seven, change to *tous les jours,* pointing out the sun symbol, and *tous les soirs*, pointing out the moon symbol. Questions and answers may be practised between teacher and student, or student and student, e.g. – *Tu écoutes souvent la radio? – Oui, tous les jours.* Introduce the fraction code here, i.e 1/7 = *une fois par semaine,* 7/7 = *tous les jours.* These can be put onto flashcards and used for practice.

Point out the less precise expressions such as *souvent, d'habitude, normalement,* illustrating them with examples, e.g. *Je joue souvent au foot, normalement trois fois par semaine.* Less regular intervals can then be introduced such as *une fois par mois* or *une fois par an* using the calendar symbol on the OHT (or using the fraction codes: 1/31, 1/365).

Summary expressions such as *de temps en temps, quelquefois, des fois* can then be introduced, e.g.

(indicating three dates on the calendar) *Je joue au tennis de temps en temps.*

Draw attention to the distinction between *samedi* (on Saturday) and *le samedi* (on Saturdays).

4  [CD 1 track 4]

This activity revises time phrases and introduces some new vocabulary. The aim is for the students to concentrate on the notion of 'frequency'.
Première écoute aims to get students to pick out particular expressions, whilst **Deuxième écoute** (task 5) aims to get students to deduce answers and produce the correct frequency expression.

Transcript for 4 & 5

Notre reporter a interviewé des habitants de Saint Malo. La question – qu'est-ce qu'ils font le week-end?

Interviewer: Pour toi, Alain, qu'est-ce que c'est, le week-end?
Alain: Pour moi, c'est le skate. Ah oui, j'en fais tous les week-ends aussi. J'adore ça.
Interviewer: Parle m'en un petit peu.
Alain: Alors, je fais toujours du roller le week-end. Maintenant des 'in-line', les rollers actuels. J'adore!
Interviewer: Cécile, pour toi, ça consiste en quoi, le week-end?
Cécile: Ben, le samedi après-midi, je fais mes devoirs. Puis, le samedi soir, je sors avec mes copains, ou je reste à la maison et je regarde la télé. Le dimanche . . . ben . . . ça dépend, tu sais . . . normalement nous déjeunons chez mes grands-parents.
Interviewer: Régine, qu'est-ce que tu fais le week-end?
Régine: De la musique. Toujours de la musique. Depuis un an je fais partie d'un groupe.
Interviewer: Ah bon? Et tu joues de quel instrument?
Régine: De la guitare électrique, et je chante aussi.
Interviewer: Et vous jouez souvent?
Régine: Ah oui, tous les samedis après-midi.
Interviewer: Vous jouez où?
Régine: D'habitude, c'est chez Richard, le batteur. Il a un petit studio.
Interviewer: Marc, que fais-tu le week-end?
Marc: Ben moi, je suis programmeur, donc je travaille très dur. Alors le samedi matin je me réveille tard. Je prends une douche et je me relaxe. J'écoute des disques, je téléphone à mes amis. Quelquefois je déjeune dans un petit restaurant. Le soir, j'aime aller au club ou à la disco avec ma copine.

Solution
1 le week-end: Alain
2 tous les samedis après-midi: Régine
3 tous les week-ends: Alain
4 le samedi matin: Marc
5 le dimanche: Cécile

Point grammaire: Frequency
Summarises expressions of frequency, dividing them into regular and irregular occurrences.

Tip: Fillers
Aims to make students aware that not every word is essential to the meaning of the passage, and that fillers are used to make time for the speaker to think and also to keep the listener in the conversation. Using the list, the teacher could ask students: **a** which elements are time-fillers (*ah, ben, alors, euh*); **b** which ones keep the listener in the conversation (*tu sais? quoi?*). Students could listen to the recording for task 4 again and put up their hands each time they hear a filler.

Students could practise asking each other questions. In answering, they should give themselves time by inserting a filler, e.g.

– *Tu aimes surfer sur Internet?*
– *Euh . . . ben . . .oui, j'aime surfer.*

5 *Deuxième écoute*
Students choose between two answers.

Solution
1 a; **2** b; **3** a; **4** a

Point grammaire: Reflexive verbs
In practising reflexive verbs, it is essential that students should **not** convert all the verbs that they know into reflexives. A short list of very common verbs can be practised and drilled (*s'amuser → je m'amuse, se laver → je me lave*). Daily routine is a useful way of practising such verbs (*je me réveille, je me lève, je me lave, je me douche, je m'habille, je me peigne*, etc.). More able students may be able to cope with *je me brosse les cheveux, je me brosse les dents.*

Extra idea
Prepare a set of orange cards each showing an example of a verb in the present tense (*je* form) and a second set of orange cards showing temporal adverbs relating to the present, e.g. *d'habitude, le week-end, le samedi, en général*, etc. Blu-tack these to the board (time expressions on left and verbs on right) and ask students to make up sentences each with one time expression and one verb. (These orange cards – orange signifying present tense events/concepts – form part of a set of 'traffic light' cards. Red cards (past tense concepts) and green cards (future tense concepts) will appear in later units.)

6
Students complete the answer to the question, using a reflexive verb and altering the time or location suggested in the question. Answers will depend on students' choices.

Extra idea
To help students cope with a mix of reflexives and non-reflexives, extend the list of routine activities to include some non-reflexive verbs. Practise via a game in which you give the infinitive (*jouer, regarder, préparer, manger, déjeuner*, etc.). Students reply using

the first person and any student inserting a reflexive pronoun into the *je* form of a non-reflexive verb is out.

Homework opportunity

Extra Grammar Worksheet EG1 (see notes at the end of this unit) offers extra grammar practice on reflexives (present tense, *-er* verbs).

1 Using the table, students compose sentences involving time expressions and the present tense. Answers will depend on the students' choice of elements.

↕2 Students make up their own sentences from the table, using *je*. The sentences composed will be the choice of the students, but all verbs should have the silent ending *-e*, e.g.

D'habitude, j'écoute des disques.

Ça se dit comment? p.5 [CD 1 track 5]

The sound '-an-', '-en-', '-am-', '-en-', '-ent-'.

Transcript
- dimanche, vendredi, temps, grand, flan
- parent, adolescent
- de temps en temps le dimanche je mange un grand flan

Differentiation opportunities ↓ ↑

Practice with *-er* verbs. At this point **Differentiated Worksheets DW1.1A** and **DW1.1B** may be used.

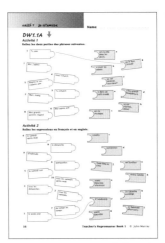

■ ↓**DW1.1A Activity 1:** Match jigsaw pieces to produce verbs with correct endings.

Solution
1 g; **2** e; **3** h; **4** f; **5** c; **6** b; **7** d; **8** a

■ ↑**DW1.1B Activity 1:** Add correct endings to incomplete verbs from memory. Then complete sentences using the verbs thus made, e.g. **1** *Je* mang**e** *au MacDo tous les samedis avec mes copains.*

■ ↑↓**DW1.1A** and **B Activity 2:** Linking time expressions with their translation.

Solution DW1.1A
1 f; **2** g; **3** h; **4** i; **5** b; **6** d; **7** j; **8** e; **9** c; **10** a

Solution DW1.1B
1 h; **2** j; **3** k; **4** l; **5** b; **6** i; **7** d; **8** g; **9** f; **10** m; **11** e; **12** c; **13** a

ICT activity

Learning objectives
- to reinforce the use of familiar verbs in the present tense;
- to provide an opportunity for students to present personal information to other members of the class using presentational software (e.g. PowerPoint).

1 Students gather information about each member of the family and what they do at the weekend.

2 Using PowerPoint they create a presentation on each member of the family, incorporating scanned or digitised images if possible.

↑3 The higher attainers should be encouraged to write in note form so that they 'talk to the presentation'.

↓4 The writing of lower attainers could be supported by tables to be completed or by a model to be adapted.

Extra idea

CM5a could be used as an OHT. Using the three-column table, students ask each other questions, partner A using columns 1 and 2 and partner B using columns 2 and 3.

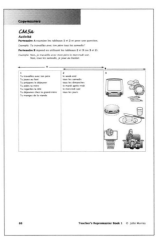

Differentiation opportunity ↑

A more demanding version of this practice could be as follows, using the lower part of **CM5**. Students look at the right-hand section of exercise 7 in the Student's Book again for a few moments and then close their books, so that they cannot see the verbs, and, working in groups, use the list on **CM5** to make up as many sentences orally as they can in a given time. One student could be appointed to count the number of sentences for each group. Additional points could be given for wholly new sentences.

Homework opportunity

Students write a brief description of a weekend. You may wish to support weaker students by giving them some verb 'starters'.

Unité 1 Pages 6–7

The reading passage on Britney Spears provides the opportunity to study a brief biography/portrait of a well-known personality. Before the passage is read, the teacher could remind students about *se prénommer*, e.g. *Je me prénomme John. Cette jeune fille au premier rang se prénomme Emily.* Then teach *surnommer*. A little prior research may be necessary to find out nicknames in the class. These could then be demonstrated thus: *Voici Nicola. On la surnomme Nicki. Et voici Trevor. On le surnomme M. Muscles.*

The exercise at the end is designed: **a** to practise sorting relevant from irrelevant information in the text; and **b** to practise the correct form of the present tense of *-er* verbs, some of which will be new to students.

9 *Transcript* [CD 1 track 6]

Britney Spears est née le 2 décembre 1981 à Kentwood en Louisiane. Elle habite maintenant à Hollywood. C'est une jeune femme qui a les cheveux longs et les yeux marron. Elle mesure environ 1m 65 et elle pèse environ 55 kilos. Ses parents se prénomment Jamie et Lynne.

Ses amis l'appellent Bit Bit. Ses hobbys préférés sont le shopping, voir des films, lire des nouvelles romantiques, et elle adore aller à la plage.

Ses sports favoris sont la natation, le tennis, le golf et le basket. Ses acteurs favoris sont Mel Gibson, Tom Cruise, Brad Pitt, Ben Affleck et Leonardo Di Caprio.

Elle aime manger des pizzas, des hot dogs, des pâtes, des cookies avec de la glace et des sandwichs grillés. Sa couleur préférée est le bleu.

Comme chanteuses elle aime Mariah Carey, Whitney Houston, Madonna, Brandy et Lauren Hill. Comme chanteurs elle aime Michael Jackson et Prince. Ses groupes favoris sont les TLC, Aerosmith et Goo Goo Dolls. Elle est influencée musicalement par Madonna, Whitney Houston, Mariah Carey et Otis Redding.

Elle s'habille chez Betsey Johnson, Bebe, A/X et Rampage, parmi d'autres. Elle aime porter des tennis, des t-shirts et des jeans, mais elle adore toujours changer de look. Elle essaie toujours de dégager une image positive.

Britney ne supporte pas ses pieds qu'elle trouve trop larges!

Exercise 9 is a gap-fill with *-er* verbs to be chosen from the list of infinitives and put into the appropriate form.

Solution

1 Britney mesure environ 1m 65.
2 Elle habite aujourd'hui à Hollywood.
3 Elle a les yeux marron et les cheveux longs.
4 Son père se prénomme Jamie et sa mère se prénomme Lynne.
5 Les copains de Britney la surnomment «Bit Bit».
6 Britney aime aller au bord de la mer.
7 De préférence, elle mange des fast-foods.
8 Elle aime/admire des chanteuses comme Mariah Carey, Whitney Houston et Madonna.

9 Elle aime/adore acheter ses vêtements chez Betsey Johnson, Bebe, A/X et Rampage.
10 Elle porte d'habitude des tennis, un t-shirt et un jean.

Differentiation opportunities

⬇**DW1.2** carries a simplified version of the text. The attached exercise already contains verbs in the correct form and students are required to complete the sentence with the missing information. You could draw attention to the verb endings.

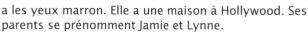

Transcript

Britney Spears est née le 2 décembre 1981. Elle mesure environ 1m 65. Elle a les yeux marron. Elle a une maison à Hollywood. Ses parents se prénomment Jamie et Lynne.

Ses amis appellent Britney «Bit Bit». Ses hobbys préférés sont le shopping, les films, la natation et aller à la plage.

Ses sports favoris sont la natation, le tennis, le golf et le basket. Ses acteurs favoris sont Mel Gibson et Leonardo Di Caprio. Comme films, elle aime *My Best Friend's Wedding*, *Steel Magnolias* et *Titanic*.

Elle aime manger des pizzas, des hot dogs, et des sandwichs grillés. Sa couleur préférée est le bleu.

Comme chanteuses elle aime Mariah Carey, Whitney Houston et Madonna. Comme chanteurs elle aime Michael Jackson et Prince.

Elle s'habille chez Betsey Johnson, Bebe, A/X et Rampage. Elle aime porter des tennis, un t-shirt et un jean, mais elle adore toujours changer de look, qui est toujours positif.

Britney n'aime pas ses pieds, qu'elle trouve trop larges!

Solution

1 Britney mesure environ 1m 65.
2 Elle habite à Hollywood.
3 Elle a les cheveux longs et les yeux marron.
4 Ses parents s'appellent Jamie et Lynne.
5 Les copains de Britney la surnomment «Bit Bit».
6 Britney aime aller à la plage.
7 De préférence, elle mange des fast-foods.
8 Elle admire des chanteuses comme Mariah Carey, Whitney Houston et Madonna.
9 Elle aime acheter ses vêtements chez Betsey Johnson, Bebe, A/X et Rampage.
10 Elle porte d'habitude des tennis, un t-shirt et un jeans.

Extra idea

Examples in the Britney Spears passage provide an opportunity to remind students that verbs such as *aimer*, *adorer* and *détester* can be followed by an infinitive. This could be practised using infinitive

unité 1 Je m'amuse

expressions such as: *jouer au foot, regarder les films à la télé, sortir avec mes copains, tchatcher sur Internet,* etc. Note that reflexive verbs will require a reflexive infinitive, i.e. *J'aime **me coucher** tard le samedi* soir.

Other regular *-er* verbs which fit this pattern are *aimer mieux* (to prefer), *compter* (to intend), *oser* (to dare) and *souhaiter* (to wish – rather formal). These could be practised using the activities mentioned:

- *Tu aimes mieux porter une robe ou un t-shirt?*
- *Tu comptes aller à la plage samedi?*

Transcript: Poème p.7 [CD 1 track 8]

Britney Spears
Sur terre
Il y a mille et une filles
Des brunes, des blondes
et des rousses
Mais c'est toi que mon cœur a choisie,
Pour passer mille et une nuits
Voilà pourquoi c'est à
Toi qui es si gentille
Toi qui es ma meilleure amie
Que je dédie ce poème,
Car c'est toi que j'aime

This short poem about Britney Spears might serve as a writing stimulus, but its main purpose is to add a short reading passage of a different genre on the same subject, giving rise to some practice on adjective agreement in task 12.

Point grammaire: Agreement of adjectives

At this point, students could examine the sentences given as examples in the Student's Book and be asked to find the adjective. Reinforce knowledge of the definition of an adjective. Attention should be drawn to the different adjectival endings. Point out that these adjectives each follow a noun, and it is the noun which influences the end of the adjective. The pattern is given in the table.

The box includes a reminder that *tout* is an adjective so it must agree with its noun. There are plenty of examples in the current context of frequency.

10

This exercise gives practice in adjective endings, including *tout*; the final adjective depends on students' choice.

1 toutes les femmes . . .
2 tous les garçons . . .
3 toutes les filles . . .
4 tous les hommes . . .
5 tous les professeurs . . .
6 tous les chiens . . .

Differentiation opportunity

One student could suggest an adjectival phrase, e.g. (*un professeur horrible* or *une fille blonde*), and the others could write it down. This simple form of dictation aims to establish that agreements mustn't be forgotten, even if they are not always audible when spoken.

Unité 1 Pages 8–9

11 Transcript and Solution [CD 1 track 9]

Céline est née à Charlemagne au Québec, Canada. **Agée** de cinq ans, elle chante avec ses 13 frères et sœurs. En 1983 elle est la **première** Canadienne à recevoir un disque d'or. Elle a aussi chanté la **belle** chanson-titre du dessin animé *La Belle et la Bête* de Walt Disney. Aujourd'hui la planète **entière** connaît sa version de *My Heart Will Go On*, chanson-titre du film *Titanic*. Au cours des années elle a connu un succès **fabuleux**.

Point grammaire: *Avoir, être* and adjectives

The two verbs *être* and *avoir* (see paradigms on **CM6**) could be printed in large format and mounted on the wall where they can clearly be seen. Students can thus familiarise themselves with them and refer to them when needed.

Draw attention to adjectives such as *premier, entier* and *beau.* A preliminary activity could be to predict the feminine form, and then to see how it actually turns out in the grammar section.

12

Using the table, students talk or write about stars that they like and don't like. Some thought should be given to the endings of the adjectives, so students should not attempt to rush this exercise, but aim to produce accurate sentences. The feminine forms *belle* and *travailleuse* are given.

Differentiation opportunities

At this point **DW1.3A** and **DW1.3B** could be used.

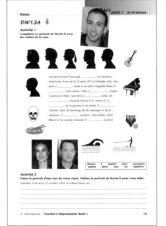

■ ↓**DW1.3A Activity 1:** Students complete a gap-fill article on Howie D, using verbs given in the box.

Solution

Howard Dwaine Dorough **est** un chanteur américain. Il est né le 22 août 1973 à Orlando, USA. Son père **s'appelle** Hoke et sa mère **s'appelle** Paula. Il **a** trois sœurs. Elles s'**appellent** Angie, Caroline et Polly. Son frère s'**appelle** John. On **surnomme** Howard «Howie D» et «Sweet D». Il **joue** de la guitare et du piano. Il **aime** chanter, faire du bowling, du ski nautique et de la natation. Il **adore** sa mère, Tom Hanks, Demi Moore et la cuisine chinoise! Il **déteste** la mort.

■ ↑**DW1.3B Activity 1:** Students write an article on Howie D, using the CV given and referring to the Britney Spears portrait (which is the same as that on page 6 of the Student's Book) as a model. Verbs to use are given at the top of the sheet.

■ ↑**DW1.3B Activity 2:** Students are asked to produce a portrait of a favourite star, modelled on the Howie D and Britney Spears texts. In order to prepare for this task some preliminary work using the grid on **CM7** with headings such as *famille, sports, TV/ films, instruments,* etc. could be used to assemble the sort of vocabulary which will be necessary, whoever the choice of star. This master could be left on view as an OHT while the students rough out their biographies.

ICT opportunities

Research could be done for **DW1.3B Activity 2** using teenage magazines (e.g. *Salut, Hit & News, Jeune et Jolie*) or the Internet. Once the biography has been drafted it could be checked by the teacher, and suggested corrections incorporated into a re-draft using word-processing or a DTP package with down-loaded or scanned images.

La lettre de Sophie

13

Students correct the spellings on Sophie's letter as a computer spell-check would do.

Solution

Je m'appelle Sophie et j'ai un problème. Je suis **sportive** mais je suis très **nerveuse**. Je suis **amoureuse** d'un garçon de ma classe. Il est **sportif** aussi et il est très sympa. Il a les yeux **bleus** et les cheveux **blonds**. Il est vraiment très **intelligent** et très **gentil**, mais quelquefois il est un peu **réservé**. On fait du skate ensemble le week-end mais je trouve difficile de l'inviter à sortir avec moi. Le samedi après-midi nous sommes toujours ensemble. Il est vraiment **beau** et je l'adore. Que faire?

14 [CD 1 track 10]

Students identify the order in which the advertisements are discussed (**1**) and which option is finally chosen (**2**). Note: the option is **not** the last item mentioned.

Transcript

Claude: Alors, c'est ton anniversaire dans deux semaines. Anne et moi, nous allons te payer une excursion. Qu'est-ce que tu veux faire?
Paul: C'est gentil ... mais ... ben ... je sais pas, moi.
Anne: Tu veux aller à la disco?
Paul: Ah, non. On va à la disco tous les samedis. C'est vraiment nul!
Claude: Mais il y a ce club-discothèque *L'Aéronaute.* C'est ouvert jusqu'à deux heures du matin. Ça ne te dit pas?
Paul: Ah oui. Deux heures du matin. Figure-toi la réaction de mes parents!
Anne: Tu as envie d'aller au cinéma?
Paul: Pas tellement.
Anne: Il y a *Scream 3* au cinéma Le Vauban.
Paul: Ah, non, tu sais que je déteste les films d'épouvante.
Claude: Mais il y a d'autres films. Tu pourrais aller voir *Les Acteurs,* par exemple, à 20 heures 30, et puis on pourrait aller au café ensemble.
Paul: Écoute, hein ... il n'y a pas de bons films cette semaine-là ... vraiment, je ne veux pas aller au cinéma ...
Anne: OK. Mais regarde, il y a ce bateau-restaurant. On pourrait faire une croisière ...
Paul: Mais, Anne, je vais avoir seize ans ... pas soixante ans, hein? Les croisières comme ça, c'est pour les parents ... et les grands-parents.
Anne: Mais regarde. Il y a une piste de karting à Saint-Méloir.
Paul: Les karts? Ah oui! Un après-midi de karting ... super! J'adore les karts! Et on peut louer des karts en groupe pour une heure. Ouais!!
Claude: Mais regarde. Le kayak. Tu as envie de faire un stage d'initiation? C'est pas trop cher. Une demi-journée ... 20 euros.
Paul: Mais non ... je ne sais même pas nager. Non, j'aime mieux le karting. Et c'est pas trop cher, non? ... 12 euros les 10 minutes ... Regarde, il y a un numéro de téléphone. Tu peux téléphoner?
Anne: Mais oui ... bien sûr ... Enfin!

Solution

1 b, d, a, c, e; **2** c

Point grammaire: Imperatives

Tu and *vous* imperatives. Students will be familiar with various sorts of commands from classroom language but this consolidates the point.

The teacher can play *Bring me the head of Alfredo Garcia!*, asking students to bring various strange objects which the students must rush up and draw on the board, e.g. *Apporte-moi deux kayaks et un igloo. Vous* form commands are addressed to pairs of students. Students then take over the ordering role. Alternatively, give each student four Lego blocks of different colours and instruct them, e.g.

Posez le bloc bleu sur la plaquette rouge. Attachez le bloc jaune à la plaquette rouge. Posez la plaquette bleue sur la plaquette rouge.

Pairs can then practise using the *tu* form, with one student trying to build the twin of the object made by the other.

15 [CD 1 track 11]
Students listen to an answerphone message and note the details.

Transcript
Merci de nous avoir appelés. La piste est ouverte entre mars et octobre. Les heures d'ouverture sont les suivantes. Du lundi au vendredi, la piste est ouverte de neuf heures jusqu'à vingt heures.

Le samedi et le dimanche, la piste est ouverte de dix heures à dix-sept heures. Nos tarifs sont les suivants: adultes, 12 euros les dix minutes, enfants de huit ans à quinze ans, 9 euros les dix minutes. Pour de plus amples renseignements, visitez notre website **www.karting.france.fr** ou téléphonez à notre bureau pendant les heures d'ouverture. Merci.

Solution
Jours d'ouverture: Tous les jours
Heures d'ouverture: lundi–vendredi: 0900–2000h
samedi–dimanche: 1000–1700h
Tarifs: Adultes 12€/10 minutes; enfants 8–15ans 9€/10 minutes.
Informations/supplémentaires: Visitez le website ou téléphonez au bureau

ICT activity
Learning objective
• to provide an opportunity for interested students to read for pleasure.

1 Students are given the URL **www.nomade.fr**
2 They enter 'karting' as the search word.
3 Students are then asked to choose one of the top ten sites found in their search.
4 They then note 10 important facts they have learned from the site.

For lower attaining students the teacher will have to guide students to one or two sites they have researched themselves and provide those students with a gapped text.

16
This task practises the formation of imperatives, with a variety of *tu* and *vous* forms offered in skeleton sentences.

17
This is an open-ended task, which offers an opportunity for differentiation.
You could make use of this rubric for practice in identifying imperatives. Students use leaflets from a nearby tourist office in Britain to produce a

summary of entertainment available, producing short documents similar to the five pictures used for task 14, giving names, opening hours and prices where applicable.

ICT activity
Learning objectives
• to reuse the vocabulary learned on the topic of the information office in a French speaking country in the context of their home region;
• to produce a word-processed document giving information about attractions in their town/region.

1 List the main tourist attractions in the area.
2 Brainstorm what information would be helpful for a foreign visitor who wanted to visit those attractions.
3 Ask students to select three or four attractions to research on-line or through brochures.
4 Students word-process the information in tabular form.

Unité 1 Pages 10–11
Checkpoints
Test
The **Test** checks students' skills in the grammatical goals of the unit:
• using the present tense of regular -er verbs
• saying when and how often you do something
• using the present tense of reflexive verbs (e.g. *s'habiller*)
• using *avoir* and *être* in the present tense
• using adjectives to describe people and things
• using imperatives to give instructions

Solution
1 a On **joue** au football **deux fois par semaine**. [2]
  b Nous **écoutons** de la musique **six fois par semaine**. [2]
  c Alain **bricole une fois par mois**. [2]
  d Anne **mange** chez sa tante **deux fois par mois**. [2]
  e Les garçons **surfent** sur Internet **tous les jours**. [2]
2 Tous les jours, plusieurs fois par semaine, deux fois par semaine, plusieurs fois par mois, deux fois par mois, une fois par an. [3]
3 Le samedi Michèle se **réveille** très tard. Elle se **lave** les cheveux et puis elle **regarde** la télé. [3]
4 a Howie D et Britney Spears sont très **doués**. [1]
  b Les vedettes de rock n'ont pas de vie **privée**. [1]
  c Céline Dion est très **célèbre**. Elle est **canadienne**. [2]
5 **Réservez** vos places à l'avance. **Téléphonez** à notre bureau ou **visitez** notre website. **Demandez** nos tarifs aujourd'hui. **Notez** les détails. [5]

Total [25]

Quiz

The **Quiz** checks students' knowledge acquired in the unit, about:

- leisure time in France
- music celebrities and their leisure interests

Solution

1 Ils travaillent au collège.	[1]
2 Any five of: on s'amuse, bricole, jardine, regarde la TV, écoute de la musique, parle avec ses copains, surfe sur Internet, lit, tchatche, fait du sport, fait de la musique.	[5]
3 Any three of: on passe le dimanche en famille, déjeune chez les grands-parents, passe beaucoup de temps à table, parle, mange, se relaxe.	[3]
4 a Le 2 décembre	[1]
b Kentwood	[1]
c Jamie et Lynne	[2]
d Any two of: Mel Gibson, Tom Cruise, Brad Pitt, Ben Affleck, Leonardo Di Caprio	[2]
e Any three of: des pizzas, des hot dogs, des pâtes, des cookies, de la glace, des sandwichs grillés	[3]
f Any two of: des tennis, un jean, un t-shirt.	[2]
5 a *La Belle et la Bête*	[1]
b *Titanic*	[1]
c Un disque d'or.	[1]
	Total [23]

Projets

A This portrait of a friend or someone that the student admires is an opportunity to practise third person singular verbs (including *avoir* and *être*) and adjective agreements. Short sentences have been given as examples, but as far as possible these should be expanded to the best of the student's ability. Example: *Elle habite à Kirtley dans un bungalow tout près du supermarché.*

B This gives the opportunity to draw together the various points treated in this chapter. While students will write most of the piece in the *je* form, there are opportunities to use the third person (singular and plural) to talk about their friends, family and relations.

C Students prepare a brochure on a weekend in the UK. This is an open-ended task, building on the simpler description written for task 11 in this unit. Students could use the various tables and grammar explanations throughout the chapter as reference material on which they can draw.

ICT opportunity

The brochure could be prepared using word-processing or a DTP package. The Internet could be used for pictures which could be downloaded. Alternatively, pictures could be scanned and pasted in. This could also form the basis of a piece of coursework for GCSE.

ICT Unit round-up activity

Learning objectives

- to practise skimming and scanning when reading;
- to complete a word-processed document providing detailed information about a chosen actor or singer.

1 Using the grid **CM7** or something similar students use **yahoo.fr** as a search engine.

2 They choose media as an area and key words *acteur/artiste*.

3 They then choose someone of interest and find out as much as possible about that person under the headings on the grid.

⇩ Limit the choice in advance and ensure that the sites available for those actors or singers are accessible linguistically to students.

EGW1 teaching notes

Copymaster **EGW1** offers a differentiated version of a text using reflexive verbs.

Activity 1 is a cloze text with the correct forms of the verbs given below.

Activity 2 gives the verbs in the infinitive form. The exercise is done on a photocopy of the sheet. More able students should use Activity 2 and copy out the text for writing practice. The teacher could gloss *se prénommer*, e.g. *Je me prénomme John. Cette jeune fille au premier rang se prénomme Emily.*

EGW1 Solution (applies to both activities)

Je **m'appelle** Isabelle Dufour et j'ai quinze ans. Je voudrais correspondre avec un garçon ou une fille de mon âge. J'ai une sœur qui **se prénomme** Jeanne . . . Nous **nous intéressons** toutes les deux au skate et nous en faisons tous les weekends. Le vendredi soir, je **me couche** tôt, car je suis toujours fatiguée. Le samedi matin on **se réveille** assez tôt. D'habitude je **me lave** les cheveux et je **m'habille** en survêtement et baskets. On déjeune, et puis, hop! en route pour le skatepark. Dans notre quartier le skate **se popularise** et il y a pas mal de jeunes au parc quand nous y arrivons. Il y a un garçon qui **s'appelle** Marc. Il **se spécialise** en 'in-line'. Moi j'aime la rampe, sorte de grand U en bois. C'est très énergique, ça! À la fin, on rentre chez nous et nous **nous douchons** car nous avons vraiment chaud!

Si tu **t'intéresses** au skate, écris moi bientôt!

unité 2
En forme!

Contexts
- popular sports in France
- sports personalities
- record holders
- fitness and exercise
- healthy lifestyles

Grammar
- using high numbers
- making comparisons using adjectives
- recognising masculine and feminine nouns
- using the perfect tense with *avoir* to say what you did/have done
- using the verb *passer* with *à* to say how much time you spend on something
- using *on*
- using *il faut* and *devoir* to say what you must do

Pronunciation
- 'r'
- 'u'
- 'ou'

Unité 2 Pages 12–13

Presentation ideas
The first article deals with the most popular sports in France. As a preliminary to this, revise the names of sports using flashcards or **CM1**. Emphasise the need to include the definite article (*le, la, l'*). Then ask the students to predict the popularity of sports in France before they see the article. Under the heading *Popularité des sports en France*, write the numbers 1–12 and ask the students to suggest which sports occupy which position. When the article has been read, the positions can be compared, e.g.

Pour nous, le ski est numéro 8. Ici c'est numéro 3.

 [CD 1 track 12]

Students find French expressions in the text.

Transcript

Sports: les plus populaires
Il y a 1 600 000 joueurs de football en France: le football est le sport le plus populaire.

Les sports dans l'ordre d'importance:
Le football, le tennis, le ski, la pétanque, le judo, le basketball, le rugby, le golf, le hand-ball, l'équitation, la voile, la natation.

En France, environ 75 pour cent des hommes et 50 pour cent des femmes pratiquent un sport régulièrement. Seule la télévision est plus populaire que les activités physiques. Les sports les plus populaires sont les sports d'équipe (football, rugby, etc.) et de compétition (ski, tennis, golf, etc.). Les

sports de découverte et d'aventure (le VTT, la randonnée, le canoë-kayak) sont aussi très populaires.

Le football
Le football est le sport le plus populaire de la planète et déchaîne les passions, surtout au Brésil et en Italie! La dernière Coupe du Monde du vingtième siècle s'est jouée en France en 1998.

Solution
1 joueurs de football
2 environ 75%
3 dans l'ordre d'importance
4 la voile
5 plus populaire que
6 le sport le plus populaire
↕7 joueurs de tennis
↕8 joueurs de basketball
↕9 environ 20%
↕10 le sport le plus populaire du monde

Tip
A brief reminder about the most difficult 'tens' numbers.

Ça se dit comment? p.12 [CD 1 track 13]
Once the method suggested has been tried, ask students to look at the 'R' section of the vocabulary in the back of the Student's Book and to pronounce as many words as they can in two minutes while their partner listens. The partner then attempts to beat this time. They should concentrate on the initial 'r' rather than total accuracy.

Transcript
- Sport, populaire, pratiques, rugby, randonnée.
- Un rat rouge a rongé les roues de ma Renault rouillée.

Tip: Masculine and feminine nouns
As regards endings, point out that it is easier to tell the gender from the written form, where the ending is visible, rather than from the spoken form where the ending is not usually heard. If students need to guess a gender when speaking or writing, then they are more likely to be right than wrong if they choose the masculine, as 61% of nouns in French are masculine.

2
Identifying the gender of a list of sports nouns.

Solution
le basketball, **le** squash, **le** parachutisme, **la** danse, **le** kendo, **la** luge, **le** surf, **la** plongée, **la** pétanque, **le** badminton, **le** kayak, **le** hockey, **le** sprint.

3

In this game, each time a student takes a turn he or she gives an opinion on the last activity mentioned, and adds one more opinion on a new activity. An element of time pressure makes this more motivating: pairs have to note the activities mentioned and each pair aims to mention as many as possible in a given time limit – say, two minutes. Alternatively, students could work in threes with the third person keeping the list of activities mentioned.

Presentation ideas (comparatives)

Some preliminary revision may be done with the notion of height. Use drawings or an OHT to illustrate, or ask students to stand by the whiteboard and mark their height. Then model sentences involving comparatives, e.g. *Philip est plus grand que Mark. Anne est plus grande que Sarah.* Practise *vrai? ou faux?* using the heights marked (*Mark est plus grand que Philip.* Answer: *Faux.*) Then model the *moins* construction. *Mark est moins grand que Philip. Sarah est moins grande qu'Anne.* For *aussi ... que*, take one mark as a measure and try to find a student who is the same height. Then model *Laura est aussi grande que Sarah.*

Differentiation opportunity ⬇

A height game. The aim is to get a line of students graded by height. Take one student as a model at the front of the class. A second student comes out and stands beside him/her. Students watching simply say *plus grand(e)* or *moins grand(e)*. A third student goes and stands by Student 1 and is compared first with him/her. Students say *plus grand(e)/moins grand(e)* and Student 3 is then compared with Student 2 if necessary. He/she then takes an appropriate position in the line, etc.

The more complicated construction *Philip est plus grand que Jenny* can then be attempted.

Point grammaire: Comparatives and superlatives of adjectives

This explains the three forms of the comparative of adjectives(*plus/moins/aussi ... que ...*). Before the box in the Student's Book is used, the preliminary board work, above, could be adapted thus:

If '*Philippe . (+) grand . Mark*' means '*Philippe est plus grand que Mark*', what does '*La télévision . (+) populaire . le sport*' mean?

The explanation in the Student's Book of *moins* may be done in a similar way, using the symbol (−), and *aussi* by using (=).

4

Students decide if sentences in the task are true or false and correct the false ones.

Solution

1 F: La pétanque est moins populaire que le tennis.
2 F: Le football est plus populaire que le basket.
3 F: Le ski est plus populaire que le rugby.
4 F: Le judo est plus populaire que le golf.

5 V
6 F: les sports d'équipe sont plus populaires que les sports de découverte.

5

Check examples against the five sports personalities' heights which, in order, are:

Cédric Pioline: 1.88m
Christophe Moreau: 1.86m
Zinédine Zidane: 1.85m
Marie-Jo Pérec: 1.80m
Jacques Villeneuve: 1.68m

Students then compare themselves, e.g. *Moi, je suis moins grand(e) que Zinédine Zidane.*

ICT activity

Learning objectives

- to reuse the language on comparatives in the context of comparing prices;
- to use the Internet to do comparative research on prices;
- to present their findings to the rest of the class e.g. . . . *sont plus chers en France qu'en . . .*

1 As a class students list what they spend their money on. Agree on the price(s) in England.
2 Allocate two or three items to a pair of students.
3 Students then visit an appropriate site, e.g. **nomade.fr/contenu/thematiques/shopping** to find out the prices in France.
4 Students then report back costs and comparisons.

Differentiation opportunity ⬇ ⬆

■ ⬇**DW2.1A** Pair work. This worksheet practises comparatives in a different context, namely numbers and prices. Each student has half of the prices, and must communicate with his/her partner. Once the prices for each pair of articles is known, students agree on a comparison, e.g.

Le Disque de Britney Spears est plus cher que le disque des BackStreet Boys, or *Le disque des Backstreet Boys est moins cher que le disque de Britney Spears.*

■ ⬆**DW2.1B** works in the same way but has more complex vocabulary and higher numbers.

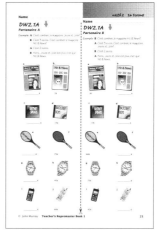
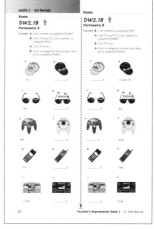

Unité 2 Pages 14–15

Point grammaire: Comparatives and superlatives of adjectives

Preliminary work may again be done with height, using the markers on the board, e.g. *Mark est plus grand que Stephen, Stephen est plus grand que Darren, mais Philip est le plus grand.* Alternatively, show a *Guinness Book of Records* to the class and read a few prepared translations, *e.g. Thrust SSC est la voiture la plus rapide du monde* emphasising *le/la plus . . .* to give the idea of the biggest, smallest, etc. Once this has been established, ask for opinions: *Quel est le sport le plus ennuyeux du monde? Quelle est la matière scolaire la plus ennuyeuse du monde?* Write *le/la plus rapide, le plus ennuyeux, la plus ennuyeuse* on the board as a point of reference.

Try to get students to use a framework such as **Je pense que** *X est le sport le plus ennuyeux du monde* or **À mon avis,** *Y est la matière scolaire la plus ennuyeuse du monde.* Write these on the board and leave them there for the first few attempts and then rub them off.

6

Students complete a gapped text using *le, la* and *les.*

Solution
À part **le** football, **le** tennis est **le** sport **le** plus populaire de France. Puis on a **le** ski et **la** pétanque. **Le** numéro cinq des Français, c'est **le** judo, et puis en sixième position on a **le** basketball. **La** moitié des Françaises et **la** majorité des Français pratiquent un sport.

7

Identify the tallest/smallest individuals among the sports personalities shown.

Solution
Cédric Pioline est le plus grand.
Jacques Villeneuve est le plus petit.

8

Students match people and things to world records. This exercise depends on a process of elimination and deduction, plus some grammatical awareness (*la* v. *les*). The ambiguity of the name Sandy Allen may lead to a revision of first attempts.

Solution
Sandy Allen = la femme la plus grande du monde.
Lockheed SR-71 = l'avion le plus rapide du monde.
Helen et Alice Walton = les femmes les plus riches du monde.
Titanic = le film le plus coûteux du monde.
Otto Acron = un des hommes les plus forts du monde.

9  [CD 1 track 14]
Students listen for sports mentioned and for ways of asking and expressing opinions. You could carry out some preliminary work on opinions, asking students to produce adjectives with positive meanings (*passionnant, excitant, intéressant, fascinant, merveilleux,* etc.) and those with negative meanings (*ennuyeux, barbant, fatigant, bête, compliqué,* etc.)

Differentiation opportunity
A simpler activity which could prepare weaker students for task 9: give the above list of adjectives to students in random order and ask them to sort them into positive and negative. Add any others that you think appropriate. If you read the words aloud with appropriate intonation and mime, students will be able to understand whether they are positive or negative. Students could then tick any of these adjectives that they hear on tape, before listening for expressions of opinion on a second run-through.

Transcript
Notre reporter a interviewé des jeunes du Collège Aux Quatre Vents, ainsi que leur professeur. Il a demandé leur opinion sur le sport.

Interviewer: Adèle, tu penses que le football est important?
Adèle: Moi, je pense que le football est le sport le plus passionnant du monde.
Interviewer: Et Philippe, tu trouves que le foot est passionnant?
Philippe: Non, pour moi c'est le sport le plus ennuyeux du monde.
Interviewer: Qu'est-ce que tu aimes alors?
Philippe: Moi, j'aime le hand-ball.
Interviewer: Ah, bon?
Philippe: Oui, je trouve que c'est le sport le plus excitant du monde.
Interviewer: Anne, toi aussi, tu aimes le hand-ball?
Anne: Non. C'est barbant. C'est peut-être le sport le plus barbant du monde.
Interviewer: Et John. Tu es anglais, non?
John: Oui. Je fais un échange en ce moment.
Interviewer: Et qu'est-ce que tu aimes comme sport?
John: Le cricket. Pour moi, c'est le sport le plus fascinant du monde.
Interviewer: Et le plus compliqué aussi, hein! Aline, pour toi, quel est le sport le plus excitant du monde?
Aline: La natation. À mon avis c'est le sport le plus intéressant du monde.
Interviewer: Et, vous M. Leclerc, vous êtes professeur de sport. À votre avis, quel est le sport le plus important du monde?
M. Leclerc: Moi, je pense que tous les sports sont importants. À mon avis, l'activité la plus importante du monde, c'est l'activité physique. Voilà.

Solution
1 le football, le hand-ball, le cricket, la natation
2 **a** je pense que; **b** je trouve que; **c** pour moi; **d** à mon avis; **e** tu penses que? **f** tu trouves que?

Extra idea

Using the expressions used for asking and giving opinions, students could interview each other and ask/express opinions on sports/school subjects/people/TV/events, using the adjectives which they assembled for the preliminary work to the listening exercise, e.g. *Tu penses que la Coupe du Monde est l'événement le plus passionnant du monde?*

Ça se dit comment? p.14 [CD 1 track 15]

In addition to the words given on the page, students could practise some common words and abbreviations beginning with '*u*'. These could be written on an OHT or on the whiteboard:

Ukraine, Ulster, unisexe, université, urgent, usine, utile, UEFA, UHT, USA, UV

Transcript
– Une, lu, bu, vendu, grue.
– L'urubu a vu une tortue poilue.

10

This exercise involves a short survey (**CM8** may be used for this purpose) and the class could be given a time limit in which to carry it out, e.g. five minutes. Once this has been done, students write out the list in order of popularity.

Differentiation opportunity↟

More able students can go on to write five sentences and compare results (Question ↟5). Insist that the three expressions given are used.

Extra ideas

1 Practice using **CM9** photocopied onto card and cut up. Students each have three comparison cards: '*plus*', '*moins*' and '*aussi*'. They take two noun cards and one adjective card and try to make sentences using comparatives, e.g. mon *frère/moins/intelligent/Howie D* = *Mon frère est moins intelligent que Howie D.* The sentences can be reported to the teacher, a partner or group.

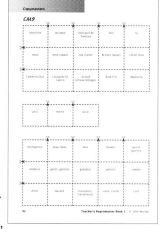

↟More able students may be asked to write down the full form of their sentences.
2 Carry out a survey on students' tastes in TV programmes, pop stars or foods. Students could write conclusions at the foot of their survey sheets and these could be mounted as a display, e.g.

Britney Spears est moins populaire que Robbie Williams.
  Les feuilletons sont plus populaires que les documentaires.

11

Students look at photos of sports and express their opinion on which is the most dangerous, most exotic, etc. Answers will depend on students' opinions.

Tip: Masculine nouns

Some reminders about deducing gender from noun endings, and a list of the most common -e endings that are masculine.

Differentiation opportunity↟

The other masculine forms ending in -e are -ice (except *la justice, la police, la malice*), -isme, -iste, and -logue. Since most of these are cognate forms with English, students could work out how to say things in French which they didn't know before, e.g. (organism = *organisme*, biologist = *biologiste*).

Solution

le sommaire, la glace, la bibliothèque, le privilège, le fromage, la classe, la voiture, la piscine, le sondage.

12

Students predict which are the most popular sports in which people participate in the UK. The actual order may be found on **www.english.sport.gov.uk.** The sports are:

walking 44.5%; swimming 24.8%; keep fit 12.3%; snooker/billiards 11.3%; cycling 11%; weight training 5.6%; association football 4.8%; golf 4.7%; running 4.5%; bowls 3.4%.

Having found out the answer, they design a poster in French to illustrate their findings.

Differentiation opportunity↡ ↟

↡Give the students the above list of sports (without the percentages) in random order and ask them to predict the correct order of popularity. Stress the fact that it is the number of participants that is in question.
↟Students could use both the French and the English lists on their poster if they wished. Some conclusion could be added at the bottom, e.g. *Le football est moins populaire en Angleterre qu'en France.*

ICT activity

Learning objectives

- to reinforce the language on sports by sending a questionnaire or series of questions to students in another school;
- to practise sending e-mails;
- to produce a presentation on their findings.

1 As a class, decide the content and the format of the questions to be asked. They might want to ask name, ages, favourite sport, how often played, etc.
2 Students e-mail these questions either in the body of the e-mail or as an attachment to students in another school. If you have a partner school with e-mail facilities in France this would be ideal. Alternatively, you might involve older students in your own school or in a neighbouring school.
3 Students cut and paste the responses of their 'partner' into a word-processed document, changing first to third person.
4 Students then make an oral presentation of their findings about their 'partner' to the rest of the class.

Unité 2 Pages 16–17

The article on page 16 is set out like a sports interview from a magazine. The emphasis is on recent events and there are numerous examples of the perfect tense.

Transcript

Interviewer: Marcelo, vous avez semblé très confiant cette semaine.
Marcelo: Oui, j'ai joué très offensif contre Alberto Costa. Je suis très confiant, et c'est pour ça que j'ai gagné.
Interviewer: Vous allez jouer contre Berasategui aujourd'hui. Vous l'avez battu à Rome, non?
Marcelo: Oui, j'ai joué contre lui la semaine dernière et j'ai gagné 7–6, 6–2.
Interviewer: Vous avez été opposé à Carlos Moya d'Espagne au tournoi de Sankt Pölten il y a deux semaines, non?
Marcelo: Oui, et j'ai été éliminé. Mais j'aime la compétition. J'aime jouer. Moya a très bien joué.
Interviewer: Vous êtes content de votre victoire sur Alberto Costa?
Marcelo: Oui, ce match a prouvé que je suis en forme. Je suis très content. Et mon manager aussi! Nous avons célébré notre victoire ensemble avec une bouteille de champagne!

Point grammaire

Since *avoir* is so important for the formation of the perfect tense, some revision is appropriate at this point.

Differentiation opportunity ⬇

Students of lower ability may require revision of the forms of *avoir*. A question and answer session could

begin with the topics of family and pets (*Tu as des frères ou des sœurs? Tu as des animaux?*) in order to elicit *j'ai* and *je n'ai pas*. Reporting by students on what others have said will produce *il/elle* and *ils/elles* forms, e.g.

Catherine a des frères ou des sœurs? – Oui, elle a deux sœurs. Patsy et Ruth ont des animaux? – Oui, elles ont des chats.

The Q/A session could then extend to cars/motorbikes/sports equipment/boyfriends/girlfriends, practising the same construction.

Display **CM6** (lower half) which shows the present tense of *avoir* or ask the students to reconstruct the whole verb on the board.

Extra ideas

1 Write a date on the board to illustrate *le week-end dernier*, and then give an account of what you did. At the end ask *oui/non* questions, e.g. *J'ai joué au tennis?* and write the forms that occurred in your presentation on the board, e.g. *J'ai joué…, j'ai regardé…, j'ai écouté…* The degree of explanation offered here will depend on the ability of the class.
2 Prepare a set of ten red cards each showing an example of a verb in the perfect tense (*je* form) and a second set of red cards showing temporal adverbs relating to the past: *hier, avant-hier, il y a trois jours, la semaine dernière*, etc. Blu-tack these to the board (time expressions on the left and verbs on the right) and ask students to make up sentences, each with one time expression and one verb. (These red cards – red signifying past events/concepts – will have several other uses later.)

13 📖✏️🎧 [CD 1 track 16]

Students complete the perfect tense sentences with the appropriate form of *avoir* (**1**) and then decide whether sentences in the exercise are true or false (**2**).

Solution

1 a Marcelo Rios **a** accordé une interview à Tennis International.
 b «Je n'**ai** pas été très confiant, et c'est pour ça que j'**ai** perdu.»
 c Rios **a** été opposé à Berasategui à Sankt Pölten il y a deux semaines.
 d Rios et son manager **ont** été très contents.
 e Costa **a** joué très offensif.
 f Marcelo Rios **a** été éliminé par Costa.
 g Marcelo et son manager **ont** célébré la victoire ensemble.
 h Le match **a** prouvé que Marcelo est un excellent joueur.
2 a V; b F; c V; d V; e F; f F; g V; h V.
⬆3 b «J'**ai été** très confiant, et c'est pour ça que j'**ai gagné**.»
 e **Rios** a joué très offensif.
 f Marcelo Rios a été éliminé par **Moya**.

14 [CD 1 track 17]

A volleyball sports commentator talks about Laurent Capet of Paris–Volley who has just (2001) celebrated his 29th birthday. The text has many words with the sound 'ou', e.g. *jouer, joueur, groupe, Coupe, tournoi, toujours, aujourd'hui* (see **Ça se dit comment?**), plus a range of perfect tenses (mainly -*er* verbs) and some expressions of opinion/ comparatives as covered earlier in the unit.

Transcript

Interviewer: Champion de France depuis trois ans, Laurent Capet a fêté samedi son vingt-neuvième anniversaire. Il a fêté aussi la victoire, car samedi dernier, le premier mai, en fin de tournoi, Paris–Volley a gagné son match contre Poitiers, 17 à 15. Capet lui-même a marqué neuf points. Laurent, une bonne semaine pour vous, alors?

Capet: Ouais . . . ouais . . . je pense que nous avons très bien joué. Nous avons été très performants et nous sommes très contents d'être champions. Au début du tournoi, notre groupe était assez faible, à mon avis, mais nous avons bien travaillé et samedi le moral était bon. Nous étions plus en forme que nos opposants . . . Et voilà, la Coupe est à nous maintenant. Aujourd'hui c'est un jour de repos et on se relaxe.

Interviewer: Et les neuf points que vous avez marqués, vous en êtes content?

Capet: Ouais . . . en plus c'était mon anniversaire samedi!

Interviewer: Et vous avez bien fêté les deux événements?

Capet: Ben . . . samedi soir, on a mangé dans un bon restaurant . . . et on a consommé pas mal de vin! Et moi, j'ai décidé d'acheter une nouvelle voiture, un peu plus chère que ma voiture actuelle, quoi!

Solution

Nom	Laurent Capet
Âge	29 ans
Points marqués dans le match	9
Date du match	le premier mai
Qui a gagné	Paris–Volley
Les célébrations (3 choses)	On a mangé dans un bon restaurant. Ils ont consommé beaucoup de vin. Il a décidé d'acheter une nouvelle voiture.

15

Linked to **Ça se dit comment?** the order in which the 'ou' words appear is: *tournoi, joué, groupe, Coupe, aujourd'hui*

Ça se dit comment? p.17 [CD 1 track 18]

Transcript

– Tout, doux, joujou, glouglou.
– Les joues des joueurs sont couvertes de boue.

Differentiation opportunity ⬇ ⬆

At this point **DW2.2A** and **2.2B** may be used. These are cloze exercises based on a simplified form of the article.

- ■ ⬇**DW2.2A:** Students choose the correct perfect tense verb from among those supplied.
- ■ ⬆**DW2.2B:** Students fill the same gaps but the verbs are not supplied.

Solution

Interviewer: Laurent Capet **a fêté** samedi son vingt-neuvième anniversaire. Il **a fêté** aussi la victoire, car samedi dernier, Paris–Volley a gagné son match contre Poitiers, 17 à 15. Capet **a marqué** neuf points. Laurent, une bonne semaine pour vous, alors?

Capet: Ouais . . . ouais . . . À mon avis, nous **avons joué** très forts. Au début du tournoi, notre groupe n'était pas fort, mais on **a travaillé** dur et samedi le moral était bon. Nous **avons joué** plus offensifs que nos opposants. Aujourd'hui c'est un jour de repos et on se relaxe.

Interviewer: Vous **avez marqué** neuf points. Vous en êtes content?

Capet: Oui . . . et c'était mon anniversaire samedi.

Interviewer: Et vous avez célébré ensemble les deux événements?

Capet: Oui, samedi soir, on **a mangé** dans un bon restaurant. Et moi, j'**ai décidé** d'acheter une nouvelle voiture.

ICT activity

Learning objectives

- to use search strategies for an effective search on the Internet;
- to understand details from Internet sources using context and other clues;
- to present that information in a different format.

1 The class decides the headings under which they want to search for information.
2 Students search the Internet to find the web-site of a famous French sportsman or woman.
⬇3 Students complete a grid designed by the teacher based on the agreed headings.
⬆4 Students write an interview with that person including a range of information.

Tip: *On*

Here the use of *on* to replace *nous* is stressed. Remind students that *on* needs the third person singular of the verb (cf. Unit 1) and then give a number of sentences to transform into the *on* form, e.g. *Nous avons bien travaillé. Nous avons gagné. Nous avons fêté la victoire. Nous avons mangé dans un restaurant. Nous avons consommé beaucoup de vin.*

Then ask students what they did last weekend or during the last holidays, requiring them to begin *On a . . .* They can then practise this student to student.

Extra idea

Students could work in pairs using **CM10** (grammar battleships) to practise the perfect tense. They choose a time expression (horizontal axis) and a verb in the perfect tense (vertical axis). They mark their own choices first by shading eight squares, and then play Battleships by marking hits and misses with X and O.

EGW2 (see full notes at the end of this unit) offers extra grammar practice on the perfect tense.

Differentiation opportunities ↓ ↑

↓ For students of lower ability, provide small cards with a number of holiday activities in the perfect tense: *J'ai visité . . ., J'ai joué . . ., J'ai regardé . . ., J'ai mangé . . ., J'ai dansé . . ., J'ai dragué . . ., J'ai aimé . . ., J'ai quitté . . .* Ask them to put them into an appropriate order for a holiday and to think of appropriate endings to the sentences. Some students may need help with possible endings.

They could write a short report on an imagined holiday using these sentences, if this is within their capability.

↑ As extension work, students could complete the story of the holiday using the verbs suggested.

16

Group work using the material in the Student's Book. Questions are put by students to individuals or pairs of students (thus practising *tu/vous* and *je/nous* forms). Answers will depend on students.

17

Students are asked to prepare an article about themselves when they are famous. They could write down some basic details first, e.g. name, age, height, family, team played for, match won last weekend, celebrations, etc. They could then be encouraged to use comparatives (e.g. *je suis donc plus grand(e) que mon frère*) before moving on to weekend events. Here they have the opportunity to say what they usually do (see Unit 1) and what they did last weekend, using the perfect tense.

Unité 2 Pages 18–19

The text on page 18, which gives advice on getting fit, practises the use of *devoir* and *il faut*. Students could be asked what sort of formulae they might expect to find in an article in English of this type. When they read the article, they could then be asked what they think *on doit* and *il faut* mean.

18 📖 [CD 1 track 19]

Students' comprehension of the advice is tested by asking them whether Danny, shown in the cartoon, is following the advice or not.

Transcript

Jeunes sportifs
Le courrier sportif.
Danny de Saint-Omer nous demande:
– *Je ne suis pas très en forme. Je trouve que le fitness, c'est bon, mais j'ai peur d'avoir un accident. Qu'est-ce qu'il faut faire pour éviter les accidents?*
Nous avons des conseils essentiels à offrir à Danny:
- **On doit** bien se préparer par la pratique régulière d'un sport.
- **Il faut** s'échauffer par des exercices ou massages.
- Pendant l'effort, **on doit** boire régulièrement de l'eau.
- **Il faut** faire une pause si on est fatigué.
- **On doit** porter des protections pour les sports à risque.

Solution

1 Oui; **2** Non; **3** Oui; **4** Non; **5** Oui

Point grammaire: The verb *devoir*

It is useful to draw attention to the fact that *devoir* is one of several verbs which change their vowel sound throughout the singular and in the third person plural. The verb has been set out in such a way as to emphasise this, on **CM11**.

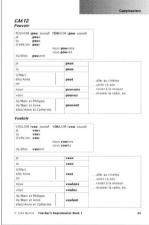

See **CM12** for the other two main modal verbs that follow this pattern: *pouvoir* and *vouloir*.

19

Students work out the requirements for particular sports. Several answers are possible.

1 le cyclisme, la course automobile, le motocyclisme, le hockey sur glace, le cricket, le ski, le football américain, le kayak, le VTT;
2 la natation, le water-polo, le ski nautique;
3 la course automobile, le motocyclisme;
4 le football, le rugby, le hockey, le hockey sur glace, le basketball;
5 l'équitation, le polo, les concours de chiens de berger (sheepdog trials);
6 la course automobile, le hockey sur glace, le patin à glace, le cricket, le football (gardien de but);
7 l'athlétisme, le football, le tennis, le rugby, le cricket, le volleyball;
8 le football.

20  [CD 1 track 20]

To ease students into this listening task, ask them to indicate (saying *oui/non*) whether they are likely to hear the following words in an interview with a swimmer: *natation, casque, piscine, vélo, nager, régulièrement, protéines, frites, en forme, le matin.*

Students listen to the cassette or CD – a local radio interview with a swimmer who describes her training and fitness regime.

Transcript

Interviewer: Ici Radio Corsaire. Vous écoutez Programme Jeunesse. Bonjour. Aujourd'hui nous parlons à Yvette Jansen, championne junior de natation. Yvette Jansen, que faites vous pour rester en forme?

Yvette: Ben . . . il faut s'entraîner régulièrement . . . chaque jour, quoi! Normalement je nage deux fois par jour, une fois le matin, une fois le soir. Alors, je me lève de bonne heure . . . vers six heures . . . et je vais à la piscine. Je passe une heure à nager et puis je rentre à la maison et je prends le petit déjeuner. Si on fait beaucoup d'exercice, il faut bien se nourrir. Donc, je dois manger beaucoup de céréales, mais très peu de graisse . . . et puis . . . pendant la journée . . . ben . . . bon ben . . . il faut manger des légumes, beaucoup de légumes, et bien sûr, des protéines . . . de la viande, des œufs, quoi! Si on désire garder la forme . . . et la ligne . . . on ne doit pas trop boire . . . de l'eau minérale, oui, ça va, mais pas d'alcool, hein?

Interviewer: Et que faites-vous pour vous relaxer?

Yvette: Ben . . . quelquefois je promène le chien ou je fais une promenade toute seule. J'aime bien respirer de l'air frais. Et puis . . . euh . . . J'aime bien jouer au tennis. De temps en temps je passe la matinée à faire du tennis.

Interviewer: Et vous vous couchez de bonne heure?

Yvette: Ah oui. Je n'ai pas le temps de sortir. Je me couche vers dix heures chaque nuit. Je dors environ huit heures, et puis, hop, à six heures je me lève de nouveau!

Interviewer: Yvette Jansen, merci bien.

Solution

1 Students produce sentences on what the swimmer Yvette Jansen says. Sentences will depend on students' interpretations but could include:
   a Il faut s'entraîner régulièrement.
   b On doit bien se nourrir.
   c Je dois nager deux fois par jour.
   d Il ne faut pas boire d'alcool.
   e On ne doit pas manger beaucoup de graisse.
   f Je ne dois pas me coucher tard.
2 Je passe une heure à nager.

Tip: *Passer + à* + infinitive

Since the perfect tense has now been revised, it would be useful to practise the perfect of *passer + à* + infinitive. Students could be asked how they spent their time yesterday/last weekend, e.g.

– *Comment est-ce que tu as passé ton temps le week-end dernier?*
– *J'ai passé une heure à regarder la télé, et j'ai passé deux heures à faire mes devoirs.*

Differentiation opportunity

This practice could be a preliminary to the extension activity Question 2 in task 21. Practice with the third person could be achieved by asking how their father/mother/friend spent the evening/weekend or what the family did, e.g.

On a passé deux heures à ranger le garage.

21

1 Students say or write down how long they spend on activites in a normal week.
2 They say how long they spent on activities last weekend.

22

1 Students choose which items give good advice.

Solution

b Il faut manger beaucoup de fruits et de légumes.
c Il faut pratiquer un sport.
g Il faut dormir 7 ou 8 heures chaque nuit.
i Il faut sortir et respirer de l'air frais.

2 Students suggest other pieces of advice about staying fit. Examples:

Je pense qu'on doit passer une heure par jour à faire du sport.
À mon avis, il faut se promener tous les jours.
Moi, je crois qu'on doit nager deux fois par semaine.
Je pense qu'il ne faut pas boire d'alcool.

ICT activity

Learning objectives

- to understand details from a selected website using context and other clues;
- to reinforce students' understanding of what constitutes a healthy diet;

- to design a poster to support a 'healthy eating campaign'.

1 Teacher familiarises her/himself with the website: **perso.club-internet.fr/chpavie/index.htm** – which contains a range of information and graphics on diet.

2 Teacher gives the students an outline for the content of the poster.

3 Students visit the website and download text and graphics which they then incorporate into their posters.

↓4 Lower attainers might be given the headings of the five areas necessary for a healthy diet and be asked to find examples from the website.

Differentiation opportunities ↓

DW2.3 uses *il faut/il ne faut pas* in a different context, namely what you might need to do in order to be happy. It shows jumbled illustrations and phrases. These are linked together before the phrases are put into the table under the positive and negative columns.

Students compare various foods and say which are more delicious/healthy, etc., and add a further comment using a comparative.

Unité 2 Page 20

24 [CD 1 track 21]

An article about a 'fat camp' in the USA.

Transcript

Les enfants du Coca-hamburger

Aux USA 30% à 40% des enfants sont obèses.

Les hamburgers sont le plat le plus populaire chez les enfants américains, et le Coca est la boisson la plus aimée.

À Camp Shane, à 150 kilomètres de New York, 350 enfants, agés de sept à dix-neuf ans, sont soumis à des activités physiques intenses (six heures de sport par jour) et un régime sévère.

Les enfants passent entre trois et neuf semaines à Camp Shane.

Le coût? 500 dollars les sept jours.

Scott dit: «Ici c'est dur, mais je voudrais être plus mince.»

Ici, les enfants apprennent à dire «non» devant une portion de frites ou une glace au chocolat. Adieu, les hamburgers, adieu, le Coca!

Presentation idea

Number revision would be a useful preliminary here, perhaps using the number cards described in Unit 1.

Students read the article and complete the table with a number or numbers.

Solution

1	$500	Prix d'une semaine à Camp Shane
2	7–19 ans	Âge des enfants
3	150 kilomètres	Distance entre Camp Shane et New York
4	6	Heures de sport par jour
5	30%–40%	Pourcentage des enfants obèses
6	3–9	Semaines passées à Camp Shane
7	350	Nombre d'enfants à Camp Shane

Tip: Cognates

Points out the direct relationship between French and English words ending in *ité/*-ity, respectively.

Solution

1 activity; **2** électricité; **3** identity; **4** majorité; **5** density; **6** qualité; **7** reality; **8** obésité; **9** intensity; **10** capacité

25 [CD 1 track 22]

Students listen to an interview with Guy who has been to Camp Shane. The interview includes examples of *-er* perfect tenses, a comparative and opinions. Students could first listen and just write down the missing word(s) in rough, before copying the sentences and inserting what they have heard.

Transcript

Interviewer: Guy, tu as passé combien de temps à Camp Shane?

Guy: J'y ai passé six semaines.

Interviewer: Et comment as-tu trouvé le régime là-bas?

Guy: Ben, j'ai trouvé que le régime est dur, très, très dur.

Interviewer: Tu as fait beaucoup de sports, alors?

Guy: Oui, tous les jours. Le football, j'ai aimé, mais on a dû nager aussi, et ça, j'ai vraiment détesté. Je trouve la natation plus difficile que le basket.

Interviewer: Tu as fait d'autres sports?

Guy: Oui, du basket et de la voile. C'était bien tout ça, surtout la voile.

Interviewer: Et combien de kilos as-tu perdus?

Guy: Moi, j'ai perdu quinze kilos.

Interviewer: Super!

Guy: Ah oui, mais mon copain André, lui, il a perdu vingt kilos. Il faut le voir maintenant. C'est un squelette!

Solution

1 a Guy a quitté le camp après six semaines.
  b Il a trouvé que le régime est dur.
  c Il a aimé le football, mais il a détesté la natation.
  d Il a fait du basketball et de la voile.
  e Guy a perdu 15 kilos, et son ami a perdu 20 kilos.

2 Students invent a set of rules for Camp Shane. You could give some key words to get them thinking, e.g. *eau minérale, Coca Cola, salades*.

Solution

Students' own choices, but answers could include:

On doit boire beaucoup d'eau minérale.
On ne doit pas boire de Coca Cola.
On doit dormir 7 à 8 heures chaque nuit.
On ne doit pas manger de frites.
Il faut faire de l'exercice.
Il faut manger des salades.
On ne doit pas manger de glaces.
On doit se coucher à dix heures.
On ne doit pas rester au lit.
On ne doit pas passer des heures à regarder la télévision.

26 ✐
Students describe an imaginary weekend at Camp Shane. This exercise gives practice in the use of the perfect tense.

Homework opportunity

The use of *devoir* and *il faut* could be extended to other contexts such as school, youth club and the workplace. Short sets of rules could be composed for each.

Unité 2 Page 21

Checkpoints

Test

The **Test** checks students' skills in the grammatical goals of the unit:

* making comparisons using adjectives
* recognising masculine and feminine nouns
* using *on*
* using the perfect tense with *avoir*
* using *il faut* and the verb *devoir* to say what you must do

Solution

1 a Le football est plus fatigant que la natation. [1]
  b Le français est plus facile que le chinois. [1]

  c Les jus de fruits sont moins populaires que le Coca. [1]
  d Le jogging est moins coûteux que la voile. [1]
  e La lecture est aussi/plus/moins passionnante que la danse. [1]

2 a L'Allemagne est le pays **le** plus riche d'Europe. [1]
  b Le «Blackbird» est l'avion **le** plus rapide du monde. [1]
  c La baleine bleue est la baleine **la** plus lourde du monde. [1]
  d Les Alpes sont les montagnes **les** plus hautes de la France. [1]

3 Open-ended task: write three comparatives. [6]
4 Masculin ou féminin? sport (m), natation (f), voile (f), rugby (m), danse (f) [5]
5 a Vendredi matin, elle a joué au tennis. [1]
  b Samedi matin, elle a fait de la natation. [1]
  c Dimanche après-midi, elle a fait de l'équitation. [1]
  d Lundi matin, elle a joué au football. [1]
  e Mardi soir, elle a joué a badminton. [1]
6 a Tu **dois** rester à la maison. [1]
  b Nous **devons** partir maintenant. [1]
  c Les filles **doivent** partir aussi. [1]
7 Open-ended task: write six pieces of advice under these two headings:

On doit/On ne doit pas [6]
Il faut/Il ne faut pas [6]

Total [40]

Quiz

The **Quiz** checks students' knowledge acquired in the unit, about:

* popular sports in France
* sports personalities
* record holders
* fitness and exercise
* healthy lifestyles

Solution

1 Le football [1]
2 La natation est moins populaire que le tennis [1]
3 Le golf [1]
4 Le tennis [1]
5 Sandy Allen [1]
6 Roland-Garros [1]
7 a le volleyball [1]
  b le tennis [1]
  c l'athlétisme [1]
  d pilote, Formule 1 [1]
  e le cyclisme [1]
  f le football [1]
8 a Camp Shane [1]
  b 7–19 ans [1]
  c $500 [1]

Total [15]

Projets

A Students design a poster giving advice about fitness. Websites on sport and fitness may be found by consulting **www.nomade.fr.** These posters could be mounted around the school.

B Students compare two sports or sports personalities. They could say if one sport is more difficult, easier, etc. than the other. Sports personalities could be compared in terms of height, weight, speed, strength, etc.

C Students describe a sport by responding to prompt questions. Note the use of *il faut* and *on* to convey generalities.

EGW2 teaching notes

EGW2 provides extra grammar/homework on the perfect tense.
Activity 1 uses a gapped account of a water-sports holiday. Students insert the correct form of *avoir*. You could give students a copy of **CM6** (*avoir*) for reference. **Activity 2** extends this, inviting abler students to continue the story and suggesting verbs they could use.

Solution

André Leconte a passé ses vacances au bord de la mer à Dinard. Les vacances **ont** duré du 20 juillet au 2 août. Il a fait des sports aquatiques. Le premier jour, André **a** rencontré Stéphanie, et ils **ont** décidé de faire de la plongée. André et Stéphanie **ont** parlé de leur séjour.

«Au début, j'**ai** trouvé la plongée assez difficile,» dit André.
«Oui,» répond Stéphanie, «mais tu **as** essayé!»
«Après, nous **avons** commencé à faire de la planche à voile. Ce n'était pas facile!»
«Tu as raison,» répond Stéphanie. «Les autres membres du groupe **ont** trouvé la planche assez facile. Pour moi, c'était très difficile!»
«Le premier jour **a** été fatigant, mais le soir on **a** dansé à la disco.»
«Le lendemain, André et moi nous **avons** regardé du ski nautique. Fantastique!»
«L'après-midi, le groupe **a** joué au water-polo. Notre équipe a gagné!»
«Ah oui, les deux semaines **ont** vite passé. On **a** essayé toutes sortes de sports. C'était vraiment super!»

unité 3
Boulot

Unité 3 Pages 22–23

The opening two pages focus on revision of the verb *pouvoir* and presents a text in the form of a magazine article relating to the use of the Internet for educational purposes.

1 Transcript [CD 1 track 23]

Vous nous demandez ...

Cécile: Moi, je suis en 3ᵉ et je veux être programmeuse, mais j'ai des problèmes en calcul. Où est-ce que je peux trouver de l'aide?

Réponse: Tu as un ordinateur chez toi, Cécile? Tu sais, maintenant on peut étudier toutes les matières scolaires en ligne ... ou presque. Tu dis que tu as des problèmes en calcul. Il y a beaucoup de sites web éducatifs où tu peux trouver des puzzles, des jeux et des tests. Oui, le monde d'Internet, c'est à toi! Maintenant, nous pouvons faire des études scolaires à la maison. Est-ce qu'on peut faire ses devoirs à l'aide d'Internet? Bien sûr! On peut trouver toutes sortes d'informations à l'aide d'un moteur de recherche. Mais on ne peut pas rester à la maison tout le temps! Il faut aller au collège, bien sûr. Là, vous pouvez consulter vos professeurs. Les professeurs peuvent vous offrir des conseils et ils peuvent vous guider. Oui, le monde change, mais il faut continuer à travailler!

Solution
1 C'est une **jeune fille** qui écrit cette lettre.
2 Elle ne comprend pas le **calcul**.
3 Il y a un **grand** nombre de sites web éducatifs.
4 Il est **possible** de faire des recherches à la maison.
5 Il faut **continuer d'aller au collège**.
6 Les **professeurs** sont capables de vous aider.

Tip

This explains the numbering system of the French secondary and tertiary education systems. Information could also be given on the primary system. The classes in the primary system are:

CP = Cours préparatoire
CE1 = Cours élémentaire 1
CE2 = Cours élémentaire 2
CM1 = Cours moyen 1
CM2 = Cours moyen 2

(French children start school at the age of six.)

Since students should be able to talk not only about themselves, you could ask them to say in which class their friend, sister or brother is at present. They could also say what they did in any given year. Avoid the imperfect, e.g.

En sixième, j'ai commencé à apprendre le français.
En cinquième j'ai étudié ...

Ça se dit comment? p.22 [CD 1 track 24]

Very common words with this sound are: *mon, ton, son, sont, on, bon, onze, long.* You could revise the -*an*- sound from Unit 1 (page 5) and ask students to combine words to illustrate the difference in sound, e.g. *Le monde est très grand. Il faut avoir un contact avec la France.*

Transcript
- on, monde, pouvons, maison, information, consulter, conseils, continuer
- comprendre, nombre
- Bon nombre de longs camions sont sur le pont d'Avignon.

2

Finding synonymous expressions.

Solution
1 on peut; **2** beaucoup de; **3** à la maison; **4** bien sûr; **5** on ne peut pas rester; **6** il faut

Differentiation opportunity ⬆

Some practice on the notions of **possibility** and **impossibility** could follow this exercise:

– *Il est possible de faire du foot au collège?*
– *Oui,* **on peut** *jouer au foot tous les jours.*
– *Il est possible de faire du théâtre tous les jours?*
– *Non,* **on ne peut pas** *faire du théâtre tous les jours.*

Similarly, revision of *devoir* and *il faut* (Unit 2) will help:

– *Il faut arriver arriver au collège à 9 heures?*
– *Non,* **on doit** *arriver à 8h 40.*

Point grammaire: The verb *pouvoir*

CM12 shows the forms for the present tense of *pouvoir* (and *vouloir*, covered later in the unit). This may be made into an OHT, issued as a reference tool to each student or enlarged and used as a classroom poster. Remind students that the three singular forms sound the same and the *ils* form has the same vowel as these. The *nous* and *vous* forms resemble the infinitive.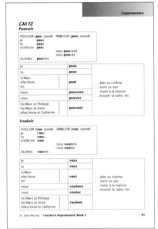

The verb could be set out on the board as for *devoir* (Unit 2).

Differentiation opportunities

⬆ More able classes may revise the whole paradigm of *pouvoir* (see Grammar, page 150). The activity symbols from **CM1** could be used.

An extension activity would be to add the contrary using *devoir*:

– *On ne peut pas manger en classe. On doit manger dans la cantine.*
– *On ne peut pas porter un pull rouge. On doit porter l'uniforme scolaire.*

This could become a writing activity, possibly in the form of a poster. Alternatively, students could make up a list of 'interdictions' for their teachers:

Les profs ne peuvent pas fumer. Ils doivent faire de l'exercice.

⬇ Students of lower ability may concentrate firstly on *je* and *tu*, e.g. under the heading 'What I can do at home': *Moi, je peux téléphoner à mes copains. Et toi, tu peux téléphoner à tes copains, Sam?*
Follow this with third person singular forms, getting students to report what they have just heard (*Susie peut tchatcher sur Internet*) followed by third person plural forms (*Susie, Daniel et Sam peuvent tchatcher sur Internet*). *Vous* and *nous* may also be practised by using the activity symbols from **CM1**, e.g.

– *Vous pouvez écouter de la musique, Darren et Emma?*
– *Oui, nous pouvons écouter de la musique.*

Once this is established, try *Qu'est-ce que vous pouvez faire, Sam et Linda?* eliciting, *Nous pouvons écouter la radio*, etc. Ask students to make up other activities beginning *Nous . . .* This could cover activities done at school or in a youth club.

 3

Practice of the use of expressions of time and frequency (see Unit 1) and positive and negative forms of *pouvoir*. For both Questions 1 and ⬆2, the sentences made up will be of the students' own choice, but all should contain correct forms of *pouvoir*.

Extra idea

Task 3 could take the form of producing a Community College leaflet for French visitors/exchange partners explaining what activities are available to the local community. This is an opportunity to use ICT (scanning, word-processing).

Tip: Tu and *vous*

The basic rule in French is: call your friend, each of your family members and your dog *tu*; call everybody else *vous*! This concept is not easy to grasp, despite practice in early years. More able students may be able to grasp this if you explain that most of the major European languages have the distinction between the informal one-person form and the polite/plural forms and that only English has the one-size-fits-all pronoun.

	Singular informal	Plural informal	Singular polite	Plural polite
Spanish	tú	vosotros	Usted	Ustedes
German	du	ihr	Sie	Sie
Italian	tu	Lei	Voi	Loro
French	tu	vous	vous	vous
English	you	you (lot)	you	you

 4

Draw attention to the formality or informality of the situation and the number of persons addressed.

Solution
1 **Vous pouvez** m'aider, Monsieur?
2 **Tu peux** m'aider, maman?
3 **Vous pouvez** travailler dans la bibliothèque, Aline et Marie-Jo.
4 **Vous pouvez** entrer maintenant, Monsieur, Madame.
5 **Tu peux** sortir ce soir, Paulette?

 5

Two-choice questions based on the numbers in the *Quelques chiffres* text.
Decimals and percentages have been dealt with in Unit 2. Practise the pronunciation of the numbers in the box by asking: *Nombre d'enseignants en France? Pourcentage des élèves dans le privé?*

Practise numbers using the number cards described in Unit 1. Add a few with decimal points or percentages, e.g. 4,1; 13,7; 25%; 100%.

Solution
1 b; **2** b; **3** a

Extra idea

While you are dealing with *majorité*, introduce *minorité* and ask which words ending in *-ité* students can remember from Unit 2 (Tip, page 20). Students could compose a poem or rap with words rhyming in *-ité*, e.g.

On va à l'université, Étudier l'électricité, Faire des activités, Avec la majorité.

Unité 3 Pages 24–25

These two pages focus on jobs.

Presents short advertisements such as might be found in the *Offres d'emplois* column of a local newspaper. The form of each advert is similar, with a final comment at the foot of each. Students match the requirements to the jobs.

Solution
1 b; **2** d; **3** c; **4** a; **5** e

 [CD1 track 25]

Students listen to five people talking about their experiences of work.

1 They assign one of the five advertised posts to each person. This work could be done individually or in pairs.
2 Students give a reason for each match.

Transcript

Christine: Moi, j'ai travaillé dans un café pendant les vacances. Donc, je connais les boissons alcoolisées et non-alcoolisées . . . Et on servait des plats chauds aussi . . . omelettes, crêpes, etc. J'aime ce travail . . . le contact avec le grand public . . . les conversations, tout ça.

Kamel: Moi, j'ai travaillé en colonie de vacances . . . c'était bien, quoi . . . J'étais responsable d'un groupe de jeunes pendant la journée . . . et le soir, ben, quelquefois on passait des disques, on dansait, on s'amusait, quoi. C'était chouette.

Benoît: Moi, je distribue des journaux. Je dois me lever de bonne heure pour faire ça. Quelquefois on change de tournée . . . donc, je connais bien la ville . . . les routes, les petites rues, les coins, les recoins et je connais beaucoup de gens aussi. C'est bien.

Alice: Mes parents ne me donnent pas d'argent de poche. Donc, je fais du baby-sitting . . . pour trois familles. J'adore ça! . . . les petits, j'aime bien, même quand les bébés pleurent . . . c'est pas trop difficile et ça me fait de l'argent de poche.

Gérard: Moi, je ne cherche pas un emploi à plein temps . . . c'est juste pour les vacances . . . euh . . .

j'ai travaillé dans une boulangerie – pas comme boulanger. Non, je servais les clients. En septembre je vais à l'Université de Rennes pour étudier les maths . . . j'aime bien les maths.

Solution
a Christine – serveuse; **b** Kamel – animateur; **c** Benoît – distributeur; **d** Alice – garde d'enfants; **e** Gérard – caissier

Differentiation opportunity

More able students could explain their choice, e.g.

X peut travailler comme Y parce qu'elle/il a fait/été/travaillé . . . etc.

Extra idea

A discussion on qualities necessary for the jobs. Students could say what sort of experience might qualify people for the posts advertised. Students could look at the *petites annonces* of a local paper and pick out jobs that they recognise or use a dictionary to find out those that they don't.

1 Students complete the table with the correct form of the noun, using the Tip as a guide (see Student's Book, page 24).

Solution

Masculin	Féminin
électricien	**électricienne**
instituteur	institutrice
vendeur	**vendeuse**
boulanger	boulangère
chanteur	**chanteuse**
infirmier	infirmière
caissier	**caissière**

2 Students insert appropriate nouns from the table into the gapped sentences.

Solution
a boulanger; **b** chanteuse; **c** instituteur; **d** vendeuse (*or* caissière); **e** infirmier

 [CD 1 track 26]

Preparation for this could include asking students what sort of weekend work they do, how many hours they do, what the pay is per hour, whether they have to wear special clothes or a uniform and what they think of the job. This could be set out on the board in tabular form (as for task 9). Students could be asked to predict what might appear in these columns for the exercise, i.e. numbers up to 40, prices, names of clothes, and words/ expressions giving opinions. They could then do a preliminary exercise to calculate who earns the most among the names on the board before tackling the listening exercise.

Transcript

Interviewer: Alors, Fabien, vous faites quelle sorte de travail?

Fabien: Moi, je suis disc jockey dans un club . . . ben . . . je fais 30 heures par semaine. C'est pas mal payé, hein, je gagne 17 euros à l'heure.

Interviewer: Et vous devez porter des vêtements spéciaux?

Fabien: Mais non . . . du tout . . . ben . . . d'habitude je porte un jean et un t-shirt.

Interviewer: Et ça vous plaît comme métier?

Fabien: Ah oui! J'aime bien. C'est super!

Interviewer: Merci bien. Et Maïté, que faites-vous comme métier?

Maïté: Moi, je suis boulangère.

Interviewer: Et vous travaillez de longues heures, alors?

Maïté: Oui, surtout s'il y a des problèmes. Je travaille jusqu'à 40 heures par semaine . . . je gagne 14 euros à l'heure.

Interviewer: Et qu'est-ce que vous portez?

Maïté: Ben . . . une blouse blanche et un petit chapeau blanc.

Interviewer: Et que pensez-vous de cela comme métier?

Maïté: Alors . . . D'habitude, je dois me lever à 5 heures du matin et les heures sont longues . . . c'est fatigant . . . mais c'est pas mal, quoi.

Interviewer: Bon. Valérie, que faites vous comme travail?

Valérie: Moi, je suis infirmière dans l'hôpital municipal.

Interviewer: C'est bien payé?

Valérie: Non, pas du tout. Je gagne environ 25 euros à l'heure.

Interviewer: Vous travaillez combien d'heures par semaine?

Valérie: 35 heures. C'est le maximum permis.

Interviewer: Il faut porter un uniforme?

Valérie: Oui. On porte un uniforme bleu et blanc.

Interviewer: C'est un métier qui donne beaucoup de satisfaction, non?

Valérie: Oui. J'adore le travail. J'aime le contact avec les patients.

Interviewer: Sébastien, que faites-vous comme métier?

Sébastien: Malheureusement, je suis au chômage.

Interviewer: Oh, là! Alors vous ne recevez pas de salaire, alors?

Sébastien: Non, pas de salaire, pas d'heures de travail . . . mais pas d'uniforme, non plus, hein. Mais, c'est vraiment nul, le chômage!

1 Details to be noted in the table.

Solution

⬆**2** To calculate who earns most per week, students need to multiply the hourly rate by the number of hours worked.

Solution

Valérie gagne le plus.

Point grammaire: *Savoir* and *connaître*

Ilustrate that *savoir* can be used for knowledge:

– *Qui sait l'heure?* – *Moi, je la sais.*
– *Je sais que David Beckham joue pour Manchester United.*

Also show that it can be used for skills:

– *Je sais danser.*
– *Tu sais parler allemand?*
– *John sait draguer les filles!*

Illustrate that *connaître* is used for people, towns, regions and school subjects.

– *Moi, je connais Lille.*
– *Qui connaît une célébrité?* – *Moi, je connais . . .*

10

Students complete a gapped text with the correct form of *savoir*.

1 Tu **sais** conduire une voiture?
2 Tu **connais** Paris?
3 Tu **sais** quelle heure il est?
4 Tu **connais** mon copain Michel?
⬆**5** Tu **sais** la date de la bataille de Waterloo? Non, mais demande à Michel – il **connaît** bien l'histoire.

Tip

Point out that *pouvoir* is used for physical capability, whereas *savoir* is used for a skill. The cartoon should make this clear and **DW3.1** could be used to reinforce the point.

Solution

	Profession	Heures de travail par semaine	Salaire à l'heure	Vêtements	Opinion
Fabien	disc jockey	30	17€	t-shirt, jean	Super
Maïté	boulangère	40	14€	blouse, chapeau	Pas mal
Valérie	infirmière	35	25€	uniforme bleu et blanc	Adore
Sébastien	au chômage	–	–	–	Nul

Differentiation opportunity⬇

DW3.1 provides practice in understanding the different verbs for 'to know'. Students complete the gapped speech bubbles, which they can do largely by copying from the model ones.

Solution

Marcel's boasts	**Paul's boasts**
Je peux soulever 50 kilos, moi.	Moi, je **peux** soulever 80 kilos!
Je sais tout sur le football, moi.	Moi, je **sais** tout sur tous les sports!
Je connais deux personnes célèbres, moi.	Moi, je **connais** trois personnes célèbres.
Je peux nager deux kilomètres, moi.	Moi, je **peux** nager cinq kilomètres.
Je sais jouer du piano, moi.	Moi, je **sais** jouer du piano *et* je **sais** jouer de la trompette.
Et toi, **tu** sais que tu es un idiot?	Au contraire, moi, je **sais** que je suis un génie.

1 Students match descriptions of required abilities/knowledge/skills to job titles. They have to take gender into account, to get the right answers.

Solution

a Michel; **b** Pauline (remind students that Jean is a masculine name in French.); **c** Ben et Boris; **d** Charlotte; **e** Catherine; **f** Claude

⬆**2** Students' personal responses.

12 🎧 [CD 1 track 27]

Preliminary work: This task can be used to revise household tasks, revise *devoir*, revise opinions and give reasons.

Using **CM13** (pictures of household chores) revise the names of the *corvées de ménage (faire la cuisine, faire la vaisselle, faire les lits, faire la lessive, faire le repassage, faire les courses, mettre la table, sortir les poubelles, ranger sa chambre, passer l'aspirateur, promener le chien, donner à manger au chat/au chien, laver la voiture)*. Photocopy **CM13** and ask students to match the pictures to the captions (listed below) and keep them for reference.

Practise the vocabulary by getting students to mime for each other, while their partner guesses what they are doing, e.g. *Tu fais la vaisselle, c'est ça? – Non, je ne fais pas la vaisselle* . . .

Ask students: *Qu'est-ce que tu dois faire comme corvées de ménage?* and elicit *Je dois . . .*

Ask for opinions: *Qu'est-ce que tu penses de ça?* Write useful words on the board for expressing opinions: *nul, dur, fatigant, barbant, ennuyeux, pas mal, assez intéressant, nécessaire*. Ask students to produce a sequence of sentences, e.g. *Moi, je dois faire le repassage. Je trouve que c'est vraiment dur parce que c'est barbant.*

An alternative activity would be to ask *Qui doit faire la lessive chez toi?* Elicit *C'est mon père/ma mère qui . . .*

Transcript

Interviewer: Nathalie, qu'est-ce que tu dois faire comme corvées de ménage?
Nathalie: Moi, je dois faire la vaisselle.
Interviewer: Et qu'est-ce que tu penses de ça?
Nathalie: C'est nécessaire, mais je n'aime pas, parce qu'il y a trois repas par jour, le petit déjeuner, le déjeuner et le dîner. C'est du boulot, ça!
Interviewer: Et Paul, tu donnes un coup de main à la maison?
Paul: Oui. Je dois ranger ma chambre . . . c'est moche parce que, moi, je ne suis pas très organisé . . . il y a des livres et des vêtements partout!
Interviewer: Merci. Angèle, qu'est-ce que tu fais comme travail chez toi?
Angèle: Ben . . . ça dépend . . . quelquefois je mets la table . . . j'aime bien, surtout s'il y a des invités. C'est plutôt spécial alors.
Interviewer: Et Stéphane, que fais-tu?
Stéphane: Moi, je fais la lessive . . . surtout mes vêtements de sport. Je n'aime pas ça. Je fais beaucoup de sport, et ma mère dit qu'il faut que j'organise ça.
Interviewer: Et finalement, Nicole.
Nicole: Moi, je fais presque tout – vaisselle, lessive, cuisine, etc. C'est que je suis enfant unique. Mon père est parti et ma mère travaille de longues heures. Alors, moi, je suis responsable de beaucoup des corvées.

Solution

Nathalie: **g** ☹
Paul: **b** ☹
Angèle: **f** ☺
Stéphane: **c** ☹
Nicole: **g, c, a** ☺

Unité 3 Pages 26–27

Presentation ideas

Here is some background information about the Red Cross.

> Fondateur? Henry Dunant
> Où? Genève, Suisse
> Quand? octobre 1863
> Organisation gouvernementale? Non
> Il y a d'autres organisations similaires? Oui
> Médecins Sans Frontières, par exemple

Students could be asked if they have any ambition to do voluntary work. If so, where? When? For what organisation?

Transcript

Quotidien: Quelles sont vos ambitions?

Éric: Moi, je veux travailler pour la Croix Rouge. C'est une organisation admirable qui aide les populations en danger. Elle est représentée dans 176 pays différents du monde. J'espère étudier la médecine à l'Université de Caen où je veux me spécialiser en maladies tropicales. Mon ambition est de passer deux ou trois années en Afrique et de travailler dans un hôpital. Pourquoi est-ce que je veux faire cela? Parce que je trouve qu'il faut aider les autres, surtout les pauvres. Nous habitons un pays riche, nous avons beaucoup de possessions – voitures, frigos, ordinateurs, chaînes stéréo, etc. Si on veut manger dans un restaurant, pas de problème! Mais il y a des millions de pauvres qui n'ont ni nourriture ni d'eau pure à boire. C'est scandaleux!

Quotidien: Si vous voulez avoir plus d'informations sur la Croix Rouge, consultez **www.croix-rouge.fr** sur Internet.

13 [CD 1 track 28]

Students find opposites.

Solution

1 un pays riche
2 une organisation admirable
3 il faut
4 nous avons beaucoup de choses
5 C'est scandaleux!

ICT activity

Research could be done on the website quoted in the Student's Book. A world map of countries in which the Red Cross has worked could be labelled in French, perhaps with labels giving the reason for the work: *famine, sécheresse, séisme, épidémie, inondations, guerre civile.* Appropriate photos could be scanned or downloaded.

14

Completing sentences with a single word.

Solution

1 La Croix Rouge est présente dans **176** pays du monde.
2 Éric veut travailler comme **médecin**.
3 Il trouve qu'il est **important/nécessaire** de travailler pour les pauvres.

Ça se dit comment? p.26 [CD 1 track 29]

A reminder that consonants at the ends of words are not usually pronounced. The letter *-l*, however, is an exception (but beware *réveil, soleil*!).

Transcript

– *beaucoup*
– *pays*
– *il, personnel, tropical, tel*

Point grammaire: Vouloir

The similarity of *vouloir* to *pouvoir* (both shown on **CM12**) should be pointed out, both in form and in the fact that an infinitive follows both.

15 [CD 1 track 30]

Four people talk about their plans for the future. Each person gives a reason for their wishes, using *parce que*.

Transcript

Adèle: Bonjour. Ici Adèle Bazin au Micro de Radio Corsaire. Aujourd'hui on parle du travail. Nous avons interrogé des jeunes sur leurs ambitions. Ils nous ont parlé de ce qu'ils veulent faire et de ce qu'ils espèrent acheter avec l'argent qu'ils vont gagner.

Cédric: Bonjour. Je m'appelle Cédric Dutour. Mon ambition est de devenir journaliste, parce que je veux aller aux États-Unis, voir New York, le Grand Canyon . . . tout cela . . . et je veux m'acheter une grande voiture américaine! Le métier de journaliste est assez bien payé, après tout.

Anne-Marie: Salut. Je m'appelle Anne-Marie Marcheteau. Je suis fascinée par la télévision et j'espère devenir caméraman. Je veux aller en Afrique faire des documentaires sur les lions et les autres grands chats. C'est plutôt dangereux, mais pour moi ça c'est une aventure! Comme achats . . . euh . . . je veux bien m'acheter une jeep parce que comme ça j'aurai une certaine mobilité.

Henri: Moi, je suis Henri Boiron. J'espère devenir infirmier. Je veux travailler pour la Croix Rouge ou pour Médecins Sans Frontières. Comme ça on peut visiter d'autres pays et aider les gens. Moi, je veux travailler en Inde. Mon ambition est d'avoir une belle maison à la campagne parce que je n'aime pas les villes.

Simone: Euh . . . Simone Leclerc. Bonjour. Moi, je m'intéresse à l'anglais et je veux devenir professeur d'anglais. J'espère aller habiter en Angleterre pour perfectionner mes connaissances de la langue. J'adore les cultures étrangères. J'espère m'acheter un petit bateau parce que j'aime me relaxer en faisant de la voile.

Solution
Activity 1

	Travail	**Voyages**	**Achats**
Cédric	journaliste	États-Unis	voiture américaine
Anne-Marie	caméraman	Afrique	jeep
Henri	infirmier	Inde	maison (à la campagne)
Simone	professeur	Angleterre	bateau

Solution
Activity 2
a Henri; **b** Cédric; **c** Anne-Marie; **d** Simone

Tip

This gives ways of expressing your ambitions and intentions.

Ambitions: Constructions with *espérer, aimer* and *vouloir* are listed together, as they are all followed directly by an infinitive.

The constructions *Mon ambition est de . . .* and *Mon rêve est de . . .* are linked because of their need for *de*.

Intention: *Compter* requires a straight infinitive. *J'ai l'intention . . .* and *Mon idée est . . .* require *de* before the infinitive. Draw the parallel with the above expressions for ambitions.

Students could combine minor wishes with their ambition. *Je veux aller aux États-Unis et j'espère aller à Disneyland, mais mon ambition est d'apparaître à la télé avec Brad Pitt.*

Differentiation opportunity⬇ ⬆

⬇Lower-ability students could be given only the verbs which are followed by a straight *-er* infinitive: *Je veux travailler . . .; J'espère visiter . . .*, etc.

⬆Students of greater ability could use irregular infinitives.

Useful verbs for oral practice with all the verbs expressing wish or intent would be:

Regular: *travailler, aller, visiter, voyager, rencontrer, interviewer, jouer, acheter, trouver, se marier.*
Irregular: *écrire, apparaître à la télé, faire le tour du monde, découvrir, être (riche/heureux/célèbre), avoir une famille.*

Extra practice: *Vouloir* (alternative context)

Saying what chores you do and don't want to do. Using **CM13** copied onto cards and cut up, play the following game in groups of four.

- Aim: to collect a full set of chores.
- Have one full set of cards per student and one photocopy of the master-sheet per student.
- Shuffle cards and distribute equally.
- Students look at their cards and place those that they are given onto the appropriate picture on the photocopy. They retain any duplicates.

- Each student then attempts to get rid of duplicates by saying *Moi, je ne veux pas (faire la cuisine).*
- Any student requiring the card answers, *Moi, je veux (faire la cuisine)*, and then receives the appropriate card.
- The winner is the first to complete the set.

Differentiation opportunity⬇ ⬆

⬇**DW3.2A and** ⬆**DW3.2B** could provide useful preparation/practice here. The short biographical tasks could also be a good basis for a piece of written coursework or practice for the GCSE speaking presentation.

16

Students reformulate the information given in the third person singular or plural, using a given construction (*vouloir, aimer, espérer, compter, avoir l'intention de*).

Solution
1 Fabienne espère travailler dans le domaine de l'éducation.
2 Valérie aimerait programmer des ordinateurs.
3 Antoine voudrait travailler dans les médias.
4 Marie-Paule compte travailler dans un bureau.
5 Jeanne et Sylvie espèrent visiter d'autres pays du monde.
6 Édouard et Agathe ont l'intention d'aider les malades.

17

You may wish to supply a list of jobs for students to choose from – here are some:

plombier; électricien; sportif; restaurateur; policier; secrétaire; informaticien; programmeur; soldat; marin; chef de cuisine; homme/femme d'affaires.

As for the exercise recommended in the Tip (page 26), the following verbs may be useful:

Regular: *travailler, aller, visiter, voyager, rencontrer, interviewer, jouer, acheter, trouver, se marier.*
Irregular: *écrire, apparaître à la télé, faire le tour du monde, découvrir, être (riche/heureux/ célèbre), avoir une famille.*

Other words and expressions which may be useful are: *intéressant, fascinant, passionnant, dangereux, bien payé, nécessaire.*

Point grammaire: Comparative of adverbs

Revise how adverbs of manner are formed, firstly using adjectives that show a distinct feminine form, e.g. *actif, attentif, lent, soigneux.* Then look at adjectives that end in *-e* in both genders, e.g. *facile, rapide.* Point out, too, that *vite* is an adverb, even though it looks like an adjective.

With *mieux,* draw the comparison with *bon,* emphasising that *bien* means 'well' and *bon* means 'good'.

Illustrate examples of adverbs in use with actions, e.g. *Il y a un bruit dans le couloir. La porte s'ouvre lentement. Et voilà Dracula!* Point out that adverbs are usually positioned close to the verb, often just after it.

18 ✎ Solution

1 Julie observe plus attentivement que Michel.
2 Les techniciens travaillent aussi soigneusement que les serveurs.
3 On peut répondre plus vite par courrier électronique que par lettre.
⬆4 Les Médecins Sans Frontières sont aussi bien connus que ActionAid.

Unité 3 Pages 28–29

Presentation idea

Have job advertisements from French newspapers posted on the walls and adverts from English newspapers which advertise jobs requiring French and/or other languages. These should be a permanent feature. Point them out as an introduction to this section.

The *petite annonce* for Radio Corsaire is the introduction to a sequence in which Alain Chasseur applies for a job, is interviewed, and begins his work as a local radio reporter.

For comprehension purposes students could be asked to complete the following, copied from the board:

> Poste
> Ville
> Éducation
> Adresse de Radio Corsaire

Other terms are explained in the vocabulary. The concept of the CV should be familiar to students completing the Record of Achievement, but **CM14** and **CM16** may prove useful in any case.

Students could examine Alain's CV (**CM14**) and work out what details are required and in which order. Note that experience is listed chronologically, starting with the most recent.

Tip

Attention is drawn to the use of *vous* in formal letters. You could point out that *veuillez* is a form of *vouloir* used only for very formal requests.

19 📖

This is a formal letter and the comprehension questions are on its format rather than its content. **CM15** shows the layout of a formal letter and may be used as a template.

Solution

1 Adresse: en haut à gauche
2 Destinataire: à droite
3 La ville et la date
4 Monsieur
5 Veuillez agréer, Monsieur, l'expression de mes sentiments distingués.

Differentiation opportunity ⬇ ⬆

Students could be shown the formal phrases that are to be found in the letter. They could then use **CM15** and **CM16** (the CV template) to write an application for one of the jobs advertised on page 24.

20 🎧✎ [CD 1 track 31]

Students listen to an answerphone message and note the details. Revision of the alphabet would be a useful preliminary.

Transcript

Bonjour. Ici les bureaux de l'administration de Radio Corsaire. Nous avons reçu votre lettre et nous voulons vous inviter pour un entretien. Cet entretien aura lieu le 8 novembre à 9h00. Vous serez interviewé par Monsieur Parizet. Ça s'écrit P-A-R-I-Z-E-T. Ce sera dans la salle numéro 16 au premier étage. Voulez-vous bien confirmer votre acceptation de cette offre par téléphone ou par écrit, s'il vous plaît. Merci bien.

Solution
Date: 8 novembre; Heure: 9h00; Interview avec: M. Parizet; Salle: 16; Étage: premier; Confirmation: par téléphone ou par écrit.

Extra practice

Practise alternative details with different names, dates, times, room numbers and floors. Pair work: students could be given an outline of the above message with blanks which one partner fills in. He/she then reads this to their partner, who fills in the blanks according to what he/she hears. Students change roles for a second round.

Point grammaire: Possessive adjectives

At this point no specific mention is made of the possessive adjectives for plural **subjects** (*notre*, *votre*, *leur*); although *votre* is mentioned, this is in the context of its use as a formal second person singular.

21 [CD 1 track 32]

Practice of first person possessive adjectives.

Transcript
Bon . . . qu'est-ce que je vais porter . . . voyons voir. Oui, je vais porter **mon** complet gris . . . avec **ma** nouvelle chemise bleue et **ma** cravate jaune. Mais **mes** chaussures sont trop vieilles . . . je vais en acheter de nouvelles. Et s'il pleut? Bon . . . je vais porter **mon** imperméable . . . et je vais prendre aussi **mon** parapluie.

22 [CD 1 track 33]

In this follow-up, second and third person possessive adjectives are also needed.

Transcript
Brigitte: Alors, c'était comment, **ton** interview?
Alain: C'était vraiment super. M. Parizet m'a parlé de **mon** expérience. Et **mes** qualifications l'ont impressionné.
Brigitte: Est-ce que **ses** questions étaient difficiles?
Alain: Non, et je pense que **mes** réponses étaient assez bonnes.
Brigitte: Et tu as l'air assez chic avec **ta** cravate jaune, non?
Alain: Oui, peut-être. Regarde, tu aimes **mes** nouvelles chaussures?
Brigitte: Oui, elles sont belles. Bon, qu'est-ce que tu prends comme boisson, **mon** chéri?

23 [CD 1 track 34]

Students read the text. Explain any difficulties of vocabulary (e.g. *costume, simplement, avant de*). They then listen to four mini-dialogues involving job applicants and identify which rules each one is ignoring.

Transcript
1 **Père:** Comment ça s'est passé aujourd'hui, l'interview?
 Rachel: Pas très bien – tout d'abord, je suis arrivée en retard.
2 **Mère:** Mais, Richard, tu ne peux pas porter ce t-shirt là.
 Richard: Mais si, j'adore le jaune.
3 **Réceptionniste:** Bonjour, Mademoiselle, comment vous appelez-vous?
 Jeanne: Je m'appelle Jeanne Muret.
 Réceptionniste: Ah bon, mais je ne trouve pas votre nom sur la liste. Vous avez confirmé votre rendez-vous?
 Jeanne: Oh, peut-être pas . . .
4 **Interviewer:** L'interview est terminé . . . avez-vous des questions à me poser?
 Richard: Euh, non, non, je ne crois pas.

Solution
1 c; **2** b; **3** a; **4** g

24 [CD 1 track 35]

Presentation idea

Before the account of Alain's day, you could quickly run through your own routine for the days thus far (*je me suis levé(e)*, etc.) in order to accustom students' ears to the past tense of reflexive verbs.

Alain reports on the events of the day and there follows a recording of the interview with M. Parizet. Students complete M. Parizet's form. At the end students make a judgement as to how well Alain performed in the interview.

Transcript
Alain: Ouf, quelle journée . . . oh là là! Je me suis réveillé à six heures ce matin. Je me suis levé et je me suis douché, mais n'ai pas pu manger . . . j'étais si nerveux! Alors, je me suis calmé un peu et je me suis mis en route pour les studios de Radio Corsaire. La réceptionniste m'a accueilli et m'a fait entrer dans le bureau de M. Parizet . . .
M. Parizet: Alors, Monsieur, vous vous appelez Chasseur, c'est ça?
Alain: Oui, Monsieur. C'est exact. Et je me prénomme Alain. Alain Marc.
M. Parizet: Quel âge avez-vous?
Alain: J'ai vingt ans, Monsieur. Je suis né le 16 octobre 1980.
M. Parizet: Vous dites dans votre lettre que vous travaillez pour *Le Marché*, petit journal publicitaire. Quel est votre salaire annuel en ce moment?
Alain: Je gagne 20 000 euros par an.
M. Parizet: Hmm. C'est pas beaucoup, hein? Et vous espérez gagner combien dans un nouveau poste?
Alain: Je veux gagner un minimum de 24 000 euros. C'est raisonnable, non?
M. Parizet: Oui, oui. Ici un reporter gagne 25 000 euros par an. Bon. Parlez-moi un petit peu de vous-même. Qu'est-ce que vous faites pour vous relaxer, par exemple?

Alain: Ben, j'aime le foot . . . euh . . . les sports en général et j'aime lire, surtout des romans anglais, et j'aime écrire aussi. Je trouve que c'est important si on est journaliste.

M. Parizet: Vous parlez bien l'anglais et l'allemand, je vois. Vous parlez d'autres langues?

Alain: Oui, je parle espagnol, mais pas très bien . . . mais je veux bien me perfectionner.

M. Parizet: C'est bien. Pourquoi est-ce que vous voulez travailler pour Radio Corsaire?

Alain: Tout d'abord, je veux travailler pour Radio Corsaire, parce que je trouve que c'est une excellente station de radio locale. Puis, je me passionne pour le reportage. Alors, je veux devenir le meilleur reporter à la radio. J'espère attirer beaucoup de nouveaux auditeurs pour la station.

M. Parizet: Bon. Très bien, M. Chasseur, mon appréciation de vos compétences et de vos ambitions est la suivante. Tout d'abord je pense que . . .

Solution

Nom: Chasseur.
Prénoms: Alain Marc.
Âge: 20 ans.
Langues: anglais, allemand, espagnol.
Salaire actuel: 20 000€.
Poste actuel: Journaliste.
Ambitions: Travailler pour Radio Corsaire; attirer de nouveaux auditeurs; être le meilleur reporter à la radio.
Appréciation: (*Depends on student, but probably*) Excellent.

Tip: Questions

Question words are very important. Have a set of double-sided flashcards with a French question word on one side and the English on the other. Practise them regularly, giving only two seconds to give the meaning/translation. Make this a competition in which the students try to beat the teacher. If they fail to answer within two seconds, the teacher gets the card. Students could make up questions suitable for a job interview using both yes/no and information questions with *vouloir* or *espérer*, e.g.

Est-ce que vous voulez voyager?
Pourquoi est-ce que voulez voyager?
Combien est-ce que vous espérez gagner?
Où est-ce que vous voulez travailler?

They could then practise questions and answers in pairs, using *je veux* and *j'espère* in the answers. An extension activity would be to report back in speech or writing on what answers others gave, e.g. *Terry veut travailler aux États-Unis parce qu'il veut être riche.*

Unité 3 Pages 30–31

25 [CD 1 track 36]

This is a report by Alain Chasseur on a fire in a local factory. The text contains examples of verbs taking *être* in the perfect tense, including some reflexives. The comprehension questions involve cardinal numbers.

Transcript

Alain: Ici Radio Corsaire, Alain Chasseur au micro. Je suis sur les lieux d'Arkitex, petite usine à l'extérieur de Dinard, où un incendie s'est déclaré à neuf heures ce matin. Une secrétaire a téléphoné à la caserne des sapeurs-pompiers et une voiture de pompiers est arrivée ici à 9h14, suivie d'une ambulance. La plupart du personnel est sorti avant l'arrivée des pompiers, mais quand on les a comptés dans la cour, il manquait une des secrétaires, une certaine Mlle Ducros. Donc, un des pompiers est monté au premier étage. Dans la cour, nous avons tous attendu avec impatience. Quatre minutes plus tard, le pompier est descendu, portant Mlle Ducros. Il est sorti dans la cour sous les applaudissements du personnel. Mlle Ducros est montée dans l'ambulance, qui est partie tout de suite. Le personnel (ils sont trente-six) qui travaille chez Arkitex est donc sain et sauf. Une demi-heure plus tard, l'incendie éteint, la voiture de pompiers est partie. Ici Alain Chasseur, Radio Corsaire.

Solution

1 L'incendie s'est déclaré à **neuf** heures.
2 Les pompiers sont arrivés à **neuf heures quatorze**.
3 **Un** des pompiers est monté au premier étage.
4 Il est descendu **quatre** minutes plus tard.
5 Tout le personnel, qui consiste en **trente-six** personnes, est sain et sauf.

Point grammaire: *Le passé composé*

Before this section is tackled, students could be given a list of verbs which take *être* (except *rester*) and asked to find what they have in common (they are verbs of motion – *naître* and *mourir* can be classified as moving from one world to the next!).

26

Students choose the right caption for each picture. Each caption is an example of the perfect tense with *être*.

Solution

• Un pompier **est entré** dans le bâtiment – **b**
• Le pompier **est sorti** du bâtiment, portant Mlle Ducros – **d**
• La voiture de pompiers **est arrivée** à l'usine – **a**
• Le pompier **est monté** au premier étage – **c**
• Enfin, la voiture de pompiers **est partie** – **f**
• Les pompiers **sont remontés** dans la voiture – **e**

Differentiation opportunity ⬆

Once the Point grammaire has been tackled, students could be asked to rewrite this story, doubling the number of vehicles and characters.

27

Students' answers will vary, but all should contain correct forms of the *passé composé*.

Differentiation opportunity ⬆

Ask abler students to come up with pairs of questions and answers using the *être* perfect tense verbs given in task 25. Attention may be drawn to the fact that *tu* questions will require *je* answers, whereas a *vous* question will require *je* or *nous*, depending on the context given. Third person questions will require third person answers.

Homework opportunity

The following exercise would be suitable as a homework task.

28

This account is to be rewritten in the *passé composé*.

Solution

23h10   Deux cambrioleurs **sont entrés** dans une bijouterie à Avranches.
23h20   Des gendarmes **sont arrivés** à la bijouterie. Trois gendarmes **sont entrés** dans le bâtiment et **sont montés** au premier étage.
23h25   Un des gendarmes **est descendu** et **est sorti** de la bijouterie avec un des cambrioleurs.
23h30   Les deux autres **sont sortis** de la bijouterie. Ils sont montés dans la voiture qui **est partie** à toute vitesse.

Differentiation opportunity ⬆

Students could be given the following task:

Imaginez que vous êtes une des femmes pompiers qui ont assisté à l'incendie à l'usine Arkitex ou une femme gendarme qui a assisté à l'incident à la bijouterie. Écrivez un rapport pour votre chef, donnant les détails de vos activités ce jour là.

Example: *Je suis arrivée à la caserne à 8h30. L'alarme a sonné. Je suis montée dans la voiture, qui est partie à 8h47 ...*

This report not only gives practice in using the feminine forms of the past participle, but also makes it clear that police and fire work are not simply jobs for the boys!

29 [CD 1 track 35]

This newspaper article is a written version of the radio report on the fire (task 24), but contains a number of errors. You will need to replay the tape once or twice to allow students to spot the errors.

Differentiation opportunity ⬇ ⬆

⬇ The errors could simply be identified and counted.
⬆ More able students could correct the errors.

Solution

À **9** heures du matin, hier, vendredi, un incendie s'est déclaré dans l'usine Arkitex dans la zone industrielle de Dinard. A **9 heures 14**, **une** voiture de pompiers **est arrivée sur** les lieux. Quelques minutes plus tard, **une ambulance est arrivée**. Deux pompiers se sont précipités dans le bâtiment pour chercher le personnel de l'usine. **Un pompier est monté** au premier étage, où **il a** trouvé une des secrétaires.

Il est descendu, portant Mlle Dufour. **Il est sorti**, sous les applaudissements du personnel assemblé devant l'usine. **Mlle Dufour est montée dans l'ambulance**. **L'ambulance est partie**. **La voiture** de pompiers **est restée** devant l'usine encore une demi-heure, puis **elle est partie**.

Point grammaire: Reflexive verbs

Examples of the **perfect tense of reflexive verbs** have already been given on the cassette/CD for task 24 and in the above newspaper item.

The difference between the present and perfect tenses may be illustrated by two columns of verbs, e.g.

D'habitude je me réveille à sept heures. | *Hier, je me suis réveillé à huit heures.*
Normalement, je m'amuse à la disco. | *Hier, je ne me suis pas amusé – c'était nul!*
En général, Anne se couche à dix heures. | *Hier, elle s'est couchée à deux heures du matin!*

Homework opportunity

EGW1 Activity 1 could be used again at this point to repractise reflexive verb present tenses before students try to tackle reflexives in the perfect.

Differentiation opportunity ⬇ ⬆

The pair of worksheets ⬇**DW3.3A** and ⬆**DW3.3B** may be used here to practise the perfect tense. In ⬇**DW3.3A** the gap-fill passage has verbs supplied.

Solution

Je me suis **levée** ce matin à six heures. Je me suis **douchée**, j'ai **mangé** le petit déjeuner et je suis **partie** en voiture pour le studio. Je suis **arrivée** au studio vers 9h00. Le téléphone a **sonné**. C'était Éric, le producteur. De mauvaises nouvelles – une explosion dans une maison à Bourges. J'ai **envoyé** un mél à un correspondant et puis je suis **montée** dans l'hélicoptère de TF1. Quand il est **arrivé** à Bourges, j'ai **interviewé** un certain M. Leclos. J'ai **écrit** mon scénario sur ordinateur. J'ai **présenté** mon reportage à 18h00. Une heure plus tard, l'hélicoptère est **reparti**. **Arrivée** à Paris, je suis **rentrée** à la maison. Très **fatiguée**, je me suis **couchée** de très bonne heure!

In ⬆**DW3.3B** the text is an open-ended narrative writing task based on the same prompts.

30 🖉🖊

La journée d'Alain. Students recount Alain's heavy day. The verbs all require *être*. Once roughed out, the text could be recorded. More able students could write this as a diary entry. Girls might like to write it as if from a female reporter's point of view.

EGW3 could be used at this point – it practises *être* and *avoir* perfect tenses in a text on the same theme as the above exercise, but in a context more closely connected with business. (See full notes on **EGW3** at end of unit.)

Tip

Organising things by pairs of opposites (or negatives and positives) is a proven way of securing and revising knowledge. In addition to the comments listed here, students could do further work to find opposites, e.g. verbs: *aller/venir, rester/partir, monter/descendre*; adjectives: *petit/grand, bavard/timide, intelligent/bête*; prepositions/adverbs: *dedans/dehors, en bas/en haut*.

Once students have learned or revised these pairs, they could be put onto charts, or hung as mobiles.

31 🎧🖊 [CD 1 track 37]

A number of people discuss their attitude to their jobs.

Transcript

1: Moi je suis médecin. Je trouve que c'est un boulot qui est très stressant, mais ça donne beaucoup de satisfaction.

2: Je suis scientifique. À mon avis, c'est un boulot qui est très stimulant.

3: Moi, je suis électricienne. Je pense que c'est assez facile, mais ça donne peu de satisfaction.

4: Moi, je suis maçon. C'est un boulot très difficile et très stressant. Ça donne beaucoup de satisfaction quand même.

5: Moi je suis bibliothécaire. Je trouve que c'est très relaxant.

Solution

		Profession	Opinion
1	M. Martin	Médecin	Stressant. Beaucoup de satisfaction
2	Mlle Muret	Scientifique	Stimulant
3	Mme Vauban	Électricienne	Facile. Peu de satisfaction
4	M. Gilbert	Maçon	Difficile, stressant; beaucoup de satisfaction
5	Mme Maloux	Bibliothécaire	Relaxant

32 🖉⬆

Solution

A 21h le soleil **s'est couché**. A 21h10 je **me suis levé** – je **suis sorti** de mon cercueil. Je **me suis brossé** les dents très soigneusement, parce qu'elles doivent être blanches et propres. Je **me suis rasé** – c'est difficile parce que je ne vois pas mon visage dans le miroir. Je **me suis peigné** – dans ma profession, il faut être chic! Je **suis parti** pour le village. Je **suis arrivé** à la maison d'une jeune fille, et je **suis entré** dans sa chambre par la fenêtre. Elle ne **s'est pas réveillée**. Je **me suis approché** du lit . . .

Unité 3 Pages 32–33

Checkpoints

Test

The **Test** checks students' skills in the grammatical goals of the unit:

- using *pouvoir* and *savoir*
- using *vouloir*
- making comparisons using adverbs
- using the perfect tense with *être*

Solution

1	– Maman, je **peux** sortir ce soir?	[1]
	– Non, tu ne **peux** pas. Tu dois finir tes devoirs.	[1]
	– Mais, maman, la mère de Philippe dit qu'il **peut** aller au cinéma ce soir.	[1]
	– Bon, vous **pouvez** y aller tous les deux, mais tu dois finir tes devoirs avant, OK?	[1]
	– D'accord!	
2 a	Alain Chasseur **veut** être reporter.	[1]
b	Est-ce que vous **voulez** faire le tour du monde?	[1]
c	Mes copains **veulent** faire du travail volontaire.	[1]
d	Moi, je **veux** aller aux États-Unis.	[1]
e	Est-ce que tu **veux** aller au café ce soir?	[1]
3 a	On arrive plus facilement avec le bus qu'avec le train.	[2]
b	Le TGV roule moins vite que Thrust 2	[2]
c	Moi, je travaille plus rapidement que ma sœur.	[2]

4 a Paul **est arrivé** au bureau à neuf heures.   [2]
  b Hélène **est arrivée** juste après Paul.   [2]
  c Ils **sont entrés** dans le bâtiment.   [2]
  d Paul **est monté** au premier étage.   [2]
  e Hélène **est montée** au deuxième.   [2]
  f Ils **sont descendus** à une heure.   [2]
5 a Sandrine est **arrivée** au travail à 9h30.   [1]
  b Les deux directeurs sont **restés** dans la cantine.   [1]
  c Anne et Simone sont **parties** à 6h00.   [1]
  d Moi, je suis **rentré(e)** à 5h30 (*agreement according to sex of student*).   [1]
6 a Elle **s'est levée** à 7h00.   [1]
  b Elle **s'est douchée** et elle **s'est habillée.**   [2]
  c Elle **est partie** pour le studio à 7h45.   [1]
  d Elle **est arrivée** au studio à 8h15.   [1]
  e Elle **a préparé** son programme entre 8h15 et 12h.   [1]
  f Elle **a déjeuné** à midi.   [1]
  g Elle **est retournée** au studio à 13h00.   [1]
  h Elle **a écouté** une répétition entre 14h et 16h.   [1]
  i Elle **a participé** à une conférence à 16h.   [1]
  j Elle **est rentrée** à la maison à 18h.   [1]
  k Elle **a dîné** à 20h.   [1]
  l Elle **s'est couchée** à 22h30.   [1]
Total [48]

Quiz

The **Quiz** checks students' knowledge acquired in the unit, about:

- the school system in France
- jobs in France
- a French CV
- a French business letter and job application
- voluntary work and organisations

Solution

1 F: la 3e = Yr 10   [1]
  V: la terminale = Year 13   [1]
2 au lycée   [1]
3 au lycée professionnel   [1]
4 4,5 millions d'élèves en primaire   [1]
5 6 millions d'élèves en secondaire   [1]
6 10 élèves/1 professeur   [2]
7 Il y a plus d'élèves dans le secteur public.   [1]
8 On dit *vous* quand on parle à son professeur.   [1]
9 Dans une lettre formelle on écrit à la fin *Veuillez agréer, Monsieur, l'expression de mes sentiments distingués.*   [1]
10 a 176 pays   [1]
   b C'est une organisation médicale.   [1]
14 Un CV, c'est un Curriculum Vitae.   [1]
15 a restaurant, café, bar   [1]
   b magasin, supermarché   [1]
   c club, disco, boîte   [1]
Total [16]

Projets

A Students write a prose portrait of Patrick Legrand using the notes given in his CV. For differentiation purposes, phrases and expressions could be given, e.g. *Je m'appelle, J'ai travaillé, Je veux . . .*

B Students note what they can do at present and what they hope to be able to do in 10 years' time. This is an opportunity to practise the verbs *savoir* and *espérer*. Having written these lists, they compare them with those of a partner, and give a brief commentary as shown in the Student's Book.

C Preliminary work. Work out the questions necessary to conduct the survey. *Qu'est-ce que tu fais comme travail? Combien d'heures est-ce que tu travailles? Combien est-ce que tu gagnes par heure?*

  Once the survey has been carried out, some mathematical work is required to calculate the totals and to see who earns the most.

  ⇧ Students could extend their work for **Projet C** by giving their opinions on their findings, e.g. *Je pense que David est très mal payé. C'est pas juste.*

EGW3 teaching notes

Sheet **EGW3** provides extra grammar/homework on the perfect tense (*avoir* and *être* verbs).

Solution

09h00 M. Hervé a téléphoné à M. Denis.
09h30 M. Hervé a dicté une lettre à Mlle Leclerc.
10h00 Mlle Leclerc a posté la lettre.
10h15 Le PDG est arrivé.
10h30 M. Hervé a envoyé un mél à la Société Michelin.
12h00 M. Hervé a présenté des données à une conférence des directeurs.
13h00 M. Hervé a déjeuné avec M. Denis et le PDG.
13h30 M. Hervé et le PDG sont partis pour Clermont-Ferrand.
14h00 M. Hervé et le PDG/Ils ont visité l'usine Michelin.
16h00 M. Hervé et le PDG/Ils ont négocié un contrat.
18h00 Le PDG a signé le contrat.
20h00 M. Hervé et le PDG ont dîné dans un restaurant.
22h00 M. Hervé est rentré à la maison.

unité 4
Communications

Contexts
- TV in France
- radio in France
- using the Internet
- multimedia
- French newspapers and magazines

Grammar
- using direct object pronouns instead of repeating nouns
- using the present tense of *finir* and *dire*
- using indirect object pronouns: *lui* and *leur*
- using negatives: *ne . . . jamais* and *ne . . . plus*

Pronunciation
- '*i*'
- '*s*', '*ss*'
- '*-e*', '*-é*', '*-è*'
- final *-l*

Revision in this unit includes:
- making comparisons
- the perfect tense
- asking and giving times in French

Unité 4 Pages 34–35

The opening two pages focus on direct object pronouns in the context of French television viewing habits.

1  [CD 1 track 38]

This task picks up on comparatives (*plus, moins, aussi*) as practised in Unit 2. Note the use of *plus de/moins de* with nouns.

Transcript

Mille heures devant la télé

En moyenne, les Français passent 1001 heures par an devant la télévision. Au total, ils passent plus de neuf années de leur vie devant le petit écran (ils passent six années au travail). Les enfants passent 800 heures par an à l'école – et 800 heures devant la télé! En général, on passe trois heures par jour à regarder le petit appareil au coin du salon. Mais les enfants sont moins fascinés par la télévision. Pourquoi? Parce qu'ils ont maintenant des magnétoscopes et des consoles de jeux qui se branchent sur le téléviseur. Les enfants ne sont pas passifs – ils préfèrent l'interactivité.

Solution

1 Les Français passent **plus** de 1000 heures par an à regarder la télé.
2 Ils passent **moins** de temps à travailler qu'à regarder le petit écran.

3 Pour les enfants, le temps passé à l'école est **aussi** long que le temps passé devant la TV.
4 Les enfants sont **plus** fascinés par les consoles de jeux que les adultes.
5 Ils sont **plus** actifs que les adultes.

2

1 Students find the French expressions in the text.

Solution

1 **a** en moyenne
  b au total
  c un appareil
  d la télévision; la télé; le petit écran
  e magnétoscope
  f console de jeux
  g se brancher sur

↕ 2 Students translate two sentences into French, referring back to the text.

Solution

a En moyenne, on passe trois heures par jour à regarder la TV.
b Les enfants français passent 800 heures par an devant la TV.

Presentation ideas

Using **CM17**, revise the types of programmes that can be seen on television. Point out that it is important to learn programmes using the singular indefinite article (for gender) where possible, but that after expressions of opinion (*j'aime, je déteste*, etc.) the plural follows: *J'aime les documentaires, mais je déteste les jeux télévisés.*

As students are unlikely to be familiar with French TV programmes, use English ones as a starting point, e.g. *EastEnders, c'est quelle sorte d'émission?* Then point out that clues in the titles of French programmes may be used to guide people to the type of programmes that they are (see also task 4): *Événements Sports, Bon appétit, bien sûr, Des chiffres et des lettres.*

TV schedules can be found in daily papers on the Net. Students could attempt to identify types of programmes from their titles.

Differentiation opportunity ⬇

⬇ **DW4.1** could be used here to reinforce understanding of TV programme types. In **Activity 1** students draw lines to link programme types with the matching symbols, and then in **Activity 2**, they choose one of the expressions from the box to express their opinion about each programme type.

3  [CD 1 track 39]

Students listen to the recording and note which programme type they hear.

Transcript

Numéro 1: Oui, oui . . . et voilà, vous avez gagné dix mille francs! Dix mille francs!

Numéro 2: Regardez de près. Cet animal est très timide. Il sort la nuit et il chasse les souris et les insectes. On le voit rarement le jour.

Numéro 3: En région parisienne, il fera très froid – environ trois degrés. Des chutes de neige sont prévisibles sur toute l'Île-de-France.

Numéro 4: Le Président de la République est arrivé à Londres ce soir pour des négociations sur l'économie avec le Premier Ministre britannique. Demain, M. le Président poursuivra son tour d'Europe; il ira en Allemagne et puis en Italie.

Numéro 5: Mais regardez, Dracula, le jour se lève. Voilà le soleil! Les vampires ne supportent pas le soleil. C'est la fin, Dracula, la fin!

Numéro 6: Bonsoir, je suis sur les lieux de l'accident de la route dans le petit village de Sainte-Marie-sur-Cher dans laquelle deux personnes ont trouvé la mort. La tragédie, c'est que c'était le premier jour de leurs vacances dans la région.

Solution

1 e un jeu télévisé; **2 g** un documentaire; **3 a** la météo; **4 c** le journal; **5 h** un film d'horreur; **6 j** un reportage

4

In this exercise students use linguistic and cultural clues to match the type of programme to the title.

Solution

Ligue des Champions: À qui la victoire dans le football?

Le Juste Prix: Des gens ordinaires gagnent des milliers d'euros.

Le genie d'Hercule Poirot: Un détective belge à la recherche d'un meurtrier.

Les Volcans Tueurs: Documentaire sur la géologie et les catastrophes.

L'Homme au Masque de Fer: Film classique français. Qui est le prisonnier royal?

Differentiation opportunity ⬇ ⬆

A follow-up writing exercise could be to write:

⬇ **a** some key words (French words, English proper names disallowed!); or

⬆ **b** a one-line description

relating to a British TV programme and then to ask a partner to guess which programme it is, e.g. for 'London's Burning':

⬇ **a** *feu, explosion, Londres, pompiers*

⬆ **b** *À Londres, des pompiers combattent une explosion.*

Ça se dit comment? p.34 🎧 [CD 1 track 40]

Practice of the French pronunciation of 'i'.

Transcript

– À qui la victoire dans le football le plus passionnant du monde?
– Des gens ordinaires gagnent des milliers de francs.
– Un détective belge à la recherche d'un meurtrier.
– Documentaire sur la géologie et les catastrophes.
– Film classique français. Qui est le prisonnier royal?
– Si six scies scient six cigares, six cent six scies scient six cent six cigares.

Other useful words to practise this sound are: *Ibiza, ici, idée, idiot, igloo, il, île, illustration, imaginer, imiter, Irak, Iran, Irlande, Islande, Israël, Italie, italique.*

Point grammaire: Direct object pronouns

Students usually have more difficulty with the positioning of pronouns than with the actual substitution of pronoun for noun. Try putting the words of the example sentences in the Point grammaire onto individual cards and blu-tacking them onto the board:

Do the same for the other examples and ask students if they can see what's happening. More able students will be able to cope with the

Tu	regardes	**le**	**football?**

Do the same for the answer.

Je	regarde	**le**	**football**

Point out **football** is a repetition, and remove it.

Je	regarde	**le**

This now corresponds to the English order 'I watch it'. Now move *le* to its correct place.

Je	**le**	regarde

generalised notion that little words precede big words in French (pronouns before verbs, articles before nouns, etc.).

Presentation ideas: Negatives with pronouns

Suggest that direct object pronouns stick to their verbs like glue and cannot be separated. So where can we put *ne . . . pas*? Try turning the example sentences in the first part of the Point grammaire into negatives.

Play a game orally practising pairs of the type: *Tu aimes les feuilletons? – Je ne les aime pas.* Only negative sentences are allowed. Anyone who says *Non* is out! A hooter or bell livens this up.

 [CD 1 track 41]

1 Students listen carefully to identify the right articles and pronouns.

Transcript/Solution

1 a Tu aimes **les** feuilletons australiens?
  b Ah, oui, je **les** adore. Et toi, que penses-tu de la musique à la télé?
  c Moi, je **la** déteste. Je **la** trouve ennuyeuse.
  d Tu aimes **le** magazine sportif *Sports Événements*?
  e Non, je ne **l'**aime pas.

2 Students deduce the pronoun before checking their answers by listening to the second conversation.

Transcript/Solution

  a Et que penses-tu du journal du soir? Tu **l'**aimes?
  b Non, je **le** déteste, c'est barbant!
  c Et que penses-tu des documentaires? Tu **les** préfères?
  d Oui, je **les** trouve vraiment intéressants!

Differentiation opportunity ⬇ ⬆

⬇**DW4.2A** and ⬆**DW4.2B** could be used here.

■ ⬇**DW4.2A** revises time expressions while familiarising students with phrases using direct object pronouns, as they have to say how often they watch each of their six favourite programmes. The time expressions are supplied for them to choose from, and an example phrase is given including the direct object pronoun.

■ On ⬆**DW4.2B** students are working with the same concepts but have to produce two sentences, the second of which (supplied in gapped form) requires the insertion of the direct object pronoun.

Tip ⬆

In preparation for the harder elements of tasks 6 and 7, the Tip explains agreement of adjectives with their pronouns.

This point may confuse some students, who should simply attempt replies with:

• *C'est* + adjective or
• *ils/elles sont* + adjective, where the agreement is easier to deal with.

ICT activity

Learning objectives

• to listen for gist and detail;
• to make notes;
• to edit text for factual inaccuracies.

1 This activity makes use of the listening text above.
2 Students listen to the recording, making notes of what they think is significant. Lower attainers could be supported here with a grid to be completed.
3 Students then open a word-processed file which contains a factually inaccurate version of the interviews.
4 Students correct the factual inaccuracies and rewrite the dialogue as a narrative using the third person.

6

Students interview their partner using Yes/No questions (*tu aimes . . .?*). Partners answer using whichever form of response they are able to produce – a few may manage the agreed pronoun/adjective pattern, but most will be using *c'est* + adjective or possibly *il est* + adjective.

Extra ideas

1 Students may be interested to know more about French TV, for example: France has six terrestrial TV channels – *France 1*, *France 2*, *France Régions 3* (*FR3*), *Canal+* (a subscription channel), *La Cinquième* and *Arte* (*La 5* broadcasts until 7.00 p.m. and *Arte* then takes over), and *M6*. *FR 3* is the most popular channel. There is a huge variety of cable and satellite stations, of which the most popular include *RTL9* and *Eurosport*.
2 Students could look through a TV schedule from *Télé 7 Jours* or *TV Magazine* to see what they can recognise (English/American programmes; programmes whose titles give a clue as to what they are). They could see if they could characterise the different channels, e.g. *FR3* = regional programmes, *Arte* = arty/intellectual programmes, M6 = Music and entertainment.

Teacher's Guide 1 © John Murray

ICT activity

Learning objectives

- to use authentic materials from the Internet to find out about TV programmes in France;
- to make comparisons between TV viewing in France and in England.

1 The teacher downloads a selection of up-to-date TV listings. A starting point here might be the TV section on **yahoo.fr.**

2 Students scan the listings to find out what type of programmes are being shown. Students then present their findings (in tables in Word), e.g.

Name of programme	Type

 [CD 1 track 42]

Students listen to a dialogue in which father and daughter discuss which programmes to watch. Father gives reasons why she can/can't watch them – educational/too violent/finishes too late, etc. *Pouvoir*, *vouloir* and direct object pronouns are used, and *finir* is introduced, in preparation for work on the next page. Key words are given, but students have to match them with the right programme and speaker to complete the grid.

Transcript

Amélie: Papa, je peux regarder ce film ce soir? . . . *La Femme Flic* . . . ça a l'air intéressant.

Papa: Ah non, les films comme ça, ils sont trop violents. Non, il y a trop de violence à la télévision maintenant. Pourquoi est-ce que tu ne veux pas regarder *Tintin et le lac aux requins*? Les dessins animés comme ça, moi, je les trouve vraiment excellents. Il n'y a pas assez d'émissions comme ça.

Amélie: Mais papa, c'est vraiment nul, c'est pour les enfants. Alors, si on regardait ce documentaire sur l'amour et le mariage? Ça doit être éducatif, non?

Papa: Ah ça, non! Ça, c'est vraiment pour les adultes . . . en plus ça finit trop tard . . . 23 heures 30, tu vois? Ah, non! Mais regarde, il est 8 heures. L'heure du journal . . . Moi, je veux le regarder. Et toi? C'est toujours intéressant, le journal.

Amélie: C'est toujours barbant, le journal!

Papa: Alors, si on regardait une vidéo . . .?

Solution

Émission	Opinion d'Amélie	Opinion de son père
La Femme Flic (film)	intéressant	trop violent
Tintin et le lac aux requins	excellent	nul
Amour et Mariage (documentaire)	éducatif	pour les adultes (finit trop tard)
Le Journal de 8 heures	barbant	intéressant

Unité 4 Pages 36–37

Point grammaire: Verbs like *finir*

Students will already be familiar with *Tu as fini? Qui a fini? Si vous avez fini . . . Finissez cet exercice et puis . . . Finis ce que tu fais . . .*

See page 146 for the complete verb. Other verbs in this group include *saisir* (to seize), *remplir* (to fill), *punir* (to punish) and *choisir* (to choose). The latter verb will be familiar, but can be practised by getting a student to remove an object or picture from the OHP: *Choisis un objet/une image . . . Elle a choisi X ou Y? Qu'est-ce qu'elle a choisi?*

Students look at a TV schedule and correct the following statements which are all false. Apart from the vocabulary of TV programmes, familiarity with *avant/après*, *durer plus/moins* and *comique/sérieux* is necessary.

Solution

a M6 Kid est une émission jeunesse qui **finit** à 11h20.

b La météo dure **cinq** minutes et finit à **11h55**.

c Le journal commence à **11h55** et dure **trente-cinq minutes**.

d A 12h30 on peut voir un match de **golf**; cela finit à **13h10**.

e Fréquenstar est un magazine de musique; il finit à **18h55**.

⬆**f** Les Nouveaux Professionnels est une série policière qui **finit** à 17h40.

⬆**g** Cyrano de Bergerac **commence** à 18h55 et dure **plus** de deux heures.

Practice with numbers and times is necessary before this exercise is tackled. Use an OHT of a digital clock (draw a simple two-box grid and overlay it with various possible combinations of numbers – **CM74**. Practise with numbers ending in *cinq*. Insist on the use of *quinze, trente* and *quarante-cinq* for digital time (not *et quart, et demie, moins le quart*).

Differentiation opportunity ⬇ ⬆

⬇**DW4.3A** and ⬆**DW4.3B** provide extra practice at this point.

■ ♦ **DW4.3A** is an information gap exercise and covers types of TV programmes. Students will need to know time: *À X heures ...*, the construction *il y a*, and the expression *sur TF1, sur France 2*, etc. Students exchange information and complete the grid.

Solution

	TF1	**F2**	**F3**	**M6**
18.00	FILM	DOCUMENTAIRE	JEU	PROGRAMME DE SCIENCE-FICTION
19.30	MAGAZINE DE MUSIQUE	SÉRIE POLICIÈRE	PROGRAMME DE CUISINE	CONCERT DE ROCK
20.00	JOURNAL et MÉTÉO	JOURNAL	ÉMISSION SPORTIVE	FEUILLETON AMÉRICAIN

■ ♦ **DW4.3B** is an information gap activity for students of higher ability.

Scenario: A TV producer has muddled his papers for the evening's schedule. He has the times of the programmes, the types of programmes to be broadcast, their length and their titles, but the information has become jumbled.

Students examine the times on their sheet and listen to each other giving details of the lengths of the programmes. Emphasise that the *Durées* given refer to their *partner's* sheet, and they must listen and work out what programme fits where. This enables them to fit them into the schedules and report back. Once they have the schedules, they listen to the titles and allocate them to the programmes.

Solution

Heure	**Programme**
18.00	Émission sportive
18.35	Magazine régional
19.00	Documentaire
19.55	Météo
20.00	Journal
21.00	Film
22.30	Jeu
23.00–23.45	Concert

Extra idea

For extra practice of times, you could use **CM19**. Students give starting times, duration and finishing time of a programme. Partners deduce which programme is being talked about. Or the time of a programme can be given by one partner and the other has to give details of start, duration and end. Alternatively, this could be run as a real information gap where Student A tests Student B without the book (but with less to remember – just starting times, for example).

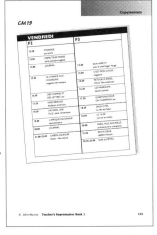

10 🎧 *Transcript* [CD 1 track 43]

Au téléphone

Maïté: Allô, Maïté Deschamps à l'appareil.

Pierre: Salut, Maïté, ici c'est Pierre. Écoute, dis-moi, on sort ce soir?

Maïté: Bon, je ne sais pas, je dois me laver les cheveux ...

Pierre: Mais tu peux faire ça demain, allons, tu ne sors pas assez ... à quelle heure finis-tu ton travail?

Maïté: Bien, en général nous finissons à 18h, mais aujourd'hui je ne finis pas avant 18h30.

Pierre: Mais c'est parfait, on se rencontre à 7h et on choisit un film. Ça va?

Maïté: Bon, ça va, tu m'as persuadée! À bientôt.

Au café

Pierre: Bon, qu'est-ce que tu veux voir? *Les Vampires de Paris*, par exemple?

Maïté: Mais tu sais, je les déteste, les films d'horreur! Je ne dors jamais après ... Toi, tu choisis toujours des films terribles. Et regarde, ça finit à onze heures. C'est trop tard, n'est-ce pas?

Pierre: Bon, cette fois c'est toi qui choisis le film.

Maïté: D'accord. Peut-être *Voyage Mystérieux*, ou bien *Mission Improbable* ...

Pierre: Je les ai déjà vus.

Maïté: Il y a le film classique au cinéma Gaumont – c'est *Jean de Florette*, un film de Gérard Depardieu. Tu l'as déjà vu aussi?

Pierre: Non, je ne l'ai jamais vu mais c'est très vieux, ce film ...

Maïté: Tu sais, moi Depardieu, il me plaît, oui, j'adore ses films. Tu ne l'adores pas, Depardieu? Oui, j'ai choisi, je t'en prie, allons voir *Jean de Florette*.

Pierre: Bon, bien sûr, je sais que cet homme te fascine. Mais regarde, ça finit à onze heures dix – ce n'est pas top tard?

Maïté: Oh, non, si ce n'est pas un film d'horreur, pas de problème!

Solution

1 Pierre.
2 a; **3** b; **4** c; **5** c

11 📖

A mixture of comprehension and logic, in effect placing the evening's events in sensible order.

Solution

1 le film commence à 19h15
2 on arrive au cinéma à 19h00
3 le film finit à 21h00
4 on choisit un film à 18h30
5 on se rencontre au café à 18h15
6 on finit son travail à 18h00
7 on sort du cinéma à 21h10

12 🎧 📖 [CD 1 track 44]

The strip cartoon on page 37 illustrates the use of some other direct object pronouns (*me, te, vous*).

Papa: Rachel! Tu ne peux pas écouter la radio quand tu fais tes devoirs!

Rachel: Quoi? – attends – je ne t'entends pas!

Papa: Mais ça ne m'étonne pas! Baisse le son! Comment peux-tu te concentrer?

Rachel: Mais ça m'intéresse – et la radio m'aide à me concentrer! Toi, tu ne me laisses rien faire! Tu m'énerves, toi! Ne me tracasse pas, hein!

Radio: Et maintenant, chers auditeurs, votre émission favorite: «Ça vous intéresse?»

Papa: Ah, bon – «Ça vous intéresse?» ça m'amuse beaucoup!

Papa: Oh zut!

Rachel: Tu peux te concentrer, papa, la radio ne te dérange pas?

Presentation ideas

To make the link between the text, the following task (12) and Point grammaire, quiz students briefly on the content of the text, to make sure they have understood the positive/negative import of key phrases, for example:

- *Est-ce-que Rachel aime écouter la radio? Comment savez-vous cela – qu'est-ce qu'elle dit?*
- *Papa dit à Rachel «Baisse le son». Il demande, «Comment peux-tu te concentrer?». Quelle est la réaction de Rachel. C'est positif? Elle est heureuse? furieuse? difficile? Comment savez-vous cela – qu'est-ce qu'elle dit?*
- *Est-ce que le père de Rachel aime écouter «Ça vous intéresse?» Comment savez-vous cela – qu'est-ce qu'il dit?*

More assimilation of pronoun phrases via the process of identifying positive/negative/neutral opinions. Note that there is one example of a *jamais* construction here; the explanation and practice of these constructions comes on page 38 of the Student's Book.

Solution

Positif	Négatif	Ni l'un ni l'autre
C'est rigolo!	Ça m'ennuie	Ça m'est égal
Ça m'intéresse beaucoup	Je ne veux pas le voir, merci	Ça m'intéresse un peu, mais pas trop
Les dessins animés? Ça m'amuse bien	Les reportages? Je ne les regarde jamais	

Point grammaire: Direct object pronouns

Revise the position of *le*, *la* and *les* as object pronouns.

Show flashcards/OHTs of activities (**CM1**, **CM2**, **CM13**) and ask students double questions such as *Tu aimes le football? Ça t'intéresse?* In answer to *Oui*, say *Oui, ça m'intéresse aussi*, and to *Non*, *Non, ça ne m'intéresse pas (non plus)*. Write up *Ça m'intéresse*, *Ça ne m'intéresse pas*. Then ask a student, *Les documentaires, ça t'intéresse, toi?* and elicit one of the above answers.

Use three cards with the English words 'It interests me'. Move 'me' to a pre-verbal position to parallel the French. Ask students to comment on its meaning and the order. Move on to *Ça vous intéresse, Nicole et Kim? – Oui, ça nous intéresse.*

13

Students unscramble short, jumbled sentences.

Solution

1 Mon père ne m'écoute pas.
2 Allô. Oui, je vous écoute.
3 Mon frère t'amuse beaucoup.
4 Ta sœur nous embarrasse.
5 Je trouve que ces émissions m'ennuient.
6 Je pense que cette émission vous intéresse.

14

Students decide on the order of importance of these statements for them and compare with a partner. They could see which statements come in exactly the same position in their list: *X arrive en 7ᵉ place pour nous deux.*

Tip

Students could try and tune the departmental radio to a French station on long wave. If done on the hour, they should be able to discover which station they have found. *Radio Monte Carlo* is always obtainable on long wave.

ICT activity

Learning objectives

- to be able to sort data and enter it appropriately on a spread sheet or database;
- to present that data in graphical form.

1 The teacher provides the students with the results of a 'survey' (see below) in which people have been asked to state what type of TV programmes they like.

2 Students enter the data. If using Excel, they have two headings – the TV programme and the number of people who like it.

3 They then present this information as a pie or bar chart using the chart as a stimulus for talk.

Personne A	les feuilletons australiens, les magazines sportifs
Personne B	les magazines sportifs, les magazines de jardinage
Personne C	les feuilletons australiens, les films
Personne D	les feuilletons australiens, les magazines sportifs
Personne E	le journal du soir, les documentaires, les magazines de jardinage
Personne F	les documentaires, les magazines sportifs
Personne G	les magazines de jardinage, les films
Personne H	les feuilletons australiens, les émissions comiques
Personne I	les magazines sportifs
Personne J	les feuilletons australiens, les magazines de jardinage
Personne K	le journal du soir, les films, les magazines de jardinage
Personne L	les feuilletons australiens, les magazines de jardinage
Personne M	les feuilletons australiens, les magazines sportifs, les documentaires
Personne N	les émissions comiques, le journal de soir, les documentaires
Personne O	les feuilletons australiens
Personne P	le journal du soir, les documentaires
Personne Q	les magazines de jardinage, les magazines sportifs
Personne R	les magazines sportifs, les émissions comiques
Personne S	les feuilletons australiens, les magazines sportifs
Personne T	les feuilletons australiens, les émissions anglaises

Unité 4 Pages 38–39

Avec Internet, c'est vite fait!

This cartoon is provided simply for reading, but if you want to exploit it, see the list of possible task types for extra exploitation on page vii of this Teacher's Guide.

15 📖 [CD 1 track 45]

Students use what they have just been told about *ne ... jamais* constructions to help them match the five people in the left-hand column with the descriptions on the right.

Transcript

1 Tu as jamais surfé sur Internet? Ça t'intéresse?
2 Non, ça ne m'a jamais intéressé. Je n'ai pas le temps!
1 Mais c'est vraiment utile – et rapide aussi! Ça peut aider avec le shopping, par exemple.
2 Comment est-ce qu'on fait ça?
1 Ce n'est pas difficile. Il faut tout simplement choisir un site-web – Amazon, par exemple, puis on doit cliquer sur un produit, disons . . . un CD, et voilà!
2 Bon, mais il faut payer, non?
1 Bien sûr, quand on a choisi son produit, on le paie avec la carte de crédit. Par exemple, la semaine dernière j'ai trouvé un site intéressant et j'ai acheté un logiciel pour mon ordinateur.
2 Et comment est-ce que tu l'as trouvé, ton logiciel?
1 Euh, je sais pas, il n'est pas encore arrivé . . .

Tip

To introduce the concept of *ne ... jamais*, here are some ideas.

- Ask students to ask you Yes/No questions involving activities (not opinions or feelings), e.g. *Vous regardez le football à la télé?* Answer the first few with *Jamais!* (shaking head and arms furiously). Then add a full answer: *Jamais! Je ne vais jamais au pub! Pas le samedi, pas le dimanche, pas en semaine. Jamais!*
- Ask them what they think *jamais* means. Then show some some sentences such as *Je ne vais pas au pub*, rub out *pas* and change to *Je ne vais jamais au pub*. Students see that *jamais* goes in the same place as *pas*.
- Now ask students the sort of questions that they asked you. They must not say *Non*, but must give full answers with *jamais*. Anyone saying *Non* is out.
- The same pattern can be applied with perfect tense examples.

Solution

1 e; 2 d; 3 f; 4 b; 5 a; c is a distractor.

16 📖 [CD 1 track 46]

This is the sort of text that appears in on-line magazines such as *Funky Magazine*, a French Canadian one. The real thing is sometimes a bit too hot for classroom use. If students want to get *un cyber-copain* or to read authentic teenage French material, they could try **www.kazibao.net**. This is a magazine for youngsters of all ages. It is closely supervised and a code of conduct must be observed in all correspondence on the Net. Parental consent should be sought before the address is given.

The present text has many examples of *me* as both direct and indirect pronouns, as well as *lui* and *le (l')*.

Transcript

Bonjour, je m'appelle Célia et j'ai un problème. Il y a trois mois, j'ai rencontré un gars sur Internet. Je lui envoie des méls tous les jours. Quelquefois, je lui parle au téléphone des heures et des heures. De temps en temps il me téléphone. Il me dit qu'il m'aime. Je n'oublie jamais de lui envoyer un mél ou de lui téléphoner, mais la semaine passée j'ai été malade et je ne lui ai pas téléphoné, et je ne lui ai pas envoyé de mél, non plus. Aujourd'hui, je lui ai téléphoné, mais il ne me croit pas. Il pense que je ne l'aime plus, mais ce n'est pas vrai. J'ai téléphoné à ses parents et je leur ai expliqué le problème. Ils me disent qu'ils ne peuvent pas m'aider. Que dois-je faire?

Solution

1 Je lui envoie des méls.
2 Je lui parle au téléphone.
3 Il me téléphone.
4 Il me dit qu'il m'aime.
5 Je n'oublie jamais de lui envoyer un mél.
6 Je ne lui ai pas téléphoné.
7 Je ne lui ai pas envoyé de mél.
8 Aujourd'hui je lui ai téléphoné.
9 Il pense que je ne l'aime plus.
10 Je leur ai expliqué le problème.

17 📖✏ Solution

This will depend on students' own views of the situation.

Point grammaire: Indirect object pronouns

Pick out *Il me dit qu'il m'aime* and *Ils me disent qu'ils ne peuvent pas m'aider*. Use 'say to' rather then 'tell' to illustrate the idea of 'to' in these sentences.

Pass a ball or other object round the class. *Voici Sharon. Je lui passe le ballon. Et voilà Wesley. Sharon lui passe le ballon*, etc. Demonstrate *Anthony m'envoie des méls*, and then *Moi, je lui envoie des méls*. Elicit from students that *lui* can mean 'to him' and 'to her'. Try similar exercises for *leur*.

Ask for comment on the position of *lui* and *leur*. By this time students should be getting the idea that direct and indirect object pronouns precede the verb.

Mnemonic: PVC = Pronouns before Verbs in most Cases.

Presentation ideas

- Say that you are going to give presents to various people *J'offre un cadeau à* . . . single names, pair/group/plural names, e.g. *à Jean et à Jeanne; à ma mère; à ma copine; à mes copains; à mes frères; au directeur; aux élèves; à mes grands-parents.*

- Put two column headings on the board – *singulier* and *pluriel* – and ask students to come up and copy an item into the correct column.
- As they fill them in, comment *Oui, je lui donne un cadeau* or *oui, je leur donne un cadeau . . .*
- When the columns are completed, add *lui* at the foot of the *singulier* column, and *leur* at the foot of the *pluriel* column.

18

Students choose the right form of the pronoun, which is indirect in all cases.

Solution

a – Oui je **lui** parle tous les jours.
b – Oui, nous **leur** envoyons des méls tous le temps.
c – Oui, je **lui** ai répondu.

EGW4 Activity 1: (See full notes at the end of this unit) offers extra practice in the use of *lui* and *leur*.

19

Students answer questions in the perfect tense; the answers require indirect object pronouns.

Solution

1 Oui, je **lui** ai téléphoné.
2 Oui, je **leur** ai écrit.
3 Oui, il **lui** a parlé.
4 Oui, je **lui** ai téléphoné.
5 Oui, il **m**'ont parlé.
6 Oui, il **nous** a donné des devoirs.

Point grammaire: The verb *dire*

It is important that the perfect tense should be demonstrated, so that students can report speech. Ask one student to give you a sentence, e.g. *Je n'aime pas les documentaires.* Pretend not to have heard and and ask another student to report: *Qu'est-ce qu'il a dit?* Give students: *Il a dit que/Elle a dit que . . .* on the board.

↑ *Le bruit court:* An alternative game is to ask students to make up a rumour going round on one of the soaps (*EastEnders, Brookside, Neighbours,* etc). Use the present tense of *dire*, e.g. Student 1: *Lindsay dit que Jimmy est fou.* Student 2: *Jackie a dit que Lindsay a dit que Jimmy est fou.* Student 3: *Max a dit que Jackie a dit que Lindsay a dit que Jimmy est fou,* etc. This is best played in small groups.

20 Solution

1 Qu'est-ce que tu **as dit**?
2 Mon père **a dit** que je peux sortir samedi soir.
3 Alain **dit** qu'il va à Paris la semaine prochaine.
4 Mes professeurs **ont dit** que je travaille assez bien.
5 Vous **dites** qu'il y a un train à quelle heure?
6 Yannick **a dit** qu'il espère retourner en Bretagne.

EGW4 Activity 2: (See full notes at the end of this unit) offers extra practice in use of object pronouns and *dire*.

Unité 4 Pages 40–41

These two pages look at multi-media and some associated problems. The first article comes in the form of a problem page letter from a parent and the newspaper's answer.

Transcript

J'ai lu avec intérêt votre sondage sur les enfants et les jeux vidéo. Mon fils Pierre a neuf ans et il passe beaucoup de temps à jouer sur ordinateur. Il a plusieurs jeux vidéo. Maintenant, il ne joue plus au foot, il ne sort plus, il n'écoute plus la radio. Il ne regarde plus la télé – il préfère brancher sa console sur le téléviseur. Il ne s'intéresse plus à rien, sauf à l'ordinateur! Il commence à être difficile – il ne veut jamais aller à l'école, il ne veut pas manger les plats que je prépare. Il veut manger des fast-food devant l'écran. En ce moment il ne porte pas de lunettes, mais il a des problèmes de vue. Que faire?
Monique, Lille.
Votre fils est typique de la génération actuelle – la génération «joystick». Les enfants et les adolescents qui passent trop de temps à jouer sur ordinateur deviennent solitaires, moroses même. Les copains ne leur sont plus d'importance. Les jeux vidéo ne constituent pas une activité sociale. On ne doit pas laisser un enfant rester des heures devant un ordinateur. Il est essentiel de limiter l'accès à l'ordinateur. Fixez une période spécifique où Pierre peut faire ses jeux vidéo. Il doit sortir avec ses copains. S'il ne veut pas manger, tant pis pour lui! Vous ne devez pas préparer d'autres plats pour lui. Quant au problème de la vue, Pierre doit aller voir votre opticien le plus tôt possible.

21 📖 [CD 1 track 47]

Students decide if the statements given are to be found in the letter or the answer. The verbs *vouloir*, *devoir* and *pouvoir* are revisited, and the notion of *ne . . . plus* introduced.

Solution

dans la lettre: 1, 2, 4, 6
dans la réponse: 3, 5, 7, 8

Ça se dit comment? p.40 🎧 [CD 1 track 48]

A reminder about when the -s is silent in French, when it is pronounced as English '-s' and when as English '-z'.

Further examples of the -z pronounciation are: *dose, laser, Moselle, la Tour de Pise, séisme.* Then point out the liaison between *les* or *des* and the initial vowel of the following noun.

Transcript

- ses, sondage, solitaire, sortir, sur
- passer, laisser
- console, constituer
- plu**s**ieurs, fantai**s**ie
- les‿enfants, les‿adolescents, de**s**‿heures
- Six scientifiques ont passé de longues heures à analyser les espèces rapportées de Saturne.

Point grammaire: Ne . . . plus

In order to introduce *ne . . . plus* mount some photographs of yourself as a child on a sheet of sugar paper. These should be photos of activities. If poses are used, attention should be drawn to the clothes or the hairstyle. Show the photos to the class. (This is a 'stirring' activity and is always good for a laugh!) For each photo explain: *Quand j'étais petit(e), je . . . Maintenant je ne . . . plus.* Emphasis should be on the present rather than the imperfect which is incidental here. Write a few sentences on the board with the year at the top. *Je ne regarde plus Bob the Builder. Je ne mange plus de biscottes Farley's. Je ne bois plus de Coca Cola.* Ask students what they think *ne . . . plus* means. Point out its similarity to *ne . . . pas* and *ne . . . jamais.*

Ask students what they no longer do. Leave the frameworks *Je ne regarde plus . . ., Je ne mange plus . . ., Je ne joue plus . . .,* etc. on the board.

Ask others to report on what has been said: *Angela ne joue plus avec ses poupées.*

Alternative contexts: How have the town and the school changed in recent years? *Il n'y a plus de boulangerie. Le cinéma n'est plus là. Mme Brown n'est plus ici. On n'étudie plus l'espagnol.*

Homework opportunity

Students could stick photographs/scanned pictures of themselves when younger into their books, with a comment under each relating to the activity portrayed. This avoids the need for the imperfect. All three negatives could be used. *Je ne joue plus au foot. Je ne mange jamais de chocolat maintenant. Maintenant je n'aime pas les bananes.* Alternatively, this could be done on A4 sheets and mounted as a display with word-processed comments.

22

Students complete sentences using one of the three negative forms, according to the code. The sentences contain pronouns which must be kept within the negative framework.

Solution
1 Pierre ne joue jamais sur ordinateur.
2 Moi, je n'ai plus accès à Internet.
3 Mes parents n'aiment pas le fast-food.
4 Yannick ne sort plus avec ses copains.
5 Tu n'aimes plus les jeux vidéo?
6 Je ne lui parle jamais.
7 Anne ne leur parle pas.
8 Il ne me téléphone plus.

23 [CD 1 track 49]

Students listen to a radio doctor discussing with a mother the advantages and disadvantages of multi-media. The verbs *vouloir, pouvoir* and *devoir* are revisited, and the vocabulary of communications is reinforced.

Transcript
Speakerine: Bonjour. Aujourd'hui, nous avons dans le studio le Docteur Philippe Lejeune qui va nous parler des multi-médias et des problèmes des jeunes. Mme Adèle Martin, mère d'un garçon de onze ans, a des questions à lui poser. Mme Martin!

Mme Martin: Merci. Docteur, est-ce que je peux donner accès à Internet à mon fils?

Docteur: Oui et non. Internet est vraiment bien en ce qui concerne les informations. Mais le problème c'est les sites pornographiques et racistes. Vous devez être là quand il surfe sur le web.

Mme Martin: Est-ce que les jeux vidéo peuvent causer des problèmes?

Docteur: Les jeux vidéo sont très bons pour la coordination. Le problème c'est qu'ils sont très, très mauvais pour la concentration.

Mme Martin: Mon fils veut avoir un téléphone portable comme cadeau d'anniversaire.

Docteur: Alors, les téléphones portables . . . la communication est bonne . . . mais ils émettent des micro-ondes comme un four à micro-ondes, et ça, c'est dangereux.

Mme Martin: Que pensez-vous des CD-ROM?

Docteur: Ah, ça, c'est pas une question médicale . . . bon . . . vous avez des encyclopédies sur CD-ROM et ça c'est bien . . . mais les enfants n'utilisent plus leurs livres.

Speakerine: Merci bien, Docteur.

Solution

	Bon points	Mauvais points
Accès à Internet	informations	sites racistes/ pornographiques
Jeux vidéo	bon pour la coordination	mauvais pour la concentration
Téléphones portables	bonne communication	micro-ondes
CD-ROM	encyclopédies	on n'utilise plus les livres

24

This exercise brings together practice of pronouns and negatives. There are several pairing possibilities.

25

This exercise brings together the points mentioned in task 24, and *c'est* + adjective.

Differentiation opportunity and homework opportunity

Differentiation will be largely by outcome, but preliminary work could involve a pie chart being drawn on the board divided into the different media.

⬇Students could verbally practise forming sentences using phrases given in the exercise.

⬆Before attempting the written version, more able students could be given linking expressions:

En plus	*Au contraire*
D'ailleurs	*Par contre*

Tip ⬆

C'est + adjective is such a useful construction that it's worth enabling students to use it correctly, pointing out it does not require agreement. Many students, of course, won't be helped by drawing attention to this, but it may be a relevant point for your more able students.

Unité 4 Pages 42–43

Presentation idea

It's helpful if there can be a selection of French newspapers and magazines available. Alternatively, access them via the Internet as suggested below.

ICT opportunity

The teacher might find it convenient to download and provide hard copies of examples of materials prior to starting this part of the unit. Alternatively, they could bookmark examples of sites to show students on-line.

Some suggested starting points are **www.momes.net/education**, **www.apreslecole.fr**, and the *médias journaux* sections of **yahoo.fr**.

Students could be given access to these and asked to decide into which category they fall: *journal national quotidien, journal régional quotidien, magazine.* The latter category can be sub-divided into: *magazines sportifs/de jardinage/de musique,* etc. If newspapers are not to hand, many can be downloaded from the Internet.
(**www. addresses: Libération**, etc.)

Transcript
La presse: les journaux
Il y a environ 50 titres aujourd'hui dans la presse nationale et régionale. Les trois grands titres quotidiens sont:

Journal	Lecteurs
L'Équipe	1 855 000
Le Parisien	1 633 000
Le Monde	1 513 000

On peut les acheter partout en France. On achète 230 journaux pour mille habitants en France.

En général, ce sont les hommes qui lisent les journaux (60% des lecteurs). D'habitude ils aiment les lire le matin. La durée moyenne de lecture est de 30 minutes par jour.

En ce qui concerne la presse régionale (par example Ouest-France), il y a environ 40 titres. Les gens des régions préfèrent les acheter pour leur contenu d'intérêt local.

26 📖✏

By linking the figures to what they represent, students also practise association between figures and written forms of numbers.

Differentiation opportunity ⬇

Before tackling task 26, students of lower ability could be asked to convert the written forms of the numbers into figures.

Solution
1 b; **2** i; **3** h; **4** g; **5** f; **6** c; **7** a; **8** d; **9** e

27 📖🔊✏ ⬆

Students find out a bit about the three main dailies by matching their titles to their descriptions, which have heavy hints in them!

Solution
1 *Le Monde*
2 *L'Équipe*
3 *Le Parisien*

28 🎧✏ [CD 1 track 50]

Students listen to a journalist explaining why the circulation of newspapers has gone down. They note their answers in English.

Preliminary work: Before they listen, ask students to suggest words that they might hear in the recording (list them on the board). You might like to prompt: *journal/journaux, les nouvelles, la radio, la télévision, regarde, on lit/on ne lit pas;* think about possible reasons for a decline in newspaper reading.

Transcript for 28 and 29
Pour les grands journaux quotidiens, c'est difficile aujourd'hui. On n'a plus le temps de lire. On ne peut pas lire quand on travaille, mais on peut écouter la radio. En voiture aussi, on peut écouter la radio, mais on ne doit pas lire le journal! En plus, vous avez les informations sur l'ordinateur, sur Internet. Vous cliquez . . . et hop! voilà . . . vous avez les nouvelles. Maintenant, vous avez tous les grands journaux sur Internet.

Et puis . . . euh . . . le soir . . . euh . . . on mange et on regarde la télé. On ne lit pas le journal, en général. Mais les journaux régionaux sont toujours populaires. Les gens aiment les journaux régionaux, les nouvelles régionales, parce que c'est local.

Solution
1 People no longer have time to read.
2 You can listen to the radio while working or driving, but you can't read the paper.
3 You can get information, including news, on the Internet.
4 In the evening people eat and watch TV (they don't read the paper).
5 People prefer local newspapers.

29 [CD 1 track 50]

This task is useful practice for the Higher GCSE oral presentation. (The words supplied would be legitimate as notes which the student could have with them in the exam.)

Ça se dit comment? p.42 [CD 1 track 51]

The difference between the various *-e* sounds is problematic for English speakers. Since *-é* often begins words, students could look through a given page of a dictionary in this section and attempt to pronounce words.

As *-è* is less common, practise the conjugation of *acheter*, *préférer* and *répéter* purely for pronunciation.

Transcript

- général, durée, Libération, représenter
- achète, frère, père, mère
- je préfère, je répète
- L'infirmière préfère utiliser une épée pour piquer les malades terrifiés dans le derrière.

Point grammaire: Word order with pronouns

The image of the sandwich is useful. Draw a baguette sandwich – end on – in perspective, with modal verbs, verbs of feeling and verbs of intention in the top half, *le*, *la* and *les* as the filling, and transitive verbs (*regarder*, *écouter*, *acheter*, *visiter*, *lire*, etc.) in the bottom half. This can be copied and kept for reference.

30

Students complete the replies by inserting a direct object pronoun. Some sentences are negative. In the last two ↟ questions the infinitive has to be added also, to complete the replies.

Solution

1 Non, je ne veux pas **le** lire.
2 Oui, nous aimons **les** lire.
3 Oui, il espère **l'**acheter.
4 Non je ne compte pas **les** regarder.
↟5 Non, nous détestons **les écouter**.
↟6 Oui, je **les écoute tous les jours**.

31 [CD 1 track 52]

Presentation ideas

1 Magazine covers (or Internet printouts) could be mounted on the wall with word-processed labels: *Cousteau Junior – un magazine sur les animaux; Salut – un magazine de musique*, etc.
2 As this item focuses on where people read magazines, you could do a pre-listening exercise. Ask students to predict places they might expect to hear, given the theme of the recording (e.g. *à la maison, au café, au travail, au collège, chez le dentiste/le médecin, dans le train/le métro*).

Differentiation opportunity ⬇ ⬆

To help weaker students, put some of the above key words on the board, and ask them for a couple more.

⬇1 Students identify the order in which the places where people read are listed.
⬆2 More able students listen again and note the percentages given. Revision of the fact that the decimal point is a comma (*virgule*) in French would be a useful preliminary.

Transcript

On lit la majorité des magazines à la maison – 81,2%. On en lit 8,2% chez des amis ou des voisins. La lecture au travail est populaire aussi – on lit 5,2% des magazines là où on travaille. Dans les salles d'attente, par exemple dans les gares, on lit 2,2% des magazines. On en lit 1,6% chez le marchand de journaux ou en librairie, 1,2% dans les transports publics, 0,5% chez le coiffeur, 0,5% dans un café, un restaurant ou dans un hôtel.

Solution

1 c, d, g, f, e, h, a, b
2 **c** 81,2%; **d** 8,2%; **g** 5,2%; **f** 2,2%; **e** 1,6%; **h** 1,2%; **a** 0,5%; **b** 0,5%

32

Students could first look at the names of the magazines and decide what they are about. They then match magazines to people's interests.

1 Photo, Vidéo 7
2 Auto Moto
3 Parents, Famille Magazine
4 Mon jardin et ma maison
5 France Football, L'Équipe Magazine
6 Géo, Science et Vie

Unité 4 Pages 44–45

Checkpoints

Test

The **Test** checks students' skills in the grammatical goals of the unit:

- using direct object pronouns instead of repeating nouns
- using the present tense of *finir* and *dire*
- using indirect object pronouns: *lui* and *leur*
- using negatives: *ne ... pas*, *ne ... jamais* and *ne ... plus*

Solution

1 Les documentaires sont assez populaires en France, mais ce sont les adultes qui (**a**) **les** préfèrent, plutôt que les jeunes. Les jeunes connaissent assez bien Internet et ils (**b**) **le** trouvent très utile pour leurs études scolaires. Les adultes (**c**) **l'**utilisent moins. Ils préfèrent la télévision. Ils (**d**) **la** trouvent plus réconfortante.

Les jeunes au contraire aiment tous les médias. Ils (**e**) **les** connaissent depuis leur toute jeune enfance. [5]

2 – Tu as vu cette émission sur le Canada hier?
– Non, je ne **l'**ai pas vue. C'était bien? [1]
– Oui, c'était formidable. Tu as vu le journal à 8h00?
– Non, je **le** regarde jamais. [1]
– Mais, comment as-tu trouvé la présentation sur le foot?
– Moi, je **l'**ai trouvée très bonne. Je **la** regarde tous les jeudis. [2]
– A propos, tu as fini tes devoirs de maths?
– Oui, je **les** ai finis. [1]
– Je peux emprunter ta copie?
– Non, je **l'**ai prêtée à Catherine. [1]
– Zut! Tu peux me donner les réponses, peut-être?
– Désolé, je **les** ai oubliées. [1]

3 a Je **dis** toujours bonjour au professeur. [1]
b On **dit** que le match est annulé. [1]
c Cette émission **finit** à quelle heure? [1]
d Les cours **finissent** normalement à cinq heures. [1]

4 a Je **leur** ai prêté une calculatrice. [2]
b Je **lui** ai passé une note. [2]
c Je **lui** ai donné de l'argent. [2]
d Je **leur** ai offert des cadeaux. [2]

5 a On **n'**aime **jamais** les mauvais professeurs. [2]
b Je **ne** sors **plus** avec Angéline. [2]
c Pourquoi est-ce que tu **ne** veux **pas** être pompier? [2]
d Tu **ne** vas **jamais** en France? [2]

6 a Non, je ne veux pas **lui** téléphoner. [2]
b Non, je n'aime pas **les** envoyer. [2]
c Oui, je vais **leur** écrire. [2]
d Oui, je veux **l'**acheter. [2]

Total [40]

Quiz

The **Quiz** checks students' knowledge acquired in the unit, about:

• TV in France
• radio in France
• French newspapers and magazines

Solution

1 non [1]
2 trois heures [1]
3 les adultes [1]
4 Hercule Poirot [1]
5 La station de radio française la plus populaire en France est France-Inter. [1]
6 Any two of: *L'Équipe, Le Parisien/Aujourd'hui, Le Monde, Le Figaro* [2]
7 Il y a environ 40 journaux régionaux; Ouest-France [1]

8 Any two of: *Cousteau Junior* – pour les jeunes qui aiment les animaux
Science et Vie Junior – pour les jeunes qui s'intéressent aux sciences
Salut – pour les jeunes qui aiment la musique et la mode
Les Clés de l'Actualité – pour les jeunes qui s'intéressent à tout. [6]

Total [13]

Projets

⬇**A1**/⬆**A2** Differentiated work, based on a survey of television preferences.
B Interview pair work on use of the Internet, leading to a 100-word written report.
C Describe a favourite magazine or newspaper (50 words).
⬆**D** Describe why radio is important to you.

EGW4 teaching notes

Sheet **EGW4** provides extra grammar/homework on the core points of the unit.

Activity 1 practises *lui* and *leur* in the context of identifying who gets which Christmas present.

Solution

1 (Exemple) Non, il **lui** offre **un ballon de foot**.
2 Non, il **lui** offre un vélo.
3 Non, il **leur** offre **une bouteille de cognac**.
4 Non, il **lui** offre **un livre**.
5 Non, il **leur** offre **un jeu vidéo**.
6 Non, il **lui** envoie **une carte**.
7 Non, il **leur** envoie **une carte**.

Activity 2 practises direct object pronouns, negatives, *finir* and *dire*.

Solution

– Tu aimes cette émission, grand-mère?
– Non, je ne **l'**aime pas. Elle **finit** à quelle heure?
– À 8 heures. Et puis tu as les actualités.
– Et elles **finissent** à quelle heure?
– À 8h30. Tu veux regarder un film?
– Non, je **n'**aime **pas** les films.
– Alors, tu veux regarder un documentaire?
– Comment? Qu'est-ce que tu **dis**?
– Je **dis**, EST-CE QUE TU VEUX REGARDER UN DOCUMENTAIRE?
– Non, les documentaires, je ne **les** regarde jamais. Non, je vais me coucher. Bonne nuit!

unité 5
Allons-y! Le Québec

Background information on Quebec

Le Québec is the French-speaking Eastern Province of Canada. Its capital is also called Québec, or Quebec City in English. The second city is Montréal. Of the 7.2 million inhabitants of the region, 5.6 million are francophone.

The French explorer Jacques Cartier, a native of Saint-Malo, arrived in Quebec in 1534. The area was originally occupied by French settlers until Canada was conquered by the British. Some of the Canadian French from the more easterly provinces went south to Louisiana, where their descendants still live (and some are francophone).

The majority of the population are concentrated along the banks of the St. Lawrence river. This area is less harsh than the north, which has an Arctic climate. The area has a number of hi-tech industries such as IT, telecommunications and aerospace in addition to the more traditional industries such as logging, paper, tourism and engineering.

There are 11 native tribes in the region, known as *les Premières Nations* or *les Autochtones*. Efforts are being made to preserve the cultures of these native peoples who represent 1% of Quebec's population.

Unité 5 Pages 46–47

Point d'info

The map shows the position of Quebec in relation to the rest of Canada and lists the main cities and geographical features. A more detailed map is provided on **CM21**. Brief facts on population and language are given. You could add some of the above facts as background before starting work on the exercises, as students may be curious as to why French is spoken in a country which has many British connections and which is a member of the Commonwealth.

As an alternative, **CM20** could be used. This is the text of the above notes, but in French. This could be exploited in one or more of the following ways.

- Students complete a grid giving details, e.g. population, francophone population, languages, major cities, industries, native cultures.
- You could block out a certain category of word, e.g. adjectives, and supply them in a separate jumbled list for a gap-fill.
- Students pick out important vocabulary from English prompts, e.g. French-speaking, inhabitants, explorer, native (n.), Louisiana, information technology, telecommunications, aerospace, logging, engineering, etc. These could be incorporated into gapped sentences, skeleton sentences or be used in a summary of the text.
- For differentiation, the text could be cut up and attached to photos taken from brochures or the Internet to form a display/brochure.

1  [CD 1 track 53]

This exercise requires students to examine the grid of facilities available in wild-life reserve/leisure parks. Students read the e-mail and decide where Patricia went.

Transcript

Salut! Me voici au Québec – en vacances. Tu sais, les Québécois aiment les activités en plein air. Ce matin je suis allée nager avant le petit déjeuner. Hé! Il fait froid ici! Après, mon père et moi, nous sommes allés voir des animaux typiques de la région – l'orignal, par exemple. Cet après-midi nous sommes allés au bord de la rivière – papa a attrapé un poisson – moi, j'ai décidé de faire du canot! Demain on va faire du ski. Bons baisers.
Patricia

Solution

Port-Daniel

2

Students read the spiral and separate out the invidual sports which number among the most popular in Quebec.

Solution

le hockey; la natation; la pêche; le ski; le patinage sur glace; la randonnée; la voile; le VTT; le surf des neiges; le lacrosse; le hockey sur glace.

3  [CD 1 track 54]

Students read the short advertisement for a nature park and a list of five types of *amateur*; they decide to whom it does **not** apply.

Transcript

Les parcs du Québec

Découvrez les 20 parcs du Québec. Ces parcs existent pour la protection des régions naturelles du Québec et ils offrent à leurs visiteurs une grande diversité d'activités en plein air.

Solution

4 Les amateurs de musique.

 [CD 1 track 55]

Four students are shown, each with different likes and dislikes about leisure. Because they will have to relate the first person statements they hear to the third person version on the page, you may wish to prepare students by drawing their attention to key words before playing the tape.

1 Students match the third person descriptions to the first person statements on the tape.

Transcript

Paul: Moi, j'aime bien rester en forme. Je fais du patin. Mais je n'aime pas la musique.

Angèle: Moi, j'adore la musique et j'aime danser. Le sport? Ça ne m'intéresse pas.

Ahmed: J'aime être en plein air. Je m'intéresse aux animaux et à l'environnement.

Magali: Je pense que la musique et les sports sont vraiment ennuyeux. Je trouve le passé du Canada fascinant.

Solution

a Angèle; **b** Magali; **c** Ahmed; **d** personne; **e** Paul.

2 Students study the four advertisements below and decide who wants to go where.

Solution

Paul veut aller au Taz Skatepark.
Angèle veut aller à Groove Society.
Ahmed veut aller au Parc Jean Drapeau, à la Biosphère.
Magali veut aller au Musée McCord.

5 [CD 1 track 56]

Canadian French uses many English words and expressions. In this exercise, students match the Québécois French to the pictures and add the 'standard' French word if they can.

Transcript

Ben, c'est dull ici. Quelquefois on prend mon char, puis on va dans un bar. Je prends une draffe, tu sais, puis on jase. Puis on fait le party, peut-être, ma blonde et moi. C'est l'fun! Mais, elle, elle aime magasiner, et ça peut coûter un bras. Elle a besoin d'un tchum riche. À tantôt!

Solution

dull = image 5 – ennuyeux
mon char = image 1 – ma voiture
une draffe = image 11 – une bière
jase = image 4 – bavarde/parle
on fait le party = image 3 – on fait la fête
ma blonde = image 2 – ma copine
c'est l'fun = image 6 – c'est super!
magasiner = image 7 – faire des courses
coûter un bras = image 10 – être/coûter cher
un tchum = image 8 – un copain
à tantôt = image 9 – à tout à l'heure

⬆ More able students could be asked to rewrite the Quebec teenager's monologue in standard French (this is on tape so that the Québécois and French pronunciation can be compared if you wish).

Solution/Transcript [CD 1 track 57]

Ben, c'est **ennuyeux** ici, tu sais. Quelquefois on prend **ma voiture** et on va dans un bar. Je prends **une bière**, tu sais, et on **bavarde**. Puis **on fait la fête**, peut-être, **ma copine** et moi. **C'est super**! Mais, elle, elle aime **faire des courses**, et ça peut **être cher**. Elle a besoin d'un **copain** riche. **À tout à l'heure!**

Unité 5 Pages 48–49

Point d'info

This gives some brief statistics on the number of tourists in Quebec, most of whom are Québécois.

6 [CD 1 track 58]

Students read the advertisement for a Director of Tourism in Montreal. They then listen to the four candidates who are interviewed for the post and decide which one would be best. All but one have one factor which excludes their being employed. For easier access to the task, you may wish to do a bit of whole-class work on identifying the key words, before they listen.

Transcript

1 Je m'appelle Albert Jourdain. J'ai trente-six ans, et j'ai été Directeur de Tourisme dans une ville française. Je suis né en France, et donc je parle couramment le français. Je suis très dynamique et on a eu beaucoup de succès dans notre région. J'habite au Québec depuis deux ans, et je connais assez bien cette région.

2 Je m'appelle Louis Picard. J'ai 40 ans. Je suis francophone, mais je ne parle pas très bien l'anglais. Je connais très bien la région, surtout la ville de Québec. J'ai travaillé pendant quinze ans dans le commerce et je comprends bien les problèmes du financement du tourisme.

3 Bonjour. Je m'appelle Isabelle Kanapé. J'ai 38 ans. Je suis née à Québec . . . donc je suis francophone de naissance . . . J'ai fait des études en Angleterre et je parle couramment l'anglais. J'ai travaillé en France, dans l'industrie et le commerce. Depuis cinq ans je suis Directrice de Tourisme pour la ville de Québec, et pour moi, le tourisme, c'est ma vie. Je suis très enthousiaste pour cette profession! Je pense que nous devons attirer de plus en plus de touristes dans notre très belle région . . .

4 Hi! My name's Paul Chevrette. I'm Canadian . . . from Vancouver actually . . . euh . . . We don't have much use for French over that side of the country, so I guess I can get by in Quebec without any French . . . after all, everybody speaks English these days, so I don't see that as being a problem . . . Euh . . . when do I start?

Solution

Mme Kanapé. Reasons: M. Jourdain doesn't say he speaks English and he only knows Quebec fairly well; Louise Picard doesn't speak English very well; Paul Chevrette doesn't speak French, obviously doesn't know Quebec (and has a bad attitude!).

 [CD 1 track 59]

Students read part of a web page for Télévision–Radio Canada which broadcasts from Montreal. They listen to the tape and identify the programmes being discussed – the titles are 'bleeped' out on the cassette.

Transcript

Interviewer: Qu'est-ce que vous aimez comme émissions à la télévision?
Garçon: Moi, j'adore (*bleep*). Ah oui . . . quelquefois il y un certain drame . . . mais en général très rigolo. Je m'amuse toujours à le regarder.
Interviewer: Et vous, vous avez d'autres émissions favorites?
Femme: Oui, je m'intéresse à tout ce qui est culture . . . donc un programme que j'aime bien c'est (*bleep*). Oui, j'aime me relaxer, surtout le dimanche.
Interviewer: Et les séries, vous les aimez?
Jeune fille: Ben, je dois dire que, comme des millions d'autres téléspectateurs, je suis une vraie fan de (*bleep*). J'ai regardé toutes les séries jusqu'à maintenant, et la nouvelle série va être super!
Interviewer: Et le sport?
Homme: Ben . . . euh . . . je suis très sportif et j'aime bien les émissions sportives . . . donc . . . cette semaine . . . je vais m'installer devant (*bleep*) . . . ça va être un événement passionnant, je crois.

Solution

– le Monde de Charlotte
– MC
– 4 et demi
– Finale de la Coupe Québécoise

Students are given a two-minute time limit to make up as many words as possible from the phrase *comédie dramatique*. These could include: *car, carte, comique, dire, dit, drame, ma, Marc, mardi, me, mec, média, midi, or, ouate, Rome, que, tard,* etc. You could award a prize for the largest number of correct words.

ICT activity

Learning objectives

- to use search strategies for an effective search on the Internet;
- to scan for key words;
- to download/print an appropriate recipe.

1 The class considers the range of dietary likes and dislikes that exist, e.g. vegetarian/only eats fish/loves pasta, etc. and lists them.
2 Students are asked to find a suitable québécois recipe for one particular dietary requirement.
3 Teacher guides students to **www.toile.qc.ca** and tells them they have to search this site for a suitable recipe.
4 Students download their chosen recipe into a word document and add a glossary of any unfamiliar terms so that it can be readily understood.

 [CD 1 track 60]

This page gives some information on the native tribes of Quebec. They are usually referred to as *les autochtones*, but the alternative name of *les Premières Nations* will be much easier for students to understand. The eleven tribes are (in French) Abénaquis, Algonquins, Attikameks, Cris, Malécites, Micmacs, Montagnais, Naskapis, Hurons–Wendat, Mohawks and Inuit.

Transcript

Les Premières Nations
Ce sont les tribus natives du Québec. Il y en a onze, qui comprennent les Algonquins, les Micmacs, les Mohawks et les Inuits. En juillet et en août, les tribus célèbrent leur culture et leur histoire. On chante, on danse, on joue de la musique, on raconte des histoires et des légendes. Il y a aussi des compétitions pour les femmes et les jeunes – par exemple, dresser une tente, faire un feu, préparer du thé, porter un canot et participer à des courses.
  Les jeunes jouent un rôle actif dans les cérémonies traditionnelles. Ils portent des costumes spéciaux avec des plumes, des masques et des vêtements multicolores.

Solution

1 Il y a moins d'une douzaine de tribus natives.
5 Les jeunes participent aux cérémonies.

Extra idea

Many words from the native languages of America have entered both English and French. Using **CM22**, students use the definition clues given to complete the grid with the words in rows 1–6 and reveal the mystery word 7.

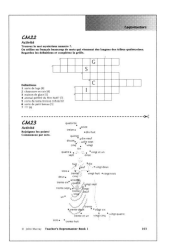

Solution

					7			
1	T	O	B	O	G	**A**	N	
2	M	O	C	A	S	S	**I**	N
3			I	G	L	**O**	O	
4				C	A	**R**	I	B	O	U
5			W	I	G	**W**	A	M	
6			K	A	Y	A	**K**		

10 📖

Students first work out the code used to spell MOHAWK. The 26 letters of the alphabet are assigned a number (D = 1, E = 2, F = 3, G = 4, H = 5, I = 6, J = 7, K = 8, L = 9, M = 10, N = 11, O = 12, P = 13, Q = 14, R = 15, S = 16, T = 17, U = 18, V = 19, W = 20, X = 21, Y = 22 Z = 23 A = 24, B = 25, C = 26).

Solution

Tribu 1 CRI
Tribu 2 NASKAPI
Tribu 3 HURON–WENDAT
Tribu 4 ABÉNAQUI

Extra idea

CM23 is a dot-to-dot picture. The key is given in the form of numbers appearing as words, and this provides an opportunity to revise high numbers.

Possible projects/coursework

A Students could research the life of the native tribes using encyclopedias, the Internet and information gathered from libraries, tourist offices and the Quebec government office. This could be done in groups, with each group researching a different tribe. The results could be collated into a display, perhaps using native drawings and patterns as borders.

B Another possible topic could be ice hockey, a top sport in Canada of course, but increasingly watched on TV in the UK.

Further information

Information on the tribes and on all aspects of Québécois culture is available from:

Quebec Government Office,
59 Pall Mall,
London SW1Y 5JH.

Useful websites include:
La toile du Québec: **hhtp://www.toile.qc.ca**
Ministère de l'Éducation: **http://www//.meq.gouv.qc.ca**
Office national du film du Canada:**http://www.nfb. ca**
Canadian National Tourist Office:
http://www.tourisme.gouv.qc.ca
First Nations: **http://www.autochtones.com**

unité 6
Le grand départ

Contexts
- French holiday destinations
- hotels and camping in France
- holiday activities
- safety advice on a French beach
- giving/accepting/rejecting invitations

Grammar
- using *à* and *en* to talk about places
- using *du . . . au . . .* to talk about dates
- using *-re* verbs
- using the verbs *prendre* and *mettre*
- using *qui* and *que* to say 'the . . . which/who/that'
- asking questions using *quel* and *lequel*
- using *ce/cet/cette/ces* and *celui/celle/ceux/celles*, to say 'this, these' and 'this one, that one'

Pronunciation
- '*-t*' as '*-ss*'
- '*-t*', '*-d*'

Revision in this unit includes:
- numbers, times and dates
- asking questions

Unité 6 Pages 50–51

The opening spread focuses on the favourite holiday destinations of the French. Since 80% of French holidays are taken within *l'hexagone*, the unit concentrates on France rather than holidays abroad.

Presentation ideas

A good preliminary activity would be to revise basic points of the geography of France, using outline map **CM24** and overlays **CM24a** and **CM24b**. If you start with major cities, this gives an opportunity for practice of the points of the compass, e.g. *Lille est dans le sud?* (oui/non); *Toulouse est dans le nord-est ou le sud-ouest?* (alternatives); *Où est Bordeaux?* (open question). Use overlay of the Alpes, Vosges and Pyrénées mountains and practise *sont: Les Vosges sont dans le nord-est ou le nord-ouest?*, etc. An overlay of the main rivers may be used to remind students of their names and locations: *Seine, Loire, Rhône, Dordogne.*

The first article gives some statistics and some brief indications of the attractions of key holiday regions of France.

1 [CD 2 track 1]

Transcript

80% des Français passent leurs vacances en France. Pourquoi? Parce qu'il y a une si grande variété de paysages et d'activités à voir et à faire! Plus de 1,5 millions de vacanciers français choisissent le département du Var comme destination en été.

Numéro 1: Moi, je vais en Bretagne, parce que j'adore les fruits de mer, les crêpes et le cidre!

Numéro 2: Moi, je vais à Bordeaux, parce que j'aime faire de la voile.

Numéro 3: Nous allons dans le Var, parce qu'il fait si beau en été!

Numéro 4: Moi, je vais dans les Alpes pour faire des sports d'hiver et des randonnées dans la montagne.

Solution

1 La **majorité** des Français passent leurs vacances en France.
2 Bordeaux est sur la côte **ouest** de la France.
3 Dans le département du Var, il fait un temps **superbe**.
4 En Bretagne, dans le **nord-ouest**, on peut très bien manger.
5 Le département des Alpes-Maritimes est une région **montagneuse**.

Tip

Introduces the concept of *départements* and mentions that you can spot the origin of a French car by the department number in its registration.

If you feel it is appropriate, you could point out that the *département* names are often linked with natural features, e.g. *Alpes–Maritimes: la partie sud des Alpes est près de la mer.*

CM75 is a map and list of the French *départements* with their numbers, which you could use for number/pronunciation practice.

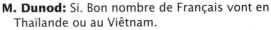

Presentation ideas

2 [CD 2 track 2]

Familiarise students with country names by playing a verbal quiz game, asking '*l'X, c'est dans quel continent?*' Write the five continent names *l'Europe, l'Amérique, l'Afrique, l'Australasie, l'Asie* up on the board. Test first of all with the countries that are mentioned in the transcript below (but in a more mixed order). Then add some others, e.g. *la Chine, le Niger, le Portugal, le Japon, la Finlande,* etc. This verbal work provides some good pronunciation practice because of the visual closeness of the French and English forms.

Revise the general rule that nouns ending in *-e* are feminine. This can then be linked to the gender of countries (*le Maroc – terminaison en -c, c'est masculin; l'Espagne – terminaison en -e c'est féminin*) and in turn to the *en/au(x)* distinction: *Je vais au Maroc; Je vais en Allemagne.*

Extra points you might mention: *le Canada* ends in a vowel other than *-e*, hence it is masculine. The two most common plural countries are *les Pays-Bas* and *les États-Unis*. Others include *les Antilles, les Canaries* and *les îles Anglo-Normandes* (the Channel islands)

Transcript

Interviewer: Oui, c'est Radio Corsaire et vous écoutez Studio Vacances. Ce soir notre invité est M. Hervé Dunod, auteur du nouveau livre *Les Français ne partent pas en vacances*. M. Dunod, c'est pas vrai, hein? Les Français partent en vacances comme les autres Européens, non?

M. Dunod: Oui, c'est vrai, mais 80% des Français restent en France – ils ne partent pas à l'étranger. Seuls 20% des Français visitent un pays étranger.

Interviewer: Et où est-ce qu'ils vont, ces Français qui ne restent pas en France?

M. Dunod: La destination préférée des Français, c'est l'Espagne, et puis, après cela, ils choisissent d'aller en Grande-Bretagne. Ils aiment aller à Londres, bien sûr. Et puis, il vont en Italie, en Belgique et en Allemagne. Ce n'est pas loin, après tout!

Interviewer: La majorité des Français préfèrent rester en Europe, alors?

M. Dunod: Oui, c'est ça, mais l'Afrique du nord est populaire aussi. On va surtout au Maroc et en Tunisie, mais aussi au Sénégal. Là, on est sûr de trouver le soleil!

Interviewer: Les Français n'aiment pas tellement l'Asie, alors?

M. Dunod: Si. Bon nombre de Français vont en Thaïlande ou au Viêtnam.

Interviewer: Et ces Français qui aiment parler français, ils ne vont plus au Canada?

M. Dunod: Si, mais récemment le Canada est moins visité par les Français, sauf le Québec, qui est une région francophone.

Interviewer: Et vous, M. Dunod, où est-ce que vous allez passer vos vacances cette année?

M. Dunod: Dans le département du Var – comme la majorité des Français! Oui, je vais à Nice.

Interviewer: Merci bien, M. Dunod. Et bonnes vacances!

Solution

1 Le Maroc; l'Espagne; le Sénégal; le Viêtnam; le Canada; la Belgique; la Grande-Bretagne; la Tunisie; l'Italie; l'Allemagne.

2 Belgique, Allemagne, *or* Italie – pas loin; Canada – récemment moins visité, *or* on va au Québec; Afrique *or* Tunisie *or* Sénégal – soleil; Grande Bretagne – aller à Londres.

Point grammaire: 'To' and 'in'

The distinction in the use of *en, au, aux* and *à* with country names.

3 Solution

1 Cette année-ci, nous **espérons** aller **en** Tunisie.
2 Moi, je ne suis **jamais** allé **à** Madrid.
3 Moi, j'ai une correspondante qui **habite aux** États-Unis et une autre **qui** habite **au** Canada.
4 Moi, j'ai **passé** d'excellentes vacances **à** Paris.
5 Nous avons l'**intention** d'aller **en** Italie l'année **prochaine** ou peut-être **au** Maroc.
6 La semaine **dernière** j'ai été **aux** Pays Bas, **à** Amsterdam.

4

Open-ended task.

5

This task and the Tip pick up on the use of *si* in the interview (task 2). To help with the difficult concept of using a different word for 'yes', practise it in the context of revising basic points of French geography, using **CM24, CM24a, CM24b**. Give students a selection of statements, some positive, some negative to which to reply *oui* or *si*, e.g.

Nice est dans le sud; Paris n'est pas la capitale de la France.

Ça se dit comment? p.51 [CD 2 track 3]

Pronunciation of the letter '*-t*' as '*-s*' in words ending *-tion*.

Transcript

–destination, conversation, addition, solution, réaction, intention, réception

Extra idea

You could combine practice of the pronunciation point with some word-building: prompt students with a series of words which have a related word ending in -tion; students should try to come up with the -tion word. The exercise also serves to underline that most -tion words in French are feminine. Some starters:

prononcer	la prononciation
inventer	l'invention
fascinant	la fascination
considérer	la considération
imaginer	l'imagination
fabriquer	la fabrication
déterminer	détermination

 [CD 2 track 4]

Students listen to a discussion between four teenagers about their holiday plans. They pick out the destinations suggested and the reasons for going there.

Transcript

Alain: Bon, alors, on a trois semaines, du 20 août au 12 septembre. Moi, je pense aller dans le Var . . . le soleil . . . les plages . . . Qu'en penses-tu, Michèle?

Michèle: Oh Alain, je ne suis pas d'accord. On est allés dans le Var en famille, l'année dernière. En plus, il fait trop chaud là-bas pour moi – tu sais, Alain, je ne supporte pas le soleil.

Alain: Oui, peut-être, mais où est-ce que tu veux aller donc – en Norvège?

Michèle: Mais non! Moi, je voudrais aller en Angleterre. Je ne suis jamais allée à Londres . . . je voudrais voir la Tour de Londres, Big Ben, tout ça. Tu es d'accord, Juliette?

Juliette: Oui, mais trois semaines à Londres, c'est trop long! Dans une grande ville, imaginez le bruit, les voitures, la pollution! Oh, non . . . moi, j'aimerais aller en Irlande . . . c'est si tranquille, si romantique . . . la campagne, les montagnes . . . Qu'est-ce que tu penses, Daniel?

Daniel: Moi, je veux aller à Ibiza . . . pour la musique . . . quoi . . . sensass . . . ouais . . . là on peut danser, draguer un peu . . . n'est-ce pas, Juliette?

Juliette: Pas question, Daniel. Moi, j'ai une bonne idée . . . on passe quelques jours à Londres, disons du 20 août au 24, puis une semaine en Irlande . . . du 25 août au premier septembre, et enfin le reste de nos vacances . . . dans le Var! Il ne fera pas trop chaud en septembre.

Alain et Michèle: Oui, d'accord/Là tu as raison/Ça va.

Daniel: Mais vous êtes sûrs que vous ne voulez pas aller à Ibiza, même pour un week-end?

Alain, Juliette et Michèle: Pas du tout! Absolument pas! Pas question!

Solution

1

	Destinations préferées	Raisons
Alain	Var	soleil, plages
Michèle	Angleterre, Londres	Tour de Londres, Big Ben
Juliette	Irlande	C'est tranquille, romantique, la campagne, les montagnes
Daniel	Ibiza	danser, draguer

2 Londres, Irlande, Var.
20–24 août à Londres; 25 août – 1 septembre en Irlande; le reste des vacances: dans le Var.

↕3 Personal response.

Tip

Phrases for expressing (dis)agreement were used in the discussion and are given, with some others, in the Tip.

Extra ideas

Play the task 6 recording and ask students to pick out who uses which of the opinion phrases in the grid. This could be done in a 'fun' but more elaborate way by preparing cards showing different combinations of about six of the expressions, and play Bingo, using the recording.

(Dis)agreement could be practised by your suggesting some holiday destinations of varying desirability. ↕ More able students might be able to answer using *Si*, if you frame your questions negatively.

Unité 6 Pages 52–53

This spread deals with hotel accommodation and offers a variety of information and language connected with facilities, booking and problems.

1 Students match symbols to meanings.

Solution

a Parking.
b Chiens admis.
c Tennis.
d Jardin.
e Ascenseur.
f Bienvenue aux enfants!
g Piscine.
h Télévision.
i Téléphone dans les chambres.
j Chambres accessibles aux handicapés physiques.
k Restaurant.

Presentation ideas

To practise the use of hotel accommodation/ facilities symbols, use enlarged photocopies from **CM25** as a set of flashcards with a symbol on each.

Divide the class into two teams. Ask a student to time exactly one minute while you flash cards for one team who call out the meaning. The second team attempts to beat the number of correct answers. To practise languages, use pictures of national flags. Establish which country is which and then sort out the languages (*En Allemagne on parle?*)

This would be a good opportunity to make students aware that Flemish (*le néerlandais*), as well as French, is spoken in Belgium, and that in addition to French, German and Italian are spoken in Switzerland. (There's more on this theme in Unit 12.)

1 Students use the authentic hotel entry to write a brief description of the hotel, with the help of some phrases given to guide them.
2 Students look at the national flags and give the language spoken.

Solution
anglais, allemand, hollandais, espagnol, italien

Extra ideas

Students could work in pairs, one partner having the details of a hotel in symbolic form. The other partner asks questions about facilities: *Il y a un parking? Les chambres sont équipées d'une télévision? Est-ce qu'on parle anglais?* This partner then draws the symbols when he/she has the answers.

Homework opportunity

From this could come a second activity, the description of a Fawlty Towers-style hotel which lacks any facilities at all. This would give students the opportunity to use negatives. The writing could be in the form of a script for a telephone conversation between an unhelpful staff member and a potential customer, e.g.

- *Vous avez une piscine?*
- *Non, nous n'avons pas de piscine.*
- *Vous avez un ascenseur?* etc.

9 [CD 2 track 5]
Preparatory work. Using **CM26**, revise rooms, nights at hotel, etc.

Presentation idea

Use **CM27** to teach students the French Post Office Code for the alphabet. This may be practised with flashcards, each with a letter on one side, and the name on the other. Students shown 'B' say 'B comme Berthe'. Students shown 'Berthe' say 'B'.

Students complete Franck Moulot's details.

Transcript
Réceptionniste: Allô. Hôtel du Château.
M. Moulot: Bonjour, Mademoiselle. Je voudrais réserver une chambre, s'il vous plaît.
Réceptionniste: Oui, c'est pour combien de nuits?
M. Moulot: C'est pour cinq nuits du quinze au dix-neuf juin. Ça va?
Réceptionniste: Pas de problème, Monsieur. Vous désirez une chambre individuelle ou une chambre double?
M. Moulot: Une chambre individuelle, s'il vous plaît, avec douche et WC privatif.
Réceptionniste: Oui, Monsieur. C'est à quel nom?
M. Moulot: Moulot.
Réceptionniste: Comment ça s'écrit?
M. Moulot: M-O-U-L-O-T.
Réceptionniste: D comme Désiré?
M. Moulot: Non. T comme Thérèse.
Réceptionniste: Ah, bon merci.
M. Moulot: C'est combien par nuit?
Réceptionniste: 50 euros, plus 0,7 euros de taxe.
M. Moulot: Le petit déjeuner est compris?
Réceptionniste: Non, Monsieur, c'est en supplément.
M. Moulot: Bon, merci bien, Mademoiselle.
Réceptionniste: Je vous en prie, Monsieur.

Solution
Nom: **MOULOT** Prénom: **Franck**
Chambre **individuelle**
Du **15** au **19 juin**
Douche ✓   Bain
WC privatif   Oui ✓ Non
Petit déjeuner   Oui ✓ Non

Tip

le + date; *du/au* for periods of time between two dates.

Students are reminded that '**on** the sixth of June' is le *six juin* (no 'th'). Hence '**from** the sixth of June' = *du six juin*.

Extra idea

Practise the correct form with well-known dates, e.g. birthdays, Christmas Day, Boxing Day, New Year's Day. More variable dates used could be the FA Cup Final, the end of term, the date of the French exchange, a big pop concert at Wembley, the date of the school drama production (*Ça commence le . . . et ça finit le . . .*), the start of the football season or the duration of a championship.

10

Students use the flow chart to make up hotel dialogues, filling the gaps with appropriate details. If the department has internal phones or a classroom phone set, this can be made more realistic by the added element of not being able to see the person speaking. This sort of activity may be suitable for small groups, depending on your class. The 'receptionist' could note the details of the various calls.

ICT activity

Learning objectives

- to use search strategies for an effective search on the Internet;
- to understand details using context and other clues;
- to choose appropriate hotels for groups with particular needs.

   1 The teacher provides students with a range of scenarios (see the example below) of groups looking for hotels.
   2 Students decide on a destination in France and search the information on hotels. Alternatively, choose **yahoo.fr** and use the key word *hôtel*.
   ⬇3 Lower attainers could be provided with checklists to make their search easier. Suggested scenario: *trois jeunes, pas riches, piscine essentiel, pas besoin de petit déjeuner . . .*

Homework/ differentiation opportunity ⬇ ⬆

■ ⬇**DW6.1A** Students sort out a jumbled dialogue, putting questions in one column and answers in another. There are various possibilities for a logical order. They practise the dialogue and then change the details.

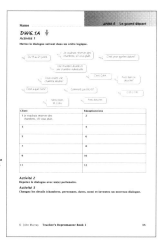

■ ⬇**DW6.1B** Students write a dialogue between M. Colin and a hotel receptionist. The requirements in M. Colin's diary do not match the rooms available. Expressions such as *Nous n'avons pas de . . .* and *Je peux vous offrir . . .* could be given as preliminaries. A decision will have to be made at the end as to whether to take the rooms on offer.

11 [CD 2 track 6]

Students listen to a radio advertisement for a special offer on hotels in Saint-Malo and note the details in English.

Transcript

Vous venez à Saint-Malo? Venez passer votre première nuit et nous vous offrons la deuxième! Oui, deux nuits d'hôtel pour le prix d'une! Du 21 septembre au 31 octobre, la deuxième nuit vous est offerte si vous arrivez le vendredi ou le samedi. Demandez notre brochure 'Bon week-end à Saint-Malo' et présentez-la dès votre arrivée à la réception de l'hôtel. Pour de plus amples renseignements, téléphonez à l'Office de Tourisme de Saint-Malo, 02 99 56 64 48.

Solution

Any four of the following:

- Two nights in a hotel for the price of one.
- Between 21st September and 31st October.
- You must arrive on a Friday or a Saturday.
- Obtain your brochure and present it at the hotel reception desk.
- For further information, phone the Tourist Office at Saint-Malo.
- Telephone number: 02 99 56 64 48.

12 Transcript [CD 2 track 7]

M. Férien: Rachel, tu m'entends . . .?
Rachel: Est-que je l'entends? Ça dépend . . .
M. Férien: Rachel, tu m'entends, tu vas mettre la table, s'il te plaît? Réponds-moi!
Rachel: Désolée, je ne t'entends pas.
M. Férien: Elle n'entend rien avec ce vacarme-là, elle ne me répond jamais . . . Rachel, à table!? Tu m'entends?
Rachel: Oui, attends, j'arrive!

Solution

1 Tu m'entends?
2 Ça dépend
3 mettre la table
4 désolé, je ne t'entends pas
5 ce vacarme
6 elle n'entend rien
7 elle ne répond jamais
8 à table
9 attends
10 j'arrive

Point grammaire: Regular *-re* verbs

The regular *-re* verbs *attendre*, *répondre*, *entendre*, are displayed on **CM28**.

Points to note:

- the *-d* is never heard in the singular forms;
- past participles end in *-u* (*j'ai attendu*, etc.);
- *prendre* (and its compounds) and *mettre* look like ordinary *-re* verbs, but they do not follow this pattern – they are featured later in the unit, on pages 56 and 58.

13 🎧✏️ [CD 2 track 8]

Students listen to a telephone conversation involving problems of waiting, hearing and replying. They complete the gaps in the sentences with appropriate verbs.

Transcript

M. Désirat: Oh là . . . mais répondez, hein? . . . Ça fait trois minutes que j'attends . . . ah . . .
Réceptionniste: (*totally muffled speech*)
Désirat: Je n'entends pas . . . allô? Est-ce que vous m'entendez? . . .
Réceptionniste: Allô. Hôtel de la Plage . . . Vous m'entendez maintenant . . .?
Désirat: Oui, oui . . . je vous entends. Passez-moi le directeur, s'il vous plaît.
Réceptionniste: Attendez . . . je vous le passe.
Désirat: Attendez . . . attendez . . . zut . . . on attend toujours . . .
Directeur: Allô . . . oui . . .
Désirat: Allô . . . écoutez . . . qu'est-ce que vous dites? . . . je n'entends pas.
Directeur: . . . on est complet, vous m'entendez bien . . .? OK . . . Au revoir.
Désirat: Ah, zut!

Solution

1 Il **attend** depuis trois minutes.
2 On ne **répond** pas.
3 Il n'**entend** pas le réceptionniste.
4 Il doit **attendre** pour parler au directeur.

Presentation idea

For *entendre*, practise repetition between pairs. One partner whispers or silently mouths something connected with hotels, e.g. *Je voudrais réserver une chambre* or *Est-ce qu'il y a une piscine?* The other requests a repeat – *Qu'est-ce que tu dis? Je n'entends pas.* Further practice is possible using intra/interdepartmental phones or even two tins and a piece of string!

For *répondre*, point out that, like *dire*, *écrire* and *téléphoner*, *répondre* is followed by *à*: *répondre à quelqu'un/à une lettre/au téléphone.*

14 🎙️✏️

Students complete gapped sentences with the correct form of *attendre*, *entendre*, or *répondre*.

Solution

1 Oui, il **attend** sa petite-amie.
2 Le téléphone sonne, mais on n'**entend** pas.
3 Pardon, mais je n'**entends** pas.
4 R.S.V.P = **Répondez** S'il Vous Plaît.
5 **Attendez** ici, s'il vous plaît.
⬆6 Est-ce que vous avez **entendu** la sonnerie?
⬆7 Ils ont **répondu** à mon mél.

Tip ⬆

Explains the construction **present tense + *depuis*.**

15 ✏️⬆

Tests use of present tense with *depuis*. Answer choices are open-ended.

Unité 6 Pages 54–55

The introductory text gives a brief outline of the stars system for camping. This will enable students to judge the quality of the campsites in the following exercises. There are no questions directly based on this text.

Transcript

Les campings
Dans les guides touristiques, les campings ont des étoiles. Voici le système:

Une étoile – Assez bon – lavabos, douches froides, WC, bacs à vaisselle.
Deux étoiles – Bien aménagé – douches chaudes, prises électriques, lavabos, gardé le jour.
Trois étoiles – Confortable – emplacements équipés électriquement, magasin, service de boissons, gardé en permanence – site éclairé la nuit.
Quatre étoiles – Grand confort – arbres, fleurs, salle de réunion et de jeux.

16 📖 [CD 2 track 9]

Facilities listed for three campsites whose star rating has to be worked out from the information in the text.

Camping de la Plage: ***
Camping de la Fôret: ****
Camping des Rochers: *

17

These are extra symbols not previously used in the section on hotels. Students attempt to identify the meaning of as many as possible in a one-minute time limit.

Solution

1 bar; **2** garderie/crèche; **3** électricité; **4** golf; **5** pêche; **6** volleyball; **7** magasin/supermarché; **8** équitation/centre équestre; **9** machines à laver/laverie; **10** voile.

18

Students use the symbols in the description of the campsite to answer questions which involve words related to the symbol. They give a reason for their answer.

Solution

1 Oui. Le site est équipé d'électricité.
2 Oui. Il y a un magasin.
3 Oui. Il y a une garderie.
4 Oui. Il y a une piscine.
5 Non. Il n'y a pas de rivière/de lac.

Presentation idea

Add these symbols to your set of flashcards, copying them up from **CM29**. Practise campsite cards individually and then mix them with hotel cards for revision.

ICT activity

Learning objectives
- to understand details using context and other clues;
- to use the information found as a stimulus for a letter describing a holiday on a campsite.

1 Teacher provides students, if necessary, with a choice of websites. This could be done as hard copy or as sites bookmarked for student use. A good starting point could be: **www.campingclub.asso.fr.**
2 Students then draft the letter. ⬇Lower-attaining students could be given a model letter which they can amend.
3 ⬆Higher-attaining students make notes on facilities. ⬇Lower attainers are given grids to complete.

19  [CD 2 track 10]

For a preliminary activity use copymaster **CM26** again to practise the vocabulary of nights, people, accommodation and vehicles.

Students listen to the cassette and complete the table with the details required.

Transcript

Client 1
Client: Vous avez de la place? C'est pour une tente.
Gardien: C'est pour combien de personnes?
Client: Deux. Mon mari et moi.
Gardien: Et c'est pour combien de nuits?
Client: C'est pour trois nuits.
Gardien: Vous n'avez pas de voiture?
Client: Non, on est à pied. On fait des randonnées dans la montagne.

Client 2
Client: Vous avez un emplacement pour une caravane?
Gardienne: Bien sûr. Vous êtes combien de personnes?
Client: On est trois adultes.
Gardienne: Et c'est pour combien de nuits?
Client: Alors . . . lundi, mardi, mercredi, jeudi . . . donc quatre nuits.
Gardienne: Et vous avez là une Peugeot. . . .
Client: 405.

Client 3
Client: Vous avez des emplacements? C'est pour deux tentes.
Gardien: Oui. Vous êtes combien?
Client: Quatre. Deux adultes et deux enfants.
Gardien: Et c'est pour combien de nuits?
Cliente: C'est pour une semaine
Gardien: Ben, pour une semaine il faut réserver, quoi. Heureusement, il y a de la place. Vous avez une voiture, je suppose?
Cliente: Oui. Une Renault Mégane.

Client 4
Client: Est-ce que vous avez de la place? C'est pour une tente.
Gardienne: Oui. Vous êtes combien de personnes?
Client: Je suis seule.
Gardienne: C'est pour combien de nuits?
Client: C'est juste pour une nuit. Je suis en route pour la côte.
Gardienne: Oui, il y a de la place. Vous avez quelle marque de moto?
Client: Une Harley-Davidson.

Solution

	Tente	Caravane	Personnes	Nuits	Véhicule
Cliente 1	1	non	2	3	–
Client 2	0	oui	3	4	Peugeot 405
Client 3	2	non	4	7	Renault Mégane
Cliente 4	1	non	1	1	Harley-Davidson

20 [CD 2 track 11]

Students read the list of rules (4 × *il est interdit de*, 3 × *il faut*) and identify the rule which has been broken.

Transcript

1 Fifi, viens ici . . . pas dans le lac! Fifi, non!

2 Mais regarde celui-là! Il lave des assiettes dans le lavabo! C'est dégoûtant, ça!

3 Mais baissez le son . . . Vous entendez . . . Il est minuit . . . Zut! On ne m'entend pas!

4 Phou, ça pue . . . et il y a une cigarette ici . . . mais c'est dangereux, ça!

5 Sortez, s'il vous plaît! Vite! Vous n'avez pas quatorze ans, il me semble!

6 Chéri, t'as pas vu mes boucles d'oreille, tu sais, les gros diamants? Je les ai laissées ici, sur la table . . .

Solution

1 F; **2** D; **3** B; **4** A; **5** C; **6** G; E is a distractor.

Differentiation opportunities ↓ ↑

↑ In addition to simply identifying the rule, students could explain what has happened using *on*: *On a . . .; On n'a pas . . .; On a oublié de . . .*

↓ ↑ To practise writing information on booking, students could be given either an outline booking form (**CM26**) with gaps to complete, or a more difficult task, having only details of place, dates, composition of group and expected time of arrival, with students asked to write a booking letter.

Presentation idea

Revise the flags of EU countries. This could be done in two ways:

Display different flags and ask *C'est quel pays?* **CM62**, which shows an outline map of Europe, could be displayed also to remind students of the locations and French names of the countries.

Describe flags, e.g. *C'est un tricolore. Les raies sont verticales. Les trois couleurs sont le vert, le blanc et l'orange. C'est donc . . .?*

CM62
Carte de l'Europe

© John Murray **Teacher's Repromaster Book 1**   141

21 [CD 2 track 12]

Students listen to the cassette and identify the tent or caravan being talked about and the nationality of the occupants. This text revises prepositions (*devant, derrière, à côté de*) and introduces the relative pronouns *qui* and *que*.

Transcript

Papa: Ça va, Cécile. Tu t'es fait des copains?

Cécile: Oui. C'est vraiment international ici, tu sais, papa. J'ai déjà rencontré une Anglaise, un Hollandais, un Allemand, et bien des autres . . .

Papa: Ah bon?

Cécile: Oui. Regarde. Tu vois la voiture rouge? Eh bien, ces sont des Allemands. Il y a un garçon super qui s'appelle Helmut . . . et puis tu vois là . . . la voiture blanche?

Papa: La voiture blanche qui est derrière la tente orange?

Cécile: Non, tu vois la voiture blanche qui est *devant* la tente orange? Ça c'est à Philippa . . . elle est anglaise. La voiture qui est derrière la tente orange est à Chiara . . . elle est Italienne.

Papa: Et qui a la caravane verte à côté de la Renault bleue?

Cécile: Oh, il y a un Hollandais qui s'appelle Jan. Et la voiture rouge que tu vois là . . . derrière la caravane blanche . . . alors là, tu as un Espagnol . . . vraiment chouette!

Papa: Et tu connais les gens de la caravane bleu clair?

Cécile: Oui, c'est un couple français qui s'appellent M. et Mme Depardieu. Ce sont des gens que je ne connais pas. M. et Mme Depardieu . . . Papa, tu ne penses pas . . .?

Solution

a 3; **b** 6; **c** 1; **d** 4; **e** 5; **f** 2

Point grammaire: *Qui/que*

The relative pronouns *qui* and *que* are not easy for English speakers, few of whom use '(to) whom'! The following tip may help. Before a verb or *ne*, use *qui*. Before a noun or a pronoun (*je*, etc.) use *que*.

The distinction between object and subject pronouns is not made here because it would make the tip too complex for many; however, for your more able students, the explanation that *qui* is the subject, and *que* is the object may be appropriate.

22

Receptive work with *qui/que*: unjumbling sentences which contain them.

Solution

1 Natasha sort avec le garçon que j'aime.

2 Où est l'emplacement que nous avons réservé?

3 Nous cherchons le camping 'Soleil' qui a trois étoiles.

4 Voilà la tente que Marcelle veut acheter.

23

Students link two sentences into one, using *qui* (they will use *que* in task 24).

Solution

1 Tu vois la voiture rouge qui est derrière la tente.
2 Tu connais les gens qui ont la caravane bleue.
3 Tu vois la voiture verte qui est là-bas.
4 Les Hollandais qui ont la tente d'à côté s'appellent Seuren.
5 Tu aimes la fille qui a les cheveux longs et bruns.

24 *Solution*

1 La boisson que j'aime, c'est l'Orangina.
2 La voiture que je préfère, c'est une Audi.
3 La matière que je ne supporte pas, c'est la biologie.
4 Le garçon que je déteste, c'est Louis.

25

An extension activity in which students choose one of the provided endings and invent their own 'middle sections', using *qui* or *que* as given.

Extra idea

CM30, the campsite scene, can be used for:

- simple revision of holiday/ camping/leisure vocabulary and/or;
- practice of prepositions to express position and/or;
- practice of relative pronouns *qui/que* to identify objects/people in relation to each other.

Unité 6 Page 56

This page deals with holiday activities. The main grammar point is the verb *prendre* and its relatives.

26 [CD 2 track 13]

In this activity students listen to the cassette and put the activities into the right order. Most of them contain an example of *prendre*.

Transcript

Ça fait du bien d'être en vacances . . . on prend le temps de se relaxer. Moi, je me lève tard. Je prends une douche et puis . . . euh . . . quelquefois je prends

le petit déjeuner devant la télé. J'aime bien ça . . . Bon, il ne faut pas se presser, donc on peut prendre le bus pour aller en ville, faire du shopping. J'aime bien aller au marché. Je prends le temps de regarder . . . peut-être que je m'achète un jean ou un foulard . . . puis . . . euh . . . à midi je prends le déjeuner dans un restaurant ou dans un café . . . puis, l'après-midi, bon, je reprends le bus pour rentrer. Le soir . . . ben . . . je prends un bain . . . et puis . . . hop! À la disco.

Solution
c, b, a, d, f, h, e, g

Extra idea

Use **CM32** to prompt phrases with *prendre*.

Point grammaire: *Prendre*

See page 150 and **CM31** for full conjugation of *prendre*. On this page, attention is focused on idiomatic uses of the verb, particularly where the use contrasts with English. It is important that students should be aware that *prendre* is the 'parent' of a family of verbs, of which three common ones are given.

27 *Solution*

Personal choices – an open-ended activity.

28

Combines practice of *prendre* and *à* with places, in the context of holiday vocabulary.

Solution

1 Il prend le bus qui va à la plage.
2 Elles prennent le bus qui va à Avignon.
3 Ils prennent le bus qui va à Lorient.
4 Ils prennent le bus qui va à Valence.
5 Elle prend le bus qui va à Calais.
6 Ils prennent le bus qui va au Futuroscope.

Unité 6 Page 57

Two types of holiday are advertised here. The listening exercise contains examples of the main grammar point (*quel?*), as do the questions on the texts.

The meaning of *quel* can be communicated by tone of voice (questioning) or by suggesting answers, e.g. *Quels animaux? Des lions, des tigres?*

29  Solution

1 **a** ballon
2 **b** le pont d'Avignon
3 **a** la Provence
4 **b** le parc naturel régional du Lubéron
5 **b** natation, monter à cheval, pêche
6 **a** les chambres pour deux personnes (doubles)

Transcript [CD 2 track 14]

Vacances en montgolfière

Voler, c'est magique! Vous flottez, vous glissez. Un vol en montgolfière, c'est vraiment magnifique. Observez les villages, les voitures, les moulins, petits comme des jouets. Flottez au-dessus de la Provence, descendez vers le pont d'Avignon. Remontez dans l'air. Ici vous n'entendez rien. Tout est tranquille.

Par monts et par vallées – Vacances en VTT dans le parc naturel régional du Lubéron

Centre du Mont Sainte-Victoire – Hôtel – Restaurant – Centre VTT
- 120 km de sentiers et chemins
- 6 circuits (bleu, blanc, rouge)
- Garage à vélos
- Location VTT
- Chambres à louer: individuelle 40€, double 55€ la nuit
  À proximité: piscine en plein air, centre équestre, pêche en rivière

30 [CD 2 track 15]

Students listen to three short dialogues about choosing holidays. They deduce from synonymous expressions within the text which advertisement is under discussion. The text contains various instances of *quel?* and forms of the demonstrative adjective *ce*. The relative pronouns *qui* and *que* are also revisited.

Transcript

Numéro 1
A: J'adore le vélo, tu sais, mais tu vois les détails supplémentaires?
B: Quels détails?
A: Ces détails au bas de la page . . . là . . . je ne sais pas monter à cheval et je ne sais pas nager.
B: Non, mais c'est pas obligatoire, tu sais. D'habitude, on passe toute la journée dans la montagne.

Numéro 2
A: Alors, Christophe, tu as fait ton choix?
B: Pas encore. J'ai toujours des questions.
A: Par exemple? De quelle brochure est-ce que tu parles?

B: Cette brochure-ci. On dit qu'il y a des animaux sauvages . . . ça doit être dangereux, non?
A: Oh, non. Il y a des guides experts.

Numéro 3
A: Un voyage comme ça . . . oui . . . ça m'intéresse beaucoup. Mais quels vêtements est-ce qu'il faut porter . . . Il fait très chaud là-bas en été.
B: Oui, mais on monte très haut, donc il fait froid. Alors, tu mets un pull comme ce pull que tu portes maintenant . . . et euh . . . un anorak, je suppose, et une casquette.

Solution

1 B; 2 ni A ni B; 3 A

Point grammaire: 'Which', 'this', 'that'

Both *quel* and *ce* are dealt with here, since it is logical to treat both question and answer at the same times. *Quel*, of course, poses few problems of pronunciation, since the four forms are similar. Note the liaison in *Quels animaux?*

To practise *quel/ce* in question and answer form distribute a number of items (newspaper, magazine, record, walkman, cassette, minidisc, cap, sunglasses, mobile phone). Students check the gender of their item.

Practise dialogues thus:

Student 1: *J'ai un journal.*
Teacher: *Quel journal?*
Student 1: (holding it up) *Ce journal – L'Équipe.*
Student 2: *Moi, j'ai une casquette.*
Teacher: *Quelle casquette?*
Student 2: (holding it up) *Cette casquette Nike.*

Differentiation opportunity ⬇

⬇ **DW6.2** provides support/easier practice in using *quel* with demonstrative adjectives to ask and answer questions.

Solution

1 Quelle – **Cette**
2 Quel – **Cet**
3 Quelles – **Ces**
4 Quels – **Ces**
5 Quelles – **Ces**
6 Quel – **Ce**
7 Quelle – **Cette**
8 Quels – **Ces**
9 Quelle – **Cette**
10 Quel – **Ce**
11 Quel – **Cet**
12 Quelles – **Ces**

31

Students practise the grammatical forms of *quel* and *ce.* This could be done orally first, followed by practice in writing. The latter part of the exercise will bring out the differences in spelling.

Solution

Questions	Réponses
Quelle visite?	Cette visite.
Quel centre de vacances?	Ce centre de vacances.
Quels animaux?	Ces animaux.
Quelle montgolfière?	Cette montgolfière.
Quel hôpital?	Cet hôpital.
Quelles brochures?	Ces brochures.
Quelle attraction?	Cette attraction.

32 [CD 2 track 16]

Students listen to an account of a holiday in Provence in which a teenager has undertaken two of the activities advertised in the brochures. They note the good and bad points in two lists.

Transcript

Cet été on est allés en Provence . . . ben . . . c'était génial. Pour la plupart du temps ... ouais. Un jour nous avons fait un vol en montgolfière, mon père et moi ... Super! Le problème, c'est que au début j'ai eu le mal de l'air. Heureusement je n'ai pas vomi, hein ... mais à la fin, c'était vraiment bien. On est montés très haut ... euh ... donc il faisait très froid. Çe n'était pas très agréable ... mais la vue ... oh, la vue! C'était vraiment magnifique, tu sais ... on a vu le pont d'Avignon ... et les montagnes. C'était super-chouette! Et puis on a passé quelques jours dans le centre VTT du Mont Ventoux. En général, on a passé la journée dans la montagne ... il a fait très beau et très chaud ... très, très chaud. Donc, le soir, on crevait de faim ... on était vraiment fatigués, quoi. Un jour mon père et moi, nous sommes allés à la piscine d'à côté et enfin, oui enfin ... j'ai appris à nager. En effet, c'est simple ... mais je n'aime pas avoir de l'eau dans les yeux ... mais pour moi, c'est un petit triomphe, en fin de compte.

Unité 6 Pages 58–59

These two pages cover beach safety, invitations to go out and eating and drinking at a café. There are many examples of imperatives, and the verb *mettre* makes its appearance in several forms.

The leaflet offers some simple but practical advice for the beach.

33 [CD 2 track 17]

Students identify the people breaking particular rules.

Transcript

Protégez-vous!
Vous allez à la plage! Super! Mais faites attention ... même à la plage en pleines vacances il y a des dangers.

Soleil
Règle numéro 1: Ne prenez pas de bains de soleil entre midi et trois heures – le soleil est au plus chaud.
Règle numéro 2: Mettez un chapeau.
Règle numéro 3: Les enfants doivent mettre une chemise en coton.
Règle numéro 4: Mettez-vous à l'ombre.

Mer
Règle numéro 5: Si vous ne savez pas nager, restez au bord de l'eau.
Règle numéro 6: Faites attention aux marées.
Règle numéro 7: Ne plongez jamais des rochers.

Feu
Règle numéro 8: N'allumez jamais un barbecue les pieds nus – mettez des chaussures.

Objets aigus
Règle numéro 9: Attention! Il y a quelquefois du verre cassé sur les plages – même des seringues. Mettez des sandales.

Solution
a 7; **b** 5; **c** 6; **d** 1; **e** 3; **f** 8; **g** 9; **h** 2

Differentiation opportunity

More able students could explain exactly what is being done, or has been done, e.g. *Le petit garçon ne porte pas de chemise en coton.*

Point grammaire: Mettre

The full paradigm of the verb *mettre* is given (with *prendre*) on **CM31**. Students will probably recognise classroom uses of this verb – *Mettez vos sacs par terre. Mettez vos cahiers sur ma table, s'il vous plaît.* Other uses given here include *se mettre* (to place oneself), *se mettre à* (to begin) and the use of *mettre* meaning *to put on* (also practised on **DW6.3A** and **DW6.3B**, see below).

34

Students choose the correct verbs (*mettre* or *prendre*) according to the sense of the sentence. Both present and perfect tense forms are used.

a S'il fait chaud je **mets** un t-shirt et un short.
b Quand on est en vacances on **prend** le déjeuner sur la plage.
c Quand je suis revenu de la plage hier, j'**ai pris** une douche.
d Mes parents **ont pris** le temps de se détendre.
e Nous **avons pris** le bus pour aller de l'hôtel en ville.

Differentiation opportunities⬇⬆

⬇**DW6.3A** practises *mettre* by prompting students to match clothes to activities and say what each person puts on. First of all they revise the necessary clothes vocabulary by matching words to pictures in **Activity 1**. Then they complete sentences with suitable clothing for the activities and sports (**Activity 2**).

Solution

1 Exemple: Pour jouer au tennis, Isabelle **met** un short, un t-shirt et des baskets.
2 Pour jouer au foot, Pierre **met** un short, un t-shirt et des chaussures de football.
3 Pour faire une randonnée dans la montagne, je **mets** des chausettes, des bottes et un pull.
4 Pour faire du vélo, nous **mettons** un short, un T-shirt, des gants et des baskets.
5 Pour ranger le garage, Susanne et Georges **mettent** un short, un t-shirt, des gants, une casquette et des baskets.
6 Pour se bronzer à la plage, les garçons **mettent** un maillot de bain, des lunettes et de l'huile solaire.

⬆**DW6.3B** also practises *mettre* but in a different context. The Férien family are moving house and Mme Férien issues instructions as to what goes where. Students use her list as a reference to write her instructions. To do this correctly they also have to put the direct object pronoun in place.

Solution

1 **Tu le mets** dans le salon.
2 **Tu les mets** dans la salle à manger.
3 Non, **tu le mets** dans le salon.
4 **Vous les mettez** dans le salon.
5 **Tu la mets** dans le salon.
6 **Tu la mets** dans la cuisine.
7 **Vous les mettez** dans la cuisine.
8 Non, **tu le mets** dans la cave.

35 🎧✏️ *Ça ne va pas*

Students describe the after-effects of a day at the beach from which they have returned, sunburnt with a cut foot and a headache. They explain what they did and did not do. This gives them the opportunity to use the perfect tense of the verbs in the leaflet as well as negatives, e.g. *Je n'ai pas appliqué de crème solaire. J'ai plongé d'un rocher.*

36 📖🎧

This text can be used in the form of a quiz like those in teenage magazines. A points score is allocated to each answer depending on its power to attract or interest the other person.

Ask students to read out the letters of their three chosen favourites, what the sentence says, and to note the letter. Then, give them the score for each sentence and ask them to add up their own totals. The totals give an indication of the likely success of each questioner.

Scoring

a 7; **b** 0; **c** 8; **d** 4; **e** 2; **f** 5; **g** 10; **h** 6; **i** 5; **j** 0

18+: Tu réussiras ton flirt.
14–18: Pas mal. N'abandonne pas.
10–14: Tu n'essaies pas assez.
0–10: Tu dois améliorer ta technique!

Tip

This picks up on constructions with the infinitive that are useful in invitations.

37 🎧✏️

Students use the invitations in the Tip and the vocabulary from *Tu sais draguer* to make up invitations to go out. Personal choices.

Differentiation opportunity⬆

Students make up further invitations to go to other places and to do other things.

38 📖✏️

Students deduce suitable invitations based on the cartoon of the girl's various attempts to interest the boy. Several variants are acceptable in each case.

Extra idea

You could give studnts some phrases for accepting or rejecting an invitation:

'yes please'	'no thanks'	reasons/excuses/put-offs
volontiers	non, je regrette	je suis très occupé(e)
je veux bien	non, merci	je ne peux pas parce
d'accord	désolé	que ...
pourquoi		peut-être plus tard/
pas?		demain ...

EGW6 practises the language of invitations and snacks (see full notes at the end of the unit).

39 📖🎧 [CD 2 track 18]

Students listen to the cassette and note the choices of the two speakers. The dialogue contains examples of *lequel* and *celui* in their various forms.

Transcript

Alain: Ouf! Il fait chaud. Tu as envie d'aller au café?

Madeleine: Oui. Pourquoi pas? Moi, j'ai envie d'une glace.

Alain: Bonne idée! . . . Bon. Voilà le menu. Oh . . . il reste seulement deux parfums . . . chocolat ou café . . . lequel préfères-tu?

Madeleine: Moi, je préfère le chocolat.

Alain: Moi, le café. Tu veux un jus de fruits?

Madeleine: Oui, je veux bien.

Alain: Orange ou pomme . . . tu préfères lequel?

Madeleine: Pomme, s'il te plaît.

Alain: Bon et pour moi, orange. Tu sais, j'ai faim. Je vais prendre une crêpe. T'en veux une aussi?

Madeleine: Oui, je veux bien.

Serveur: Et voilà. Deux jus de fruits, deux glaces, deux crêpes. Bon appétit.

Alain: Merci bien. Alors. Les glaces. Laquelle est au chocolat? . . . Celle-là, je pense. Et celle-ci, au café, est à moi.

Madeleine: Merci bien.

Alain: Et les crêpes. Laquelle est au citron? Celle-ci ou celle-là? Ah, c'est celle-ci. Alors, bon appétit!

Madeleine: Bon appétit. Et merci bien.

Alain: Il n'y a pas de quoi. Dis donc . . . T'as envie d'aller au cinéma ce soir?

Solution

	À manger	**À boire**
Alain	1 une glace, parfum café 2 une crêpe	un jus de fruits (orange)
Madeleine	1 une glace, parfum chocolat 2 une crêpe	un jus de fruits (pomme)

Point grammaire: 'Which one?', 'this one', 'that one' ⬆

The table sets out both the interrogative pronoun *lequel* in its various forms and the demonstrative pronoun *celui* in its corresponding forms. The distinction between *-ci* and *-là* is indicated. Intended for receptive understanding only, though the following task reinforces it.

Extra idea ⬆

EGW6 Activity 2 practises *lequel* in the context of choosing food in a café (see full notes at the end of the unit).

40 ✐ ⬆

Students practise the correct forms of the interrogative pronoun and the demonstrative pronoun.

1 Celui-là.
2 Ceux-ci.
3 Celui-ci.
4 Lequel
5 Lequelles
6 Lesquels

Presentation ideas

To practise this point, have two sets of pictures consisting of, for example, pairs of footballers, motorbikes, cars, pop singers, cinema stars, etc. Put the masculine nouns on blue card and the feminine ones on pink. Pin one of each pair at one end of the classroom and one at the other. Stand by one set and ask students. *Alors, Il y a deux motos. Laquelle est-ce que tu préfères – celle-ci ou celle là?* Then get students to ask the questions and give the answers.

Unité 6 Pages 60–61

Checkpoints

Test

The **Test** checks students' skills in the grammatical goals of the unit:

• using *à* and *en* to talk about places
• using *du . . . au . . .* to talk about dates
• using *-re* verbs
• using the verbs *prendre* and *mettre*
• using *qui* and *que* to say 'the . . . which/who/that'
• asking questions using *quel* and *lequel*
• using *celui, celle, ceux, celles* to say 'this one, that one'

Solution

1 a Qu'est-ce que tu dis? Je n'**entends** pas
    très bien. [1]
  b Vous **attendez** l'autobus juste devant le
    camping. [1]
  c Le directeur de l'hôtel ne **répond** jamais
    à mes lettres. [1]
  d Quand le téléphone sonne, c'est toujours
    moi qui **réponds**! [1]
2 a J'**ai entendu** ce que vous avez dit. [1]
  b Sandra **a attendu** une demi-heure au
    cinéma [1]
  c Nous **avons répondu** à toutes vos
    questions. [1]

3 a Qu'est-ce que **tu** mets pour sortir ce soir? [1]
  b **Je** mets un t-shirt et un pantalon. [1]
  c **Nous** prenons le petit déjeuner à quelle heure? [1]
  d D'habitude, **Jérôme** prend le bus de huit heures pour aller au travail. [1]
  e **Mes parents** ne me prennent jamais au sérieux! [1]
  f **Vous** me prenez pour un idiot? [1]
4 a Je connais quelqu'un **qui** parle six langues. [1]
  b Il faut utiliser les bacs à vaisselle **qui** se trouvent derrière les toilettes. [1]
  c Il a essayé de draguer cette fille **qui** est avec ses parents. [1]
5 a La tente **que** tu cherches est bleue. [1]
  b Les boissons **qu'**on vend sont froides. [1]
  c La jeune Espagnole **que** j'ai rencontrée est très aimable. [1]
6 a Saint Raphaël est **dans** le Var. [1]
  b Cet été on va **en** Espagne. [1]
  c J'espère passer quelques jours **à** Paris. [1]
  d Nous allons faire du ski **dans** les Alpes. [1]
  e Cette année je dois rester **en** France. [1]
7 a Nous allons rester à Biarritz du 1 au 14 août. [2]
  b On espère être à St Malo du 6 au 12 juin. [2]
  c Mes amis sont restés à Lorient du 27 septembre au 4 octobre. [2]
⬆8 Quelles invitations préférez-vous? Celles-là. Quels campings va-t-on visiter? Ceux-ci. Quel hôtel préfères-tu? Celui-là. Quelle brochure est-ce que tu lis? Celle-ci. [8]
⬆9 a On a le choix de deux hôtels. **Lequel** préfères-tu? [1]
  b Il me reste cinq chocolats. Tu peux en avoir deux. **Lesquels** veux-tu? [1]
  c Tu peux acheter un maximum de cinq cartes postales. **Lesquelles** vas-tu prendre? [1]
  d Il faut choisir entre deux destinations. **Laquelle** est la meilleure, à ton avis? [1]
  Total [42]

Quiz

The **Quiz** checks students' knowledge acquired in the unit, about:

• French holiday destinations
• hotels and camping in France
• holiday activities
• safety advice on a French beach

Solution

1 80%. [1]
2 Le Var. [1]

3 Any two of: Grande-Bretagne, Espagne, Italie, Belgique, Allemagne, Maroc, Tunisie, Sénégal, Thaïlande, Viêtnam. [2]
4 a restaurant [1]
  b chiens admis [1]
  c piscine [1]
  d ascenseur [1]
  e jardin [1]
  f bienvenue aux enfants [1]
  g tennis [1]
  h chambres accessibles aux handicapés physiques [1]
5 a a hot air balloon [1]
  b a mountain bike [1]
  c a national/regional nature reserve or park [1]
6 Two 'do's and three 'don'ts' on the beach: any from task 33 on page 58 of the Student's Book. [5]
  Total [20]

Projets

A Ideal as a piece of written coursework.
B This could be the basis of a speaking presentation or a piece of written coursework.
C A piece practising a Higher writing task with a narrative/imaginative input.

Extra idea

Students are given leaflets on hotels, youth hostels or campsites. They then discuss which is better for their holiday under various headings:

Comment sont les services? Qu'est-ce qu'on peut faire? On peut prendre le petit déjeuner/le déjeuner/le dîner? Il faut réserver? Lequel est-ce que tu préfères? Pourquoi?

ICT unit round-up activity

Learning objective

• to search an on-line database of restaurants to find a match for specific requirements. Suggested website: **www.amatable.com** (French version!)

1 The teacher will need to familiarise him/herself with the site.
2 The teacher demonstrates the use of the website to the students, showing the need to be clear about region, town, price range, type of food, etc.
3 Students are then given a series of groups for whom they need to find a restaurant, e.g. want a restaurant in Finistère near to Brest, want to pay between 10 and 20 euros, would like to eat seafood, would like a terrace if possible and would like to eat in the evening.

EGW6 teaching notes

Sheet **EGW6** provides extra grammar/ homework on invitations and *lequel/celui-ci,* etc.

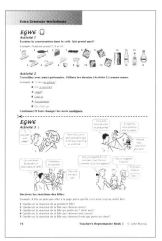

Activity 1 🎧

[CD 2 track 19]

Two boys and two girls are in the campsite café. They are all having difficulty choosing, thus making good use of interrogatives and demonstrative pronouns.

Exemple: Francine: 1, 9, et 16.

Transcript

Érik: Moi, j'ai grand'faim. Je prends un sandwich et du gâteau, je suis gourmand, moi. D'abord, quels sandwichs y a-t-il?

Francine: Il y a des sandwichs au fromage, au jambon, au thon. Moi, je ne prends pas de sandwich, mais lequel prends-tu, Érik?

Érik: Je vais prendre le jambon. Et du gâteau aussi, mais lequel . . .

Annette: Peut-être celui-là, au chocolat?

Érik: Non, pas celui-là, je préfère celui-ci, aux pommes.

Francine: Tu n'aimes pas le chocolat?

Érik: Si, mais je n'en veux pas aujourd'hui. Tu ne prends pas de gâteau, Francine?

Francine: Si, je prends un éclair, mais j'ai pas encore choisi mes chips. Je crois que je prends . . . celles-là, au fromage. Annette, les chips, tu en prends? Lesquelles?

Annette: Oui, j'en prends . . ., euh . . . à l'oignon, je crois. Dominic, quel sandwich prends-tu?

Dominic: Celui-là, au fromage, et celui-ci, aux crevettes. Je n'aime pas le gâteau. Et les boissons, lesquelles voulez-vous?

Francine: Pour moi, celle-ci, l'Orangina. Annette? Qu'est-ce que tu prends?

Annette: Je prends celle-ci, l'eau minérale.

Érik: Mais laquelle: gazeuse?

Annette: Oui, gazeuse. Euh . . . et une tarte aux fruits. Bon. Et Dominic, tu prends une boisson? Laquelle veux-tu?

Dominic: Un Orangina . . . non, un Coca, celui-ci.

Érik: Moi aussi, je prends un Coca.

Solution

Francine prend 7, 9, 16.
Érik prend 2, 6, 13.
Annette prend 8, 10, 15.
Dominic prend 1, 4, 13.

Activity 2 🗣

Pair work testing ability to offer/accept/reject a range of invitations. Makes use of the pictures for Activity 1.

Activity 3 📖 🎧 ⬆ [CD 2 track 19]

Two boys attempt to pick up girls at a campsite. This revises infinitive constructions and combines them with acceptance/refusal phrases.

Transcript

Frame 1

Boy 1: Tu veux aller à la plage?

Girl 1: Non, merci, je ne peux pas parce que je me suis trop mise au soleil hier . . .

Frame 2

Boy 2: Vous avez envie de jouer au ping-pong?

Girl 2: Je regrette, nous sommes très occupées.

Girl 3: Désolée, mais . . . peut-être plus tard . . .

Frame 3

Boy 1: Ça vous dirait de prendre un snack au café?

Girl 4: Volontiers, je veux bien.

Girl 5: D'accord, pourquoi pas?

Boy 1: Moi, je m'appelle Érik et mon ami, c'est Dominic. Comment vous vous appelez?

Girl 4: Moi, je m'appelle Francine.

Girl 5: Et je suis Annette.

All: Salut!

Solution

1 Exemple: Elle ne peut pas aller à la plage parce qu'elle s'est trop mise au soleil hier.

2 Ça ne l'intéresse pas beaucoup et elle dit qu'elles sont trop occupées.

3 Elle s'intéresse un peu, mais elle dit «peut-être».

4 Elle est enthousiaste, elle veut bien.

5 Elle est d'accord, mais pas très enthousiaste.

unité 7
La France en huit jours

Contexts
- the Channel Tunnel, Eurostar and Le Shuttle
- travelling by French train and Métro
- car hire and driving on French roads
- cycle hire in France and the *Tour de France*
- hitch-hiking
- air travel in France
- regions of France

Grammar
- using prepositions: *de, à, en, entre, dans* in expressions of time
- using the verb *venir* and others like it
- using the pronoun *y*
- using the perfect tense with pronouns
- using strong pronouns *moi, toi*, etc.

Pronunciation
- '-c-', '-ç-'
- '-g-'

Revision in this unit includes:
- using *aller* to refer to future events
- times and numbers

This unit takes the form of a journey round France made by Phileas Fogg, the great-great grandson of Jules Verne's famous hero in *Le Tour du monde en 80 jours*. The unit covers various means of transport and some of France's major cities and regions. **CM33** shows Fogg's complete route and means of transport, so you could use it periodically, perhaps revealing a part at a time, as you progress through the unit.

CM33
La route de Phileas Fogg

© John Murray Teacher's Repromaster Book 1   115

Unité 7 Pages 62–63

Since the introduction refers to Jules Verne's *Le Tour du monde en 80 Jours*, students should be made aware of the book. (The English language film starring David Niven is available on video. Students could watch the section which takes place at the Reform Club in order to understand the reference.)

Transcript [CD 2 track 20]
Dans le livre de Jules Verne, en 1872, le célèbre Phileas Fogg a fait le tour du monde en 80 jours. Aujourd'hui, son arrière-arrière-petit-fils, qui s'appelle aussi Phileas Fogg, est à Londres où il parle avec des amis. Lui, aussi, il va faire un voyage.

Reform club member: Le tour de la France en 8 jours? Impossible, Fogg!

Fogg: Mais si, c'est possible et je vais faire ce voyage! Je vais partir demain! Je vais utiliser tous les moyens de transports possibles. Je vais visiter Paris, Strasbourg, Marseille, Toulouse et Rennes et je vais revenir en Angleterre dans 8 jours.

Tip
Students could first revise *aller* by means of a two-team game. Members of one team give a subject (*je, tu, Philippe, Sarah et Mandy*, etc.), members of the other team give the correct form of *aller* (*vais, vas*, etc.) and members of the first team complete the sentence with a destination. Thus: *André et moi – allons – à Paris*

Extra idea
To practise *aller* + infinitive, select a number of alphabet cards. Now one team selects a subject, and the other has to find a destination to match the letter that you hold up. Thus: (card B) *Vous – allez visiter Bordeaux*; (card M) *Les filles – vont visiter le Maroc*.

EGW7 Activity 2 also practises *aller* + infinitive, but it also practises the time expressions covered on page 68 of this unit, so you may prefer to use it at that stage. (See full notes on **EGW7** at the end of the unit.)

1

A pairing exercise for receptive practice of the future with *aller*, bringing in also a bit of practice of times.

Solution
1 e; **2** a; **3** f; **4** d; **5** b; c is the distractor.

2

You could revise means of transport through flashcards. Firstly, just obtain the names of the means of transport. Then ask students to practise, *Je vais prendre . . .* As a memory test and for practice, other students could report on what has been said. *John va prendre le train; Tracy va prendre le bus.*

N.B. Hovercraft services across the Channel ceased in 2000. These craft are now used only on the Isle of Wight route.

1 Pour aller de Lyon à Alger, on va prendre l'avion.
2 Pour aller de Paris à Londres, on va prendre l'avion.
3 Pour aller de Londres à Lille, on va prendre l'Eurostar.
4 Pour aller de Plymouth à Santander, on va prendre le ferry.

Teacher's Guide 1 © John Murray

3 [CD 2 track 21]

The listening text gives some background information on the Channel Tunnel. You could ask students who have travelled either on Le Shuttle or L'Eurostar if they prefer the Tunnel or a ferry, and why. This gives the opportunity for justifying an opinion and using comparatives, e.g. *Je préfère le Tunnel parce que c'est plus rapide; Je préfère le ferry parce que c'est plus confortable.*

Transcript
Le Tunnel sous la Manche
Pour passer en France, Phileas Fogg va à la gare de Waterloo et prend un train Eurostar. À Folkestone dans le Kent, on entre dans le Tunnel sous la Manche. Ce tunnel, long de 50,5 kms a été construit entre 1987 et 1994. Les voitures et les camions prennnent Le Shuttle, train spécialement conçu pour transporter toutes sortes de véhicules. Le voyage sous la Manche dure environ 25 minutes. La vitesse maximale de l'Eurostar en France est de 300 km/h.

Solution
1 Longueur: **c** 50, 5 km.
2 Date de commencement de la construction: **b** 1987.
3 Date d'ouverture publique: **c** 1994.
4 Train-piétons: **a** L'Eurostar.
5 Train-véhicules: **b** le Shuttle.
6 Vitesse maximale de l'Eurostar: **c** 300 km/h.

Ça se dit comment? p.62 [CD 2 track 22]

Draw a parallel with English. The letter 'c-' is hard before '-a', '-o' and '-u': cat, cot, cut. It is soft before -e and -i: ceiling, city.

Transcript
– ce, Cité, celui-ci, Nancy
– Catherine, comme, culottes
– ça, leçon, reçu
– Ça alors! Catherine, à Nancy, a reçu cette carte-ci de sa cousine de Besançon.

ICT activity

Learning objectives
- to reuse the language of the unit focusing on question forms;
- to create a questionnaire;
- to e-mail that questionnaire to a partner school or give to another class in the same school;
- to present the outcomes in written form.

1 Teacher presents a series of headings to the class that they need information on:

pays preféré; moyen de transport préferé; activités préferées.

The students are then asked to formulate the questions they would need. ⬆ Higher attainers could be asked to do follow-up questions on reasons.

2 The questions are then e-mailed in the body of the e-mail or as an attachment to a second group of students.
3 Students then write a summary of the information they have received. ⬇ Lower attainers would need a writing frame to support their work, e.g. *Mon partenaire s'appelle . . . Il aime voyager . . . Il préfère . . . En vacances il aime . . .*

4 [CD 2 track 23]

The poster illustrated here gives a brief idea of the workings of the Paris Métro, and the cartoon includes some of the vocabulary for negotiating the Métro.

One ticket covers a *section urbaine*, and this includes all the stations within Paris. Métro lines are known by the names of the stations at each end of the line, e.g. *Direction Clignancourt*. A map is therefore a real necessity! The line numbers are not usually used. *Une station de correspondance* is a station where one can change between lines.

The listening exercise uses names which the students have already seen and heard.

Transcript
Femme: Pour aller à Cité s'il vous plaît?
Contrôleur: C'est la ligne Porte de Clignancourt – Porte d'Orléans.
Femme: C'est quelle direction?
Contrôleur: Direction Porte d'Orléans.
Femme: Il faut changer?
Contrôleur: Oui. Vous avez une correspondance à Châtelet.
Femme: Il faut combien de tickets?
Contrôleur: Un ticket, Madame.

Solution
Destination: Cité
Ligne: Porte de Clignancourt – Porte d'Orléans
Direction: Porte d'Orléans
Correspondances: 1
Tickets: 1

Extra idea

For pronunciation practice and specifically to prepare students for working on ⬇ **DW7.1A** and ⬆ **DW7.1B**, use the following Métro station names, which are the ones they will be using on the worksheets.

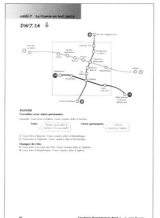 

Bibliothèque François Mitterand Bourse Châtelet
Étienne Marcel Galliéni Gare de l'Est
Gare de Lyon Les Halles Madeleine Opéra
Pont de Levallois Porte d'Orléans
Porte de Clignancourt Pyramides Quatre septembre
Réaumur Sébastopol République
Sentier Strasbourg St-Denis

Differentiation opportunities ↓ ↑

At this point ↓**DW7.1A** and ↑**DW7.1B** could be used. This shows sections of lines on the Paris Métro with the end stations marked. In a pair-work exercise, students ask each other how to get from one station to various others.

- ↓**DW7.1A** involves only *C'est la direction . . .*
- ↑**DW7.1B** involves *Prenez la ligne X, direction . . . Changez . . .* and students are then encouraged to set each other some more questions.

Tip ↑

pour + infinitive = in order to
Pour aller à . . .? How do I get to . . .?

Point grammaire: Prepositions

To reinforce prepositions, they can be practised with double-sided, English–French flashcards and/or by means of simple illustrations on the wall, e.g. (picture of section of Paris Métro) *Bourse est **entre** Quatre Septembre et Sentier.*

Extra idea

The use of *Pour aller à . . .* will be already familiar. Practise with other contexts: *Pour envoyer un mél? Il faut connecter sur Internet; Pour réussir ses examens? Il faut travailler.* Some of these could be put on the wall as illustrations.

Students complete the sentences with prepositions chosen from the list:

1 Phileas Fogg va **de** Londres **à** Paris.
2 Il a passé **par** le Tunnel **sous** la Manche.
3 Il a pris le Métro **pour** aller **à** la Gare de l'Est.
4 Il a demandé des informations **sur** le Métro.
5 Il est parti **sans** ses bagages.

To practise the above point, you could invite students to test your local knowledge by asking the way to local shops/facilities etc., e.g.

Pour aller à Blockbuster Video, s'il vous plaît?

Unité 7 Page 64

Presentation ideas

Paris has six main rail stations.
Trains from the North, including the Channel ports (except Dieppe and Le Havre) arrive and depart from the Gare du Nord.

Trains to/from the east (Alsace) use the Gare de l'Est.
Trains to/from the south and south-east (Nice, Italy) use the Gare de Lyon.
Trains to/from south-west (Bordeaux, Toulouse, Spain) use the Gare d'Austerlitz.
Trains to/from Lower Normandy (including Le Havre) and Dieppe use the Gare Saint Lazare.
Trains to/from Brittany use the Gare Montparnasse.

CM35 shows the relative positions of these stations. Ask students to work out which station they would have to go to, e.g.

– Vous allez à Lille, dans le nord. – Il faut aller à la Gare du Nord.

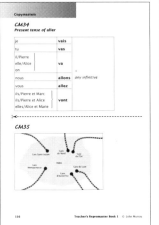
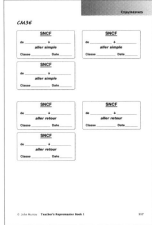

– Vous allez à Strasbourg. – Il faut aller à la Gare de l'Est.
   Teach or revise ticket types with the use of the 'tickets' on **CM36**. On these can be written (for example) *Paris – Strasbourg: 1ère classe* or *Lille – Paris: 2ème classe.* Give the vocabulary *un aller simple, un aller-retour, en première classe, en deuxième classe.* Smaller versions can be given to students to practise with, e.g. with six different cards, they shuffle them, place them face down, turn then over one at a time and order the ticket that turns up. Alternatively, in pair work, the cards are all placed face up. The 'passenger' states his/her requirements and the 'booking clerk' picks out the right ticket.
   Using **CM37**, teach/revise the station. Ask students where you need to go for specific things, e.g.

–Le train de Strasbourg part à quelle heure?
– Allez au bureau de renseignements.

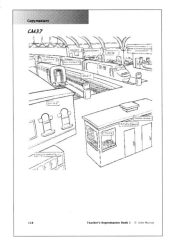

6
Solution
1

Départ		Arrivée		Type de train / Quai	Durée
PARIS EST	15:54	STRASBOURG	19h49	Train / 4	Exemple: CHOIX 1 (3h55m)
PARIS EST	16:48	STRASBOURG	20:59	Train / 3	CHOIX 2 (**4h11m**)
PARIS EST	17:45	STRASBOURG	**21:15**	TGV / 5 Réservation essentielle	CHOIX 3 (3h30m)
PARIS EST	18:47	STRASBOURG	22:55	Train / 4	CHOIX 4 (**4h08m**)
PARIS EST	**20:07** (25.07)	STRASBOURG	00.02 (26.07)	Train / 3	CHOIX 5 (3h55m)

2 Choix 3.

7 [CD 2 track 24]

Present briefly the sort of problems that could occur, e.g. *retard, restaurant fermé, détournement, incident technique.* These phrases could be written on the board and glossed, e.g. *retard: on n'arrive pas à l'heure.*

Transcript
1 Nous avons le plaisir d'informer nos passagers que la voiture restaurant va ouvrir dans deux minutes.
2 Ce train a environ 17 minutes de retard. Il arrivera à Strasbourg vers 21h35.
3 En raison d'un incident technique, il n'y aura pas de bar dans ce train.
4 Par suite d'un déraillement au niveau de Châlons, ce train sera détourné par Reims et Charleville. Par conséquent, il arrivera à Strasbourg avec une heure et demie de retard.

Solution
1 ☺; **2** ☹; **3** ☹; **4** ☹

8 [CD 2 track 25]

Students read a short text on Strasbourg and assign three of five titles that could be used for sections of the text.

Transcript
Venez à Strasbourg!
Strasbourg est la capitale de l'Alsace et de l'Europe. Ici vous allez trouver le nouveau siège du Parlement Européen. Venez visiter la belle cathédrale et les collections artistiques des musées de la ville. Vous aimez manger? Strasbourg est la capitale des gourmands: vins d'Alsace, chocolats et les célèbres gâteaux strasbourgeois. Les touristes viennent des quatre coins du monde pour trouver la vie de la ville la nuit – bars, discos, clubs – tout est là. Moi, je reviens ici chaque année. Venez découvrir Strasbourg!

Solution
Strasbourg culturel   Strasbourg gourmand
Strasbourg touristique

9
Solution
1 chocolats, gâteaux
2 vins d'Alsace
3 Parlement Européen
4 musées, cathédrale
5 aller dans un bar, une disco, un club

Point grammaire: *Venir*

The useful construction *venir* + infinitive, e.g. *Viens regarder! Venez voir!* is mentioned here. Explain to students that no 'and' appears in the French.

Differentiation opportunity ⬇

⬇**DW7.2** practises *venir* and *revenir* in the relatively familiar and accessible context of saying where you come from.

Solution
Activity 1
1 Exemple: Je viens de France.
2 Je viens de Maroc.
3 Je viens d'Irlande.
4 Je viens d'Allemagne.
5 Je viens de Québec.
6 Nous venons de Belgique.

Activity 2
1 Exemple: Il revient du Sénégal.
2 Elle revient de Viêtnam.
3 Ils reviennent de Thaïlande.
4 Il revient d'Angleterre.
5 Elle revient de Turquie.
6 Elles reviennent de Grèce.

Activity 3
1 Exemple: Je reviens du Sénégal.
2 Je reviens de Viêtnam.
3 Nous revenons de Thaïlande.
4 Je reviens d'Angleterre.
5 Je reviens de Turquie.
6 Nous revenons de Grèce.

Unité 7 Page 65

Presentation ideas

- Use **CM38** to teach/revise vocabulary relating to the car. This can be used for a memory test: give the students two minutes to commit the parts to memory and then test them. Alternatively, use a copy of **CM38** with the labels obscured, for a beat-the-clock attempt to put the labels in place.

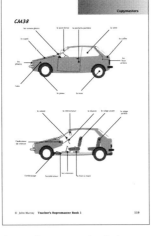

- Ask students to give a mime plus sound of the various parts of the car, while others guess what's being referred to. Alternatively, ask them to use the words in a way which shows what they mean, e.g. *KLAXON!!!*; (creaky voice) *capot*; (getting faster) *roue-roue-roue-roue*, etc.

N.B. *direction* has two meanings (direction/steering), as does *vitesse* (speed/gear).

10 [CD 2 track 26]

Students listen to the car-hire salesman explaining the virtues of the various cars to Phileas.

Transcript

Fogg: Qu'est-ce que vous pouvez m'offrir comme voitures à louer?
Agent: Eh bien, nous avons cette superbe Peugeot 406, avec freins assistés, direction assistée, boîte de vitesse automatique, vitres électriques . . .
Fogg: Oui, oui, mais quelle est la vitesse maximale?
Agent: 180 km/h . . . Mais vous savez . . . il y a des limites sur les routes françaises!
Fogg: Oui, oui. Et cette Opel Vectra. Vous la recommandez?
Agent: Mais bien sûr! Là vous avez une vitesse maximale de 185 km/h, avec direction assistée, freins assistés, CD . . .
Fogg: Et la Renault Mégane?
Agent: Une excellente voiture. Là encore, CD, direction assistée, freins assistés, vitesse maximale de 190 km/h.
Fogg: Et la Renault Clio?
Agent: Vous avez les freins assistés et les vitres électriques, mais pas la direction assistée. La vitesse maximale est de 175 km/h.
Fogg: Bon, je prends la Mégane.

Solutions
1

Marque et modèle	Freins assistés oui/non	Direction assistée oui/non	CD oui/non	Vitres electriques oui/non	Vitesse maximale
Exemple Peugeot 406	oui	oui	non	oui	180 km/h
Opel Vectra	oui	oui	oui	non	185 km/h
Renault Mégane	oui	oui	oui	non	190 km/h
Renault Clio	oui	non	non	oui	175 km/h

2 Le choix de Phileas: Peugeot 406. Raison: Vitesse maximale de 190 km/h, c'est la plus rapide.

Ça se dit comment? p.65 [CD 2 track 27]

Draw a parallel with English. 'g-' is hard before '-a', '-o' and '-u': garage, golf, gun. It is sometimes (but not always) soft before '-e' and '-i': gentle, gin. In French '*g-*' is always soft before '-*e*' and '-*i*'.

Transcript

- Mégane, garage
- rouge, engin
- nous mangeons, nous voyageons, une Peugeot
- Tu as garé la Mégane et la Peugeot rouge dans le garage? Génial!

11 [CD 2 track 28]

French road signs: speed limits.

1 Students work out which speed limit applies. *Une route à quatre voies* could be drawn on the board, so that students can see that it corresponds to a dual carriageway.

Solution
50 km/h – En ville
90 km/h – Autres routes
110 km/h – Route à quatre voies
130 km/h – Autoroutes

Transcript

Agent de police: Cette voiture est à vous, Monsieur?
Phileas: Non, c'est une voiture de location.
Agent de police: Vous avez vos papiers?
Phileas: Oui. Voilà.
Agent de police: Merci. Ah, vous êtes anglais! Vous avez votre passeport?
Phileas: Oui, je vous l'ai donné avec ces papiers.
Agent de police: Ah bon. M. Fogg, c'est ça?
Phileas: Oui, c'est ça.
Agent de police: Voilà vos papiers. Vous avez excédé la limite de vitesse, Monsieur. Sur les autoroutes, c'est 130 km/h. Vous avez fait du 150 km/h. C'est une contravention. Vous devez payer une amende de 45 euros. Immédiatement.
Phileas: Immédiatement?!
Agent de police: Oui. 45 euros, s'il vous plaît.
Phileas: Ah zut. Voilà. Je peux avoir mon passeport?
Agent de police: Je ne vous l'ai pas rendu?
Phileas: Non.
Agent de police: Voilà. Et bonne route, Monsieur!

Teacher's Guide 1 © John Murray

2 Phileas has broken the *autoroute* speed limit. He was doing 150 km/h.

12 📖✏️

Students choose the correct answer for the meaning of the sign. The wording involves various ways of expressing the fact that something is permitted or forbidden. If students need to remind themselves about how these verbs work, refer them back to Unit 2 page 18 and Unit 3 page 23.

Solution

1 b; **2** a; **3** a; **4** b; **5** a

13 📖✏️

Students note ways to express the fact that something is permitted or forbidden.

Vous devez	*Vous ne pouvez pas*
Il est obligatoire de	*Il vous est interdit de*
Vous êtes obligé de	*Il ne vous est pas permis de*
Il faut	*Vous n'avez pas le droit de*

Point grammaire: The pronoun *y*

Tells students what '*y*' represents and reminds them that pronouns normally go before the verb.

14 🎧✏️

Students insert *y* in the correct position.

Solution

1 Oui, il **y** va.
2 Oui, il **y** arrive demain.
3 Non, ils n'**y** vont pas.
4 Oui, j'**y** suis né(e)/Non, je n'**y** suis pas né(e).
5 Oui, on **y** est arrivé hier/Non, on n'**y** est pas arrivé hier.

Tip

Explains that all car makes and models are feminine.

Unité 7 Page 66

15 🎧✏️ [CD 2 track 29]

The pictures show various problems which might afflict a driver. These should be practised and learned. Miming with noises can be a motivating way of practising these things. Students guess what is being mimed.

Students listen to the cassette and correct the mechanic's errors on the form.

Transcript

Fogg: Allô . . . Garage Martin? . . . oui, oui, je suis en panne. Le problème? C'est les freins . . . ils ne marchent pas. Un accident? Non, mais je ne peux

pas continuer. La marque? C'est une Renault . . . et le modèle . . . une Mégane . . . une Mégane bleue. Où suis-je . . . ben . . . sur la nationale 83 entre Strasbourg et Sélestat. Ça s'écrit S-É-L-E-S-T-A-T . . . oui, c'est ça . . . C'est M. Fogg . . . non, non! F-O-G-G . . . Fogg . . . oui . . .

Solution

Nom du conducteur: M. Fogg.
Marque: Renault.
Modèle: Mégane.
Couleur: Bleu.
Situation: N83 entre Strasbourg et Sélestat.
Problème: Freins.

16 🔈

Open-ended speaking activity in which students practise a dialogue between a driver and a mechanic.

Extra idea

Use **CM39**, which shows the main motorway network of France linking main cities, to practise compass points and directions. You could add motorway numbers and then ask students, for example, *Je voyage en direction de l'ouest, et je vais arriver à Rennes dans une heure. Je suis sur quelle autoroute?*

17 📖✏️

This short exercise is informative and offers students the opportunity to recognise cognates and the fact that some words may give a hint to their meaning.

Solution

1 d; **2** c; **3** a; **4** b

Point grammaire: Agreement of past participles ↑

Agreement of preceding direct objects (but not indirect objects) when using the perfect tense. To explain this, remind students about adjective agreement after pronouns, e.g. *Les documentaires? Je les trouve **fascinants**.* This may make it easier for them to remember to 'agree' the past participle, especially if you link it to a few examples which include adjectives: *Je **les** ai trouvés **fascinants**.*

The final step is sentences without adjectives: *Les documentaires? Oui, je **les** ai vus.* You could use the card technique outlined above (page 66), with adjective/past participle endings on separate small cards so that they can be easily attached to their word.

18

Solutions

1 a Non, je ne l'ai pas **vue**.
  b Non, c'est Marc qui l'a **choisie**.
  c Oui, je les ai **vues**.

2 a Oui, il les a trouvés.
  b Non, il ne l'a pas faxée.
  c Oui, il les a reçus.

Tip

Non-agreeement of indirect object pronouns.

Differentiation opportunity

DW7.3A practises the use of direct or indirect object pronouns with single gap-fills.

Solution

1 l'
2 l'
3 les
4 vous
5 vous (**nous** also acceptable here)
6 vous (**nous** also acceptable here)

DW7.3B practises the use of direct or indirect object pronouns with gap-fills, some sentences requiring a pair of pronouns (see following Extra idea on pronoun order).

Solution

1 l'
2 l'
3 les
4 l'
5 me l'
6 nous l'ont **envoyé**.
7 nous les a pas **rendus**.

Extra ideas

- **EGW7 Activity 3** practises distinguishing between direct and indirect object pronouns. (See full notes on **EGW7** at the end of the unit.)
- None of the pronoun agreement tasks (on this page of Student's Book) include more than one pronoun, as the agreement point in itself is quite hard enough! However, if you have a very able group you may wish to explain to them the correct sequence of pronouns where there are two or more pronouns in a sentence. See notes below.

N.B. Pronouns before verbs is a useful tip for statements and questions (not imperatives).

Remind them that if the sentence is negative, all the pronouns and the verb stay **inside** *ne . . . pas*, e.g. *Vous avez laissé le triangle rouge dans le garage? Non, je ne l'y ai pas laissé. Le voici!*

Presentation idea

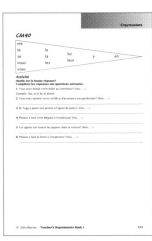

Make use of the traditional 'triangle' showing the order of pronouns on **CM40** (which also provides a separate exercise on this point). Photocopy the triangle onto cards and trim the cards to the shape of the triangle. Then cut the triangles into vertical strips (their columns). Distribute these strips randomly among the students, making sure that you are not left with any odd strips. Students attempt to reconstruct the triangles by exchanging information about cards and fitting them together.

They are not allowed to put them together until they have stated what they have got, e.g.

- *Moi j'ai **lui**, **leur**.*
- *Et moi, j'ai **y**. Ça va ensemble?*
- *Non. James, qu'est-ce que tu as?*
- *Moi, j'ai **le**, **la**, **les**.*
- *Regarde. Ça va avec **lui**, **leur**, etc.*

Once the triangle has been established, the rule may be explained.

Solution to task on CM40

1 Exemple: Oui, je le lui ai donné.
2 Non, je ne le leur ai pas montré.
3 Oui, il le lui a passé.
4 Oui, il l'y a louée.
5 Non, ils ne les y ont pas trouvés.
6 Oui, il la lui a faxée.

Unité 7 Page 67

19

Students examine two documents about Lyon and decide if the information is given in Document A, B or both.

Solution

1 Pommes lyonnaises: Document A.
2 Tramway: Document B.
3 Métro: les deux.
4 Shopping centre: Document A.
5 Car: les deux.
6 Pedestrian: Document B.
7 Cyclist: Document B.
8 Bus: Document B.

20 🎧✏️ [CD 2 track 30]

Before playing the tape for the first time, write the following words, scattered, on the board:

champs, (collines), (déserts), montagnes, ponts, routes, rues, villages, villes.

Call two (able) students to the front. As the tape plays, the two students listen for these words and try to be the first to rub off each word as it is heard (pause the tape as necessary).

Students listen to the cassette again and note the details. The terms VTT and VTC are explained.

Transcript
Agent: Vous voulez louer un VTC ou un VTT?
Fogg: Quelle est la différence?
Agent: Un VTC, c'est un vélo tous *chemins*. Donc, c'est pour les villes, les routes, les villages, quoi? Ça coûte 10€ les 24 heures. Pour une semaine, c'est 45€. Vous devez aussi payer une caution de 150€.
Fogg: Et le VTT?
Agent: Un VTT, c'est un vélo tout *terrain* . . . alors, c'est pour les champs, les collines, les montagnes, les terrains difficiles, vous comprenez? Alors, ça coûte 12€ les 24 heures, 55€ la semaine. Et vous payez une caution de 185€.
Fogg: Bon, je prends le VTC s'il vous plaît.

Solutions
1 **a** 10€; **b** 12€
2 **a** 45€; **b** 55€
3 **a** 150€; **b** 185€
4 Il choisit le VTC.

21 🗣️

Students work in pairs. One chooses the cost for a day and a week and decides on a deposit. The other asks the questions given and notes the answers. Students then change roles.

Differentiation opportunity ⬇️ ⬆️

This role-play can be extended into the context of holidays, hiring e.g. a canoe, skis or a sailboard.

⬇️ For less able students, this would probably need the support of given prices as well as the prompts.

⬆️ For more able students, a few pictures or a suitable brochure would give them some ideas as to what to hire, and they could be encouraged to look up others – they could include outrageous items such as a yacht or a helicopter, which would produce some useful practice of higher numbers.

22 📖🎧 [CD 2 track 31]

Despite Channel 4's efforts to bring it to the consciousness of the British public, not all students will realise the passion with which the Tour de France is followed in France. An outline is given here.

Transcript
En passant par la ville de Lyon, M. Fogg est entouré de cyclistes. Qu'est-ce qui se passe? Oui, c'est le Tour de France! Et on part vers Marseille!

Le Tour de France est l'événement sportif le plus populaire de France. La route du Tour change chaque année, mais il y a toujours des étapes qui passent par les montagnes. Le leader porte toujours un maillot jaune. Le coureur qui a le plus de points porte un maillot vert. Le 'roi des montagnes' (le leader dans cette étape) porte un maillot aux pois rouges, le leader dans la catégorie jeunes porte un maillot blanc.

Solution
1 le coureur qui a le plus de points
2 le leader dans la catégorie jeunes
3 'le roi des montagnes'
4 le leader

ICT activity
Learning objectives
• to reinforce the language of the 'Tour de France';
• to encourage students to take responsibility for a class project;
• to exploit the completed data for oral recap.

1 Teacher sets up a word-processed document with tables, the headings of which correspond to the categories of the race.
2 Each group of students is responsible for collecting the information on the leaders on a specified day and entering it into the document.
3 They could use a range of sources: Internet, teletext, TV or radio to access that information.
4 At the end of the race the document is printed out and exploited for language work, e.g. *Qui a porté le maillot jaune le plus souvent? . . .*

Unité 7 Page 68

23 📖🎧 [CD 2 track 32]

Students read the six facts about Marseilles and match a picture to each fact.

Transcript
Six faits sur Marseille
1 Marseille est le deuxième port français (Le Havre est le premier). D'énormes pétroliers arrivent ici.
2 Marseille est très bien connu pour le football. Son équipe s'appelle Olympique de Marseille.
3 Ici on fabrique des automobiles.
4 L'industrie chimique aussi est importante.
5 Marseille est célèbre pour son Musée de la mode.
6 Le sinistre Château d'If est situé sur une île dans le port de Marseille.

Solution
1 d; 2 b; 3 f; 4 e; 5 a; 6 c

24 🎧 [CD 2 track 33]

Phileas decides to take a flight from Marseilles to Toulouse. Students listen to the announcement that he hears.

Transcript

Speakerine: Nous avons le regret d'informer les passagers que le vol AF 679 dont le départ était prévu pour 16h45 a été retardé de 55 minutes en raison d'un incident technique.

Fogg: Zut! C'est mon vol à moi le AF 679. Encore un retard!

Solution

1	Numéro du vol	AF 679
2	Heure de départ	16h45
3	Problème	55 minutes de retard / incident technique

Point grammaire: Prepositions of time

The prepositions covered here are: *à, entre* and *dans*.

Extra idea

EGW7 Activities 1 and **2** practise time expressions and could be a lead-in to or reinforcement of the tasks on this page. (See full notes on **EGW7** at the end of the unit.)

25 🎧 [CD 2 track 34]

Students listen to these sentences and note the preposition that is used.

Transcript

1 Je compte arriver chez vous **entre** 13 et 14 heures.
2 Le vol AF 679 va partir **dans** 3 minutes.
3 Nous allons partir **dans** 10 minutes.
4 Nous allons arriver à Toulouse **entre** 10 heures et 10h10.
5 Le vol Air France va attérir **à** 17h16.

26 👁✏

Students complete gapped sentences with an appropriate preposition.

Solution

1 à; 2 dans; 3 entre; 4 dans

Extra idea

Use an OHT of a digital clock to practise 24-hour times: a simple two-box grid overlaid with various combinations of numbers (**CM74**). Practise converting 'o'clock' p.m. times to 24-hour p.m. times and vice versa by showing an analogue (dial) clock face and asking students to give the p.m. time, e.g. *Neuf heures* (*Vingt et une heures*). Then ask students to convert a digital time from an OHT to analogue time on a clock face, e.g. *23 heures* (*11 heures*).

Differentiation opportunities ⬇ ⬆

CM41 shows a departures screen in Marseilles airport, providing an opportunity for practice of 24-hour times and other expressions of time.

⬇ Make statements such as *Je pars à 13h* and ask *Je vais où?* Then move on to giving the students sentence starters, e.g. *Le vol pour Paris part à . . .*, which they have to complete by giving you the time.

⬆ More able students could add phrases such as *il y a un retard de . . . On part à l'heure.*

Unité 7 Page 69 [CD 2 track 35]

The cartoon shows Phileas in a queue at the baggage check-in. The family and the officials argue over which bag is whose. The dialogue shows the use of disjunctive (strong) pronouns after *c'est* and after prepositions.

Transcript

Mère: C'est à toi, Viviane, cette valise?
Petite fille: Non, c'est à moi ! Donne-la-moi, Viviane!
Check-in girl: Ce sont à vous, Messieurs-dames, tous ces bagages?
Père: Oui, tout ça est à nous.
Check-in girl: C'est qui, Mademoiselle Hugo?
Les deux filles: C'est moi.
Fogg: S'il vous plaît, Messieurs-dames, . . .

Point grammaire: Strong pronouns

Suggest that a number of things have happened, both good and bad. Students claim responsibility or blame others. It may work more effectively if you limit the number of pronouns to start with to *moi/toi/lui/elle*.

– *Quelqu'un a gagné 150 000 euros. C'est qui?*
– *Moi!*
– *Quelqu'un a cassé une fenêtre. Qui a fait ça?*
– (pointing) *Lui!*

Suggested events:

Quelqu'un a: eu 20 sur 20
lavé ma voiture
rangé la salle de classe
apparu à la télé
enregistré un disque
obtenu l'autographe de sa star préférée
volé £10 000
dépassé la limite de vitesse
endommagé la voiture de son père
perdu ses devoirs
insulté un agent de police

27 📖✏️

Students answer the question with the translation of the pronoun indicated.

Solution

1 moi; **2** lui; **3** nous; **4** toi; **5** elles; **6** eux

Tip

The use of strong pronouns after *à* in the possessive sense can be practised in the classroom with personal possessions gathered from students and then redistributed:

– *Ce sac est à toi, Melanie? – Oui, il est à moi/Non, il n'est pas à moi.*
– *Voilà Roger. Cette trousse est à Roger? – Oui, elle est à lui,* etc.

28 📖✏️

Students substitute a strong pronoun for the noun(s) in bold.

Solution

1 elle; **2** eux; **3** elles; **4** nous; ⬆**5** lui; ⬆**6** à eux, à nous

Unité 7 Page 70 [CD 2 track 36]

29 📖🎧

Toulouse is a dynamic and growing city, not only as the hub of the south-west region so popular with visitors, but also as a modern industrial centre – it is the headquarters of France's space research. It is also fast becoming a city of intellectuals, with more students than any other university town in France. This short text mentions four major industries. Students assign the pictures to the appropriate industry.

Transcript

Toulouse: ville d'aujourd'hui, ville de demain.
Ses Industries: l'informatique, le spatial, la pharmaceutique, la biotechnologie.

Toulouse est la ville de demain. Les voyages à Mars vous intéressent? La médecine est pour vous une passion? Vous aimez travailler avec les ordinateurs? Alors, venez travailler à Toulouse.

Solution

1 le spatial
2 le pharmaceutique
3 la biotechnologie
4 l'informatique
5 le pharmaceutique
6 le spatial
7 la biotechnologie
8 l' informatique

Differentiation opportunity ⬆

Students could write their own short leaflet on local industries or agriculture, using the questions of the text as a framework: *X vous intéresse(nt)? X est pour vous une passion? Vous aimez travailler avec X?*

⬆ More able students could perhaps include constructions of the type: *C'est une industrie qui . . .* and *X est plus important/moins important que . . .*

30 🎧 [CD 2 track 37]

Phileas goes to the *gare routière* to catch a coach. Students listen to find out why he cannot do so. The aim of the text is to ensure that students understand the word *grève* (a definition and a reason are given).

Point out that *car* is a *faux ami*. Practise with three cards showing *une voiture, un bus* and *un car*. See how fast students can respond to a flashed card.

Transcript

Agent: Oui, Monsieur?
Fogg: Bonjour, Madame. Je voudrais prendre un car pour Rennes, s'il vous plaît.
Agent: Pour Rennes? Vous voulez voyager aujourd'hui, Monsieur?
Fogg: Oui.
Agent: Désolée, Monsieur, mais ce n'est pas possible. Tous les chauffeurs de car sont en grève.
Fogg: En grève?
Agent: Eh . . . oui. Ils ne travaillent pas depuis le vingt juin. Ils protestent contre leurs conditions de travail. Mais si vous voulez voyager la semaine prochaine . . .?
Fogg: Impossible, Madame, impossible.

Solution

b les chauffeurs ne travaillent pas (une grève)

31 🎧 [CD 2 track 38]

Phileas decides to hitch-hike to Rennes. The aim of this text is to illustrate that a southern French accent is different from the standard.

Students should listen for the rolled R's and the pronunciation of final mute 'e's. Nasal vowels may present a problem. This is typified in the phrase *le vin blanc*, pronounced as *le veng blung*.

Students note details of the driver and journey.

Transcript

Fogg: Oh, c'est pas facile, faire de l'auto-stop. Une heure, et je suis toujours là. Ah, voilà un camion qui s'arrête!

Camionneur: Où tu vas, mon ami?

Fogg: À Rennes. Vous allez à Rennes, Monsieur?

Camionneur: Non, je vais à Roscoff. Mais je vais passer par Rennes. T'as de la chance, hein. Allez, monte!

Fogg: Merci bien. C'est très gentil.

Camionneur: Il n'y a pas de quoi. Mais c'est assez loin, Rennes, hein. 400 kilomètres, quoi.

Fogg: Oui, je le sais. Mais il n'y pas de cars, aujourd'hui. Les chauffeurs sont en grève.

Camionneur: En grève, hein? Eux, ils sont en grève, mais moi je travaille.

Fogg: Alors, vous allez à Roscoff en Bretagne. Vous êtes Breton?

Camionneur: Non, je suis Toulousain. J'ai toujours habité à Toulouse. Mais tu n'es pas français, hein?

Fogg: Non je suis anglais.

Camionneur: Ah, les Anglais! Moi, je parle français. L'anglais, je comprends pas. Ni les Anglais, hein? Ils aiment la bière chaude . . . moi j'aime le vin . . . le vin blanc . . . Mais je n'en bois pas quand je suis au volant, bien sûr!

Solution

1 Destination du camionneur: **Roscoff**.
2 Distance de Rennes: **400 km**.
3 Origine du camionneur: **Toulouse**.
4 Langue parlée par le camionneur: **français**.

Tip

Remind students that not everybody in France has the same accent. In Burgundy, for example, people roll their R's more, e.g. *une bouteille de bièRRRe*; and in the south people pronounce all the syllables of a word, e.g. *un-e bou-teill-e de bièr-e*.

Unité 7 Page 71

32 📖✏ [CD 2 track 39]

This short text gives a brief outline of Brittany. While agriculture and fishing remain an important part of the region's economy, the telecommunications industry has become very important, with its centre at Lannion in Finistère. Tourism is of course also of major importance. Brittany is second only to the Var as a holiday destination for the French. The Breton language is mentioned – it may be worth drawing the parallel with Welsh.

Transcript

La Bretagne
Situation: à l'extrême ouest de la France.
Capitale régionale: Rennes.
Villes principales: Brest, Lorient, Saint-Brieuc, Morlaix.
Industries: automobiles, électronique, agriculture, pêche, tourisme (2e zone de France).
Gastronomie régionale: crêpes, galettes, fruits de mer, gâteaux, cidre.
Langues: français, breton (à l'ouest).

Students complete sentences to give a summary of the information on the region, practising the use of *y*.

Solution

1 La plus grande ville de Bretagne est Rennes.
2 On y fabrique des automobiles et des produits électroniques.
3 En été, il y a beaucoup de touristes.
4 On y mange des crêpes, des galettes et des fruits de mer.
5 On y boit du cidre.
6 On y parle français et breton.

ICT activity

Learning objectives

• to use search strategies for an effective search on the Internet;
• to understand details from Internet sources using context and other clues;
• to present that information in a different format, using graphics and, if possible, sound.

1 The teacher identifies with the students the names of some of the most popular tourist regions in France.
2 The students are given the following headings on a word-processed document:

   Les villes; La géographie; La culture; Sports et loisirs; Commerce et industrie.

3 They then use the Internet to research information about their chosen region, cutting and pasting appropriate text and downloading appropriate graphics.
4 Students might be encouraged to e-mail their chosen region for information.
5 Students then present this information to the rest of the class.
⬆6 Higher attainers could be asked to use their presentation as a prompt and be asked to include a specified number of more complex constructions.
⬇7 Lower attainers could script their presentation more closely and use this as an opportunity to draft and redraft on the word-processor.

33 (headphones/pencil) [CD 2 track 40]

Students listen to a radio interview in which Phileas talks about the good and bad points of his tour. Expressions of opinion are revisited.

Transcript

Alain Chasseur: Bonjour. Ici Alain Chasseur au micro de Radio Corsaire. Aujourd'hui, notre invité spécial dans le studio est M. Phileas Fogg, le célèbre voyageur anglais. M. Fogg, vous allez retourner en Angleterre aujourd'hui. Quelles ont été vos impressions de la France?

Phileas: Tout d'abord je dois vous remercier de votre superbe hospitalité. Les Français ont été très accueillants envers moi, oui, très très hospitaliers. En général, j'ai trouvé que les transports publics sont excellents. Les trains sont, en général, très rapides. Sur les routes, j'ai trouvé que les policiers sont très stricts en ce qui concerne les limites de vitesse . . . c'est pas bon, ça, hein? Et, en plus, je suis tombé en panne et j'ai trouvé que les réparations étaient très chères . . . très, très chères. Ça, je n'ai pas aimé! À Toulouse aussi j'ai eu un problème . . . une grève de chauffeurs de car . . . ça, j'ai trouvé vraiment embêtant.

Alain: Et maintenant vous retournez en Grande-Bretagne et à son climat terrible . . . pluies, brouillard . . . tout ça.

Phileas: Oui, c'est vrai. Je trouve que le climat de la France est préférable, surtout dans le sud . . . oui, là, vous avez un climat superbe. En fin de compte, cette tournée a été très réussie.

Solution

Bons points	Mauvais points
1 hospitalité superbe	1 policiers stricts
2 trains rapides	2 réparations chères
3 climat superbe	3 grève des chauffeurs

Tip ⬆

The tip picks up on the inverted question form in the text to remind students of this usage.

34 (book/pencil)

The final stages of Phileas's journey are given in jumbled order, and students rewrite them in the correct order to summarise his return to London.

Solution

5, 1, 4, 3, 2

Unité 7 Pages 72–73

Checkpoints

Test

The **Test** checks students' skills in the grammatical goals of the unit:

* using prepositions: *de, à, en, entre, dans* in expressions of time
* using the verb *venir* and others like it
* using the pronoun *y*
* using the perfect tense with pronouns
* using strong pronouns *moi, toi*, etc.

Solution

1 a Si vous **venez** à Strasbourg, vous allez pouvoir visiter la cathédrale. [1]
  b Beaucoup de touristes **viennent** à Toulouse chaque année. [1]
  c Cette brochure **contient** des informations intéressantes. [1]
  d J'adore cette ville! J'**y reviens** le plus souvent possible. [1]
  e Les petites villes bretonnes **deviennent** très populaires. [1]
2 b, d, a, c [4]
3 a Oui, je **les ai envoyés**. [2]
  b Oui je **les ai recommandés**. [2]
  c Oui, **je l'ai achetée**. [2]
  d Oui, **je les ai achetés**. [2]
4 a Qui a fait ça? – **Moi!** [1]
  b Tu vois? Ce cadeau est pour **toi**. [1]
  c Tu es sorti avec tes copains? – Non, je ne suis pas sorti avec **eux**. [1]
  d Tu connais Rachel? Je vais au cinéma avec **elle**. [1]
  e J'aime bien Alain. Je sors avec **lui** demain. [1]
5 a Le voyage dure **de** 13h **à** 15h50. [2]
  b **À** 17h, on prend le train pour Paris. [1]
  c L'Office de Tourisme est ouvert **entre** 9h et 16h. [1]
  d Il est 12h. On va arriver à 12h30, donc **dans** une demi-heure. [1]
⬆6 a – Oui, j'**y** habite. [1]
  b – On **y** arrive dans 10 minutes. [1]
  c – Non, nous n'**y** allons pas cette année-ci. [1]
  Total [30]

Quiz

The **Quiz** checks students' knowledge acquired in the unit, about:

* the Channel Tunnel, Eurostar and Le Shuttle
* travelling by French train and Métro
* car hire and driving on French roads
* the *Tour de France*
* regions of France

Solution

1 1994 [1]
2 Le Shuttle [1]
3 la Gare du Nord [1]
4 un ticket [1]
5 une station de Métro où on change de ligne [2]
6 Alsace [1]
7 On peut (y) louer une voiture. [2]
8 Any two of: lignes de métro; lignes de tramway; zones piétonnières; réseau de bus; système de contrôle de voitures; réseau de pistes cyclables [2]
9 le leader [1]
10 dans le sud [1]
11 Olympique de Marseille (OM) [1]
12 On ne travaille pas [2]
13 Rennes [1]
14 Any three of the following: automobile, électronique, agriculture, tourisme, pêche [3]

Total [20]

Projets

A Give weaker students a sheet with the list of headings, as in the profile of Brittany on page 71, so that they simply have to complete it by adding relevant information, rather than feeling that they have to start from scratch or do lots of writing before they even start.

B Students write a short text based on the Strasbourg text and using some phrases involving *venir*.

⬆ Some categories could be given, e.g *aspects culturels, aspects gourmands, aspects touristiques* and students could be encouraged to think what might go into these categories.

⬇ Suggestions could be given to guide weaker students. *Aspects culturels: musées, galeries, salles de concert; Aspects gourmands: restaurants, cafés, cuisine régionale; Aspects touristiques; magasins, discos, bars, clubs.*

Students could choose some elements from these to produce sentences such as: *Venez manger dans nos restaurants superbes. Venez danser dans nos clubs exotiques.*

C ⬆ More able students could write longer dialogues but perhaps fewer, ⬇ less able simply do fewer.

EGW7 *teaching notes*

Sheet **EGW7** provides extra grammar/homework on the core points of the unit.

Activity 1

This practises time expressions.

Solution

Exemple: Phileas Fogg est parti **à** 7 heures du matin.
1 Il va arriver à Strasbourg **dans** moins de quatre heures.
2 Il va prendre un avion **dans** une demi-heure.
3 Cet avion va arriver à Toulouse **entre** 10 heures et 10 heures et demie.
4 Phileas espère rentrer chez lui **en** moins de huit jours.

Activity 2

This practises time expressions again, but alongside practice of *aller* + infinitive.

Solution

Exemple: Non, il va partir demain.
1 Non, elle va prendre le train pour Lille cet après-midi.
2 Non, je vais réserver une chambre ce matin.
3 Non, ils vont acheter les billets demain.
4 Non, je vais téléphoner au restaurant dans deux minutes.

Activity 3 ⬆

This practises distinction between direct and indirect object pronouns (third person only). The last question requires preceding direct object agreement.

Solution

1 Exemple: Oui, je les connais.
2 Oui, je leur parle de temps en temps.
3 Non, je ne leur ai pas parlé hier.
4 Oui, je lui ai téléphoné hier.
5 Non, je ne l'ai pas vu hier.
6 Oui, je les ai vus hier.

unité 8
Échange scolaire

•Contexts
- French school exchanges
- education in France
- weather forecasts
- planning days out
- alcohol
- dealing with ailments in France
- planning parties

Grammar
- using possessive pronouns to say 'mine' 'his', etc.
- using the pronoun *lequel*
- using the future tense of irregular verbs
- using the pronoun *en*
- using verbs followed by *à* or *de*
- using the relative pronoun *dont*

Pronunciation
- 'qu-'
- '-eu', '-oeu-'

Revision in this unit includes:
- using comparatives
- using the perfect tense
- agreement of adjectives
- the pronoun *lequel*

This unit is set within the context of French exchange between a (fictional) school in Belfast and a (fictional) *collège* in Saint-Malo.

Unité 8 Pages 74–75 [CD 2 track 41]

These two pages explain the nature of a school exchange and covers the choosing of a pen-friend. Personal interests are revisited and house and home are covered.

Presentation/differentiation opportunity ⬆

Before they listen to the tape, ensure that students have understood the *fiche*. Ask less able students to complete a few short sentences, giving them the starters below.

John habite . . .
Il a . . .
Son père est . . . et sa mère est . . .
Il a une . . .qui s'appelle Sophie.
Il aime . . .
Il n'aime pas . . .
Il ne mange pas de . . .
Il a une allergie, c'est . . .

⬆ More able students could be asked to write a brief paragraph about John, and prompted to write in the third person by being given just the first couple of starters.

Transcript

Voici John qui veut faire un échange scolaire avec un élève du Collège Jacques Cartier à Saint-Malo. Mais qu'est-ce qu'un échange scolaire? John nous l'explique.

Qu'est-ce qu'un échange scolaire? C'est simple. Vous passez quelques jours chez un jeune Français ou une jeune Française, et, en retour, votre correspondant(e) passe du temps chez vous. Quand vous êtes en France, vous avez la possibilité de visiter une école, de faire des excursions et de parler français! D'abord, il faut compléter une fiche avec vos détails. Voici la fiche que j'ai complétée.

 [CD 2 track 42]

Students now listen to a *correspondance sonore* in which three French students talk about themselves.

1 They note the answers to the questions on the three students. In Question 2 they then predict which *correspondant* John will choose, and justify their choice.

Transcript

Joël: Salut. Je m'appelle Joël Monnet et j'ai quinze ans. J'habite à Saint-Malo, et je suis en 3e au Collège Jacques Cartier . . . euh . . . mon père est professeur de maths et ma mère est secrétaire. Nous habitons dans un appartement au centre de Saint-Malo. C'est un tout petit appartement avec deux chambres. Je n'ai pas de frères . . . ni de sœurs . . . Ben . . . J'aime le football . . . oui, je me passionne pour le football, surtout pour l'Olympique de Marseille. Je ne parle pas très bien l'anglais . . . mais je suis fort en maths. Bon . . . voilà.

Simon: Bonjour. Je m'appelle Simon Letimônier et j'ai quinze ans. J'habite à Paramé . . . c'est un quartier de Saint-Malo. J'aime bien le sport, mais je suis handicapé . . . je suis dans un fauteuil roulant . . . je fais du basket, et j'aime la natation. J'adore regarder le football à la télé . . . J'aime bien Manchester United et Chelsea . . . Je suis passionné de musique . . . je joue de la guitare électrique . . . j'aime bien le rock. J'aime aussi les jeux vidéo. Je suis assez fort en anglais.

Arnaud: Salut. Je m'appelle Arnaud Conan. J'ai quinze ans. J'habite dans un petit village près de Dinan, mais je vais au Collège Jacques Cartier. Je voudrais bien correspondre avec quelqu'un qui a les mêmes intérêts que moi . . . c'est-à-dire, la musique classique et le jazz. Je joue du saxophone et je fais partie d'un trio de jazz. Je ne suis pas sportif . . . je déteste les sports!

Solutions

1

		Joël	Simon	Arnaud
a	Quel âge a-t-il?	15	15	15
b	Son père/ mère sont . . .?	prof/ secrétaire		
c	Il habite où?	St-Malo	St-Malo	près de Dinan
d	Ses hobbys	football	basket, natation, regarde le football (Man.U et Chelsea). rock, joue de la guitare électrique, jeux vidéo	la musique classique et le jazz, joue du saxophone
e	Autres détails	pas fort en anglais, fort en maths	handicapé, en fauteuil roulant, assez fort en anglais	pas sportif

2 John chooses Simon. Reasons: both fans of Manchester United, both like rock music, and John lives in a bungalow, so OK for wheelchair.

Extra idea

CM42 could be used either for students to fill in their own details or, more interestingly, to make up a character and ascribe interests, etc. to that character. The completed sheets could be collected up and redistributed. Students could then decide, either by reading or by discussion, who would made make the best partners for an exchange. This activity could be a preliminary to task 2.

Students present or record a brief presentation about themselves. Alternatively, they could use one of the characters made up using **CM42**.

If one half of the class were to record these *correspondances sonores*, the other half could use the other completed **CM42** to try find appropriate partners. This then becomes a Reading/Listening exercise.

 [CD 2 track 43]

Before attempting this exercise, students need to be sure of vocabulary relating to the house.

Presentáion idea

CM43 shows a typical French house. The expressions *en haut, en bas, au premier étage, dans*

la cave could be revised. Use **CM43** as an OHT and a small OHT of the figure of a burglar (*Christophe le Cambrioleur*) also provided on **CM43**. Place the burglar in the various rooms and ask the students to tell you what the burglar took from the room. Students could then tell you to which room he went next and what he stole there. This gives opportunities to use: *Christophe le cambrioleur est entré dans . . . Il est sorti de . . . Il est monté . . . Il est descendu . . . puis . . . ensuite . . . après cela . . . Il a pris . . . Il a volé . . . Il a mis X dans son sac . . .,* etc. The burglar could of course be female (*Christine la cambrioleuse*). If students were to write a version of this lady's activities, this would give an opportunity to practise agreements in the perfect tense. If the two burglars operate together, plural verbs and agreements can be practised either orally or in writing.

N.B. This also introduces some adverbs of time, useful in a narrative context – this is followed up later in the unit, on page 80.

Transcript

Simon: Alors . . . comme tu vois, nous habitons dans un bungalow . . . ça ressemble un petit peu au tien. Alors, là, à gauche, c'est la cuisine . . . et voilà papa qui prépare le déjeuner . . . Salut papa, voici John . . .

M. Timônier: Bonjour. Bonjour John, je suis à toi dans deux minutes.

Simon: Bon . . . on continue . . . en face de la cuisine, c'est la salle à manger. Voici ma chambre juste à côté, et puis c'est la tienne. En face, c'est la chambre de mes parents et à côté c'est la salle de bains. Tu peux prendre une douche si tu veux . . . et tout au bout du couloir, il y a le WC . . . ce qui conclut la visite du château Letimônier. Nous espérons que cette visite vous a plu.

Solution

X = la salle à manger, Y = la chambre de Simon, Z = le WC.

 [CD 2 track 44]

Revise the contents of a teenager's bedroom: *chaîne stéréo, ordinateur, CDs, radio-réveil, livres, posters, bibelots* (ornaments), *fleurs*, etc.; plus the furniture *lit, lits superposés* (bunk beds), *table, chaise, fauteuil, armoire, commode*, etc. Students could work in pairs. One describes his/her room. The other then has to say that *Chris le cambrioleur/Christine la cambrioleuse* (see **CM43**) has stolen as many things as he/she can remember. Put a time limit on the exercise, e.g. 15 seconds.

Differentiation opportunity ⬇

Students listen to the cassette and list differences between the bedrooms of John and Simon.

CM44, which shows the two bedrooms referred to in this exercise, can be used as a visual prompt, which would also help weaker students to achieve the main objective of the exercise, which is to work out from the recording which room is whose. Leave it on display while they listen, so that they know which contrasts to listen for. (On **CM44**, the upper one is John's.)

Transcript

John: J'aime bien ta chambre . . . elle est grande . . . beaucoup plus grande que la mienne, qui est assez petite . . .

Simon: Oui, c'est pas mal comme chambre quoi?

John: En plus, la mienne est carrée . . . la tienne est rectangulaire.

Simon: Oui, il me faut de la place pour mon fauteuil roulant.

John: Et là, tu as un grand lit . . . moi, j'ai des lits superposés . . . Hé, j'aime bien tes posters . . . tu aimes les guitaristes, hein? Hendrix, Clapton . . . surtout les vieux, quoi? . . . moi, j'ai plutôt des posters de footballeurs . . . et voilà ta guitare électrique . . . je peux essayer? . . . moi, la mienne, c'est une guitare acoustique . . .

Solution

chambre de John	chambre du corres
assez petite	grande
carrée	rectangulaire
lits superposés	grand lit
posters de footballeurs	posters de guitaristes
guitare acoustique	guitare électrique

Point grammaire: Possessive pronouns

For many students an ability to use *à moi,* etc. would be adequate, and possessive pronouns could be treated as 'receptive' grammar. However, for groups where it is appropriate, the following ideas may help with explaining the tricky point that in possessive pronouns both number and gender must match the noun, not the owner.

Presentation ideas

- Mix a number of your own desk items with those of a student and then pick one out a time: *C'est à moi. C'est le mien. C'est à moi. C'est la mienne.*

Emphasise **moi** and **mien/mienne**, so that students associate the initial sound.

- If you don't want to use classroom vocabulary, share out cards showing objects: *téléphone mobile/portable, radio, disque, journal, casquette,* etc.
- Then identify the student's objects: *C'est à toi. C'est le tien/la tienne.* Emphasise the similarity of *toi* and *tien/tienne.*
- Move on to alternatives. *C'est à moi ou à toi? C'est le mien ou le tien? C'est la mienne ou la tienne?* Get the student to say *C'est le mien/la mienne.*
- Put the objects into two heaps. Point out that one heap is masculine – *le stylo, le papier, le crayon,* etc. and the other is feminine – *la – la règle, la montre,* etc. – Then hold them up alternately: *Le mien. La mienne. Le tien. La tienne.*
- Formalise the singular on the board (as in the left hand column in the Student's Book)
- Move on to plurals and demonstrate as above. *Les miens. Les tiens. Les miennes. Les tiennes.* Formalise on the board as in the right-hand column of the Student's Book.

Information about *le sien/la sienne* for the majority of students is not given except in the grammar reference section, because of the double complexity of the sex of the owner and the grammatical gender of the objects. The most able students may, of course, be able to cope with the mind-numbing complexity of this part of the system!

Differentiation opportunity ⬇ ⬆

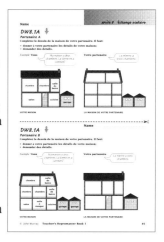

- ◼ ⬇**DW8.1A** is an information gap activity in which students find out from each other information about each others' houses – the model guides them into using first and second person possessive pronouns.
- ◼ ⬆In **DW8.1B** students again compare houses but here they use first and third person possessive pronouns in a passage written in response to a text.

A recognition exercise, in which students link the sentences which go together. Only the first person singular is covered.

Solution

1 d; **2** g; **3** a; **4** b; **5** e

6

Students complete the gapped words with the correct form of *le mien*.

Solution

1 Est-ce que tu as ta clé? J'ai oublié **la mienne**.
2 Où sont tes crayons de couleur? Je ne trouve pas **les miens**.
3 Ta mère est cool! **La mienne** n'aime pas la musique rock.
4 Si tu ne trouves pas tes lunettes de soleil, tu peux emprunter **les miennes**.

Extra idea

Students could describe houses, parents, brothers, sisters, cars, boyfriends, etc. Their partner makes a comparison, e.g.

A: *Mon frère est petit.* **B:** *Le mien est plus grand/petit que le tien.*

Unité 8 Pages 76–77

Presentation/revision ideas

These two pages cover school premises, school subjects and teachers.

- Revise the names of school subjects using symbols, or text books from other subjects. Ask students to complete sentences such as *Mr Smith est professeur de . . .? Mme Hartley-Chivers est professeur de . . .?*
- Move on to classification. *Quelles sont les sciences qu'on enseigne ici? Quelles langues est-ce qu'on peut apprendre ici?*

7

Students classify subjects into the categories on the web page.

Solution

1 Français = Langues; Biologie = Sciences; Travaux manuels = Technologie; Traitement de texte = Informatique; Histoire du jazz = Musique.
2 La Révolution française = Histoire; Théorie des harmonies = Musique; Les forces et les pressions = Sciences; Courrier électronique = Informatique.

8  [CD 2 track 45]

Since students will have an expert knowledge of their own school/college, they could put this to use. Briefly revise *au premier étage, au deuxième étage, à gauche* and *à droite*. Ask students to describe a particular block in the school. They each give you a sentence while you try to draw a plan of each floor on the board. If they make mistakes and you draw these into the plan, other students are sure to want to correct both you and the other student!

Students could copy the two diagrams on page 76, listen to the cassette and fill in the details on the plan according to what they hear.

Transcript

Simon: OK . . . on va faire un petit tour du Collège . . . à gauche . . . tu vois ce bloc-là . . . alors c'est là qu'on fait des cours de langues. Au rez-de-chaussée, il y a des salles de classes où on fait espagnol . . . le bureau du Directeur est aussi situé au rez-de-chaussée . . . puis au premier étage on fait anglais, il y a quatre salles de classe là-haut . . . et puis, finalement au deuxième étage . . . ça, c'est pour les classes de français. Bon, à droite on a le bloc de sciences et de technologie . . . en bas, on fait technologie . . . travaux manuels, informatique, tout ça . . . puis au premier étage, on a sciences naturelles . . . euh . . . chimie et biologie . . . et au deuxième étage, on fait physique . . . électricité, pressions . . . tout ça . . .

Solution

Français		Physique	
Anglais		Chimie	Biologie
Espagnol	Directeur	Technologie	

Point grammaire: *Auquel*

The relative pronoun *auquel* is likely to be a receptive point only for many students. Task 11 which follows is recognition only, and even task 12 is very formulaic. If you feel your group can get their teeth into this point, however, you may find the following ideas useful.

Presentation ideas

Following on from the previous exercises, say to students: *Donnez-moi le numéro d'une salle de classe où on fait français.* After a couple of examples like this, change to *Donnez-moi le numéro d'une salle de classe* **dans laquelle** *on fait technologie.* After a few examples, write on the board:

La salle dans laquelle on fait chimie avec M. (X) = ?
Le bureau dans lequel Mme (Y) travaille = ?

Students copy the question and give the answers. Having checked these, point out the link between *le bureau* and *dans lequel, la salle* and *dans laquelle.* Ask what would follow *le laboratoire* and *la section.* Then go on to the explanation given in the Student's Book. This also contains an explanation of the plural forms.

9

Students link matching halves of sentences containing *lequel* and its variants.

Solution

1 b; **2** a; **3** d; **4** c

10

Students give a guided tour of the school. Photos taken from the school prospectus could be photocopied or scanned and then enlarged. These could then be used for an oral presentation, and afterwards labelled appropriately for a wall display: *Voici la grande salle dans laquelle nous faisons des représentations théâtrales.*

For those with more ambitious ideas of a presentation, students could tour the school with a video camera and make a comment in each room visited.

11  [CD 2 track 46]

Students listen to extracts from lessons. Before they listen, ask them to look at the timetable which will remind them of subject names. Question 1 asks them simply to identify the subjects being taught in the three class extracts; using this information and the timetable they can work out which day it must be.

Transcript

A: Au Royaume-Uni on ne dit pas toujours *Good morning.* On dit souvent *Morning* ou même *Hello* ou *Hi. Good morning, good afternoon* et *good evening* sont des expressions plutôt formelles.
B: Bon, vous allumez l'ordinateur. Vous mettez la disquette dans le lecteur A. Vous cliquez sur l'icône Diskette A et vous double-cliquez sur le fichier que vous voulez ouvrir. . . .
C: Quelle est la différence entre un reptile et un amphibie? Alors, les amphibies peuvent respirer dans l'air et dans l'eau. Donc un crocodile est un reptile et non pas un amphibie, vous comprenez ...?

Extra idea

Ask students to listen again and pick out the vocabulary that gives the clue to the identity of the subject.

Solution

1 anglais, informatique, biologie
2 mardi

12 ⊕

Using the table given in the Student's Book, students express their opinion on a variety of school subjects, giving justification for their opinions. This enables them to use *parce que* and expressions such as *je pense que, je trouve que.*

13 🎧✏️ [CD 2 track 47]

In this exercise, students listen to French students giving their opinions of their teachers. They say why they do or do not like them and explain why.

Presentation idea

Write a number of adjectives on the board, some positive, some negative, between two columns, one marked + and the other −. Students come to the board, circle the adjective and indicate with an arrow into which column it should be placed. Suggested adjectives: *intéressant, enthousiaste, barbant, ennuyeux, strict, dur, énergique,*

passionnant, juste, lent, bête. This will prepare students for the listening, in which the teachers' qualities are sometimes given before the statement as to whether they are liked or disliked.

Transcript

A: Tu sais, les profs ici . . . ben . . . ils sont vraiment mixtes . . . par exemple, tu as Mlle Trélente . . . alors, moi, je ne l'aime pas du tout . . . elle est vraiment barbante, mais barbante . . . c'est la classe dans laquelle je m'endors . . . moi, je trouve qu'elle est bête.
B: Oui, je suis d'accord . . . mais si on prend, par exemple, M. Duroc, notre prof de maths . . . lui, il est vachement bon. Il est toujours intéressant et très enthousiaste . . . il adore les maths . . . et en classe il est toujours très juste . . . il faut travailler avec lui . . . sinon . . . hop . . . devoirs supplémentaires! J'en ai eu de temps en temps.
C: Tu as de la chance, toi, avec ton prof de maths. Le mien, c'est Mme La Tène . . . elle est plus stricte que M. Duroc, hein? . . . C'est le prof avec lequel on doit travailler le plus. Je suppose qu'elle est juste . . . et elle est très énergique . . . mais moi, je n'ai pas d'énergie pour les maths!
D: Bon, à mon avis le prof le plus ennuyeux, c'est M. Legros, le Directeur. Il est si strict . . . quand il nous parle, on tremble. Et il n'est pas juste. S'il ne t'aime pas, il te punit, quoi. C'est un mec prétentieux, je le déteste.

Solution

	Professeur	☺/☹	Raisons
1	Mlle Trélente	☹	lente; barbante; bête
2	M. Duroc	☺	intéressant; enthousiaste; juste
3	Mme. La Tène	☺	stricte; juste; énergique
4	M. Legros, le Directeur	☹	strict; pas juste

Ça se dit comment? p.77 🎧 [CD 2 track 48]

A reminder that while in most cases, '*qu*' is pronounced as 'k', the two important notable exceptions are *quoi?* and *pourquoi?* The cartoon caption has a mixture of the two sounds.

Transcript

– Qu'est-ce que c'est? Quelle quantité? Lequel?
– Quoi? Pourquoi?
– Quoi? Pourquoi est-ce que Quasimodo a quitté son quartier pour aller au Québec?

ICT activity

Learning objectives

• to reuse the language of the unit;
• to create a questionnaire;
• to e-mail that questionnaire to a partner school or give to another class in the same school;
• to present the outcomes orally.

1 Teacher decides with the class what format the questionnaire should take, e.g. *Comment est-ce que tu trouves ton prof de . . .? Strict/barbant/ juste . . .?*

2 Students create the questionnaire and send it as an attachment to a partner school or to another class.

3 Students then present the opinions of their 'partners' to the rest of the class.

⬆4 Higher attainers could be encouraged to ask follow-up questions and give reasons.

14  ⬆

This extension exercise offers the students an opportunity to reflect on the qualities of good and bad teachers. The expressions listed in the Student's Book reflect those used in the classification exercise above. Other constructions that can be used are: *on ne doit pas . . .*, *il faut* (+ infinitive) . . . ; *connaître à fond* (to have a thorough knowledge of).

Expressions used to give opinions can also be revisited: *je pense que, je trouve que, je crois que.* (Avoid *Je ne pense pas que* and *Je ne crois pas que* because the subjunctive would have to follow.)

Tip

Students may already be aware of some differences between French and UK schools, but a quiz will check/ reinforce their knowledge. They could be given the following choice of answers to allow them to have a go if they're not sure: *C'est (probablement) en France; c'est (probablement) en Royaume-Uni; tous les deux.*

On ne porte pas d'uniforme scolaire. [F]
On travaille du lundi au vendredi. [R-U]
Il y a six semaines de vacances en été. [R-U]
On travaille le samedi matin. [F]
Le 14 juillet, il n'y a pas de cours. [F]
On a des examens importants à l'âge de 16 ans. [R-U]
La rentrée des classes, c'est mi-septembre. [F]
On achète tous ses propres livres et manuels scolaires. [F]

Extra idea

CM45 shows a typical French 15-year-old's school timetable, which can be used to reinforce knowledge of French school subjects and routine. It can also be used for practice of the 24h clock, and *ça dure de ... à*, etc.

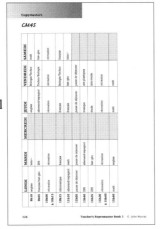

ICT opportunity

In this unit the students have had further work on the topic of school. This would be an appropriate time to extend the word-processed file started in Unit 3. Students are now able to add additional information about school buildings and give opinions about subjects and teachers.

Unité 8 Pages 78–79

These two pages introduce the simple future tense, firstly with regular verbs and then with irregulars.

EGW8 provides extra practice of the future (see full notes on **EGW8** at the end of this unit).

15 📖🎧 [CD 2 track 49]

This reading passage has a number of verbs in the future.

Presentation idea

Write the day's date on the board in one column, and then a date that falls next weekend. Explain *Aujourd'hui je travaille au collège. Samedi je ne travaillerai pas – je jouerai au golf. Aujourd'hui je mange dans la cantine. Samedi je mangerai chez moi. Aujourd'hui je ne regarde pas la télé – j'ai trop de travail. Samedi je regarderai le football à la télé.*

Repeat the verbs in pairs, pointing at the dates: *je travaille – je ne travaillerai pas/je jouerai; je mange – je mangerai,* etc. Emphasise the ending: *Vous entendez la différence: je mange – je mangerai.* Note a pair on the board and circle the R in the future tense. Explain that this sound will help students to recognise the future tense.

The recording starts slightly differently from the itinerary shown on the page. This is simply to give the aural version authenticity.

Transcript

Professeur: Silence dans la classe! M. Legros a quelque chose d'important à vous dire!

M. Legros: Le lundi 15 juin, nous allons faire une excursion scolaire avec nos amis irlandais. L'itinéraire sera le suivant.

8h30 Départ du collège. On partira à l'heure et on n'attendra pas les retardataires!

Nous allons faire un petit tour de la côte jusqu'à Cancale.

Nous descendrons ensuite vers Combourg, où nous visiterons le marché de cette jolie ville.

10h30 Visite guidée du château de Combourg. Nos visiteurs apprécieront sans doute cette superbe forteresse médiévale.

12h30 Déjeuner. Les élèves apporteront un pique-nique qu'on prendra dans le parc de la Higourdais. S'il fait mauvais, nous prendrons le déjeuner au Lycée Condorcet.

14h00 Arrivée au Mont Saint-Michel. Nous passerons l'après-midi à visiter le Mont. Nos visiteurs achèteront sans doute des souvenirs de leur journée en Bretagne.

17h00 Départ pour Saint-Malo. En route pour le collège nous déposerons les élèves qui habitent dans les villages près de la ville.

18h00 Arrivée au collège.

Having read the text, students find the information on the basis of synonyms and deduction. The sentences all contain verbs in the future tense.

Solution

1 On mangera en plein air à 12h30.
2 On passera au bord de la mer à 8h30.
3 Les Irlandais visiteront des boutiques à 14h00.
4 On partira pour Saint-Malo à 17h00.
5 On retournera au collège à 18h00.

Point grammaire

Reminding students that the R sound is characteristic of the future tense, ask them firstly to pick out verbs from the text which are in the future and then to work out the *je* form of each of these verbs.

Extra idea

Practice of the future could involve saying what you will do next weekend, or in the year 2010.

16 [CD 2 track 50]

In this exercise, students match questions to answers and have a chance to laugh at Mlle Trélente, the teacher who has got it all wrong!

Transcript

a Non, Mlle Trélente, ils en achèteront au Mont Saint-Michel!
b Non, Mlle Trélente, nous le visiterons à 10h30!
c Non, Mlle Trélente, nous y visiterons le marché!
d Non, Mlle Trélente, nous le prendrons dans le parc à Combourg.
e Non, Mlle Trélente, nous mangerons en plein air!
f Non, Mlle Trélente, nous partirons à 8h30!

Solution

1 **f**; 2 **a**; 3 **c**; 4 **e**; 5 **b**; 6 **d**

The material on the weather forecast introduces irregular verbs in the *il* form.

Presentation ideas

Revise the weather using OHT symbols from **CM46**.

These could be placed on an OHT of **CM24**.

Write *Et demain* (+ date) *ça ne changera pas* on the board as a title. Use symbols which involve irregular verbs (*il fait, il y a, il pleut, le temps est . . .*). Ask what each symbol means. In answer to *Il pleut*, say *Et demain aussi il pleuvra.* For *Il fait beau*, *Et demain aussi il fera beau*, etc.

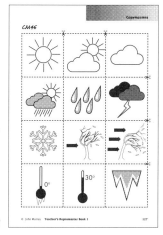

Write the present and the future of these verbs in two columns. Point out that although they are irregular, that they still have the characteristic R sound and endings for the *il* form.

17

Practice of basic weather phrases using futures in the '*demain*' parts of the sentences.

Solution

1 a; aura
2 est; sera
3 a; aura
4 fait; fera

18 [CD 2 track 51]

Students listen to 10 sentences and identify those containing a future tense. Listening for the R sound may help them.

Transcript

1 Dans les Alpes et dans le Jura, il fera beau demain.
2 Il y aura des averses dans le nord.
3 Il pleut dans les Pyrénées.
4 Hier il y a eu des chutes de neige en région parisienne.
5 Cet après-midi il fera beau au nord de la Loire.
6 Il fait très beau en Provence en ce moment.
7 Le temps sera pluvieux pour les deux jours à venir.
8 Il y a du brouillard en Bretagne.
9 Il pleuvra très fort dans les Vosges et les Ardennes.
10 Le temps sera nuageux ce matin en région méditerranéenne.

Solution

1 oui; 2 oui; 3 non; 4 non; 5 oui; 6 non; 7 oui; 8 non; 9 oui; 10 oui.

19

Students examine a weather map and say if statements relating to it are true or false.

Differentiation opportunity

Students correct those sentences which are wrong.

Solution

1 F: Le temps sera beau.
2 V.
3 F: Il y aura des nuages/Le temps sera nuageux.
4 V.
5 F: Il pleuvra.

ICT opportunity

The weather forecast for all the regions of France is readily available on the Internet: **www.meteo.fr**; students could examine real weather forecasts from this site or from French newspapers and find examples of this. They could check their conclusions against the symbols on the weather maps.

Note: French newspapers often use a codified set of symbols whose meaning is not transparent to the uninitiated. Some guidance may be needed here.

Extra idea

EGW8 Activity 2 provides extra practice of the future of weather verbs (see full notes on **EGW8** at the end of this unit).

ICT activity

Aims:

- to practise further the future using the language of the unit;
- to locate an appropriate site on the Internet for this topic.

1 Students locate sites with information on the weather (see above).
2 They download weather maps for two or three regions for the following day.
3 They import these into a document and write the corresponding weather reports.
↓ 4 Lower attainers might need a phrase bank supplied on an accompanying document or on hard copy.

20 🎧 👂 ✏️ [CD 2 track 52]

Activity 1: This listening activity draws together the future of irregular verbs, leisure activites, *à/en* with places and weather. A Tip follows on saying how many people are in a group, e.g. *Nous serons quatre.*

Transcript

Philippe: En juillet nous irons à St Jean Pied-de-Port, dans les Pyrénées. On fera du camping, comme toujours, et on sera quatre dans une seule petite tente, . . . ce sera un vrai cauchemar! Il pleuvra, comme toujours, il n'y aura rien à faire, et nous mangerons des repas exécrables. C'est toujours la même chose!

Joélie: Nous n'irons pas en vacances d'été, parce que . . . euh . . . nous faisons des économies pour aller faire du ski dans les Alpes. En février, nous irons à Méribel pour deux semaines. Nous irons en famille, et on sera six dans un appartement. Il y aura beaucoup de neige, on fera du ski tous les jours, et on aura de belles soirées d'après-ski. Ce sera fantastique!

Claudette: En août, mes copines et moi . . . on ira dans le Var, près de St Raphaël. On ira en groupe – nous serons huit! Sans doute il fera beau et chaud, et nous pourrons faire de la planche à voile, de la natation. On se bronzera, et tout ça, et sans doute il y aura de beaux mecs! . . .

Solution

Philippe: c
Joélie: c
Claudette: a

Tip

How to say how many people are/will be in a group, using *on + être*.

21 👂 ✏️

Students present the weather forecast either in speech or in writing. The former will still require at least an outline script.

ICT opportunity

Tasks 20 and 21 are an ideal springboard for use of the video camera, as the outcome resembles a genuine TV presentation. A large map of France is necessary – you could use **CM24** (with overlays **CM24a** and/or **CM24b** if you prefer) onto which weather symbols for each area can be placed.

A more ambitious project would be to use Power Point® and present a series of slides outlining the weather.

Differentiation opportunity ↓ ↑

↓ For more practice of the future in a different context, **DW8.2A** shows people on holiday and the activities that they will be doing. Students complete sentences using *je, nous* and *ils*. The only irregular verb used is *aller.*

↑ **DW8.2B** involves more activities and the weather.

Teacher's Guide 1   © John Murray

Unité 8 Page 80

On the outing undertaken on the French exchange, things do not go quite to plan, and some medical intervention becomes necessary!

22

This exercise covers the rules to be observed on the outing.

Preliminary work could involve the revision of *devoir* and the rules invented for Camp Shane in Unit 2.
Students read the rules given under the two headings *Vous devez* and *Vous ne devez pas*. They then ascribe the remaining rules to the appropriate column.
You might want to mention the *faux ami 'alcoolique'*, pointing out that *alcoolisé* is used to describe alcoholic drinks.

Differentiation opportunity

More able students could explain the reason for some rules, e.g. *Vous devez rester assis dans le car, parce qu'il est dangereux de se lever.*

23 [CD 2 track 53]

Before listening to the cassette, students could predict what the problem might be. The rules given may prompt some thoughts, e.g. *Andrew n'est pas là, Andrew a perdu son argent, Andrew est en retard*, etc.

Transcript

John: Excusez-moi, Mademoiselle, mais Andrew ne se sent pas bien.
Mlle Trélente: Comment, il ne se sent pas bien? Il est malade?
John: Euh . . . un peu . . . non, pas exactement . . . Il a mal à la tête et mal à l'estomac.
Mlle Trélente: Il a mangé son pique-nique?
John: Oui . . . euh . . . mais . . . le problème . . . c'est que . . . euh . . . c'est qu'il a bu quelque chose.
Mlle Trélente: Comment, il a bu quelque chose? Qu'est-ce qu'il a bu exactement?
John: Euh . . . de la bière, Mademoiselle.
Mlle Trélente: Comment! De la bière . . . oh, non! Mais . . . mais . . . combien de bières a-t-il bues? Une bouteille?
John: Non, Mademoiselle . . .
Mlle Trélente: . . . *deux* bouteilles . . .?
John: Non, il en a bu trois bouteilles, Mademoiselle.
Mlle Trélente: *Trois* bouteilles! Oh, c'est pas vrai, c'est pas vrai! Oh, le petit idiot! Oh, il en a bu trois bouteilles! C'est pas vrai . . . c'est pas vrai! Bon, il faut aller à la pharmacie!

Solution

1 Exemple: Andrew ne se sent pas **bien**.
2 Andrew a mal **à la tête et à l'estomac**.
3 Il **a** mangé son pique-nique.
4 Il a bu **trois** bouteilles de bière.

5 Il est un petit **idiot**.
6 On a besoin d'**une pharmacie**.

Point grammaire: En

Since *en* is a pronoun, it replaces a noun. Write two sentences on the board, e.g. *Tu as des frères – Oui j'ai un frère*. Rub out the last *frère*, and explain that as he's been 'rubbed out', he leaves a ghost in the form of '*en*' which appears in the second sentence *Oui, j'en ai un*. Outline *en* with a ghostly form. Show some examples of pairs of sentences: *Tu as des sœurs? – Oui, j'en ai deux*.
In each of the examples:

- ask students to identify the noun to which the *en* refers, and
- stress that the pronoun precedes the verb.

24

Students match questions and answers, the latter containing examples of *en*. Contextual clues in the answer help students link them to the questions.

Solution

1 c; **2** a; **3** f; **4** b; **5** e; d is a distractor.

Tip

Adverbial phrases to describe a sequence of events (as touched on with Christophe le Cambrioleur, **CM43**), starting with *Tout d'abord*, ending with *enfin* and using *puis, ensuite, après cela* and *alors*.
This could be practised with the schedule for the outing on page 78, either in the future, or as a narrative of what happened in the perfect tense.

25

Students complete Andrew's account of the events of the day. This gives an opportunity to use sequencing expressions in a narrative.

26

This leaflet points out the risk of alcohol abuse. The explanation is matched by a simplified diagram of the human body. Students match the parts of the body (a–e) to the advice (1–5).

Solution

1 d; **2** b; **3** a; **4** e; **5** c

Extra ideas

More practice of parts of the body can be based on the luckless Andrew Smethurst – perhaps choosing one student to represent him and getting others to complete phrases about his condition, e.g. *Voilà Andrew. Il ne se sent pas bien. Il a mangé beaucoup de chocolat après le pique-nique et il se sent très mal. Il a mal à . . . ? Il a écouté la radio très fort pendant le voyage et il ne se sent pas bien. Il a mal à . . .*

Unité 8 Page 81

Presentation idea

This page covers the pharmacy and instructions for the correct use of medicines. Use **CM47** and then ⬇ **DW8.3** to revise parts of the body and the construction *'J'ai mal à . . .'*.

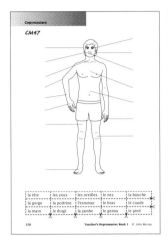

Differentiation opportunity ⬇

⬇ **DW8.3** practises the construction *avoir mal à* – in the first person via the completion of the speech bubbles, and in the third person via the completion of the captions.

Solution

1 Exemple: *speech bubble*: J'ai mal à la tête.
  Caption: Marc a mal à la tête.
2 *Speech bubble*: J'ai mal à l'estomac.
  Caption: M. Férien a mal à l'estomac.
3 *Speech bubble*: J'ai mal aux oreilles.
  Caption: Rachel a mal aux oreilles.
4 *Speech bubble*: J'ai mal aux jambes.
  Caption: L'athlète a mal aux jambes.
5 *Speech bubbles*: J'ai mal au nez!
  Caption: Les boxeurs ont mal au nez.
6 *Speech bubbles*: Nous avons mal à la gorge.
  Caption: Les chanteurs ont mal à la gorge.

27 🎧 [CD 2 track 54]

Students listen to customers in a pharmacy asking for suitable products for their complaints. Some preliminary work on the products illustrated could help students to work out what each is for, e.g.

Oxyboldine, Pour troubles digestifs – *C'est pour l'estomac.*

Paracétamol – well-known in English as pain-reliever.
Oxyboldine – 'oxy-' suggests oxygen, which suggests bubbles rising like Alka-Seltzer, a similar product.
Sparadrap – the most well-known brand of sticking plaster.
Gripponyl – 'grippe' means influenza. This is an anti-flu treatment.
Voxyl – 'voix' means voice. This is for sore throats.
Lenicalm – the ending explains this one. It relaxes those of a nervous nature.

Gel Arnica – arnica is a well-known homoeopathic remedy for bruises and can be bought in Britain in liquid and tablet form.

Transcript

Numéro 1: Je ne me sens pas bien . . . j'ai chaud et puis j'ai froid . . . puis j'ai chaud . . . j'ai de la fièvre . . . je me sens vraiment malade.

Numéro 2: Je suis très nerveuse . . . très, très nerveuse . . . je ne me sens jamais calme . . . je ne dors pas la nuit . . . oui, je suis vraiment anxieuse. J'ai besoin de quelque chose de calmant.

Numéro 3: J'ai mal à la tête . . . ça fait vraiment mal . . . oh, c'est comme un éléphant qui me marche sur la tête!

Numéro 4: S'il vous plaît, Madame . . . j'ai mal à l'estomac . . . oui, j'ai mangé du poisson au déjeuner . . . oh, j'ai très mal au cœur . . . et j'ai envie de vomir . . . excusez-moi . . .

Numéro 5: C'est que je me suis cogné le coude . . . oui, j'ai vraiment mal au coude . . . il y a une bosse, grosse comme ça . . . et un bleu énorme . . . j'ai heurté la porte . . . ça fait vraiment mal!

Numéro 6: Je me suis coupé le doigt . . . avec un couteau aigu . . . il y avait du sang partout . . . et ça saigne toujours.

Numéro 7: Je souffre d'une angine . . . J'ai mal à la gorge . . . ça fait très mal . . . oui, la gorge, ça me fait vraiment mal.

Solution

1 d; **2** f; **3** a; **4** b; **5** g; **6** c; **7** e

Ça se dit comment? p.81 🎧 [CD 2 track 55]

The letter *'o-'* is never pronounced in French like the English sound in 'photo'. The English sound is a diphthong: 'o-u'. The French vowel is a single sound.

Transcript

– photo, auto, moto, Loto, écolo

28 📖

Students match instructions on medicines to pictures. A number of cognates and near cognates will guide students in the more difficult cases.

Solution

a 4; **b** 3; **c** 1; **d** 5; **e** 2

Tip

Explains the infinitives seen in task 28, and draws attention to basic *'de'* constructions.

29 📖

Students match problems to causes, working with phrases which exemplify the *'de'* constructions.

Solution

1 d; **2** c; **3** a; **4** b; **5** e

ICT activity

Aim:

• to use the language of the unit in creative way.

1 The teacher recaps all the symptoms discussed so far. Students are then asked to suggest the name of medication to combat the illness.
2 Teacher provides a model advert, e.g. *Mal à l'estomac? Achetez . . .*
3 Students then create their own adverts with as much detail as they can. They could also be encouraged to find appropriate graphics from the Internet or from CD ROMs.
4 Results should be displayed.

Point grammaire: *Dont* ⬆

The relative pronoun *dont* is difficult for Anglophones, and in any case is not very common, except in upper registers of language. It is given here for the more able only and really only for comprehension. One way to make it a bit easier is to use the 'ghost' principle, as suggested for explaining *en* (see previous page). Students could practise it with a set phrase such as; *Le produit dont j'ai besoin, c'est . . .*, e.g. *J'ai mal à l'estomac. Le produit dont j'ai besoin, c'est Oxyboldine.* With *souffrir*, students could explain symptoms and their partner, as doctor, could define their illness, e.g. *J'ai chaud, puis j'ai froid, et puis j'ai chaud. – La maladie dont vous souffrez, c'est la grippe.*

30

Activity 1 Students link matching halves of sentences, all of which have *dont* as the relative pronoun.

Solution
1 c; **2** a; **3** d; **4** b

Unité 8 Pages 82–83

These two pages cover a party given by the French students at the end of the exchange.

31

This invitation is couched in slightly formal French.
   Students choose the correct answer from a choice of two. The verb tense is the future.

a La boum sera au collège.
b La boum sera pour les Irlandais et les Français.
c Elle finira avant minuit.
d Il faudra apporter des plats.
e Il y aura de la musique.

Point grammaire: Verbs + *de* or *à*

This covers common verbs requiring *à* or *de* before an infinitive. As a general principle, explain that *à* is often used with verbs which have a positive sense, or a sense of beginning, e.g. *commencer à, réussir à* (with the obvious exception of *hésiter*).
   Verbs which take *de* often have a sense of negativity, stopping or preventing, e.g. *finir, s'arrêter* and *empêcher* (with the obvious exceptions of *essayer* and *décider*).
   Only one verb with a direct object + *à* is used here: *inviter quelqu'un à.*
   EGW8 Activity 3 provides extra practice of this point (see full notes on **EGW8** at the end of this unit).

32

This switchboard enables students to produce a variety of possible sentences. You could ask students to try this orally as pair work. With more able students, the listening partner could decide if the ending is possible by reference to the Point grammaire or notes made from it, e.g. two columns listing verbs with *à* and verbs with *de*.

Extra idea/differentiation opportunity ⬆

Students could invent variations on these sentences, with the more able ones using sentences 7 and 8.

33

A more open-ended set of skeleton sentences.

Solution
   1 N'oublie pas **d'**informer **tes** parents.
   2 N'hésitez pas **à** prendre contact en cas **de** problèmes.
   3 Essayez **d'**arriver **à** l'heure.
   4 Nous avons décidé **d'**inviter quelques élèves **d'**autres classes.
⬆ 5 Nous **avons** invité tous nos amis **à** participer.

34 🎧 [CD 2 track 56]

Four students involved with the French exchange give their opinions. There are a number of uses of verbs with *à* and *de*.

Differentiation opportunity ⬇ ⬆

⬇ Weaker students could assign a (+) for a good exchange, a (~) for a mediocre one and a (−) for a bad one.
⬆ More able students may be able to pick out the reasons for the success or failure of the exchange.

Transcript

Alain: Alain Chasseur au micro de Radio Corsaire. Comme chaque année, le Collège Jacques Cartier fait un échange avec le Belfast College. Quelles ont été les impressions des élèves? John, comment a été l'échange pour toi?

John: Pour moi, c'était un échange réussi. J'aime beaucoup mon correspondant français. C'est un bon mec. On s'entend bien. J'ai essayé de communiquer en français. C'était bien. On s'est bien amusés ensemble. Je vais certainement revenir l'année prochaine.

Alain: Merci bien. Adèle, c'était bien pour toi aussi, l'échange?

Adèle: Ah non. C'était l'échec. Je n'ai pas aimé ma correspondante. Elle n'a pas essayé de communiquer en français. En plus, elle est très sportive – moi, je ne le suis pas. Et elle a critiqué mes fringues tout le temps. C'était un désastre. Je ne veux pas aller chez elle. J'espère que les profs vont me trouver une autre correspondante.

Alain: Oh, c'est dommage. Bon, alors, Andrew, comment c'était pour toi?

Andrew: Je me suis bien amusé. J'ai aimé mon correspondant et j'ai réussi à communiquer avec lui. Le seul problème, c'était la question des trois bouteilles de bière . . . Mais, quand même, j'espère revenir l'année prochaine.

Alain: Merci bien . . . et finalement, Céline.

Céline: Ben . . . c'était pas mal. Il y a eu de bons moments et de mauvais. Quelquefois c'était vachement cool, chouette, hein? Et puis j'ai eu des disputes avec ma correspondante. Mais j'espère que ça ira mieux à Belfast.

Solution (main points)

John: échange réussi – bonne entente avec correspondant – on s'est amusés – retour l'année prochaine.

Adèle: échec – n'a pas aimé sa correspondante – corres trop sportive – n'ira pas chez elle.
Andrew: échange réussi – a beaucoup aimé son correspondant – incident de la bière – espère revenir.
Céline: indécise – certains bons moments – disputes avec sa corres – ça ira mieux à Belfast.

Tip: De l'argot!

Slang is of course an ever-changing phenomenon, but the words listed here (*vachement, un mec, chouette, terrible, les fringues*) have really become a part of the language.

Tip

A reminder that capital letters are used on nationality words only when they are a noun, not when they are adjectival.

35 📖 [CD 2 track 57]

Students read a short article from *Le Quotidien* which sums up the successes of the visit.

Transcript

Parlez-vous franglais?

L'échange scolaire entre Belfast College et le Collège Jacques Cartier a été un vrai succès. Nos amis irlandais sont venus visiter notre ville et ses environs. Les élèves ont réussi à communiquer avec leurs correspondants et leurs parents et les commerçants de la ville. Ils ont hésité au début à parler français, mais ils ont essayé de comprendre les conversations autour d'eux. Ils ont eu l'occasion de visiter le Mont Saint-Michel et d'acheter des souvenirs de leur visite. À la boum du samedi soir, des Irlandaises ont invité des Français à danser et vice versa. Demain, c'est le départ, et il y aura certainement des cœurs brisés! Certains élèves ont déjà décidé de revenir l'année prochaine.

Solution

1 Nos amis **irlandais** sont venus visiter notre ville.
2 Ils **ont réusssi à** communiquer avec leurs correspondants.
3 Ils ont **hésité à parler** français.
4 Des **Irlandaises** ont invité des **Français** à danser.
5 **Demain**, c'est le départ.

Unité 8 Pages 84–85

Checkpoints

Test

The **Test** checks students' skills in the grammatical goals of the unit:

- using the pronoun *en*
- using possessive pronouns to say 'mine', 'his', etc.
- using the future tense
- using the pronoun *en*
- verbs followed by *à* or *de*

Solution

1 **a** Oui, j'en ai deux. [1]
   b Non, on en mange très rarement. [1]
   c Non, merci, je n'en veux pas. [1]
2 **a** Elle peut emprunter la mienne. [2]
   b Elle peut emprunter le mien. [2]
   c Elle peut emprunter le mien. [2]
   d Elle peut emprunter les miennes. [2]
3 **a** Nous **partirons** à 9h demain. [1]
   b J'espère qu'il **fera** beau pour l'excursion. [1]
   c Les élèves **auront** l'occasion d'acheter des souvenirs. [1]
   d Le car **arrivera** au Mont Saint-Michel vers 13h. [1]
   e On **aura** le temps de visiter les boutiques. [1]
   f Nous n'**attendrons** pas les retardataires. [1]
4 **a** Nous avons invité nos correspondants **à** venir à la boum. [1]
   b Pierre a décidé **de** rester à la maison. [1]
   c Aline a réussi **à** persuader Philippe **à** danser. [1]
   d David a hésité **à** demander à Céline de sortir avec lui. [1]
   e Daniel a oublié **d'**apporter la liste des invités. [1]
5 **a** les Italiens/les Italiennes
   b les Anglais/les Anglaises
   c les Espagnols/les Espagnoles
   d les Néerlandais/les Néerlandaises
   e au Portugal
   f en Irlande
   g en Allemagne
   h en Belgique [8]

Total [30]

Quiz

The **Quiz** checks students' knowledge acquired in the unit, about:

- French school exchanges
- education in France
- alcohol
- dealing with ailments in France

Solution

1 **a** On doit réserver une chambre d'hôtel quand on fait un échange. **F** [1]
   b Le choix de correspondant(e) n'est pas important. **F** [1]
   c Quelquefois on passe du temps dans une école. **V** [1]
2 Any five French school subjects. [5]
3 Any three French school cultural/sports activities. [3]
4 **a** En France, les élèves ne portent pas d'uniforme (scolaire). [2]
   b En France, les pions (les surveillants) sont responsables de la discipline dans la cour. [2]
5 estomac, foie, circulation, cerveau, vision [5]
6 Lénicalm – troubles nerveux; Paracétamol – mal de tête; Oxyboldine – troubles digestifs; Voxyl – mal de gorge; Gripponyl – symptômes de grippe. [5]

Total [25]

Projets

A Students prepare a brochure about their school for French visitors and exchange partners. This could begin with a brain-storming session in groups in which they attempt to list all the subjects taught. A copy of the school prospectus could be used as a stimulus and this could lead to dictionary work for such terms as business studies *(= études commerciales)*. As regards sports facilities, terms such as *gymnase* and *hall omnisports* may prove useful. Students could also list sites of importance, e.g. *le bureau de la Directrice, la salle des professeurs.*

B Students compare the French and the UK school systems under a number of headings. They may wish to do this in two contrasting columns of writing. They could list the suggested categories down the side of the page, with one column for France and one for the UK.

C Those students who have already participated in an exchange trip may wish to write an account. They could write about any or all of the following:

their pen-friend; the house; their room; the host family; meals; the school; the teachers; the lessons; an excursion; the weather; the town; activities; any problems.

This could be largely confined to the perfect tense, with comments being restricted to *C'était . . .* and *J'ai trouvé cela . . .*

Those students who have not been on an exchange could write an account based on the one described in the unit, as if they had participated in it.

EGW8 teaching notes

EGW8 provides extra grammar/homework on the future tense and verbs with prepositions.

Activity 1

This practises some regular and the most common irregular futures.

Solution

1 Non, je voyagerai par avion.
2 Non, mes copains m'accompagneront.
3 Non, j'irai en août.
4 Non, je serai là pour deux semaines.
5 Non, je visiterai Nice.
6 Non, je logerai dans un gîte.
7 Non, je reviendrai le 1er septembre.
8 Non, j'enverrai une carte postale à mes amis.

Activity 2

This practises the future of weather verbs.

Solution

Et voici la météo pour demain. Dans le nord il **fera** froid et il est probable qu'**il y aura** des chutes de neige. En région parisienne, **il pleuvra**, et dans l'ouest, surtout en Bretagne, il **fera** du vent. Dans le centre le temps **sera** nuageux. Sur la côte ouest, le temps **sera** orageux, et le vent **sera** fort. En région méditerranéenne, il **fera** plus beau, avec de belles éclaircies. Dans les Alpes, le temps **sera** ensoleillé, mais il **ne fera pas** très chaud, température maximale, 10 degrés.

Activity 3 ⇑

This practises choosing the right preposition for verbs taking *de/à*.

Solution

1 Nous avons essayé **d'**organiser une boum.
2 On a hésité **à** inviter Sylvie.
3 Nous avons réussi **à** avoir une trentaine de personnes à la boum.
4 Alain a oublié **d'**apporter un plat.
5 Nous avons décidé **de** commander des plats supplémentaires.
6 J'ai persuadé mon père **d'**acheter des boissons en ville.

unité 9
Le musée virtuel

Unit 9 Pages 86–87

This unit takes the form of a visit to a 'virtual museum'. Students visit exhibits on both the future (extending their use of the future tense) and the past (being introduced to the imperfect tense).

The opening two pages are an introduction to the museum, with the first page presenting the contents in the form of a web page.

The future of irregular verbs, including *avoir* and *être*, was introduced in Unit 8 and is revisited throughout Unit 9. The imperfect of *être* is presented here, with '1950' giving a contextual clue as to its meaning.

 [CD 3 track 1]

Students match French expressions from the text to their English equivalents.

Transcript
Bienvenue au musée virtuel!
Dans le musée virtuel vous allez faire un voyage dans le temps. Vous aurez la possibilité de visiter l'an 2050 et de retourner à l'an 1950. Comment sera la vie dans 50 ans? Comment était la vie de vos grands-parents il y a plus de 50 ans? Entrez ici – vous découvrirez le passé . . . et l'avenir!

Pour chaque catégorie vous avez deux possibilités. Avance: vous voyagerez dans l'avenir.
Retour: vous retournerez au passé.

Solution
1 c; **2** j; **3** i; **4** b; **5** f; **6** h; **7** e; **8** d; **9** a; **10** g

Page 87 is a general introduction to the world of the future. The text is presented as an illustration of examples of the future tense and there are no comprehension questions on it, but students could pick out the verbs and say what they mean. The Tip below reminds them about the R sound, which is a distinguishing feature of the future tense.

Transcript [CD 3 track 2]
Introduction Avance. Cliquez ici.
[F]: Comment sera la vie en 2050?
[M]: La population du monde sera de 12 000 000 000 000 de personnes.
[F]: Les villes seront énormes.
[M]: Beaucoup de gens travailleront à la maison et non pas dans un bureau.
[F]: Il y aura des robots partout.
[M]: Vous aurez la possibilité de choisir le sexe de votre bébé.
[F]: On vivra dans des maisons 'intelligentes' et robotisées.
[M]: Il n'y aura plus de voitures à essence . . . parce qu'il n'y aura plus d'essence!
[F]: Il n'y aura plus d'autoroutes.
[M]: Des astronautes visiteront régulièrement la planète Mars.
[F]: Il sera possible d'aller de France en Australie en six heures.

Tip
Two useful tips for speaking about the past. The first is the use of *il y a* to say how long ago something happened. The second is on the use of *de* when saying 'more/less than'.

Pair work choosing among six descriptions to give their opinion on the 10 predictions: *fantastique, bon, tolérable, pas important, mauvais, catastrophique*. If you want to make more of this, points could be allocated to gauge optimism about these predictions for the future: six points for *fantastique*, one point for *catastrophique*, and so on. A high score (maximum total = 60) would thus indicate the person feels things are going the right way, according to these predictions.

Tips
Tip 1 is a reminder about the potentially confusing high numbers involving thousands and millions. Add 1 000, 1 000 000 and 1 000 000 000 (*milliard*) to your set of number cards and practise them regularly, e.g. by flashing them, or asking students to guess which card you are holding. Try simple dictation to a student standing at the board e.g. 3 000; 3 000 000 000; 3 000 000. You could also try some spoken mental arithmetic (*4 000 000 + 4 000 égale combien?*).

Tip 2 is a reminder that the R sound helps to identify the future tense when listening.

3 🎧 [CD 3 track 3]

The 'museum guide' adds some further predictions for life in 2050. Students listen and note whether the topics listed in the Student's Book are mentioned (gist listening).

Transcript

En 2050 vous verrez certainement des voitures intelligentes. Elles n'auront pas besoin d'un chauffeur et elles se conduiront automatiquement.

En général, les ordinateurs et les robots feront le travail. On aura beaucoup de loisirs et on pourra bien s'amuser.

Les enfants n'iront plus à l'école. Ils resteront à la maison et ils travailleront sur ordinateur. Ils pourront envoyer leurs devoirs aux professeurs-robots par e-mail.

Heureusement, il n'y aura pas de pollution, parce qu'il n'y aura plus de voitures à essence, plus d'usines sales.

Solution

1 oui; **2** non; **3** non; **4** oui; **5** oui; **6** non; **7** non; **8** oui

Tip

At this stage, the construction *ne ... que* is used only in simple tenses with its two halves framing the verb. Practise with classroom objects or other small objects, e.g. model cars: *J'ai trois voitures ici? – Non, vous n'avez que deux voitures.* Point out that *Il y a* will give *Il n'y a que.* Practise this in a similar way to the above, or suggest sentences such as: *Il y a huit personnes dans ta famille, Sheena? – Non, il n'y a que quatre personnes dans ma famille.*

An inventory of what there 'should be' in a classroom, office or *gîte* will give students the chance to compare reality with theory, e.g. *Salle de classe: 34 chaises, 17 tables, 2 placards ... Madame, il n'y a que 33 chaises et 1 placard.*

Retour [CD 3 track 4]

This short text provides the first real contact with the imperfect and contrasts with the future images encountered thus far. The illustrations of the old-fashioned objects and scenes will make it clear that this is the past. Although there is no concentration on the forms of the imperfect at this point, students could be asked to see if they can spot a common element in all the sentences: Only the ending *-ait* is used in these sentences.

Transcript

Retour. Cliquez ici.
Et c'était comment, la vie en France en 1950?
Il y avait des tourne-disques.
En général, on avait une radio, mais pas de télévision.
On ne mangeait du bœuf que le dimanche!
L'école n'était obligatoire que jusqu'à 14 ans.

Unit 9 Pages 88–89

This 'page' of the *musée virtuel* deals with communications in the future. The main grammar point is revision of the future tense of irregular verbs which was dealt with briefly in the previous unit. Brief examples of the imperfect are given to contrast with the future, but the grammar of this tense is not explained.

4 📖 [CD 3 track 5]

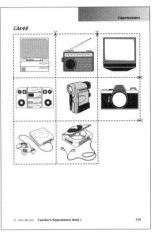

This text deals with the concept of 'convergence', though not in so many words. Revision of the names of electronic gadgets would be useful as a preliminary. Using **CM48** (the items listed in the exercise), you could revise *vouloir* and *il faut*, e.g. – *Vous voulez regarder une émission documentaire samedi après-midi. Vous avez besoin de quel appareil? – Il faut avoir une télévision.*

Alternatively, students could define the machines, e.g. *Un ordinateur? C'est pour surfer sur Internet. Une radio? C'est pour écouter de la musique.*

Transcript

Communications. Avance: 2010. Cliquez ici. Téléphone? Télévision? Ordinateur? Dans moins de dix ans vous aurez dans la poche un appareil fantastique – le vidéophone! Avec cette petite machine vous pourrez téléphoner à vos amis, et vous les verrez en même temps. Oui, le vidéophone aura un écran de télévision en couleurs. Il sera aussi possible de capter vos émissions de télévision favorites. En plus, vous pourrez vous brancher sur Internet.

Et si vous voulez vous relaxer, le vidéophone se transformera en console de jeux. Vous voulez prendre des photos? Pas de problème! Le vidéophone sera aussi un appareil-photo. Qui plus est, vous aurez la possibilité d'envoyer immédiatement ces photos à votre copain ou votre copine.

Oui, avec le vidéophone, on ne devra plus avoir cinq ou six appareils différents – un seul suffira!

Solution

Ordinateur; Télévision; Appareil-photo; Console de jeux.

Tip

A couple of phrases to help with fluency in oral and written presentations. You could play a variety of *Je suis allé au marché*, e.g.

Student 1: *Il y aura des voitures intelligentes.*
Student 2: *Il y aura des voitures intelligentes et il y aura aussi des vidéophones.*
Student 3: *Il y aura des voitures intelligentes et il y aura aussi des vidéophones. En plus, il y aura des robots partout,* etc.

Point grammaire: Future tense of irregular verbs

The future tense of *avoir, être, pouvoir, devoir and voir* are mentioned with the first person and giving examples covering all six persons.

You could ask students to spot examples of these verbs in the videophone text and say what the infinitive is.

Extra idea

Now that the future has been thoroughly introduced, add to your set of 'traffic light' cards, on which the *je* form of irregular verbs are listed. Red card indicates perfect tense, orange equals present and green now equals future. Have a set of time adverbs on appropriate coloured card, e.g. *demain, après demain, dans deux ans, à l'avenir, en 2050*, etc., on green card for the future. This indicates to students that you can only match red to red, green to green, etc., so that students are prevented from producing sentences such as *Demain je suis allé au cinéma*. Further uses for this set are outlined in other chapters.

Blu-tack the future adverbs and the future verbs on the board and ask students to make up sentences, e.g. *L'année prochaine j'aurai ... 16 ans. Dans trois ans je pourrai ... aller à l'université.*

 5

Students complete the skeleton sentences using the future tense.

Solution

1 Il
2 Vous
3 Tu
4 Philippe et Simone
5 Je
6 Nous

 **6** [CD 3 track 6]

In this exercise, students listen to three questions put to the guide in the *musée virtuel* and pick out five phrases, relating them to the three answers given. Go through the phrases with the class before playing the cassette.

Transcript

1: À l'avenir, est-ce qu'il sera possible de visiter d'autres planètes?
R: Oui, mais vous devrez attendre longtemps. On aura peut-être la possibilité de visiter Mars avant l'an 3000. On pourra certainement visiter la Lune avant 2050.
2: Dans deux ans, est-ce que je pourrai envoyer à mes copains des photos en 3-D et des hologrammes?
R: Non. Dans deux ans il ne sera pas possible d'envoyer des hologrammes avec un vidéophone. Il faudra attendre encore un peu pour cela.
3: Est-ce qu'on devra toujours aller au collège?
R: Ah non. On ne devra plus aller au collège – il n'y aura plus de collèges. On restera à la maison devant son ordinateur, et on aura accès à Internet. Ce sera très simple!

Solution

1 a; **2** c; **3** a; **4** c; **5** b

7

The cartoon shows a possible scene from life in the future in which all mechanical tasks are performed by computerised robots. Students explain or write down what will and what will not be possible/necessary.

Extra idea

CM49 could be used at this point. The poem is given in the original and in (an optional) translation. Students could: **a** illustrate the tasks to be performed by the robot; **b** find the meaning of phrases in the poem selected by the teacher; **c** write a list of tasks for the robot to do in the future (*Tu laveras la voiture, tu feras la cuisine, etc.*). More able students could attempt a poem about life in an age of computerised robots.

8

Students use the text on the videophone as a starting point and imagine what else will be possible in the future. The table lists expressions of opinion and expressions of possibility in the future tense. Some vocabulary is also given as a prompt. This exercise provides an opportunity for students to use a dictionary to find vocabulary. Answers will depend on the knowledge and ability of students.

Homework opportunity

Students make up another convergent machine, e.g. a combined computer and walkman with virtual reality helmet (*un casque à réalité virtuelle*). They could give it a name, e.g. *un walkman virtuel* and explain what one will be able to do. Start them off with phrases such as: *vous aurez, vous pourrez, on pourra, on ne pourra pas, on ne devra pas/plus ... parce que le robot le fera!* and encourage them to express opinions by giving them examples such as (*Ce sera merveilleux*) or write about the disadvantages of such machines (*Le problème, c'est que ...*).

Retour 1950 [CD 3 track 7]

This is further contact with the imperfect. Again, the tense is illustrated for passive understanding. The Tip asks students to observe that *-ait* is indicative of what used to happen.

Transcript

Retour 1950. Cliquez ici.
Et c'était comment, les communications en France en 1950?
Seulement une personne sur 100 avait la télévision.
Il n'y avait que des émissions de TV en noir et blanc.
On attendait un an pour avoir une ligne de téléphone.
En général, on voyageait en autobus ou en train.
Personne n'avait d'ordinateur individuel et les ordinateurs qui existaient étaient énormes!

You may like to add what used to happen in the decade of your own childhood using personal photos.

Unité 9 Pages 90–91

These two 'pages' of the visit look at past and future travel using cars and airships as illustrations.

9  [CD 3 track 8]

This text deals with solar and hydrogen-powered cars. Students find expressions in French which correspond to the English given. Questions ⬆6–8. require some deduction.

Transcript

Voyages. Avance: 2030.
La voiture de demain – quelques prévisions.
Dans 30 ans toutes les stations-service seront fermées parce qu'il n'y aura plus d'essence! On aura des voitures qui convertiront l'énergie du soleil en électricité. À l'avenir, il y aura beaucoup de voitures électriques et elles rouleront à une vitesse maximale de 200 km/h. En plus, elles ne pollueront pas l'environnement. Il y aura un problème – la nuit, il n'y a pas de soleil! Donc, on utilisera une batterie.

   Une autre sorte de voiture sera propulsée à l'hydrogène. Ce type de voiture aura certainement deux problèmes parce que l'hydrogène est très inflammable. Premièrement, la voiture sera une sorte de bombe roulante! Deuxièmement, il sera difficile de stocker l'hydrogène dans les stations-service à cause du danger.

Solution
   1 demain
   2 dans trente ans
   3 à l'avenir
   4 la nuit
   5 à cause du danger
 ⬆6 dans cinquante ans
 ⬆7 cause du soleil
 ⬆8 dans deux jours les magasins seront fermés

10 ✐

Students use the outline sentences to make predictions about the future, prefacing them with an expression of opinion. This is a pair-work exercise, in which partner B contradicts the statement made by partner A.

Solution

1 a Exemple: Moi, je pense que dans 20 ans il n'y aura plus d'essence. **B**: À mon avis, il n'y aura plus d'essence dans 40 ans.
   b Je pense qu'il n'y aura plus de plastiques dans 30 ans. **B**: À mon avis, il n'y a aura plus de plastiques dans 100 ans.
   c Je pense qu'il n'y aura plus de professeurs humains dans cinq ans. **B**: À mon avis, il n'y aura plus de professeurs humains dans 20 ans.
   d Je pense qu'il n'y aura plus de voitures à essence dans 10 ans. **B**: À mon avis, il n'y aura plus de voitures à essence dans 50 ans.
   e Je pense qu'il n'y aura plus de camions diesel dans 20 ans. **B**: À mon avis, il n'y aura plus de camions diesel dans 10 ans.

⬆Further examples may be possible depending on the ability of the students.

Tip

This refers students to page 119 for ways of expressing personal opinion. This would be a good point at which to revise as many ways as possible of expression of opinions, an important element at Higher Level GCSE.

Point grammaire: 'It will be'

Il sera + adjective + *de* + infinitive. This point is explained with two examples. The point is also made that the expression can be used in the present, although the imperfect is not touched on here, as students are not yet expected to use this tense actively.

11 ✐

Practice in working with sentences using the above construction, although the active work is in choosing the appropriate adjective to prove understanding of the context. (To keep the focus a bit simpler, no adjective agreement spelling changes are needed.)

Solution

   1 Il sera **difficile** de stocker de l'hydrogène parce que c'est très **inflammable**.
   2 Il sera **normal** d'acheter une voiture **électrique** – tout le monde en aura une.
   3 Il sera **possible** de faire un voyage **spatial** à la lune – si vous êtes **riche**!
   4 Il sera **facile** de faire les courses par Internet; il ne sera pas **nécessaire** d'être très **intelligent** pour faire ça!

12 [CD 3 track 9]

In this listening exercise, students note the technical details (length, load, gas, maximum speed, height of flight) of the Cargolifter, a futuristic airship. The photo should give students an idea of the craft.

Transcript

À l'avenir, il sera nécessaire d'avoir un moyen de transport économique et écologique. On aura . . . les dirigeables Cargolifter! Ces énormes ballons avanceront lentement (130 km/h), mais il sera facile de transporter de grosses charges. Le Cargolifter mesurera 260 mètres de long et il pourra transporter des charges de 160 tonnes. Il ne sera pas inflammable, parce qu'il sera rempli d'hélium et non pas d'hydrogène. Pour les passagers, il y aura de petites cabines. On traversera l'Atlantique en quelques jours. Il sera possible de dîner et en même temps d'observer la mer 200 mètres plus bas.

Solution
- Longueur: 260 m.
- Charge: 160 tonnes.
- Gaz: hélium.
- Vitesse maximale: 130 km/h.
- Hauteur du vol: 200 mètres.

Ça se dit comment? p.91 [CD 3 track 11]

The use of *y* as a vowel is covered here.

Transcript
- il y a, il y aura, l'hydrogène, l'oxygène
- Le scientifique myope combine l'oxygène et l'hydrogène.

Differentiation opportunity ⬇ ⬆

■ ⬇**DW9.1A** shows pictures of life today and life in the future. Students find the correct sentence for each picture. This entails recognition of both the present and future tenses.

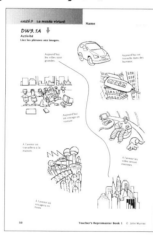

■ ⬆**DW9.1B** gives more able students an opportunity to say what will happen in the future, using *il sera possible de*. They write a caption for each of the pictures, choosing a verb from the box, e.g. *Il sera possible d'aller sur la Lune.*

Homework idea

Students could describe a journey from Britain to France in the future. They could be given futuristic transport terms such as: *l'hélibus, l'aérotrain, la voiture à propulsion magnétique, l'avion hypersonique*, and they could attempt to define such terms according to their imagination, e.g. *Un hélibus: ce sera un hélicoptère qui transportera beaucoup de passagers.* Such definitions offer a good opportunity to practise the relative pronoun *qui*.

Useful expressions could be: *on montera dans . . ., on descendra . . ., le voyage durera . . ., il sera possible de . . .*

13 [CD 3 track 10]

This short text gives some background information on the original Zeppelins. There are no comprehension questions, but students could be asked to identify imperfect verbs (see also page vii of this guide for extra exploitation ideas).

Transcript
Retour 1900/1937. Cliquez ici.
En 1900, le comte Zeppelin, un ingénieur allemand, a inventé une nouvelle sorte d'«avion» – c'était un énorme ballon propulsé.
Le saviez-vous?

- Les zeppelins flottaient dans l'air parce qu'ils étaient remplis d'hydrogène.
- Les plus grands zeppelins pouvaient porter jusqu'à 100 passagers.
- Pendant la première guerre mondiale (1914–18) les Allemands utilisaient des zeppelins pour bombarder l'Angleterre.
- En 1937 le plus grand zeppelin de tous, le «Hindenburg», a pris feu et 36 personnes sont mortes.

Point grammaire: The imperfect tense

The formation of the imperfect is outlined here. Only the singular endings and the third person plural are dealt with. It is not stated here that the basic form is the present tense *nous* form. This is perhaps best left until the whole of the tense forms of very irregular verbs have been covered. The fact that *être* is the only irregular verb in this tense is mentioned. Students could be reminded that they have been using *c'était* for a long time.

14

This is a discrimination exercise involving verbs in the future and in the imperfect. Students decide on the basis of the verb forms whether the facts given refer to 1950 or 2050.

Solution
1 2050; **2** 1950; **3** 2050; **4** 1950; **5** 1950; **6** 1950; **7** 2050

EGW9 Activity 1 provides more practice in distinguishing futures and imperfects (see notes on **EGW9** at the end of this unit).

15 [CD 3 track 12]

Students listen to three short texts in which a grandfather talks to his grand-daughter Céleste about motoring in the 1950s. The sentences all contain verbs in the imperfect. Students listen for detail.

Transcript
1 **Céleste:** Est-ce que tu avais une voiture à cette époque-là?
   Pépé: Oui, j'avais une Citroën, une vieille. Elle n'était pas très rapide, mais ... quand même ...
2 **Céleste:** Tu roulais à quelle vitesse, pépé?
   Pépé: À quelle vitesse? Alors je faisais du 70 kilomètres à l'heure ... maximum, hein?
3 **Céleste:** Tu allais au travail en voiture?
   Pépé: Oh non. J'allais au travail en autobus. Non, je sortais le dimanche après-midi ... après le, le déjeuner. Oui, je faisais des promenades en voiture ... avec mémé.

Solution
1 b; **2** a; **3** b; **4** b; **5** a

Unité 9 Pages 92–93

This 'page' of the *musée virtuel* deals with food and climate.

16 [CD 3 track 13]

This text deals with the production of food in the future. The term *génétiquement modifié* is introduced, as this is a topical issue rather than an item of GCSE vocabulary. Under Point grammaire Rappel, the full forms of the future of *aller* and *faire* are listed.

Transcript
L'alimentation. Avance: 2050. Cliquez ici.
Qu'est-ce qu'on mangera en l'an 2050? On mangera certainement des fruits, des légumes et de la viande génétiquement modifiés. Imaginez des pommes bleues, des carottes vertes ou un poulet à quatre pattes! On continuera à manger du pain, de la viande et du fromage comme aujourd'hui, mais ces produits ne contiendront pas de bactéries – est-ce qu'on sera plus sain?
    Et où est-ce qu'on fera les courses? Vous irez dans un supermarché? Non, parce qu'ils n'existeront pas. Vous utiliserez certainement Internet III, la nouvelle génération d'Internet. Vous commanderez tous vos achats par ordinateur et vous les paierez automatiquement avec une sorte de code électronique. Vos achats arriveront chez vous dans un caddy robotisé.

Solution
1 V; **2** F; **3** F; **4** V; **5** F

Tip

Draws attention to the fact that adverbs ending in *-ment* are usually placed immediately after the verb. Students could be given a series of sentences and a series of adverbs and asked to insert appropriate adverbs, e.g.

On utilisera une sorte de magasin virtuel.
On travaillera à la maison.
Nous recevrons du courrier électronique.
On voyagera sur la Lune.
probablement   régulièrement   certainement peut-être

You could remind students that this is the normal position for adverbs of frequency, e.g. *On ira souvent à l'étranger.* This knowledge is essential for **DW9.2**.

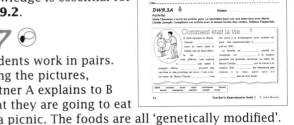

17

Students work in pairs. Using the pictures, partner A explains to B what they are going to eat on a picnic. The foods are all 'genetically modified'. Partner B chooses a positive, a neutral or a negative comment from the list.

Tip

Ça is explained as a useful word in spoken French. Further examples of its use could be:

Je n'aime pas ça.
Ça, c'est difficile.
Ça, c'est à moi, et ça, c'est à toi.

ICT activity (for average/lower attainers)

Learning objectives

- to use search strategies for an effective search on the Internet;
- to scan for key words in authentic materials;
- to understand partiality in information;
- to complete a gap-fill text on the arguments put forward by Greenpeace.

1 Teacher visits the website of Greenpeace (**www.greenpeace.fr**) and creates a gapped text to assess the comprehension of the main arguments.

2 Students visit the website and, using the key word OGM, find the solutions.

ICT activity (for higher attainers)

Learning objectives

- to use search strategies for an effective search on the Internet;
- to scan for key words in authentic materials;
- to understand partiality in information;
- to create a summary of pros and cons of GM foods.

1 Teacher directs the students to the sites of two major protagonists **www.monsanto.fr** and **www.greenpeace.fr**.

2 Using the key word OGM in their search, students should list down under the headings *pour* and *contre* some arguments supporting or opposing the principle of GM crops.

18 ⓠ ⓓ [CD 3 track 14]

The term *effet de serre* is introduced as being of topical interest rather than being GCSE vocabulary. (There is much more on environmental issues in Unit 13.)

As a preliminary to the listening, some vocabulary is given and students are asked to link two columns of nouns and adjectives, predicting what they will hear. Several solutions are possible.

Solution

dômes	enormes
êtres	humains
réservoirs	souterrains
plantes	tropicales
animaux	sauvages
organismes	génétiquement modifiés

Transcript

L'effet de serre

En 2040 il fera très chaud à cause de l'effet de serre. Certaines sections de la Terre seront recouvertes de dômes énormes dans lesquels les êtres humains vivront. Ici on cultivera des organismes génétiquement modifiés. Il est probable que l'eau sera très rare. On la gardera dans des réservoirs souterrains. On élèvera des animaux génétiquement modifiés (des vaches, par exemple). On cultivera des plantes tropicales. Il n'y aura plus de forêts tropicales, donc il y aura dans les dômes des parcs pour les animaux sauvages. Ici on trouvera des lions, des tigres, des zèbres, etc.

19

Pupils work in pairs to decide which animals go in which dome (desert, tropical, antarctic).

Solution

desert	**tropical**	**antarctic**
un chameau	un python	un morse
un âne	un tigre	un pélican
des fourmis	des fourmis	une baleine
un scorpion	un éléphant	un pingouin
	un piranha	

Differentiation opportunity ⬇ ⬆

⬆ Students prepare a presentation on a day in the life of a child of the future. They describe daily routine (*Charlotte se lèvera à . . .*), what they will eat and drink, how they will study, and what they will do for leisure.

⬇ Give the students the following starters:

Charlotte se lèvera à
(Au petit déjeuner) elle mangera
Elle travaillera
Elle jouera avec
Elle regardera
Elle ira
Elle portera

Some students may require the help of some additional nouns.

20 ⓠ [CD 3 track 15]

In this interview Alain Chasseur of Radio Corsaire talks to a 72-year-old woman, Marie-Claude Joseph, about food and shopping in 1950. Students decide whether the statements given are true or false.

Transcript

Alain Chasseur: Est-ce que vous faisiez les courses avec votre mère?

Marie-Claude: Oui, nous allions en ville tous les jours. A cette époque-là il n'y avait pas de supermarchés, donc on allait à l'épicerie faire ses achats.

Alain Chasseur: Votre mère préparait le pain chez vous?

Marie-Claude: Ah non. Non, jamais. Elle allait tous les jours à la boulangerie . . .

Alain Chasseur: Vous étiez une grande famille?

Marie-Claude: Oui, nous étions sept – j'avais deux sœurs et trois frères. Le dimanche toute la famille déjeunait ensemble.

Alain Chasseur: Et qu'est-ce que vous buviez au déjeuner, le dimanche?

Marie-Claude: Ben, du vin . . . normalement du vin de table, du vin rouge . . . mais pas les enfants, hein? Nous, on buvait de l'eau ou de la limonade.

Alain Chasseur: Et à cette époque, votre famille était riche?

Marie-Claude: Riche? Ah, non! Ça alors! Non, on était très pauvres. Mais maman faisait des efforts. On mangeait bien le dimanche.

Solution

1 a non; **b** non; **c** oui; **d** non; **e** non

2 a Il n'y avait pas de supermarchés.
  b Elle allait à la boulangerie.
  d On buvait du vin rouge.
  e Ils étaient pauvres/La famille était pauvre/On était pauvres.

Point grammaire: The imperfect tense

Although the *nous* form of the present has not been indicated as the basis for the imperfect, students now have sufficient information to work out how to translate the test sentence.

21

Match answers to questions, based on the above interview with Mme Joseph.

Solution

1 c; **2** a; **3** e; **4** b; **5** d

22

Students complete the questions and the answers of the interview, using the *nous* and *vous* forms of the imperfect.

Solution

Alain: Vous buviez du vin?
Marie-Claude: Non, nous buvions de l'eau minérale.
Alain: Vous alliez (faisiez vos courses) au supermarché?
Marie-Claude: Non, nous allions (faisions nos courses) à l'épicerie
Alain: Vous mangiez des gâteaux?
Marie-Claude: Non, nous ne mangions pas de gâteaux.

Unité 9 Pages 94–95

These two 'pages' of the *musée virtuel* focus mainly on what everyday life in France used to be like, concentrating on the imperfect tense but also practising negative constructions.

EGW9 practises these points (see full notes on **EGW9** at the end of this unit).

23 [CD 3 track 16]

This text outlines life in France in 1950. Some vocabulary is given.

Presentation idea

Preliminary work could involve revision of household appliances, e.g. *lave-linge, lave-vaisselle, four à micro-ondes.* Revise the names of the appliances using **CM48** as an OHT. Then place small OHTs one at a time on the OHP showing clothes, food (**CM60**), CD, video-cassette, etc. Ask students to produce sentences such as *Il faut utiliser le lave-linge.*

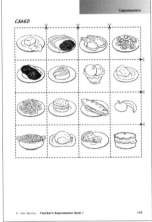

Students read the text and find the expressions listed. Questions **7** and **8** are ⬆ as they involve deduction and extension.

Transcript

Retour 1950. À la maison.

Comment est-ce qu'on vivait en France en 1950? En général, les maisons étaient froides – il n'y avait pas de chauffage central. Donc, il fallait acheter du charbon pour le feu, devant lequel on prenait un bain – il y avait peu de baignoires ou de douches. Le téléphone était assez rare, et il n'y avait que 1% des Français qui possédaient la télévision. Elle était en noir et blanc, bien sûr! Dans la cuisine, huit Français sur 100 avaient un lave-linge, et sept sur 100 avaient un réfrigérateur. Oui, on avait des radios et des fers à repasser électriques, mais on devait travailler 45 heures par semaine pour acheter de tels produits. On n'avait que deux semaines de vacances et 75% des Français ne partaient jamais en vacances. Ah, le bon vieux temps!

Solution

1 en général
2 il fallait acheter du charbon
3 il y avait peu de baignoires
4 assez rare
5 8% des Français
6 le bon vieux temps
⬆**7** on devait travailler 10 heures par jour
⬆**8** peu de Français avait le téléphone

24 ✐✎

Preliminary work could involve practice with verbs which show no irregularity in the imperfect. Using **CM50** as an OHT, students (or teacher) choose a subject (black stripes on the dartboard are subjects) and a verb (white stripes are verbs) and make a complete sentence.

To make it more difficult, the sentences could be negative and involve *ne . . . pas* or *ne . . . jamais*.

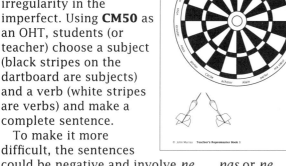

Possible solution

1 Nous **avions** un **téléphone**, mais nous n'**avions** pas de **portable**.
2 Je **prenais** un **bain**; je ne **prenais** pas de **douche**.
3 Ma mère n'**avait** pas de **lave-linge**.
4 On **écoutait** la **radio**, mais on ne **regardait** pas la **télévision**.
⬆5 Nous n'**allions** jamais en **vacances**.
⬆6 Mon père n'**avait** qu'**un vélo** – il n'**avait** pas de **voiture**.

Tip

Draws attention to the need to put the two parts of the negative on either side of the verb in the imperfect, as in the present.

Presentation idea

Students could practise this by using a simple drill, converting present tenses to imperfects.

Students must listen carefully to see if *ne . . . pas* or *ne . . . jamais* is used.

- *Nous n'allons pas en vacances (Nous n'allions pas en vacances).*
- *Nous n'allons jamais en vacances.*
- *On ne part pas en vacances.*
- *On ne reste jamais à la maison.*
- *Mon père n'a pas de voiture.*
- *Ma mère n'achète jamais de gâteaux.*

With *ne . . . que*, students could practise using the following drill:

- *On achetait du pain et des gâteaux? (Non, on n'achetait que du pain.)*
- *On achetait des journaux et des magazines?*
- *On mangeait des légumes et de la viande?*
- *On écoutait la radio et le tourne-disques?*
- *On avait le feu et un four à micro-ondes?*

ICT activity

Learning objectives

- to reuse the imperfect in a different context.

1 As a class, build up a profile of what families do/eat/watch today. Students create a word-processed file of the statements.
2 For homework they ask their parents/ grandparents what they did/ate/watched/ listened to when they were young.
3 They then amend the file by changing the verbs into the imperfect and adding any other information necessary.

25 🎧 [CD 3 track 17]

Students listen to Gérard who describes what he had to take to school with him. Students should first be made aware that there are some negatives in the text (e.g. *Il n'y avait pas de règles en plastique*) and that they should listen for the contrasting item (e.g. *une règle en bois*). There is also an example of the present tense. This excludes certain contemporary items.

Transcript

Gérard: Quand j'étais au collège, c'était très différent . . . hein? Par exemple, on avait une ardoise, sur laquelle on écrivait. Quand j'allais au collège, je devais mettre dans mon sac tout ce dont j'avais besoin . . . par exemple . . . un stylo . . . de l'encre . . . un crayon . . . une règle. Il n'y avait pas de règles en plastique à cette époque-là . . . ah non. J'utilisais une règle en bois et puis euh . . . il fallait avoir une gomme. Et pour tout ça, j'avais un porte-plumes en bois . . . c'était assez lourd . . . et puis je mettais mes livres et mon cahier de maths . . . et on n'avait pas de calculette, hein? Ah non . . . il fallait faire tous les calculs de tête, quoi? Aujourd'hui vous avez des crayons de couleur, des feutres, des bics . . . quand j'étais jeune, on n'avait pas ça . . . non . . . la vie était beaucoup plus simple.

Solution

b, c, d, f, g, h, i, j, k

26 📖 [CD 3 track 18]

Students read a text outlining school life in 1950. Some vocabulary is given. Having read the text students match the figures to the facts that they represent.

Transcript

Au collège. Retour 1950.

Il y a 50 ans l'école était obligatoire jusqu'à 14 ans. À cet âge-là on passait un examen qui s'appelait *le certificat d'études*. La majorité des enfants quittaient alors l'école. Il était difficile de continuer sa scolarité: seulement 20% des jeunes entraient au lycée à l'âge de 15 ans. Dans les classes, on ne parlait pas. Les professeurs étaient très stricts et ils punissaient les élèves qui ne travaillaient pas. Les journées étaient très longues – on finissait à 17h30 – et il y avait toujours beaucoup de devoirs. Heureusement, les vacances aussi étaient longues – 185 jours au total!

Solution

15	À cet âge on entrait au lycée.
14	À cet âge on quittait l'école.
185	Jours de vacances.
20	Pourcentage des élèves qui entraient au lycée.
17h30	Heure à laquelle les cours finissaient.

Having completed the table, students could comment on these facts and figures using *c'était* e.g.

15 ans, c'était assez jeune.

Point grammaire: Finir/punir

Attention is drawn to the fact that the imperfect is actually based on the *nous* form of the present. Verbs whose infinitives end in *-ir* (*finir* conjugation, not *sortir*) retain the *-iss-* in the middle. There is one example of this in the text (*les professeurs punissaient . . .*).

Differentiation opportunity⬇⬆

⬇**DW9.3A** and ⬆**DW9.3B** could be used here.

■ On ⬇**DW9.3A** students complete a gapped text based on Alain Chasseur's interview with Marie-Claude Joseph. The imperfect verbs to go in the gaps are supplied in a box below the text.

Solution

A cette époque-là, Marie-Claude **vivait** avec sa mère dans la vieille cité de Saint-Malo. La vie **était** très difficile. Les enfants n'**avaient** pas assez à manger. «Nous **mangions** souvent des carottes et des pommes de terre. C'est tout.» La mère de Marie-Claude **allait** tous les jours à la boulangerie pour acheter du pain. Les supermarchés n'**existaient** pas en 1950.

La famille ne **partait** jamais en vacances. On **restait** à la maison pendant les grandes vacances.

La mère de Marie-Claude **faisait** tout le travail à la maison. Elle **lavait** les vêtements des enfants à la main, parce qu'il n'y **avait** pas de lave-linge.

■ ⬆**DW9.3B** shows Alain's notes. Students write up the finished article.

Tip

This points out that material of which an object is made requires *en* in French: *en plastique*, etc. You practise this by giving students other materials and ask them to name an item made of it:

en laine, en cuir, en coton, en verre, en caoutchouc, en carton, en acier, en fer.

They could then list the items that they need for school, plus the material that they are made of, or give a list of the things that they keep in that untidy drawer full of junk that every teenager has in their bedroom!

27 🎧✏️⬆

Students are asked to write about the past and the future using negatives. This exercise brings together the future and the imperfect. Students provide a contrast in spoken or written form to the sentence.

Possible solution

1 En 2050 les professeurs ne pourront plus punir les élèves.
2 En 1950 on lisait beaucoup de livres.
3 En 1950 les vacances étaient très longues.
4 En 1950 on avait des professeurs humains (ou presque!).
5 En 2050 elle finira à midi.
6 En 2050 on ne portera rien, parce qu'on n'aura pas de cartable.
7 En 2050 on écrira tout sur ordinateur.
8 En 2050 on choisira les matières à étudier.

Homework opportunity

Students research the life of famous people, e.g. pop stars, footballers, scientists, writers to find out what their school life was like. They comment on their strengths and weaknesses:

X aimait . . .
Il/Elle n'aimait pas . . .
Il/Elle était fort(e) en . . .
Il/Elle était faible en . . .
Son professeur de . . . était excellent / nul . . .

The whole could be illustrated in the form of a strip cartoon and mounted as a wall display.

Unité 9 Pages 96–97

Checkpoints

Test

The **Test** checks students' skills in the grammatical goals of the unit:

- using the future tense
- saying what will be possible, necessary, etc.
- using the imperfect tense
- using negatives: *ne . . . plus, ne . . . jamais*
- using *ne . . . que*

Solution

1 a Beaucoup de gens **travailleront** à la maison en 2010. [1]
  b On **parlera** avec ses copains sur vidéophone. [1]
  c Nous **regarderons** des images en 3-D. [1]
  d Des astronautes **partiront** pour Mars. [1]
  e Moi, je **vivrai** dans une maison «intelligente». [1]
2 a Dans 50 ans, le monde **sera** complètement différent. [1]
  b Nous **pourrons** choisir le sexe de nos bébés. [1]
  c Il y **aura** certainement moins de voitures à essence. [1]
  d Moi, j'**achèterai** un vidéophone le plus tôt possible. [1]
  e Mes enfants **iront** peut-être sur la lune. [1]
3 a Nous aurons la possibilité de visiter d'autres planètes. **A** [1]
  b Nous n'avions pas la télévision à cette époque-là. **P** [1]
  c Mon père travaillait 12 heures par jour. **P** [1]
  d Les enfants pourront étudier chez eux. **A** [1]
  e On voyageait rarement en dirigeable. **P** [1]
  f Mon frère ira certainement en Australie. **A** [1]
  g Moi, je n'allais jamais en vacances. **P** [1]
4 a Nous habitions à Lille à cette époque-là. [1]
  b Mon père savait conduire. [1]
  c Moi, je voulais visiter l'Angleterre. [1]
  d Au collège on faisait beaucoup de devoirs. [1]
  e Mes parents étaient assez pauvres. [1]
5 Any five sentences correctly combining the elements given. [10]
6 a En 1950, on ne voyait jamais de films en 3-D. [2]
  b En 1950, on n'avait jamais la possibilité de manger des légumes artificiels. [2]
  c En 1950, on ne pouvait pas faire ses cours à la maison. [2]
⬆7 a En 2050, nous **n'**aurons **plus** de voitures à essence. [2]
  b En 2050, on **ne** restera **plus** chez soi pendant les vacances. [2]
  c En 2050, nous **ne** ferons **plus** nos achats dans un magasin. [2]
⬆8 a Non, je n'achèterai **que** deux livres. [2]
  b Non, je ne prendrai **qu'**un gâteau. [2]
  c Non, je ne regarderai **qu'**un film samedi. [2]
Total [50]

Quiz

The **Quiz** checks students' knowledge acquired in the unit, about:

- communications, past and future
- solar cars
- airships
- Internet shopping
- future foods
- home life, past and future
- education, past and future

Solution

1 dirigeable [1]
2 Any two of: l'ordinateur, la télévision, l'appareil-photo, la console de jeux. [2]
3 a électricité [1]
  b 200 km/h [1]
4 a l'hydrogène [1]
  b inflammable; difficile à stocker [2]
5 c dirigeable [1]
6 Sa charge maximale sera de 160 tonnes. [1]
7 C'est le comte Zeppelin qui a inventé le dirigeable. [1]
8 génétiquement modifié [1]
9 sur ordinateur/sur Internet [2]
10 • 1% avaient la télévision. [1]
  • 7% avaient un réfrigérateur. [1]
  • 8% avaient un lave-linge. [1]
11 En 1950, on avait deux semaines de vacances. [1]
12 En 1950, on quittait le collège à 15 ans. [1]
13 20% des élèves entraient au lycée. [1]
Total [20]

Projets

A Students interview an older person to find out what life was like when they were young. Since this will be done in English, students should prepare questions involving verbs which they can then manipulate in French, e.g. play, eat, drink, watch, go, get up, go to bed, leave, work, return. They then write up their findings using the third person of the verbs, e.g. *Mon grand-père se levait à 6 heures. Il allait au collège à pied.*

B Students imagine what life will be like for their own grandchildren. They could use the same verbs as in the above task. They could use subjects such as *mes petits-enfants, ils* and *on.* Remind students about the necessary verb endings for these subjects.

C Students research a classic or historic plane or car, and write a description of it, giving technical details.

D Students express their preference for the past or the future. They could begin their work with the sentence *Je préfère la vie au passé/à l'avenir, parce que …* The subject of the verbs could be *on.* For life in the future, the subject could be *nous.* Remind students to choose the correct set of endings (imperfect or future) according to their choice of time.

EGW9 teaching notes

EGW9 provides extra grammar/homework on the future and imperfect tenses and on negative constructions.

Activity 1

This consists of two texts in which imperfect and future sentences are interwoven. Students simply identify the 'past' sentences by underlining them.

Solution

<u>Il y a soixante ans mon grand-père était un jeune homme.</u> <u>Il habitait à la campagne avec ses parents et il travaillait dans une ferme voisine.</u> Dans vingt ans il n'y aura plus de voitures à essence. <u>Il y allait six jours sur sept, mais le dimanche il allait à l'église et il se reposait.</u> Nous verrons certainement des voitures à hydrogène ou des véhicules électriques. <u>Le soir, il n'y avait pas grand'chose à faire, mais on écoutait la radio et on jouait aux cartes.</u> Tout le monde aura un ordinateur et il sera possible de travailler à la maison. Donc, il ne sera pas nécessaire de voyager souvent. <u>Quelquefois les jeunes hommes sortaient avec les jeunes filles du village.</u> Peut-être qu'on fera des excursions en autocar électrique. Si on veut voir le monde, on aura la possibilité de regarder la télévision holographique avec des images en trois dimensions. <u>On ne gagnait pas beaucoup d'argent, et la vie était assez dure.</u> Ce sera vraiment passionnant.

Activity 2

This is based on an interview with Alain Chasseur's grandmother; students fill the gaps by completing imperfect verbs (stems are given).

- Grand-mère, quand tu ét**ais** jeune, qu'est-ce que tu aim**ais** faire?
- Ben, quand j'ét**ais** petite, nous aim**ions** aller au parc. On jou**ait** avec nos petites copines, on parl**ait** avec les adultes.
- Et le dimanche?
- Le dimanche, c'ét**ait** toujours l'église, quoi? Nous y all**ions** chaque dimanche. Et nous ne pouv**ions** pas jouer. Nous dev**ions** lire ou aider maman à préparer le déjeuner.

Activity 3

This requires students to match an appropriate ending to five sentence openers. There is sometimes more than one logical choice.

Solution

1 Quand j'étais jeune, j'allais souvent au cinéma, mais maintenant je n'y vais plus (*or* mais maintenant je n'aime que les documentaires; *or*, mais à l'avenir ce ne sera plus possible).
2 Il y a 50 ans il était possible de voyager librement sur les routes, mais à l'avenir ce ne sera plus possible.
3 J'aimais regarder les films, mais maintenant je n'aime que les documentaires.
4 Notre maison n'était pas grande, nous n'avions que quatre pièces (*or* nous n'avions pas assez d'espace).
5 Nous détestons les grandes villes, et donc nous n'allons jamais à la capitale.

unité 10
Allons-y! L'île Maurice

Background information on Mauritius

Mauritius is an independent state in the Indian Ocean. It consists of the islands of Mauritius and Rodrigues and some smaller dependencies. This unit concentrates on the island of Mauritius.

Mauritius was first 'discovered' by Arab explorers and was then visited by the Portuguese. It was the Portuguese who gave the name *dodo* to the island's most famous inhabitant, a large bird the size of a swan. This bird was so tame that it had no fear of Man. It was hunted to extinction. It was the Dutch who first settled on the island, giving it the name of a Dutch governor, Prince Mauritius van Nassau. The French claimed the island in 1715, giving it the name *Île de France*. During the 18th century many immigrant Indian workers came to the island, which fell into the hands of the British in 1810. It remained a British colony until 1968, when it became independent. It became a republic in 1992.

The present-day population is multi-ethnic with people of European, African, Indian and Chinese origin. The island has an image of harmonious multi-culturalism, but this picture hides underlying problems which exist between peoples of different faiths. The language most widely used is Creole, although the official language is English. French is widely spoken. The currency is the rupee (*la roupie*).

Mauritius has expanded its tourist industry greatly over the last decade and luxury hotels have sprung up along sea-fronts. This has sometimes led to friction with locals who no longer have access to the beaches.

Mauritius enjoys a tropical climate, and the fauna and flora are truly extraordinary, many species being unique to the island.

Unité 10 Pages 98–99
Point d'info

[CD 3 track 19]

This gives some basic information on the island. You may wish to expand on this orally by using the above information or use **CM51**, which is a slightly simplified French version of the above text. This could be used in various ways (see notes for the French text on Quebec on page 47).

The Student's Book has a small map of the island showing the principal towns, but **CM52** provides a larger, more detailed map.

Transcript
Point d'info

Vous allez visiter la belle île Maurice – un paradis tropical avec ses plages, ses forêts et ses montagnes. Elle est située dans l'Océan Indien, au sud de l'équateur et au nord du Tropique du Capricorne. Ancienne colonie française, l'île Maurice est devenue une République en 1992. On y parle anglais, français, hindi, tamil et chinois, mais la langue principale c'est le créole, une sorte de dialecte du français. La population est un peu plus d'un million d'habitants. La monnaie à l'île Maurice, c'est la roupie.

1

Students examine the map and work out the anagrams for the main towns.

Solution

1 PORT-LOUIS; **2** FLIC EN FLAC; **3** SOUILLAC; **4** CUREPIPE; **5** VACOAS; **6** TRIOLET

2

Working in pairs, students look at the advertisements for means of transport to get around the island (which is about 35 miles long by 25 miles wide). They have a budget of 8,000 rupees for transport for the week. They decide what type of transport to use in accordance with this budget. If they chose the helicopter for one day, they may have to make some decisions on savings.

Point d'info

This box adds some information about the climate.

The summer in Mauritius is hot, with temperatures up to 30º C (86º F). The humidity is intense. The winter is warm with average temperatures of 24º C (75º F). The rainy season is from January to May. Mauritius experiences the occasional cyclone.

Transcript
Point d'info: le climat

En été, il fait très chaud – la température moyenne est de 30º C. En hiver il fait moins chaud (24º). En janvier et en février il y a quelquefois des cyclones.

Extra idea

In view of the information on the climate and the picture in the book, students could decide what clothes to take with them. They should remember to include some more formal clothes for going out to restaurants, hotels, etc.

 3

Students read the text on leisure activities available on Mauritius and link the pictures to the text.

Solution

1 g; **2** f; **3** d; **4** a, c; **5** b; **6** e

 4

Students predict what they are likely to see at each of the destinations recommended by the Tourist Office for the various days of their stay.

Solution

lundi – 3; **mardi** – 5; **mercredi** – 1; **jeudi** – 2; **vendredi** – 4

 5

Students decide on a list of activities to undertake during their stay. For each day of the week, they list an activity or a place to visit.

Extra idea

This could be turned into pair work or group work once the initial lists have been drawn up. Students could suggest going to a place or doing an activity and others could agree or disagree, expressing agreement: (*Bon, OK, D'accord*) or suggesting alternatives: (*Moi, je préférerais, On pourrait, Si on allait,* etc.)

ICT activity

Learning objectives

- to write for a different audience using familiar language in a new context;
- to draft and redraft to improve accuracy.

1 Using the information available students word-process an article on their experiences on the island.
2 They should include graphics to illustrate.

The teacher suggests to the student what is incorrect in their first version and the students redraft.

Unité 10 Pages 100–101

Students read and listen to a potted history of Mauritius.

 6 [CD 3 track 20]

Students assign the correct flags representing the colonising countries/peoples to the various centuries listed. A key is given which clarifies the meaning of *drapeau* as well as identifying the less easily recognised flags.

Preliminary work could involve general revision of European flags (see Unit 6 page 52) and colours. Students could describe flags and ask others to say which flag is being described. Useful vocabulary would be: *raie, vertical, horizontal, en diagonale* and the colour words.

Transcript

Petite histoire de l'île Maurice

L'île Maurice a été découverte en 975 par Hasan Ibn Ali, explorateur iranien. Il est probable que les Portugais ont visité l'île Maurice pendant le 15e siècle. Pendant le seizième siècle, des pirates utilisaient les ports naturels de l'île. Après, ce sont les Hollandais qui l'ont occupée pendant le 17e siècle. Le nom Maurice, c'est celui du Prince Maurice de Nassau, le gouverneur des Pays-Bas. C'est en septembre 1715 que les Français sont arrivés. Ils sont restés jusqu'en 1810. C'est en septembre de cette année-là que les Anglais ont envahi l'île Maurice. La république est devenue indépendante en 1968.

Solution

1 f; **2** g; **3** c; **4** b; **5** a; **6** e; **7** d

 *7* [CD 3 track 21]

Students read and listen to a text on the dodo. They decide whether the sentences apply to the dodo or not.

As outlined in the text on the Student's Book page, this bird was about the size of a swan and had a large curved beak (see the picture in the Student's Book). It had no fear of man, and was generally clubbed to death by hunters and eaten. The bird was extinct by 1680. A skeleton may be seen in the Natural History Museum in London.

In case students want to know – the expression 'as dead as a dodo' is translated as *'tout ce qu'il y a de plus mort'*.

Transcript

Le dodo

L'île Maurice est connue pour le dodo, mais, malheureusement, vous ne pourrez plus en voir aujourd'hui, car le dodo a disparu. Quand les Portugais sont arrivés à l'île Maurice, il n'y avait pas d'habitants sur l'île. Ils ont trouvé ce gros oiseau qui était incapable de voler. Le pauvre oiseau n'avait pas peur des hommes. Les Portugais en ont mangé beaucoup. Ils l'ont appelé *dodo*, c'est-à-dire,«stupide».

Solution

1 Non. **2** Non. **3** Non. **4** Oui. **5** Non. **6** Non.

 8

Students guess which is worth most: a Mauritius two-penny deep blue stamp; flight tickets to Mauritius; or four contemporary Mauritius stamps.

Mauritius enjoyed one of the earliest postal services and issued its first stamps in 1847. Of the orange one-penny stamp, there are 15 examples in existence. There are only 12 of the deep blue two-penny stamps known to exist. As of October 2000, the value of this stamp is £550 000 (Source: Stanley Gibbons, London).

Solution

Picture 1, the old two-penny blue stamp.

Extra ideas

Without telling the students the value of the two-penny blue, you could 'auction' the stamp, either in pounds or euros, putting a reserve price of its true value on it. This would give students practice with high numbers, asking them to increase their bids until they reach the reserve price.

At this point you might like to use **CM53** with **CM52**. **CM53** is a quiz on Mauritius.

Answers are below and on the map on **CM52**. Students complete the answers, the initial letters of which spell out an important town.

Solution

Pamplemousses
Oiseau
Réserve
Timbre
Lac
Océan
U
Ile
Souillac
Port Louis

 9

Students decode some ingredients for a Mauritian chicken dish. In the recipe given in the unit, the hot ingredients have been toned down slightly (the original had four cloves of garlic and two chilli peppers, so reinstate if you wish) and the instructions simplified. The decoded words give the names of the spices in French.

10

Students now match the spices to their English equivalents.

Solution to 9 and 10

1 gousse d'ail = clove of garlic.
2 massala = massala.
3 gingembre = ginger.
4 curcuma = turmeric.
5 piment = chilli powder.
6 coriandre = coriander.

 11

The students match the appropriate pictures to the cooking instructions.

Solution

1 c; **2** b; **3** f; **4** e; **5** g; **6** a; **7** d

You could round off the unit by giving students a copy of **CM54**, which is a wordsearch using 16 items of vocabulary from the unit.

Possible projects/ coursework

• Students could try the Mauritian chicken recipe for themselves, either at home, or as part of a food technology course. To use the recipe as it stands without a translation is, of course, the most authentic exercise that they could carry out and the recipe is absolutely delicious!

• Students could use information from tourist offices or the Internet to prepare a brochure on Mauritius. They could concentrate on one particular aspect, such as tourism or wildlife. Philatelists could have a field day!

Further information

Additional information on Mauritius may be found on:

http://perso.wanadoo.fr/
http://www.multimania.com/
http://www.mauritius-island.net

unité 11
Un week-end à Paris

Contexts
- shopping in Paris's famous department stores
- fashion
- finding your way around
- major places to visit
- historical events in Paris
- eating out

Grammar
- using the conditional
- using the imperfect tense
- using contrasting past tenses
- using adverbs to say 'enough', 'too'
- recognising the pluperfect tense

Pronunciation
- '-w-'
- '-ail-'

Revision
- using irregular adjectives: *beau, nouveau, vieux*
- using the perfect tense
- using the present of irregular verbs
- describing a sequence of events
- superlatives and agreement

Unité 11 Page 102

Presentation idea
This unit examines some of the historic and modern places to visit in Paris and introduces the contrast between the perfect and imperfect tenses. The opening page shows photos of some of the well-known sites of Paris and explains what a tourist might do when visiting the capital.

Some students may have visited Paris and some may have heard of the more famous sights. To prepare for this lesson, gather any photos or postcards of Paris that you or they may have for demonstration purposes. Alternatively, Citybreaks brochures from a local travel agent will include images of several major places.

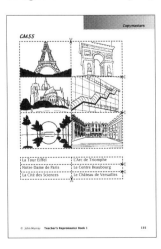 

You could also use **CM55** and **CM56** as OHTs and either elicit or explain the names of these monuments. They are:

CM55: 1 La tour Eiffel **2** L'Arc de Triomphe **3** Notre-Dame de Paris **4** Le Centre Beaubourg **5** La Cité des Sciences **6** Le château de Versailles

CM56: 7 Le Forum des Halles **8** la Grande Arche de la Défense **9** L'Opéra Bastille **10** La Pyramide du Louvre **11** Le Louvre **12** La Conciergerie

Read and listen to the introductory text.

Transcript [CD 3 track 22]
Paris! La capitale de la France
Paris: ville moderne, ville historique. Avec ses monuments, ses parcs, son architecture – historique et futuriste – Paris est peut-être la plus belle ville d'Europe. Pour les touristes, c'est le paradis. On peut visiter les musées et les expositions, se promener dans les parcs, acheter des cadeaux dans les plus beaux magasins du monde, manger dans un restaurant de luxe, danser dans une boîte de nuit.

1  [CD 3 track 23]
Students listen to the Férien family deciding what to do during their weekend in Paris. They hear a number of expressions which are in the conditional. These are dealt with in the Tip. Before playing the cassette, ask students to read the Tip, and to listen for the expressions

Transcript
Maman: Moi, je voudrais visiter le château de Versailles. C'est un des plus beaux châteaux de France.

Rachel: Ah, non, pas un château! Les châteaux sont toujours si barbants. C'est toujours vieux, vieux, vieux!

Papa: Ça ne m'intéresse pas non plus, mais toi, tu peux y aller, chérie.

Rachel: Et qu'est-ce qu'on va faire, nous deux, alors?

Papa: On pourrait aller à la Cité des Sciences. Qu'en penses-tu?

Rachel: Bof! OK, si ça te dit.

Maman: Bon, moi j'aimerais aussi aller aux Galeries Lafayette. J'adore les grands magasins!

Rachel: Moi, aussi. On pourrait acheter toutes sortes de choses.

Papa: D'accord. Moi, je vais acheter un souvenir de Paris là-bas.

Rachel: Et la Tour Eiffel? Nous devons y aller!

Papa: Ah oui. Mais maman souffre du vertige.

Maman: Pas de problème. Je voudrais bien y aller, mais je ne vais pas monter. Ah, ça, non!

Rachel: Mais moi, je vais y monter . . . même si j'ai le vertige.

Papa: Et l'Arc de Triomphe. Ça vous intéresse?

Maman: Moi, non. Je préférerais faire du shopping.

Rachel: Alors moi, j'aimerais y aller.

Papa: Moi aussi. Et Notre-Dame de Paris . . . vous voulez y aller?

Maman: Non. On n'aura pas le temps d'y aller, en fin de compte.

Rachel: Notre-Dame? La cathédrale? Moi, je ne veux pas y aller.

Papa: Moi non plus. Bon, pas de problème. On n'y va pas.

Solution

1 maman; **2** papa et Rachel; **3** maman, papa et Rachel; **4** maman, papa et Rachel; **5** papa et Rachel; **6** personne

Ça se dit comment? p.102 [CD 3 track 24]

Points out that the letter *w* has two pronunciations.

Transcript

– le week-end, le Walkman, le Web
– le wagon, le wagon-restaurant, le WC
– William a passé le week-end dans le WC du wagon-restaurant à écouter son Walkman.

Tip

Students have now heard a number of expressions using the conditional tense. These are:

Moi, je voudrais	I'd like to
Moi, j'aimerais	I'd like to
Moi, je préférerais	I'd prefer to
J'aimerais mieux	I'd prefer to
On pourrait	we could

There is no need to explain these as being in the conditional at this point. Students will meet this tense in Unit 12, at which point you could refer back to these expressions.

Practise these with an OHT of **CM55** and/or **CM56**, asking for suggestions as to where students would like to go.

Extra idea

This would be a good moment to revise *au, à la, à l'* and *aux*. You could use the places listed in task 1 as illustrations of this grammatical point, e.g. *Je voudrais aller **au** château de Versailles.*

2

Students now use the conditional expressions to carry out a structured pair-work discussion on what they would like to visit in Paris. They can model most of what they say on the dialogue they have just heard, and could be given additional support by being reminded to use the list of places in task 1. Alternatively, as a prompt, one partner could have a copy of **CM55** and the other a copy of **CM56**. The role-play may work better if students are told to decide in advance on, say, three sites, given the preferences allocated to *personne A* and *personne B*.

Unité 11 Page 103

This page introduces la Cité des Sciences. Full details can be found on the official website: **www.cite-sciences.fr**

Transcript [CD 3 track 25]
La Cité des Sciences

C'est samedi matin et la famille Férien va à la Cité des Sciences. Située au Parc de la Villette, la Cité vous offre la possibilité d'explorer la science. Ici vous avez des expositions permanentes – du vieux sous-marin *Argonaute* aux nouvelles découvertes de l'exploration spatiale. Dans la Géode, immense boule de verre, vous pouvez regarder de très beaux films sur la nature et l'univers. Dans la section Explora, vous pouvez explorer les technologies actuelles et l'environnement.

Extra idea

There is no task directly exploiting this short text (its main linguistic purpose is to exemplify the irregular adjectives in the Tip), but you could check comprehension orally by asking the following questions once students have had time to read and/or listen to the text:

- *Qui va à la Cité des Sciences?*
- *Ils vont à la Cité des Sciences le dimanche?*
- *Qu'est-ce qu'on peut explorer à la Cité des Sciences?*
- *L'Argonaute, c'est un avion? une voiture? un bateau?*
- *C'est quoi, la Géode?*
- *Qu'est-ce qu'il y a dans la section Explora?* etc.

Point grammaire

This revises the irregular forms of *beau*, *nouveau* and *vieux*. Examples of these adjectives are to be found in the above text, and a short exercise alongside gives students the opportunity to decide which is the correct form required.

Differentiation opportunities ⬇ ⬆

■ ⬇**DW11.1A** requires students simply to match captions containing irregular adjectives to events on posters. Once this has been done, attention could be drawn to the adjectives and they could be linked to their basic form by way of a reminder.

■ **DW11.1B** requires students to complete gapped captions with the correct form of irregular adjectives and to assign the captions to the correct posters.

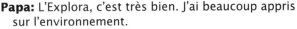

Students choose the correct form of the adjective.

Solution

1 nouvelle
2 vieux
3 belle
4 nouveau
5 vieil
6 vieilles, belle

Students decide on which level they would find the items depicted.

Solution

a 1; **b** 2; **c** 1; **d** 2; **e** 1; **f** 2; **g** 1; **h** 2; **i** 2

Extra idea

Ask students to say what else they might find under each category. They could recycle *On pourrait*, e.g. *On pourrait y trouver des animaux et des plantes.*

5 🎧 [CD 3 track 26]

Presentation idea

Intonation plays an important part in our being able to interpret the attitude of a speaker. Try saying a few sentences whose meaning may not be clear but whose import is clear from your tone of voice. Students give you the thumbs-up or thumbs-down sign according to whether what you are saying is positive or negative. They do not need to understand the meaning of these sentences, merely the attitude.

• *Ah! Comme il fait beau aujourd'hui.*
• *Que je suis malheureux/se! J'ai la déprime.*
• *Je trouve qu'il n'est pas juste qu'on doive payer des impôts.*
• *Je me fais une fête d'aller à ce concert.*

Students listen to the recording and decide whether the opinions expressed are good or bad. Less able students could simply write a tick or a cross accordingly. More able students could attempt to write down the expressions used to express these opinions.

Transcript

Papa: Quelle visite, Rachel! La Géode, c'est super!
Rachel: Oui, c'est extra! Le film était vraiment intéressant.

Papa: L'Explora, c'est très bien. J'ai beaucoup appris sur l'environnement.
Rachel: Ah, non, l'Explora, c'est moche. Je préfère voir tout cela à la télé.
Papa: Moi, je ne suis pas d'accord. Et que penses-tu de la Cité des Enfants, hein? C'est extra, à mon avis. Tu ne trouves pas?
Rachel: Ben, non. C'est pour les petits. Ce n'est pas le pied, tu sais, quand on est ado.

Solutions

	Papa	**Rachel**
La Géode?	C'est super!	C'est extra!
L'Explora?	C'est très bien!	C'est moche!
La Cité des Enfants?	C'est extra!	Ce n'est pas le pied!

Tip

This Tip gives some negative expressions: *C'était nul! C'était moche! Ce n'était pas le pied!* Other negative words in a higher register include *horrible* and *affreux*. If students are tempted to use *terrible,* you may like to warn them that it can be the highest form of praise in French slang.

6

Students imagine that they have been to the Cité des Sciences. They say what they have seen and what they thought of it. They can use the examples in the initial text or the pictures with task 4 as stimuli.

It may work better in terms of motivating students, if you make use of a recent trip/film or local attraction they may have visited, to allow them to express like/dislike opinions based on a real experience.

This is an opportunity to use *beau, nouveau* and *vieux*. Give them some examples with *de*, e.g. *Nous avons vu de nouveaux CD-ROMs* and point out to those who are able to understand that it is usual to put *de*, not *des*, before a plural adjective.

As is pointed out in the Student's Book, not every opinion should be negative. There are positive opinions in task 5 which can be reused, and by using *C'était*, students may be able to come up with more, e.g. *C'était vraiment bien!* or *C'était formidable!*

ICT activity

Learning objectives

• to use search strategies for an effective search on the Internet;
• to extract detail from an authentic source;
• to use the expressions of opinions in a new context.

1 Students are given the URL of the Cité des Sciences: **www.cite-sciences.fr**.
2 They are then asked to 'visit' one or two exhibits, watch some video clips and describe in detail, in English, what they saw.
3 They should then give an opinion of it using the expressions from the unit.

Teacher's Guide 1 © John Murray

Unité 11 Pages 104–105

The family visit les Galeries Lafayette, one of the most well known '*grands magasins*' on the Boulevard Haussmann.

7   [CD 3 track 27]

In this exercise students listen to the tape and decide, with the help of the diagram, which floors the family will visit.

Transcript

Papa: Moi, je voudrais acheter un stylo spécial, en souvenir de Paris, un beau stylo Waterman ou Parker peut-être. Comme ça, je peux écrire des lettres à mes amis.

Maman: Moi, j'ai vraiment besoin d'une nouvelle paire de chaussures . . . et j'ai soif . . . on pourrait monter prendre une tasse de thé.

Rachel: Moi, je cherche des films en cassette vidéo. Mais je ne veux pas de thé. Moi, je vais prendre un hamburger . . . un gros!

Papa: Si tu achètes beaucoup de choses, tu n'auras plus d'argent à dépenser.

Solutions

	Étage(s)
Papa	6
Maman	1; 3, 7 (restaurant floor) also acceptable
Rachel	5; 4, 7 (restaurant floor) also acceptable

Extra idea

To revise/extend shopping vocabulary, try a classroom exercise in which you call out – in as rapid succession as students' replies allow – words for products, in response to which they have to name the floor on which the product would be found.

Tip ↑

Attention is drawn to the fact that *espérer*, *acheter* and *se promener* have a sound change and a spelling change in them. These changes are highlighted in different colours.

You could remind more able students that the modal verbs *pouvoir*, *devoir*, *savoir* and *vouloir* also resemble the infinitive only in the *nous* and *vous* forms. You could ask students to work out or revise the paradigms of *répéter* or *accélérer*, *mener* or *(se) lever*.

8

This text reinforces the use of superlatives. Students link the record figures to the places.

Solution

1 La Tour Eiffel: 320 m.
2 La tour Montparnasse: 210 m.
3 Le Stade de France: 100 000 places.
4 3, rue Volta: 14ᵉ siècle.

Differentiation opportunity ↓

Task 8 could be the basis of some relatively easy writing for lower attainers, if they are asked to write a sentence for each answer.

Point grammaire: Superlatives

A reminder that:

- superlatives must agree with the noun.
- some adjectives precede and some follow the noun.

A traditional way of learning which adjectives precede is the following rhyming list, provided on the recording.

Transcript [CD 3 track 28]

méchant, mauvais, vilain, beau
petit, haut, vieux, joli, gros
gentil, nouveau, vaste et long
grand et meilleur, jeune et bon

Point out that *meilleur* does not need *le/la plus . . .* before it.

9   ↑

Students' attention to the verb form is reinforced by the matching of subject to verb, before forming the superlatives to complete the sentences.

1 **Rachel** espère voir **les plus grands** magasins de la capitale.
2 **Nous** espérons visiter **le plus vieux** château de France.
3 **M. et Mme Férien** se promènent dans **les plus beaux** jardins de la capitale.
4 Moi, **je** préférerais monter à **la tour la plus élevée** d'Europe.
5 **Vous** achetez **la plus belle montre** des Galeries Lafayette!
6 Paul, **tu** espères visiter les bâtiments **les plus historiques** de Paris?

Extra ideas

Students could now use the beginnings of these sentences to create new ones, e.g.

Rachel espère voir . . . → Rachel espère voir les sites les plus intéressants de Paris.

Students find the biggest/smallest/highest/oldest buildings in London or their own town and design an illustrated leaflet for tourists.

Homework opportunity

EGW11 Activity 1 could be used at this point; it practises perfect tense forms in the context of shopping/sightseeing in Paris (see full notes on **EGW11** at the end of this unit).

ICT activity

Learning objectives

- to use search strategies for an effective search on the Internet;
- to extract relevant detail about locations from a website on a local town;
- to write a report on a visit to a nearby town/city, reusing the language of the unit.

1 Students should be asked to find the website of a nearby town which they consider might be worth a visit.
2 They then pick out the most important tourist attractions and write a report in the past tense of a visit to the town.
⬆3 The higher attainers should be encouraged to use the new language *après avoir . . .*; ⬇lower attainers should be given some starter sentences such as: *J'ai visité . . . J'ai vu . . . J'ai mangé chez . . .*

If there is further detail about the places described, e.g. age or size, students should be encouraged to include this.

10 📖🎧 [CD 3 track 29]

Paris is known as the capital of *haute couture*. For further information on the major fashion houses, consult the French pages of, e.g. **www.chanel.com** or **www.jpgaultier.fr**.

The first text recounts the life of Gabrielle 'Coco' Chanel.

Transcript

La mode

Paris est très connu pour la mode – les parfums, les produits de beauté et «la haute couture», c'est-à-dire les robes les plus chics et les plus chères! Peut-être que vous avez entendu parler de «Chanel no. 5», mais connaissez-vous le nom de Coco Chanel? Voici l'histoire de sa vie.

Gabrielle Chanel est née en France en 1883. À l'âge de 20 ans, elle a commencé à travailler dans une bonneterie, où elle fabriquait des chapeaux. Gabrielle, qu'on surnommait «Coco», était très créative, et en 1910 elle a ouvert sa première boutique à Paris. Pour elle et pour ses amies sportives elle a inventé la mode sport. Coco ne dessinait pas ses modèles – elle les assemblait sur la cliente. En 1926, Coco a inventé «la petite robe noire», la robe la plus célèbre du monde.

Juste avant la deuxième guerre mondiale, la maison Chanel a fermé ses portes, mais en 1954, âgée de 71 ans, Coco a présenté une nouvelle collection. Elle est morte en 1971, mais la maison Chanel continue son travail. Les robes Chanel sont peut-être les plus connues du monde.

Students examine the text to find the words given as definitions:

1 les vêtements très exclusifs = la haute couture
2 établissement où on fait des chapeaux = une bonneterie
3 magasin où on achète des vêtements assez chers = une boutique

4 une personne qui achète quelque chose = un(e) client(e)

Extra idea

More use can be made of the text, including practice of numbers and the difficult point of recognising spoken dates, if you ask oral questions related to the numbers in the text. It may work best if you take things not in the order of the text, but in order of difficulty of comprehension, e.g.

- *Le Chanel no. 5, c'est quoi – un magasin? un plat chinois? un parfum?*
- *Quand Coco avait 20 ans, qu'est-ce qu'elle a fait?*
- *Quand Coco avait 71 ans, qu'est-ce qu'elle a fait?*
- *En 1926, qu'est-ce qu'elle a fait?*
- *En 1971, qu'est-ce qu'elle a fait?*
- *En 1954, elle avait quel âge?* etc.

Point grammaire: Perfect or imperfect tense?

The text contains examples of both the perfect and the imperfect tenses. The imperfect is used mainly for repeated actions here, but there are also some descriptions, e.g. *Coco était très créative.*

You could use **CM57**, on which there is a large version of the text. Explain to students that the perfect tense indicates an action which happened once, possibly suddenly, whereas the imperfect is much vaguer and is not specified as happening for a certain length of time. For these reasons, the perfect may be indicated by a 'lightning' sign, and the imperfect by a shining sun. Ask students to draw these symbols next to each verb in the photocopied text.

11 📖

1 In this exercise students identify why a particular past tense is being used.

Solution

a On la surnommait Coco = action répétée/continue.
b En 1910 elle a ouvert sa première boutique = action unique.
c Coco assemblait ses vêtements sur les clientes = action répétée/continue.
d Elle a inventé la petite robe noire = action unique.
e La maison Chanel a fermé ses portes = action unique.
f Elle assemblait ses créations sur les mannequins = action répétée/continue.

↟2 Students see an example of an imperfect tense representing a repeated or continued action in the left-hand examples. They compose the equivalent sentence in the perfect tense for single actions. The colour code of blue for imperfect and red for perfect is used.

Solution

a Elle a dessiné la petite robe noire.
b Elle a inventé le style «mode sportive».
c Elle a assemblé une robe merveilleuse sur sa nouvelle cliente.
d Après la deuxième guerre mondiale elle a présenté une nouvelle collection.

Students could examine the text for other examples of the imperfect and write equivalent examples in the perfect with introductory expressions such as *ce jour-là* or *un jour*, e.g. *On la surnommait «Coco».* → *Ce jour-là, on l'a surnommée «Coco».*

12 🎧 [CD 3 track 30]

This text reminds students about vocabulary and expressions necessary for buying clothes. Useful phrases include:

- *C'est combien?*
- *Vous n'avez rien de moins cher?*
- *Vous l'avez en (vert)?*
- *Quelle taille faites-vous?*
- *Est-ce que je peux l'essayer?*
- *Où est la cabine d'essayage?*
- *C'est trop long/court/serré.*
- *Ça me va?*
- *Ça te va à merveille.*
- *Je le/la/les prends.*

These expressions are reproduced on the vocabulary sheet for this unit (see page 12 of the Teacher's Repromaster Book).

Transcript

Rachel: Maman, est-ce que je peux avoir une nouvelle robe, s'il te plaît?
Maman: Une nouvelle robe . . . mais elles sont très, très chères ici!
Papa: Oui, mais on pourrait lui offrir une nouvelle robe en cadeau d'anniversaire, non? . . . C'est son anniversaire le mois prochain.
Rachel: Oh, papa, t'es gentil.
Vendeuse: Eh bien, Mademoiselle, nous avons cette robe en bleu. C'est une robe Chanel.
Rachel: Est-ce que vous l'avez en vert?
Vendeuse: En vert? Oui, nous l'avons en vert et en noir.
Rachel: C'est combien?
Vendeuse: 450 euros, Mademoiselle.
Rachel: Oh . . . Vous n'avez rien de moins cher?
Vendeuse: Si, nous avons cette robe Chanel à 230 euros – c'est le style classique de Chanel.
Rachel: Est-ce que je peux l'essayer?
Vendeuse: Mais bien sûr, Mademoiselle. Vous voulez quelle taille?

Rachel: 38, s'il vous plaît.
Vendeuse: Bon, la voilà. La cabine d'essayage est à gauche, là-bas.
Rachel: Qu'est-ce que vous en pensez? Ça me va?
Maman: Oui, le vert te va très bien. C'est très joli.
Rachel: C'est trop long?
Papa: Non, non, ça te va à merveille! C'est vraiment le style Chanel classique.
Rachel: Bon, je la prends. Merci bien papa, merci bien maman!

Solution

Couleur: vert; Taille: 38; Prix: 230€; Couturier: Chanel; Style: classique.

Extra idea

Fashion interests both boys and girls. Use teenage magazines for photos of the latest styles. These, when labelled, can be used as classroom decoration. French magazines will give you the latest terminology.

Unité 11 Pages 106–107

These two pages look at two aspects of the history of Paris – the Eiffel Tower and Versailles. There is further work on the difference in meaning between the perfect and imperfect tenses.

Presentation idea

Using flashcards, revise numbers, in particular hundreds and thousands. Show students a card and ask them to give you the next number or the previous number. They could also add or take away numbers. This is a valuable exercise as it involves manipulation rather than just recognition.

13 📖 [CD 3 track 31]

Students complete the technical specifications of the Eiffel Tower. A degree of logic is required. To help students to eliminate certain figures, you could ask them to find first the dates, then the height and the platforms heights. The rest follows logically.

Hauteur (mètres)	320
Poids (tonnes)	7000
Rivets:	2 500 000
Couleur	brun
Première plate-forme (mètres)	57
Deuxième plate-forme (mètres)	115
Troisième plate-forme (mètres)	274
Date de commencement	1887
Date de terminaison	1889

The following text gives a brief history of the Tower.

Transcript
Gustave Eiffel
L'ingénieur Gustave Eiffel était un génie. En 1884 il a eu l'idée de construire une tour à Paris. La tour a été ouverte pour l'Exposition Universelle, mais elle n'était pas populaire. Plusieurs personnes célèbres, comme les écrivains Alexandre Dumas (fils) et Guy de Maupassant, n'aimaient pas «cette monstruosité», et ils ont protesté contre la création de Gustave Eiffel.

Pendant la première guerre mondiale on utilisait la Tour pour faire des appels téléphoniques vers les USA. C'était le triomphe de la technologie à cette époque-là! Aujourd'hui la Tour Eiffel est le symbole de Paris. C'est l'attraction touristique la plus visitée de la capitale.

Extra idea
Make use of this text by asking *C'est qui? C'est quoi?*, e.g.

- *Il a eu l'idée de construire une tour – c'est qui?* or *Il était un génie – c'est qui?*
- *Cette construction n'était pas populaire – c'est quoi?*
- *Ils étaient écrivains – c'est qui?* etc.

Point grammaire: The imperfect tense
This concentrates on the use of the imperfect for descriptions. The verb *être* is the most common verb used for this.

14 📖
Students examine the following sentences and decide if an action or a description is involved.

Solution
1 Action; **2** Description; **3** Description; **4** Action

15 🎧 [CD 3 track 32]
Students listen to the tape and note key points of Rachel's description of her trip to the top of the Eiffel Tower.

Transcript
Ah, tu sais maman, c'était vraiment bien! On est montés au troisième étage. Au début, j'ai eu le vertige. C'était affreux, mais après quelques moments, cela a passé . . . et tu sais, la vue du sommet était superbe. C'était une vue vraiment belle, malgré la pollution . . . mais, tu sais, il faisait assez froid là-haut. Cela m'a surpris . . . j'ai voulu aller manger dans le restaurant . . . mais les prix étaient vraiment exorbitants. Est-ce qu'on peut remonter?

Solution
Vertige: C'était affreux.
Vue: La vue était superbe, vraiment belle.
Température: Il faisait froid.
Restaurant: Les prix étaient exorbitants.

16 🌀
Students imagine that they have visited several historic monuments in Paris. They use the perfect tense. They also give an opinion, using the imperfect. They could again use **CM55** and/or **CM56** or photographs in the Student's Book.

Differentiation opportunities ⬇
As in the earlier opinion-giving exercise, students may make a better start if you set them a similar task but in the context of local, real experience, first.

If you ask students to justify their opinions, weaker students could be reminded of the phrases on page 103 of this unit.

Homework opportunity
This visit to Paris could be written up in diary form, with opinions on each individual day.

17 ✏ ⬆
Students complete the postcard. The perfect tense is indicated in red and the imperfect in blue.

Solution
Chère Aline
Nous voici à Paris! Ce matin nous **sommes allés** à la Cité des Sciences. C'**était** vraiment super. Puis nous **avons visité** les Galeries Lafayette, où j'**ai acheté** une très belle robe. Cet après-midi, nous **avons décidé** de monter à la Tour Eiffel. La vue **était** magnifique. Il y **avait** un restaurant, mais les prix **étaient** exorbitants.
Bons baisers
Rachel

ICT activity
Learning objectives
- to reinforce the distinction between the use of the perfect and the imperfect.

1 Two versions of the text above could be word-processed by the teacher. One could be gapped with infinitives beneath and the other gapped with the complete verbs listed beneath.
2 Students could then work on the one which is most appropriate to their level.
3 This could then be extended by being used as a model for a postcard about a visit to another town.

18 📖 [CD 3 track 33]
The text gives a brief outline of a day at Versailles in the time of Louis XIV. Students may need some instruction in Roman numbers and in the fact that, with the exception of *premier*, monarchs are numbered with cardinal numbers. The text introduces uses of *après avoir* + past participle.

For further details on Versailles see website **www.versailles.fr**.

Transcript
Louis XIV et le château de Versailles
On appelait Louis XIV (1638–1715) «le Roi Soleil».
C'était un roi très riche et très puissant qui habitait le
plus beau palais d'Europe, le château de Versailles,
près de Paris. Une journée à Versailles était bien
ordonnée.

Students link the sentences to the pictures.

Solution
1 f; **2** g; **3** c; **4** d; **5** a; **6** b; **7** e

Ça se dit comment? p.107 [CD 3 track 34]
The letter combination *-ail-* is usually pronounced
like 'eye':

Transcript
– Versailles, l'ail, l'aillade
– À Versailles, Louis mangeait de l'ail avec de l'aillade.

Tip
To say 'after doing' something, use *après avoir* +
past participle. This is very much a higher level
construction and is not practised actively here. The
listening exercise below requires students to put
pairs of activities into chronological order
according to what is said on the tape.
   This grammar point is practised on **EGW11**,
Activity 3 (see full notes on **EGW11** at the end of
this unit).

19 *Transcript* [CD 3 track 35]
Mme Férien
1 J'ai fait le tour du château et puis j'ai visité les
   jardins.
2 J'ai visité la chambre du roi avant d'aller dans la
   chambre de la reine.
3 J'ai acheté un guide et . . . euh . . . ensuite . . . j'ai
   pris des photos.
4 J'ai fait le tour des jardins avant d'aller visiter la
   chapelle.
5 J'ai acheté des souvenirs et puis je suis sortie du
   château.

Solution
1 F; **2** V; **3** V; **4** F; **5** F

Extra idea
To make preliminary use of this text, ask students
to predict what Mme Férien might mention that she
has done; make a list of their suggestions
supplemented by your own, and ask students to
tick off the things they hear.

Unité 11 Pages 108–109

These two pages cover '*le grand axe*' from the Place de la Concorde to the Arc de Triomphe. A large-scale map of Paris or **CM58** will prove useful here to give students an idea of the layout.

Transcript [CD 3 track 36]
C'est dimanche après-midi. Rachel et son père se promènent dans le centre de Paris. Ils ont déjà visité la Place de la Concorde, où il y a des statues qui
représentent les grandes villes de France et un grand
obélisque égyptien. Pendant la Révolution Française
(1789–1793) la guillotine se trouvait ici, et beaucoup
de nobles français sont morts sur la Place, y compris
Marie-Antoinette, la femme du roi Louis XVI. À cette
époque-là, la place s'appelait la Place de la Révolution.
Actuellement, c'est le centre même de Paris.
   Il fait très beau aujourd'hui. Rachel et M. Férien
montent l'Avenue des Champs-Élysées. Cette avenue
élégante est très large et elle est bordée d'arbres. Ici
vous avez des cafés, des cinémas, des restaurants et
des magasins de luxe. Attention! Tout est très cher ici!
   En haut des Champs-Élysées vous avez la Place
Charles-de-Gaulle. Ici vous voyez l'Arc de Triomphe,
haut de 50 mètres et large de 45 mètres. Un soldat
inconnu de la première guerre mondiale y est enterré.

Extra idea
To exploit this text, you could do some oral
comprehension checking by asking some questions
once students have read/listened to the text, such
as the ones below. Alternatively, if you have a more
able group, put these questions on the board and
ask students to answer them as a listening
comprehension before they see the text.

* *Où sont Rachel et son père?*
* *Sur la Place de la Concorde, qu'est-ce que les
  statues représentent?*
* *Quelle machine d'exécution se trouvait sur la
  place pendant la Révolution Française?*
* *Comment est l'Avenue des Champs-Élysées?*
* *Qu'est-ce qu'il y a sur l'Avenue des Champs-Élysées
  – des cinémas? des garages? des bars? une piscine?
  un grand parking? des magasins? La Tour Eiffel?*
* *Quel monument très bien connu se trouve Place
  Charles-de-Gaulle?*
* *Qui est enterré ici?*

Tip

The Tip draws attention to the existence of *faux amis*. Students look at the examples and then find the meanings of the three *faux amis* listed. Other examples that could be given are:

car (m)	=	coach
chips (f)	=	crisps
conducteur (m)	=	driver
heurter	=	to bump into
lecture (f)	=	reading
pièce (f)	=	room; play; coin
stage (m)	=	training period, course

Extra idea

Using **CM58** (the simple map of central Paris), students could say where various monuments are, e.g. *La Madeleine se trouve Place de la Madeleine.*

Place names provide a good opportunity for practising pronunciation. You could do this by using some similar-sounding words or common nouns that students will already know, before they try some place names, e.g.

champs → Champs-Élysées
boule → Boulevard
glace → place
revenue → avenue
château, neuf → Châteauneuf
quart, matin → quartier latin
bon, bœuf → Pont Neuf
beau, tour → Beaubourg
phare, port → Gare du Nord

20 🎧 [CD 3 track 37]

Presentation ideas

Use **CM59** as an OHT to remind students of the basic vocabulary needed for direction finding, such as:

Tournez à gauche.
Tournez à droite.
Continuez tout droit.
Prenez la deuxième/troisième rue à gauche/à droite.
Passez le pont.
Traversez la rue/la place.

Set the classroom up with the aisles clearly defined. One student goes out of the room. Distribute large versions on card of the

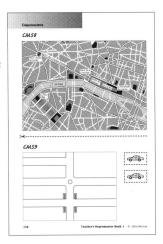

pictures from **CM55** and **CM56**. All students with one of these cards hold them up so that the others can memorise their positions. They then put the cards face down on the table. The student returns to the room and asks, e.g. *Pour aller à la Tour Eiffel?* Other students then direct him/her from memory, e.g. *Continuez tout droit. Prenez la deuxième rue à gauche. Tournez à droite.* A more elaborate version could have street names standing on tables. Students could then use then to direct the student. *Suivez la rue de Rivoli. Traversez la Place de la Concorde.*

Students listen to the recording. M. Férien and Rachel ask directions from the Arc de Triomphe to the Métro station at the Pont de l'Alma. The passer-by gives two instructions. Students select from the choice given.

Transcript

Ben . . . pour aller au Pont de l'Alma? Pas de problème. Oui, vous prenez la troisième rue à droite . . . oui, la troisième. Vous comprenez? Et . . . euh, puis vous continuez tout droit . . . la station est tout près de la rivière. Voilà. Au revoir!

Solution

Première instruction

c) 3 x →

Deuxième instruction

b) ↑

21 🎧 [CD 3 track 38]

This page deals with taking taxis and recounting accidents.

Students listen to the cassette on which the Fériens take a taxi and are involved in an accident. As a preliminary exercise, they match the French expressions to their English definitions. This doesn't give away the answer to task 22, but it does familiarise them with key phrases they will hear in the recording.

Transcript

La station de Métro Pont de l'Alma est assez loin de la Place Charles-de-Gaulle. M. Férien et Rachel décident de prendre un taxi.

Solution

1 h; **2** j; **3** g; **4** f; **5** a; **6** k; **7** i; **8** d; **9** e; **10** b. c is a distractor.

22 🎧 [CD 3 track 39]

Students identify the picture which represents what happened in the accident.

Transcript for 21 & 22

M. Férien: Vous êtes libre, Monsieur?

Chauffeur: Mais oui . . . montez . . . montez. Vous allez où, Monsieur?

M. Férien: Pont de l'Alma . . . la station de Métro, s'il vous plaît.

Chauffeur: Pas de problème . . . bon . . . Ici on tourne à droite.

M. Férien: Attention! La voiture rouge!

Chauffeur: Espèce d'idiot! Mais qu'est-ce que vous faisiez, alors?

Chauffeur de la voiture: Moi, je tournais à gauche quand vous avez tourné à droite.

Chauffeur de la taxi: Mais oui, j'ai tourné à droite. Mais vous ne regardiez pas quand vous avez tourné à gauche. J'avais la priorité. Vous n'avez pas vu le panneau? On ne peut pas tourner à gauche ici! C'est un sens unique.

Chauffeur de voiture: Mais vous ne vous êtes pas arrêté quand je tournais . . . !

Chauffeur de taxi: Écoutez, hein! Vous n'aviez pas le droit de tourner . . .

Rachel: Papa, ça va? Tu es tout blanc!

M. Férien: Oui, ça va, ça va. Je suis un peu choqué, c'est tout. Et maintenant on va être en retard.

Solution

Picture 2: Taxi turning right was hit by car turning left.

ICT activity

Learning objectives

- to reinforce the use of the imperfect;
- to show complete understanding of a familiar dialogue.

1 Teacher creates a word-processed file of the dialogue from '*Mais qu'est-ce que vous faisiez*' to '*le droit de tourner*' but in **incorrect** order.

2 Students then have to re-order the dialogue on screen.

Point grammaire: Perfect and imperfect tense

The use of the imperfect to express an ongoing action is explained here.

Presentation idea

Use **CM59** (a simplified street map) as a 'base' OHT. Use the car overlays (cut-outs on the same sheet) coloured differently with highlighter pen) to illustrate how accidents happened, e.g. *La voiture rouge tournait à gauche quand la voiture verte est sortie de la Grand'Rue.*

After showing a few examples, write some on the board, mentioning different vehicles, underlining

the -*ait* of the imperfect and circling the instance of the perfect tense. Number the actions according to sequence, e.g. *Le camion tournait à droite (1), quand la voiture bleue l'a heurté (2).* Then ask a a student to stand by the OHT and position the vehicles according to what you say. Once this has been done, students can come to the OHP and move the vehicles. Other students then explain what happened.

23 📖

Students identify the second action, i.e. the action which interrupted the ongoing action in the imperfect.

Solution

1 Rachel est arrivée.
2 Le camion s'est arrêté.
3 Une femme a commencé à traverser la rue.
4 Nous avons vu le taxi.
5 J'ai heurté la vieille dame.

Presentation idea

Designate yourself and a student as the driver and passenger of a car involved in an accident. Place two chairs at the front of a class to represent car seats. Explain in a dramatic way to the class: *Nous tournions à droite quand le camion nous a heurtés.* Give some other examples and write: *nous tournions/descendions/roulions* on the board. Designate two students as driver and passenger. Illustrate an accident on the OHT. Ask them: *Vous tourniez à gauche/à droite?* so that they have to answer, *Non, nous tournions* . . . Write *vous tourniez/sortiez/rouliez* on the board. Ask students to deduce the correct ending for *nous* and *vous* in the imperfect. This is the first time that they have dealt with forms other than the third person. Practise similar activities with *tu* and *je*. Show the whole paradigm for the imperfect.

EGW11 Activity 2 practises contrasting use of the two past tenses (see full notes on **EGW11** at the end of this unit).

24 📀 ↑

Using the table, students compose sentences about an accident in pairs. One gives an account which is then contradicted by the other. The first column of verbs is to be in the imperfect and the second in the perfect. An alternative approach could be: Students work in pairs; one composes the first part of the sentence in the imperfect, and the other completes it by choosing an appropriate ending; the first partner then has to repeat the whole sentence; they then change roles for the next sentence.

Differentiation opportunity ⬇ ⬆

⬇**DW11.2A** and ⬆**DW11.2B** use the two tenses in conjunction. Both use a different context, namely injuries sustained when working or playing.

■ ⬇**DW11.2A** requires students to match phrases to pictures and thus create sentences in which one action is interrupted by another.

■ ⬆**DW11.2B** uses the same pictures, but with skeleton sentences to complete. Students thus have to decide on the form of the verb in each of the two tenses.

Solution

Moi, j'allumais un feu . . . quand je me suis brûlé le doigt.

M. Martin montait une échelle . . . quand soudain il est tombé par terre.

Le chef préparait le dîner . . . quand soudain il s'est coupé la main.

Coralie et Alain jouaient dans le jardin . . . quand soudain Coralie est tombée à l'eau.

Nous dansions . . . quand soudain Michèle s'est foulé le genou.

Unité 11 Pages 110–111

This spread deals with suggestions about going out and eating in a restaurant. The adverbs of degree *trop*, *très* and *assez* are explained and practised.

Extra idea

Once students have had the opportunity to listen to the text, they could read the text aloud in groups of three, for pronunciation/intonation practice.

26 📖🎧 [CD 3 track 40]

Students answer *oui/non* to comprehension questions, several of which involve expressions containing adverbs of degree.

Transcript

Dimanche soir

C'est presque la fin du séjour à Paris. Qu'est-ce qu'on va faire ce soir? La famille regarde *Pariscope*.

Papa: Alors, qu'est-ce que tu veux faire ce soir, chérie?

Maman: Ben, je ne sais pas. Je suis assez fatiguée, tu sais.

Rachel: Moi, je voudrais aller à la Boule Noire. C'est une boîte de nuit vraiment super! Il y un concert de rock ce soir – ah ouais, super! – C'est les Guano Apes et Girls Against Boys!

Papa: Ah! Non Rachel, tu sais, un club comme ça, c'est très cher et ... en plus, la musique est trop forte!

Maman: Et moi, je suis trop fatiguée pour aller dans un club.

Rachel: Oh, non! Ce n'est pas juste!

Papa: Tu veux aller au cinéma, chérie?

Maman: Ça dépend, qu'est-ce qu'on passe?

Papa: Dans le cinéma du coin il y a le nouveau film de Juliette Binoche . . .

Rachel: Moi, je l'ai vu. C'est moche!

Maman: Moi, j'ai une bonne idée . . . si on allait manger dans un restaurant? Il y a un tout petit restaurant juste à côté qui n'est pas très cher. Qu'en pensez-vous?

Papa: Bonne idée.

Rachel: D'accord. Mais je préférerais aller voir les Guano Apes à la Boule Noire . . .

Solution

1 non; **2** non; **3** oui; **4** non; **5** non; **6** oui

Point grammaire: Adverbs

Explain that:

- adverbs such as *très* (very), *trop* (too) and *assez* (fairly) are used with adjectives and are placed before them, as in English;
- by putting *pas* in front of *très* and *trop* you have other possibilities for describing things.

More able students could be told either or both of the following additional points:

- *très* (very), *trop* (too) and *assez* (fairly) can also be used with adverbs.
- *trop* and *assez* can be used just with 'C'est': 'C'est trop!' (It's too much!); 'C'est assez!' (That's enough!).

27 🎧

Students decide whether the prices asked for the items illustrated are fair. They give their opinions using *assez*, *très*, *trop* and *pas trop*. Answers will depend on students' individual opinions – and their knowledge of life!

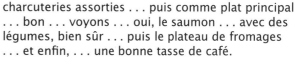

Unité 11 Page 111

Presentation ideas

Using **CM60** as an OHT, revise food as served in a restaurant. This gives the opportunity for students to express opinions (*j'aime, je n'aime pas, je préfère*) and to say what they have never tried (*je n'ai jamais essayé (de)..., je n'ai jamais mangé (de)...*). Using the categories: *Entrée, Plat principal, Fromages, Dessert*, you could ask students to say into which category they think each dish fits. This could be built up on the board. They can check their predictions by looking at the menu.

Au restaurant

Two menus are given, one *prix fixe*, one *à la carte*, the latter being more extensive (and expensive!).

Differentiation opportunity ⬇

Students could use
⬇ **DW11.3** to revise some vocabulary of restaurant food before tackling this menu and the following tasks. They tick the illustrations representing items that are mentioned in Sylvie's e-mail.

Solution

The following should be ticked:

chips; coffee; coke; egg mayonnaise; omelette; apple tart with ice-cream; pâté; pork chops; red wine; salad; salmon; steak.

28 🎧 [CD 3 track 41]

1 Students listen to the conversation on tape and decide which of the meals pictured belongs to which speaker.

Transcript

Maman: Bon ... c'est difficile ... mais je pense que je vais prendre le menu à prix fixe ... donc ... comme entrée je vais prendre les œufs durs à la mayonnaise ... puis ... le steack avec des légumes ... et comme dessert ... une glace, je pense.
Papa: Moi, je choisis à la carte ... alors ...

charcuteries assorties ... puis comme plat principal ... bon ... voyons ... oui, le saumon ... avec des légumes, bien sûr ... puis le plateau de fromages ... et enfin, ... une bonne tasse de café.
Rachel: Et moi ... je prends le pâté ... puis les côtes de porc ... avec des légumes ... puis le plateau de fromages ... et comme dessert ... je prends la tarte normande ... avec de la glace!
Papa et maman: Gourmande!

Solution

a Rachel; **b** Maman; **c** Papa

⬆**2** Students listen to the cassette again, note the prices from the menu and work out the total.

Solution
Total: 83.8€

29 ⊙

1 Students take the part of the waiter and the customer and use the menu on **CM61**. They could practise role-plays with the book open and the phrases visible. Once this has been assimilated they could try the role-play with the book closed.

Differentiation opportunity ⬇

Lower-ability students may need English versions of some of the French prompts to enable them to do the role-play.

⬆**2** Partner A decides on a budget and tells B what (s)he has available to spend. Partner B recommends various dishes from the menu. Partner A decides if this is OK or if it is too expensive. If it is too expensive, B should recommend a further, cheaper selection.

ICT opportunity

Students script a scene in a restaurant, learn it and video the sequence. This video can then be used as evidence of levels of competence achieved and as a teaching aid for future classes.

30 [CD 3 track 42]

Rachel recounts the accident while the family are eating. She makes four errors in her account. In the text, students hear examples of the pluperfect. The Tip below draws attention to this, but there is no active use of the construction.

Transcript

Maman: Explique-moi exactement ce qui s'est passé ce matin. Papa était vraiment trop choqué pour me le dire à la station de Métro.

Rachel: Eh bien ... Nous avions visité l'Arc de Triomphe ... et ... euh ... nous avions traversé les Champs-Élysées ... quand, soudain, papa a décidé de prendre un taxi. Donc ... on est montés ... et euh ... on est partis. Le chauffeur de taxi tournait à gauche ... quand, soudain, il y a eu une voiture bleue qui a tourné devant nous. Le chauffeur n'avait pas vu le panneau 'sens interdit'... et ... euh ... il nous a heurtés ... Pan! Blaf! ... Le chauffeur de taxi est descendu. Il était très calme ... et il a parlé avec l'automobiliste. Papa est resté dans le taxi ... il allait bien, quand même. Après quelques minutes on est repartis. C'est tout.

Solution

1 Elle dit que la voiture était bleue, mais c'est faux. La voiture était rouge.
2 Elle dit que le taxi tournait à gauche, mais c'est faux. Le taxi tournait à droite.
3 Elle dit que le chauffeur de taxi était très calme, mais c'est faux. Il était furieux.
4 Elle dit que papa allait bien, mais c'est faux. Il était choqué.

Tip

An example is given of the pluperfect as used in the listening text – *Le chauffeur n'avait pas vu la voiture.* No further work is done on the pluperfect at this stage (see Unit 13).

Unité 11 Pages 112–113

Checkpoints

Test

The **Test** checks students' skills in the grammatical goals of the unit:

- using the conditional tense in phrases to say what you 'would like'
- using irregular adjectives
- using superlatives
- using the imperfect tense to say what you 'were doing'
- using contrasting past tenses
- describing a sequence of events
- using adverbs to say 'enough', 'too'

Solution

1 a	Moi je voud**rais** aller à Versailles.	[1]
b	Moi, je préfér**erais** aller à la Cité des Sciences.	[1]
c	Tu aime**rais** aller à la Tour Eiffel?	[1]
d	On pour**rait** peut-être aller dans un restaurant.	[1]
2 a	de très **beaux** films	[1]
b	un **vieux** sous-marin	[1]
c	de **nouvelles** technologies	[1]
d	de **belles** expositions permanentes	[1]
3 a	C'était moche! **négative**	[1]
b	C'est vraiment nul! **négative**	[1]
c	C'était super-génial! **positive**	[1]
d	C'était extra! **positive**	[1]
e	Ce n'était pas le pied! **négative**	[1]
4 a	La Tour Eiffel est **le monument le plus élevé** de Paris.	[1]
b	Le Stade de France est **le plus grand stade** du pays.	[1]
c	3, rue Volta est **la plus ancienne maison** de Paris.	[1]
d	Le Palais omnisports de Bercy est **la plus grande salle** de Paris.	[1]

5 a Les idées de Gustave Eiffel n'étaient pas
très populaires. C [1]
  b Les constructeurs ont mis deux ans à
compléter la Tour Eiffel. A [1]
  c Une fois finie, la Tour était magnifique! C [1]
  d C'était le triomphe de la technologie. C [1]
  e On a fait des appels téléphoniques vers
les USA. A [1]
6 a Il (le bus) a heurté un motard. [1]
  b J'ai vu le car. [1]
  c Mon ami est arrivé. [1]
  d J'ai trouvé l'article. [1]
7 a C'est très cher – It's very expensive. [1]
  b C'est trop cher – It's too expensive. [1]
  c Ce n'est pas trop cher – It's not too
expensive. [1]
  d C'est assez cher – It's fairly expensive. [1]

Total [30]

Quiz

The **Quiz** checks students' knowledge acquired in
the unit, about:

* fashion
* finding your way around
* major places to visit in Paris
* historical Parisians
* eating out

Solution

1 a Le château de Versailles [1]
  b La Cité des Sciences [1]
  c La Tour Eiffel [1]
  d Notre Dame de Paris [1]
  e Les Galeries Lafayette [1]
  f La Place de la Concorde [1]
2 Au Parc de la Villette [1]
3 Gabrielle [1]
4 La petite robe noire [1]
5 (Il était) ingénieur [1]
6 À la carte [1]
7 Louis XIV [1]

Total [12]

Projets

A Students write an account of a real or imaginary
visit to Paris, saying which monuments and sites
they went to and what they thought of them.
This provides opportunities for the use of both
the perfect and imperfect tenses. A number of
phrases are given which they can incorporate
into their text.

B An account of an accident. This could be in the
first person which would give them the chance to
make comments, e.g. *C'était terrifiant!*
Students could write two versions, one from
the viewpoint of each driver. Alternatively, the
account could be written objectively in the third
person, by a witness who passes judgement, e.g.
C'était la faute du conducteur de la voiture rouge.

C Students write a mini-biography of a hero or
heroine. To assist them in this, suggest three
categories. Actions which happened once;
actions which happened repeatedly; the person's
character. Only the first category will use the
perfect tense. Some framework phrases are
suggested:
*X est né(e) en (date) . . . Son père travaillait
comme . . . Sa mère était . . . X voulait . . . Un jour
. . . X est mort(e) en (date).*

D Students research a monument or site which
interests them. This could be in Paris and need
not be a historical monument, e.g. Stade de
France. The final version could be written up in
the form of a poster for display.

EGW11 teaching notes

EGW11 provides extra
grammar/homework on
contrasting past tenses
and *après avoir.*

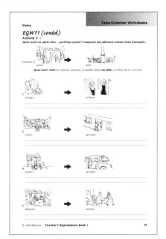

Activity 1

This offers extra practice on the perfect tense, using questions related to a tourist visit to Paris, with the gapped answers prompted by pictures.

Solution

1 Exemple: Non, merci, j'ai déjà acheté une robe.
2 Non, merci j'ai déjà mangé un sandwich.
3 Non, merci, j'ai déjà visité la Tour Eiffel.
4 Non, merci, j'ai déjà choisi une montre.
5 Non, merci, j'ai déjà mis un pull.
6 Non, merci, j'ai déjà pris un Coca.

Activity 2

This offers receptive practice of sentences containing a perfect and an imperfect tense – students choose the most logical ending for each sentence opener.

Solution

1 Exemple: Rachel choisissait une robe quand elle a vu une belle blouse verte.
2 M. Férien buvait son café dans le restaurant quand il a laissé tomber sa tasse.
3 Mme Férien visitait Versailles quand elle a vu le fantôme de Louis XIV!
4 Le taxi tournait à droite quand une voiture rouge l'a heurté.
5 Les Férien sortaient du Métro quand ils ont vu un accident.
6 Rachel montait à la Tour Eiffel quand soudain elle a eu une crise de vertige.

Activity 3↟

This practises *après avoir* based on pictures and a model sentence.

1 Exemple: Après avoir visité les Galeries Lafayette, la famille Férien est allée à la Place de la Concorde.
2 Après avoir mangé un hamburger, Rachel a acheté une robe Chanel.
3 Après avoir visité Versailles, Mme Férien a pris le Métro.
4 Après avoir monté l'Arc de Triomphe, Rachel et M. Férien ont pris un taxi.
5 Après avoir déjeuné au Petit Chat Blanc, la famille Férien est rentrée à l'hôtel.

unité 12
L'Europe

Contexts
- the geography of Europe
- food in Europe
- the languages of Europe
- the European Union
- the euro
- multicultural Europe

Grammar
- using *si* + present + future
- using the verb *croire*
- recognising the past historic tense
- using *en* and the present participle

Revision
- using adjectives
- using negatives
- using pairs of verbs
- agreeing and disagreeing
- question words

Pronunciation
- '*-oi-*'
- '*-eu*'
- '*-euil/euille-*'

This unit covers a variety of aspects of the European continent and the European Union.

Unité 12 Page 114

This page covers the geography of western Europe.

Presentation ideas

Using **CM62** as an OHT, revise the geography of Europe. Ask: *Où est la France? Où est l'Allemagne*, and get students to indicate the location on the OHT. Write the names of the countries on an overlay over the map in wipe-clean pen as they are established. Once this has been revised, run a competition between two students or teams to touch the right spot on the screen image when you (or another student) call out the name of a country.

Homework idea

CM63 presents outlines of European countries. Once the countries have been identified they can be stuck onto paper/card and used as the basis for a display. Students can add symbols or pictures of food, cars, sports personalities, etc. for each country.

Copymasters
CM63

1  [CD 3 track 43]

Students read the text and correct the comprehension sentences, all of which are false.

Transcript
La France au cœur de l'Europe
L'Europe est un continent qui est assez petit (sur les sept continents elle arrive en sixième place), mais elle est très importante. Dans le nord, le climat est froid, mais dans le sud il y a un climat méditerranéen, qui est assez chaud. Quinze pays font partie de l'Union européenne. Les pays industriels comme la France, l'Allemagne et le Royaume-Uni se trouvent dans le nord. Dans le sud se trouvent les pays plutôt agricoles comme l'Espagne, le Portugal, l'Italie et la Grèce. Ces pays sont plus pauvres que les grands pays dont l'économie est plutôt industrielle. L'Europe est un continent très varié (industries, cuisine, culture) et assez riche mais, malheureusement, la pauvreté et le chômage existent encore dans tous les pays du continent.

Solution
1 Exemple: Non, elle est assez petite.
2 Non, vous avez un climat assez froid.
3 Non, ils sont situés dans le nord.
4 Non, ce sont des pays agricoles.
5 Si, ils existent encore dans tous les pays du continent.

Tip

This draws attention to the double *-ll* in the feminine of adjectives ending in *-el*. Other adjectives which have this ending are *cruel, officiel, personnel, virtuel*. You could draw a comparison with the pronoun *elle* as being indicative of the feminine.

2

Students deduce which adjective makes sense for each gap and adapt it as necessary to agree with these feminine nouns.

1 L'agent de voyage va nous donner une opinion **professionnelle**.
2 L'Europe est un continent plutôt **industriel** qu'agricole.
3 Écoutez! J'ai des nouvelles **sensationnelles**!
4 Occupez-vous de vos affaires **personnelles**!
5 Le Var est une destination très **traditionnelle** pour les vacanciers français.
6 Pour les vacances, je ne mets dans ma valise que les choses absolument **essentielles**.

Unité 12 Page 115

This page concentrates on food in Europe. Adjectives of nationality are widely used and practised.

Presentation ideas

Using **CM60**, revise food vocabulary. Students could try to name as many items of food as possible in one minute, possibly working in pairs. Then ask students what they ate yesterday for breakfast, lunch and evening meal. In answer to various dishes, ask *C'est une spécialité anglaise?* and then *Quelles sont les spécialités anglaises?* List these on the board under the heading *Spécialités anglaises.* (You may well have to disillusion them about the origins of beefburgers and pizza!) Explain that you're going to move on to European specialities. Students could be asked if they know of specialities from countries they have visited.

This may be an opportunity for dictionary work.

Differentiation opportunity ↓

The following culinary terms are cognates or near-cognates and may help less able students, but use the opportunity also to stress French pronunciation! The words are on the recording for this purpose.

Transcript [CD 3 track 44]

Soupe, omelette, saumon, truite, pizza, hamburger, bacon, saucisse, rosbif, steack, quiche, tomate, oignon, radis, carotte, salade, riz, patate, fruit, banane, abricot, orange, cerise, yaourt, biscuit, tarte, gâteau, sandwich, margarine, chocolat, thé, café, limonade, jus d'orange, Coca, champagne, bière.

You could ask students to use these to make up a menu with a starter, main course and vegetable, fruit and dessert.

3

Students examine the pictures on the menu and decide which adjective to attach to the word *Spécialité.* There are a number of distractors.

Solution

1 Spécialité française; **2** Spécialité italienne; **3** Spécialité anglaise; **4** Spécialité espagnole; **5** Spécialité autrichienne

Point grammaire: Adjectives

The feminines of irregular adjectives are explained here, with adjectives of nationality given where possible.

Extra idea

Practise adjectives of nationality in the following way. Write pairs of sentences such as the following, to prompt the single sentence descriptions as given in the example.

– *Joélie est athlète. Elle est originaire de France.*
– *Steve est footballeur. Il vient d'Écosse.*

Use distinguishable masculine/feminine nouns such as *copain/copine, homme/femme, musicien/musicienne, chanteur/chanteuse,* ♠ *ambassadeur/ambassadrice,* ♠ *prince/princesse,* ♠ *politicien/politicienne.*

Then ask for definitions of people (Cédric Pioline, Mary Pierce, Robbie Williams, Céline Dion, or similar contemporary characters), e.g *Cédric Pioline est un joueur de tennis français.*

– *Composez des phrases selon l'exemple suivant: David Ginola est un footballeur français, mais il joue pour . . .*

4

Students complete the grid with the correct form of the adjective.

Solution

Masculin	Féminin
autrichien	autrichienne
belge	belge
grec	grecque
allemand	allemande
norvégien	norvégienne

Presentation idea

Using a poster or flashcards of the European flags with the country names concealed, ask students if they can identify the flags, e.g. *C'est le drapeau de Hollande: c'est le drapeau hollandais.* Write two columns on the board, one for countries and one for adjectives. Leave this as reference material for the listening exercise.

Differentiation opportunity ↓

With students of lower ability you could first examine the flags in their sentences with them and they decide which nationality they are. They write the basic form of each adjective, in rough e.g. 1 *français/italien.* When they listen to the tape, they delete the adjective which does not apply. They could then work on deciding on the correct form.

5  [CD 3 track 45]

1 Students identify the correct nationality adjective.

Transcript

Announcer: Radio Corsaire. Et maintenant Coucou Cuisine. Aujourd'hui, on parle de la cuisine européenne. Notre chef André a parlé avec cinq personnes du Collège Jacques Cartier au sujet de leurs plats favoris.
Interviewer: Simon, qu'est-ce que tu aimes comme cuisine européenne?
Simon: Moi, j'aime bien la cuisine italienne. Je trouve que c'est toujours très bon.
Interviewer: Merci. Magali, tu es française . . . est-ce que tu aimes la cuisine française?

Teacher's Guide 1 © John Murray

Magali: Oui . . . en général la cuisine française me plaît, mais il y a des plats que je déteste . . . le cassoulet par exemple.

Interviewer: Bon, merci. Aline, qu'est-ce que tu aimes manger?

Aline: Moi, j'adore le fromage, surtout les fromages hollandais . . . c'est très différent des fromages français.

Interviewer: Merci bien. Alors, Spirou, tu es grec, non? Tu aimes la cuisine grecque?

Spirou: Oui, j'aime bien la cuisine grecque . . . mais, les vins grecs ne sont pas très bons . . . non, moi, je préfère les vins blancs allemands. Ils sont vraiment délicieux.

Interviewer: Et finalement, nous posons une question à un professeur – Mademoiselle Trélente, est-ce que vous aimez la cuisine allemande ou la cuisine autrichienne?

Mlle Trélente: Ben . . . je ne connais pas très bien les spécialités autrichiennes, mais j'aime bien la cuisine allemande, surtout les curry-wurst . . . euh . . . les saucisses au curry.

Interviewer: Merci bien. Eh, bien chers auditeurs, la cuisine européenne, en général, est très populaire . . .

Solution

1 a Simon trouve que la cuisine **italienne** est très bonne.
 b Il y a des plats **français** que Magali déteste!
 c Aline préfère les fromages **hollandais**.
 d Spirou aime bien les vins blancs **allemands**.
 e Mlle Trélente ne ne connaît pas très bien les spécialités **autrichiennes**.

2 Four teenagers talk about particular dishes, mentioning some of the ingredients. Students deduce from which country the dish comes.

Transcript [CD 3 track 46]

Numéro 1 Patrick: Mes plats favoris sont les spaghettis . . . j'adore ça . . . et euh . . . les pizzas.

Numéro 2 Élise: Pour moi, ça doit être le rosbif . . . avec des pommes de terre rôties et des légumes.

Numéro 3 Marco: Moi, je suis très traditionnel . . . j'aime bien manger un steack . . . bien cuit . . . avec des frites . . . du pain . . . et un verre de vin rouge.

Numéro 4 Ahmed: Pour moi . . . euh . . . mon plat favori c'est la tortilla . . . et les tapas . . . et j'aime bien boire un verre de sangria.

Solution

Élise – **rosbif, pommes de terre, légumes – anglaise**

Marco – **steack, frites, pain, vin rouge – française**
Ahmed – **tortilla, tapas, sangria – espagnole**

 6

To prepare for this task, students identify the elements of the meals in the pictures. They are:

- steack, frites, vin rouge.
- pizza.
- œufs, bacon, thé.
- paëlla, vin blanc.
- escalope viennoise (escalope de porc), citron, pommes de terre.

You could also refer students back to tasks 29 and 30 in Unit 11, where the restaurant scenario was practised.

Students work in pairs, one as the waiter, one as the customer, and attempt to make up a pan-European meal, choosing elements from the different dishes. They order a meal and a drink, with the waiter using the expessions given.

Differentiation opportunities

1 The student playing the waiter could pick out an element from the order given and say, *Je regrette, mais nous n'avons plus de . . .* thus obliging the other partner to choose another element.

2 Less able students could be given the transcript for task 5 to use as a model, with certain words marked in highligher pen to indicate what should be substituted with their own choices.
  Those listening could be asked to make a choice, and justify that choice, e.g. *Moi, je vais prendre la roulade au chocolat de Tania, parce que j'aime les plats sucrés.*

ICT activity

Learning objectives

- to revise/extend the vocabulary of food;
- to research food specialities of specified countries.

1 Teacher creates a word document entitled *La cuisine d'Europe*. The document has columns with a range of headings, e.g. *pays, plats principaux, desserts, boissons.*

2 Some areas could be filled in together as above.

3 Students should then be encouraged to research, in books or on the Internet, the remainder of the document.

Unité 12 Pages 116–117

This spread covers two European countries, Switzerland and Belgium, in which languages other than French are spoken. Page 116 examines *la Suisse romande*, the French-speaking area of Switzerland in the west (Italian is spoken in the south, Romansch (*romanche*) in the canton of Graubünden, and Swiss German everywhere else). Switzerland is not a member of the European Union.

Presentation idea

Using **CM64** as an OHT, point out that Switzerland lies between France, Italy and Germany and this explains the linguistic diversity of the country. Before you do so, ask students to come up with words for any products or activities which they associate with Switzerland. Then see how many they have identified by referring to the symbols around the edge of the map which represent Swiss agriculture and industry. They are: *le secteur financier (l'argent), l'horlogerie (les coucous), l'industrie laitière (les vaches, le lait), la chocolaterie, le tourisme, les sports d'hiver, les fleurs.*

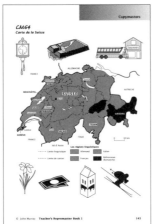

7 📖 ✏ [CD 3 track 47]

Students read/listen to the text and decide if the sentences are true or false.

Transcript

La Suisse romande

La Suisse est située au centre de l'Europe. Elle ne fait pas partie de l'Union européenne, mais elle est vraiment internationale. Dans la région qui est près de la frontière française (la Suisse romande) on parle français, mais beaucoup de Suisses savent aussi parler italien et allemand. Cette région est certainement connue pour la chocolaterie.

Solution

1 Faux; **2** Faux; **3** Vrai; **4** Faux; **5** Vrai

8 📖 ✏ [CD 3 track 48]

Students read the competition text. A process of elimination should enable them to work out the answers to the first two questions. The third is guesswork. To make this competition more real, you could ask students to write their answers on a piece of paper with their name on. You eliminate those with wrong answers, and put all the correct solutions into a hat or box. You make the draw, and could perhaps award a bar of Swiss chocolate (e.g. Lindt) as a prize.

Transcript

GRAND CONCOURS – L'ARBRE À CHOCOLAT

Les chocolatiers de la Suisse romande vous offrent l'occasion de gagner un prix incroyable

– une visite à la chocolaterie Jacques Koenig
  une superbe sélection de chocolats
– des bons à dépenser dans les pâtisseries de la région.

Il faut tout simplement deviner les bonnes réponses.

Solution

1 b; **2** b; **3** c

Tip

Show the students some language text books and say, e.g. *Voici un livre de français. Et voici un dictionnaire allemand. Tu parles allemand, Tony? Qui parle allemand? Levez la main. Et qui parle espagnol? Qui parle français?*

Having established the topic of languages, use **CM62** with an overlay of names of countries. Write two columns on the board, one for countries, one for languages. Ask: *Quelle langue est-ce qu'on parle en Angleterre?* while pointing at the map. When the answer comes write: *On parle anglais* and use this as the framework. Try to get students not to put the definite article in.

Once the list of languages has been established, ask students what languages they speak. Try to establish that it is normal for human beings to speak more than one language. The monolingual British citizen is something of a biological freak!

You may wish to mention some or all of the following countries and their languages.

Pays	Langue(s) principales
la France	le français, le breton, le provençal, l'occitan
l'Allemagne	l'allemand
l'Autriche	l'allemand
la Suisse	l'allemand, le français, l'italien, le romanche
l'Espagne	l'espagnol, le catalan, le basque, le galicien, le valencien, le majorquin
le Portugal	le portugais
l'Italie	l'italien
les Pays-bas	le néerlandais (hollandais)
la Belgique	l'allemand, le français, le flamand, le néerlandais
le Luxembourg	l'allemand, le luxembourgeois, le français
le Royaume-Uni	l'anglais, le gallois, le gaélique
la Suède	le suédois
le Danemark	le danois
la Grèce	le grec
la Finlande	le finnois, le suédois
l'Irlande	l'anglais, le gaélique irlandais

9 🎧

Students identify the flags shown and hence the language(s) spoken by the athletes.

Teacher's Guide 1 © John Murray

Solution

1 Moi, je suis Britannique. Je parle anglais.
2 Moi, je suis Français. Je parle français.
3 Moi, je suis Espagnol. Je parle espagnol.
4 Moi, je suis Allemande. Je parle allemand.
5 Moi, je suis Suisse. Je parle français/italien/ allemand.
6 Moi, je suis Italien. Je parle italien.

Extra idea

Students could find pictures of athletes from countries other than those listed in the above exercise. With these they could make a display. Some research may be necessary in order to find the languages spoken by, e.g. eastern European athletes. This provides an oportunity for work with encyclopædias, atlases and dictionaries.

10  [CD 3 track 49]

This page concentrates on Belgium and the fact of its being a bilingual country. French is spoken in the southern part of the country, known as *la Wallonie*, and covering the regions of Hainaut, Namur and Luxembourg (not the Grand Duchy, which is a separate country). Flemish (*le néerlandais*) is spoken in Flandre Occidentale, Flandre Orientale, Anvers, Brabant, Limbourg and Liège. Brussels is officially bilingual. The east–west language line was given official status in 1962.

Transcript

La Belgique
La Belgique est un pays international situé entre la France, les Pays-Bas et l'Allemagne. C'est un tout petit pays (il ne mesure que 30 500 km²), mais Bruxelles, sa capitale, est aussi la cité principale de l'Europe.

En Belgique on parle deux langues – le français et le néerlandais. On parle néerlandais dans l'ouest, le nord et le nord-est du pays et français dans le sud et le sud-est, mais sur les routes et dans les villes, tout est marqué sur des panneaux bilingues.

1 Students identify the regions where French and Flemish are spoken.

Solution

a Dans les régions bleues on parle néerlandais.
b Dans les régions rouges on parle français.

2 Students find phrases in the text to disprove the false sentences.

Solution

a Exemple: Elle est située entre la France, les Pays-Bas, et l'Allemagne.
b C'est un tout petit pays.
c Bruxelles est la cité principale de l'Europe.
d En Belgique on parle deux langues.
e Tout est marqué sur des panneaux bilingues.

11 [CD 3 track 50]

Students listen to a young Belgian explaining why he speaks four languages.

Transcript

Eh bien, moi je m'appelle Jacques Vlaminck et j'ai 18 ans. Je suis belge. Moi je suis d'une famille qui vient du nord-est du pays. Mes grands-parents parlaient néerlandais, pas français, hein? Ils n'allaient jamais en France ... ils étaient assez hostiles – plutôt négatifs, quoi – envers les Français. Ils parlaient allemand aussi. Mais moi, je suis Bruxellois, c'est-à-dire, je viens de la capitale, Bruxelles. Comme mes grands-parents, je parle néerlandais et allemand, mais, comme tous les jeunes, je parle français aussi, avec mes copains et surtout en ville ... même si je ne parle pas français chez moi. Nous, les jeunes, nous avons une attitude plus européenne, plus positive ... et je parle anglais, bien sûr ... c'est vraiment la langue internationale.

Solution

1 18.
2 Ville: Bruxelles.
3 Les quatre langues: néerlandais, français, allemand, anglais.
↑4 Attitude des grands-parents: hostile, négative.
↑5 Attitude des jeunes: plus européenne, positive.

ICT activity

Learning objectives

• to decide on the information you need to know about tourist sites before planning a visit;
• to interrogate an on-line database of places to visit in Brussels;
• to do a presentation about a tourist site.

The suggested site is
www.paluche.org/pages/somm.htm

This is part of a website intended for 'younger browsers'.

1 As a class decide what information you need to know when planning visits – how to get there, opening times, costs, refreshment facilities.
2 Students create a document with the agreed headings, perhaps in tabular form.
3 Students are then guided to the website named above and asked to find out information about two places they might visit in one day.
4 They import this information into their document, also downloading any other information or graphics they might want to complete their presentation.
5 They then complete a presentation using whatever software they deem appropriate.
6 ↓Lower attainers might need a prepared format for the language but one which still allows them opportunities for creativity in other areas, e.g. *Le matin on peut visiter ... Heures d'ouverture ...*

Point grammaire: Negatives

This is a reminder about negatives such as *ne ... pas* and *ne ... jamais* going round the verb. The expression *ne ... que* (only) is also revised.

12 📖

1 Students re-order jumbled sentences containing negatives and *ne ... que.*

Solution

a Dans le nord de la Belgique on ne parle pas français.
b Jacques ne parle jamais français avec ses copains.
c La Belgique ne couvre que 30 500 km².
d La pauvreté n'affecte pas les pays du nord.

2 Phrase 1 est vraie.

Differentiation opportunity ↓ ↑

At this point you could use ↓ **DW12.1A** and ↑ **DW12.1B**.

■ On ↓ **DW12.1A** students match sentences to consequences containing negatives. They then answer questions using appropriate negative constructions.

Solution
Activity 1: 1 g; **2** d; **3** a; **4** e; **5** f; **6** b; **7** c

Activity 2: 1 plus; **2** pas; **3** plus; **4** pas; **5** jamais

■ On ↑ **DW12.1B** students complete sentences saying what the consequence of a given situation is. They use negatives in their answers, choosing from among *ne ... pas, ne ... jamais* and *ne ... plus*. Answers will be dependent on students' abilities and imagination.
   In the second exercise, students are presented with a series of opinions and asked to contradict those with which they disagree. Answers will be dependent on students' abilities and imagination.

Solution
Students' own choice of answers for both activities.

Tip

Details of the 12 languages spoken in France may be found on **www.eurolang.net**. In 2000 the French government refused to give recognition to the minority languages, despite a Directive from the European Union. French remains the only official language.

14 ✐

Students are invited to imagine which European countries they would like to visit if they won 1,000 euros. To prepare them for this writing task, you could try the following ideas.

Presentation ideas

Using **CM62** as an OHT with an overlay of names, ask students if they would like to visit certain countries, e.g. *Tu veux visiter la Belgique?*
   Then ask them to enlarge: *Qu'est-ce que tu veux voir? Qu'est-ce que tu veux manger?* Students then work in pairs, using a photocopy of **CM62** explaining to each other where they want to go and why. At the end some students could give their presentation to the class.

Differentiation/homework opportunity ↑

More able students could do a written version of the above task. They could include reasons (*parce que, à cause de*) and opinions (*je pense que, à mon avis*).

ICT opportunity

Students doing a presentation on the same country could be videoed together, using props such as flags, posters, pictures, souvenirs. This video could be shown at parents' open evenings as a European taster.

Unité 12 Pages 118–119

These two pages cover travel in Europe.

Presentation idea

Using **CM62** as an OHT, ask the students *Quelle est la capitale de la France? Et de l'Allemagne?* etc. Write on an overlay as many capitals as they know and add those that they don't. Let them look at the completed map for one minute and then remove the overlay. Ask them to name as many countries and their capitals as they can in one minute. Then move on to task 15.

14 📖

Pairing of European country names with their capitals.

Solution
L'Allemagne – Berlin; L'Italie – Rome; La Grèce – Athènes; L'Autriche – Vienne; L'Espagne – Madrid; Le Portugal – Lisbonne; La Suisse – Berne.

15 🎧 [CD 3 track 51]

Students listen as Nicole and André discuss a route across Europe. They choose the individual routes proposed from the three given in the Student's Book. There are examples of the conditional, but no attention is drawn to these.

Transcript

Nicole: Tu vois . . . on pourrait partir de Paris, passer par Berlin . . . et ensuite . . . euh . . . si on allait à Vienne ce serait bien. Bon, voyons. Si on allait à Rome et puis . . . euh . . . on pourrait continuer sur Athènes. Après, on pourrait revenir en France, tu vois. Qu'est-ce que tu en penses?

André: À mon avis, on pourrait quitter Paris pour Berlin ... et ... euh ... puis ... après on irait directement à Athènes. Après, on pourrait passer par Rome et Vienne pour revenir à Paris à la fin du tour.

Solution

Nicole **3**; André **2**

Tip

This Tip reminds students that certain verbs may be linked to infinitives to express an intention, hope, wish, or preference. The verbs listed may be used in task 16.

16

The pictures and descriptions of European cities serve as a stimulus. Students work in pairs. Partner A proposes a European destination. Partner B disagrees and chooses another. Students could go on to say why they would prefer the other one:

Venise: On pourrait voir le Grand Canal et le Palais des Doges.

Differentiation opportunities ⬇ ⬆

Here you could use ⬇**DW12.2A** and ⬆**DW12.2B**.

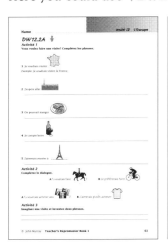

■ On ⬇**DW12.2A**, students say what they could do, would like to do, etc. on a visit to France using the expressions given and the pictures as prompts, but adding any further ideas of their own if they can.

Solution

Activity 1

1 Je voudrais visiter la France.
2 J'espère aller à Paris.
3 On pourrait manger un steack-frites.

4 Je compte boire du vin.
5 J'aimerais monter à la Tour Eiffel.

■ On ⬆**DW12.2B**, students use the pictures provided to talk about one single country. Encourage students to add more suggestions of their own.

17  [CD 3 track 52]

Nicole and André continue their discussion, concentrating this time on saving money on their travels. The comprehension questions use the construction *si* + present + future. Students choose the answer according to what they hear.

Transcript

Nicole: Si nous prenons le train de Rome à Vienne, ce sera trop cher. Je préférerais y aller en voiture.

André: Mais si on prend le train, on aura plus de temps à Vienne, tu vois. En plus, si on a une carte jeunesse, les billets seront moins chers.

Nicole: Oui, je suppose que tu as raison. Mais le logement? À mon avis, les hôtels seront trop chers.

André: On va dans les auberges de jeunesse, bien sûr. Dans une auberge de jeunesse, on fera des économies.

Nicole: Bonne idée . . . et si nous faisons des économies nous pourrons peut-être passer la dernière nuit dans un hôtel.

André: D'accord. Excellent!

Nicole: Oui, c'est décidé!

Solution

1 a; **2** b; **3** a; **4** b; ⬆**5** a

Point grammaire: Using *si*

To present this, you could write the word '*Prédictions*' on the board; then post up various things you are going to do, and practise some regular futures, e.g. *Ma sœur va se marier. Elle portera ... Son fiancé portera ... À la réception on mangera ... il y aura combien d'invités?* Or ... *Ce week-end je vais faire du foot – je porterai ...* Or ... *Qui gagnera la Ligue ... qui va marquer un but ..., croyez-vous?* (*Croyez-vous?* can be slipped in in preparation for the next two pages – it won't hinder understanding here ...)

To show that something in the present can have consequences in the future, pile up books, playing cards in a house or cans and ask: *Si j'en ajoute un(e) maintenant, ça tombera, oui ou non?* Indicate on your watch or the clock as you say *maintenant* and gesture forward to indicate the future when you say *ça tombera?*

You could prompt other future verb predictions by saying what you are going to do (*X ira à une interview lundi. Qu'est-ce qu'il portera? X travaillera dans le jardin/fera du VTT dans le Lake District ce week-end; Qu'est-ce qu'elle portera?* etc.)

EGW12 practises *si* sentences with present and future (see full notes on **EGW12** at the end of this unit).

Point grammaire: Irregular verbs

This reminds students that irregular verbs usually have irregular futures. A set of green cards with the infinitive on one side and the *je* form of the future is a useful resource for practising these. Flash the infinitive and ask the future, or flash the future and ask from which verb it comes.

18

As preparation for task 19 students match infinitives to future tenses.

Solution

devoir – je devrai; être – je serai; savoir – je saurai; aller – j'irai; venir – je viendrai

19

Students formulate complete sentences using the phrases given. There are are several possibilities.

Tip

A number of phrases for agreeing and disagreeing are given and students are prompted to make sure they understand the less obvious ones.

20

Activity 1: Using the pairs of pictures, students compose mini-dialogues, as in the example. They go on to invent some more dialogues based on the same model, but with more scope to express their own opinions: some appropriate verbs and adjectives are supplied.

Unité 12 Pages 120–121

These two pages examine the European Union and its political institutions in a non-technical way, starting with some very basic information in the Tip.

Presentation idea

Give students **CM65**, a wordsearch with 16 European country names: all of the countries are members of the EU with the exception of *Norvège* and *Suisse*, the two *intrus* which students identify for question 2 on the sheet. The 16 country names are given at the foot of the sheet so that you can supply them or not, according to the students' ability/knowledge.

Solution to CM65

1

O	L	C	W	P	A	Y	S	B	A	S	E
E	G	È	V	R	O	N	T	F	E	L	N
I	R	M	G	E	R	R	L	A	S	I	G
L	È	H	R	S	O	A	T	Z	P	O	A
A	C	F	U	S	Y	U	P	U	A	N	M
T	E	I	O	I	A	T	B	I	G	R	E
I	S	N	B	U	U	R	E	R	N	A	L
Y	F	L	M	S	M	I	W	L	E	C	L
U	A	A	E	T	E	C	N	A	R	F	A
D	G	N	X	R	U	H	S	N	P	T	H
T	O	D	U	I	N	E	E	D	È	U	S
G	B	E	L	G	I	Q	U	E	V	R	A

2 The two 'intrus' are SUISSE and NORVÈGE, the two non-EU European countries.

Some background information on the EU:

• 1951   Treaty of Paris created the European Coal and Steel Community.
• 1957   Creation of the European Economic Community (Common Market) – now known as the European Union (EU).
• 1973   Britain joins EEC.
• 1999   Creation of the euro.
• The European Parliament votes on laws to cover the whole EU. European law is superior to national law.

Presentation idea

Before listening to the tape for task 21, ask students to predict which topics might be mentioned.

21 🎧

Alain Chasseur interviews Michèle Lafontaine, a députée in the European Parliament. Students listen and note whether she mentions certain subjects. Draw attention to the two topics given in the vocabulary list.

Transcript

Alain: Madame Lafontaine, vous êtes députée au Parlement européen. Quelles sont pour vous les grandes questions qui concernent les politiques?

Mme Lafontaine: Vous avez plusieurs questions. Par exemple, il y a le logement. En Europe, il y a beaucoup de gens qui n'ont pas de logement, et ça c'est un scandale!

Alain: Oui, oui.

Mme Lafontaine: Ensuite, vous avez la question de l'emploi. En Europe il y a encore des gens qui n'ont pas d'emploi. Une autre question qui est très, très importante est celle du racisme. Malheureusement, il y a toujours des racistes en Europe.

Alain: Est-il possible de trouver une solution à ces problèmes?

Teacher's Guide 1 © John Murray

Mme Lafontaine: Oui, je pense que la solution, c'est l'éducation. Si on a une bonne éducation, on pourra trouver un emploi. En plus, on sera mieux informé sur la culture des autres, donc on sera moins raciste – du moins, je l'espère.

Solution
1 oui; **2** non; **3** oui; **4** non; **5** oui; **6** oui

Ça se dit comment? p.120 🎧

The sound *-oi* constantly turns up in *Moi, je . . .* It is not difficult to pronounce. Problems only arise in converting the written form into sound. Students could look through their vocabulary books for other instances of this spelling and try pronouncing the words.

Transcript
– moi, toi;
– la boîte, l'histoire, le roi, le poisson;
– froid;
– croire, devoir (je dois), pouvoir, savoir, vouloir;
– quoi?

Quoi? Même le roi des poissons doit faire son devoir d'histoire?

Point grammaire: *Croire*

The present tense of the verb *croire* is given in full, together the first person of the perfect tense (*j'ai cru*).

Presentation idea

Present the students with a mixture of sensible and crazy ideas. Students confirm these or contradict you and say what they believe. Give them the following phrases to introduce their replies: *Non, je ne (le) crois pas, vous avez tort/ce n'est pas possible* and *Oui, vous avez raison/c'est possible.* **N.B.** Don't let students start their sentences with *Je ne crois pas que* or they will stray into the minefield of the subjunctive!

Exemple: – *Moi, je crois que la Terre est plate.*
– *Vous avez tort. Moi, je crois que la terre est ronde.*

Suggestions for crazy sentences:

• *Moi, je crois que Londres est en France.*
• *Moi, je crois que la Belgique est en Australie. Tu me crois?*

• *Moi, je crois que la vache est une plante.*
• *Moi, je crois que le monstre de Loch Ness existe.*
• *Moi, j'ai une licorne dans mon jardin.*
• *A mon avis, Norwich City est la meilleure équipe du monde. Vous me croyez?*
• *Vous voyez cette cravate – elle m'a coûté 20 livres.*

Tip

Before students tackle task 22, they are encouraged to revise comparatives and superlatives and given a few examples as reminders.

22 🎧 ↑

Alain continues his interview. In this section, Mme Lafontaine expresses a number of opinions using *croire* and discusses the opinions of others. Students decide which statements are true.

Transcript
Alain: Pour vous, quelle est la question la plus importante aujourd'hui?
Mme Lafontaine: Moi, je crois que la question la plus importante aujourd'hui est celle de l'éducation. C'est une question d'urgence.
Alain: Les autres députés sont d'accord?
Mme Lafontaine: Oui. Par exemple . . . La pollution de l'environnement est une question qui nous concerne mais la question de l'éducation des jeunes est beaucoup plus importante. Bien des députés croient que l'éducation est plus importante que la question de la pollution. Seuls des gens éduqués pourront sauver notre planète.
Alain: Vous avez donc une vision de l'Europe unie?
Mme Lafontaine: Oui, je crois en l'unification de l'Europe. Pour moi, l'Europe unie c'est l'avenir.

Solution
Vrai: 3, 4

Ça se dit comment? p.120 🎧

This sound is uniform, with the exception of the past participle of *avoir*.

Transcript
– l'Europe, l'euro, européen, heureux, malheureux, malheureusement.
– euh

Unité 12 Page 121

This page gives a brief history of the European Union and examines the euro. The information content and grammar coverage will probably make it suitable for above-average groups only.

No comprehension questions are set on this passage which serves as an introduction to the use of the past historic (*le passé simple*).

Transcript

Pourquoi l'Union européenne?

En 1939, Adolf Hitler attaqua la Pologne, et la Grande-Bretagne déclara la guerre aux Nazis. En 1940, l'armée allemande commença à occuper la majorité des pays de l'ouest de l'Europe. La seconde guerre mondiale dura six ans, mais en 1945, la paix revint en Europe quand Hitler se tua.

Après la guerre, on décida de créer une Europe unie pour empêcher la guerre. Jean Monnet proposa la coopération européenne et en 1957 on créa le Marché Commun. Depuis ce temps-là, on a fait beaucoup de progrès.

Point grammaire: More pairs of verbs

The use of verbs paired directly with infinitives has already been revised (see page 123). Verbs which require *à* before an infinitive are introduced here. The general principle is that these verbs have a positive or inchoative (starting, beginning) sense, though there are obvious exceptions such as *hésiter*. Verbs requiring *de* are also introduced. Many of these have a sense of stopping or preventing, but this does not apply to such verbs as *essayer* or *décider*, which are very common.

To introduce these verbs, you could use **CM43** again with *Chris le cambrioleur* and *Christine la cambrioleuse* and demonstrate the following story on the OHT:

Chris a décidé d'entrer dans une grande maison. Il a hésité à ouvrir la fenêtre, mais, finalement, il a décidé de le faire. Il a ouvert la fenêtre et il est entré. Il a commencé à monter l'escalier quand il a entendu un bruit. C'était le chat! Il est entré dans une chambre et il a commencé à chercher des bijoux. Il a trouvé un collier de perles. Il a fini de chercher et il a commencé à descendre. Soudain, il a entendu un bruit. Il a essayé de se cacher. Trop tard! Il y avait quelqu'un. Chris a choisi de descendre. Devant la fenêtre il a vu une silhouette. C'était Christine!

Write on the board/an OHT those sentences that contain *à* and those that contain *de*, or use the above text, photocopied and enlarged. Underline one set of sentences in red and one in blue. Ask the students if they can see why you've grouped them like that. Explain that some verbs take *à* and some take *de*. Using the sentences, call out an infinitive, e.g. *commencer*. Students spot the preposition and call it out in answer. Formalise the infinitives in two columns with their attendant preposition.

23

Students link sentence halves according to the sense, matching sentences to the sense of the above text.

Solution

En 1939, les Allemands ont commencé à occuper la Pologne.
Les Anglais ont décidé de déclarer la guerre aux Allemands.
En 1945, les forces alliées ont réussi à battre les Allemands.
Le leader allemand a choisi de se suicider.
Jean Monnet a essayé d'unifier l'Europe.

More able students could take elements of these sentences and make up new ones, e.g. *Hitler a décidé d'occuper la Pologne. Les forces allemandes ont essayé d'occuper l'Europe.* Attention to agreement of verbs is required here.

Tip

This Tip draws attention to the use of the past historic (*le passé simple*). The verbs in this text are all in the third person singular and end in -*a*. It is stressed that students need only recognise the past historic. Attention is drawn to the fact that the past historic may be differentiated from the future by the lack of an -*r* before the -*a*.

24

In this exercise, students spot the verb in the past historic.

Solution

1 occupa; **2** essaya; **3** quitta; **4** proposa; **5** entra

Extra idea

For further practice in recognising the past historic, take simple books written for French children (but not fairy stories!) and choose a page with a good few examples. Ask students to spot these verbs and tell you the infinitive.

ICT opportunity

Use a website dedicated to young people as a source of stories.

Using **www.yahoo.fr** and key words such as *sites/enfants* it is possible to find a range of sites with reading materials for younger readers.

There are interactive sites and websites from French schools with materials put up by the students.

Some specific suggestions: **www.chez.com/magazimut/** and **www.momes.net/**. A possible extension for highest attaining students might be to encourage them to write their own stories based on some of those produced by French students.

Pourquoi l'euro?

This is a non-technical description of the euro and its function. Pictures of the notes and coins are given.

Unité 12 Pages 122–123

Thes two pages look at problems faced by the young in Europe today.

25 📖 [CD 3 track 58]

Multiple-choice reading comprehension. More able students could attempt this as a listening comprehension before reading the text, if you can persuade them not to look at it!

This article covers a tour of Europe by eight handicapped athletes using cycle-wheelchairs.

Transcript

'Nous disons «Bonjour» à la nouvelle Europe'

A: Au mois de mai, huit athlètes handicapés comptent faire le tour d'Europe en vélo-fauteuil roulant. Le tour va durer cinq semaines. L'organisateur, Antoine Aoun, nous a expliqué pourquoi les jeunes handicapés ont décidé de faire ce tour.

B: Pour nous, la vieille Europe est finie – en faisant ce tour, nous disons «bonjour» à la nouvelle Europe. En visitant plusieurs pays européens, nous espérons porter ce message à nos amis d'autres nationalités.

A: À la fin du tour, les athlètes vont visiter le Parlement européen. Le Président du Parlement a déjà encouragé les huit jeunes.

B: «En faisant ce tour, vous montrez aux jeunes Européens qu'on doit travailler ensemble pour créer une Europe unie.»

Solution

1 b; **2** c; **3** a; **4** c; **5** b

Tip

This revises question words and expressions. Others that could be revised are: *qui? combien?* and *lequel?* Additional questions on the text using these words could be put to students; e.g. **Combien** *d'athlètes vont faire ce tour?* **Qui** *va parler aux athlètes? Un des athlètes a parlé au Quotidien.* **Lequel**?

Differentiation opportunity ⬇ [CD 3 track 59]

At this point you could use ⬇**DW12.3**. Students are given a series of questions about an MEP's schedule. They are shown which future tense phrases are needed in the replies, and given pictures to prompt them in the task of completing the answers.

N.B. The questions are on the recording so that this can be done independently, using the pause button to allow time for replies.

Transcript for ⬇ DW12.3

Numéro 1: Quel jour est-ce que M. Foliot arrivera?
Numéro 2: Comment est-ce qu'il voyagera?
Numéro 3: À quelle heure est-ce qu'il arrivera?
Numéro 4: Où est-ce qu'on doit le retrouver?
Numéro 5: Comment est-ce qu'il ira à l'hôtel?
Numéro 6: Qu'est-ce que M. Foliot apportera?
Numéro 7: Qui est-ce qu'il consultera?
Numéro 8: Quand est-ce qu'il partira?
Numéro 9: Où est-ce qu'il ira?

Solution

1 M. Foliot arrivera jeudi 23 avril.
2 Il voyagera en avion.
3 Il arrivera à 21h30.
4 On doit le retrouver à l'aéroport.
5 Il ira à l'hôtel en taxi.
6 M.Foliot apportera des documents secrets.
7 Il consultera M. le Premier Ministre.
8 Il partira samedi 25 avril.
9 Il ira à Londres.

Point grammaire: *En* (= by)

Examples of *en* + present participle are given in the text and are explained here. The general rule is given that the present participle is formed from the *nous* form of the present, but no exceptions are mentioned. The point is taught here principally for recognition.

26 🎧 📖

Alain Chasseur interviews one of the athletes. His questions are heard on the tape.

1 Students find the right answers from the among those given.

Transcript [CD 3 track 60]

Alain:
Numéro 1 Pourquoi avez-vous décidé de faire ce tour?
Numéro 2 Quand est-ce que vous êtes partis?
Numéro 3 Comment avez-vous réussi à monter les collines et les montagnes?
Numéro 4 Quelles villes avez-vous visitées?
Numéro 5 Qu'est-ce que vous avez pensé de votre interview avec le Président du Parlement européen?

Solution

1 d; **2** a; **3** e; **4** c; **5** b

2 Students listen to the complete interview and check their answers.

Transcript [CD 3 track 61]

Alain: Pourquoi avez-vous décidé de faire ce tour?

Athlète: En faisant ce tour, je crois que nous avons pu porter notre message aux jeunes d'Europe.

Alain: Quand est-ce que vous êtes partis?

Athlète: Le départ a été le 8 mai.

Alain: Comment avez-vous réussi à monter les collines et les montagnes?

Athlète: En faisant un grand effort!

Alain: Quelles villes avez-vous visitées?

Athlète: Bruxelles, Paris, Berlin, Vienne et Rome. En visitant ces villes-là, nous avons pu parler à beaucoup de jeunes Européens.

Alain: Qu'est-ce que vous avez pensé de votre interview avec le Président du Parlement européen?

Athlète: En nous parlant, je crois que le Président a encouragé tous les jeunes handicapés d'Europe.

As reinforcement for work on the present participle, students could listen again to the tape and put their hands up when they hear an example of this construction. They could attempt to repeat what they hear and say what it means.

Ça se dit comment? p.122 [CD 3 track 62]

'*-euil*' is a particularly difficult sound for native speakers of English. It should be emphasised that the final *l* or *l*'s should not be pronounced.

Transcript

– Argenteuil, un fauteuil, le deuil, un écureuil, une feuille
– À Argenteuil, un écureuil en deuil est assis dans son fauteuil parmi les feuilles.

27 [CD 3 track 63]

This page deals with racism.
   Students read/listen to the text and choose the correct alternative.

Transcript

Spirou: Cela a été difficile aujourd'hui. Je suis allé au collège ce matin comme d'habitude. En arrivant, j'ai rencontré deux crânes-rasés qui ont essayé de bloquer mon passage. Ces idiots aiment faire cela. J'ai demandé à passer, mais ils ont ri. «T'es pas français, toi! La France, c'est pour les Français!» Enfin, j'ai réussi à entrer, mais ils m'ont insulté. C'est étrange, ça. Moi, je suis européen. Je suis né en Grèce et nous avons émigré en France. On est tous des Européens, non?

Quotidien: Oui, tu as raison Spirou, on est tous des Européens, mais le racisme existe toujours. Les racistes ne comprennent pas les autres. Ils sont ignorants et lâches. Tu dois continuer à combattre le racisme. L'Europe, c'est la tolérance!

Solution

1 Spirou a rencontré les crânes-rasés **en entrant au collège**.
2 Les gars ont **insulté** Spirou.
3 Spirou est d'origine **grecque**.
4 Les racistes sont **lâches**.

Point grammaire: En (= while)

This draws attention to the use of *en* + present participle to mean *on doing, while doing.*

Tip

This is a further reminder that some verbs (e.g. *aimer, devoir*) are followed directly by an infinitive.

ICT activity

The poem below is from the website of the *Association du 14ᵉ arrondissement de Paris* URL **www.sos.racisme-14.org**

Aims:
* to understand an authentic poem on racism;
* to adapt that poem;
* to reuse adjectives relating to nationality in a new context.

   1 Teacher creates a document of the poem below, adapting it as appropriate.
   2 Students are then asked to consider how they might adapt it or add to it but still keep the message.
   3 Lower attainers might be given a shorter poem with key words to be changed highlighted or additional suggestions made.

Ton Christ est juif,
Ton scooter est japonais,
Ta pizza est italienne et ton couscous marocain,
Ta démocratie est grecque,
Ton café est brésilien,
Ta montre est suisse,
Ta chemise est hawaïenne,
Ton baladeur est coréen,
Tes vacances sont turques, tunisiennes ou marocaines,
Tes chiffres sont arabes,
Ton écriture est latine,
Et . . . tu reproches à ton voisin d'être . . . étranger
. . .

28

This gives practice in using the present participle. Students choose the correct present participles from the box. (There are distractors in the box so that comprehension is necessary.)

Solution

Aujourd'hui, nous devons faire un effort pour être Européens. En **essayant** de comprendre les autres nationalités, nous réussirons à créer une Europe unie. Bien sûr, il y a des gens qui, en **hésitant** à prendre contact avec les autres, choisissent de rester isolés. Mais, aujourd'hui, en **voyageant**, les jeunes peuvent connaître les pays de l'UE. Si vous voulez avoir un emploi à l'étranger, il y a moins de restrictions aujourd'hui. En **travaillant** dans un autre pays, vous en apprécierez mieux la culture.

29 🎧 ↑ [CD 3 track 64]

Students listen to a representative of SOS-Racisme talking about racism in Europe. They choose the correct alternative from the answers given.

SOS-Racisme was founded by Harlem Désir and aims to counteract all aspects of racism. Its motto is: *Touche pas à mon pote* (Don't touch my mate). The organisation has grown immensely in recent years and is now in a position to bring court cases against those who practise discrimination. Their particular target is, of course, *le Front National*, the extreme right-wing political party.

Transcript

Notre organisation, SOS-Racisme, essaie de combattre le racisme. Il est peut-être difficile de le croire, mais on trouve des discriminations racistes dans l'accès au travail, au logement et aux loisirs. Moi, je dirais qu'il y a plus de racisme aujourd'hui. La majorité des Français sont tolérants, mais il y une minorité . . . les crânes-rasés, le Front National . . . qui sont très racistes. À mon avis, les jeunes représentent l'avenir. Il est possible d'imaginer un monde sans racisme, mais je crois qu'il y aura toujours du racisme en Europe. Malheureusement, c'est la nature humaine.

Solution

1 Il y a plus de racisme aujourd'hui.
2 La majorité des Français sont tolérants.
3 Il y aura toujours du racisme en Europe.

Unité 12 Pages 124–125

Checkpoints

Test

The **Test** checks students' skills in the grammatical goals of the unit:

- using adjectives
- using negatives
- talking about languages
- using *si* + present + future
- using pairs of verbs
- recognising the past historic tense
- using *en* and the present participle

Solution

1 **a** Il y a beaucoup de sociétés **industrielles** en Europe. [2]
  b La réalité **virtuelle** joue un rôle important aujourd'hui. [2]
  c On peut faire un stage sur l'UE dans beaucoup d'institutions **professionnelles**. [2]
  d Moi, j'aime la cuisine **grecque**. [2]
  e Nous comptons acheter une voiture **neuve**. [2]
↑2 **a** Jules; **b** Pauline; **c** Isabelle; **d** Frédérique; **e** Magali; **f** Marc [6]
3 **a** Je dois examiner la carte du continent. [1]
  b Je voudrais parler plusieurs langues européennes. [1]
  c Je compte aller en Italie. J'espère visiter Rome. [1]
4 **a** Si vous avez un passeport européen, vous pourrez visiter bien des pays. [1]
  b Si vous parlez français en Suisse, on vous comprendra. [1]
  c Si Nicole n'a pas beaucoup d'argent, elle devra passer la nuit dans une auberge de jeunesse. [1]
  d Nous pourrons faire des achats aux Galeries Lafayette, si nous allons à Paris. [1]
5 **a** En Italie. [1]
  b En achetant des CD et en les écoutant. [1]
  c En téléphonant à l'Office de Tourisme. [1]
  d Pour me relaxer! [1]
↑6 **a** Le président décida d'aller au Parlement – oui. [1]
  b Mon frère décidera ce qu'il faut faire – non. [1]
  c La France accepta la situation – oui. [1]
  Total [30]

Quiz

The **Quiz** checks students' knowledge acquired in the unit, about:
- the geography of Europe
- food in Europe
- French-speaking countries in Europe
- the languages of Europe
- the European Union and the euro

Solution

1 a Sur les sept continents, l'Europe arrive en **sixième** place. [1]
  b Les pays industrialisés se trouvent dans **le nord** du continent. [1]
  c L'Espagne et le Portugal sont des pays plutôt **agricoles**. [1]
  d La deuxième guerre mondiale a commencé en **1939**. [1]
2 Description of national dishes – open-ended task:
  a any French dish. [2]
  b any British dish. [2]
  c any Italian dish. [2]
3 Région francophone: **la Suisse romande** [1]
  Autres langues parlées: **italien, allemand (romanche)** [3]
  Deux industries importantes: (any 2 of) **le secteur financier, l'horlogerie, l'industrie laitière, la chocolaterie, la restauration, les sports d'hiver, les fleurs.** [2]
3 a La Belgique est plus grande que la France. **F** [1]
  b Tous les Belges parlent néerlandais. **F** [1]
  c Les panneaux routiers sont écrits en français et en anglais. **F** [1]
4 a FRANCE; ALLEMAGNE; ITALIE; ESPAGNE; PORTUGAL; ROYAUME-UNI; BELGIQUE; SUÈDE; PAYS-BAS; LUXEMBOURG; FINLANDE; DANEMARK; IRLANDE [13]
  b Grèce; Autriche [2]
5 a the European Union [1]
  b the European Parliament [1]
  c the euro [1]
  d a Member of Parliament [1]
  Total [40]

Projets

A Students describe a European country under the headings given. This description requires only the present tense. ⬆(A2) More able students might wish to refer to the country's history, in which case they would have to distinguish between perfect and imperfect tense.

B Students give an account of a holiday in a European country. This provides the opportunity for use of the perfect tense for actions and for imperfects in comments. If students choose to write about their intentions for next year based on these experiences, this will bring them into the realms of higher grades at GCSE.

C Students recommend a dish that they like, giving details of its nationality, ingredients and taste. A number of students could present their choices.

D Students describe an ideal European country (*l'Eurotopie*). They could explain what the country is like and give reasons for its perfection. This is an opportunity to use negatives (e.g. *Il n'y a pas de racisme et il n'y a jamais de combats entre les hooligans*). More able students could write this in the future as a vision of Eurotopia in the future.

EGW12 teaching notes

Sheet **EGW12** provides extra grammar/ homework on *si* sentences with present and future.

Activity 1

This requires students to join the halves of sentences – they have to be geographically logical.

Solution

Si vous allez à Rome, vous pourrez voir le Colisée.
Si on va à Paris, on pourra voir l'Arc de Triomphe.
Si nous visitons Venise, nous aurons la possibilité de voir le Palais des Doges.
Si vous décidez d'aller à Bruxelles, vous devrez parler français ou néerlandais.
Si on visite l'Allemagne, il sera possible d'aller à Berlin.

Activity 2

This practises the same construction, but in an open-ended exercise in which students construct their own sentences, choosing logically from the elements provided.

unité 13
La planète bleue

Contexts
- pollution: problems and action
- natural disasters: earthquakes and floods
- global warming and climate change
- animals and plants: survival and protection
- action that can be taken to protect the environment

Grammar
- using *chaque* and *chacun*
- using *si* + imperfect + conditional
- recognising the passive
- recognising verbs in the subjunctive
- using the pluperfect

Revision
- the imperfect tense
- past participles
- using pairs of verbs

This unit deals with environmental problems.

Unité 13 Page 126
This page covers energy consumption.

Presentation ideas
Use **CM66** as an OHT to introduce the vocabulary of energy and pollution (*eau, charbon, pétrole, CFC, panneau solaire*).

Students could be asked to predict how much water we use per person per day (litres), how much energy people in the northern hemisphere use annually (coal in tonnes), how much forest is destroyed annually and how much CO_2 is produced per day by a town of 24 000 inhabitants. This could be done as a guessing game. In answer to each figure you say *Plus* or *Moins*, thus enabling students to focus in on the correct figure, but stop before they reach the exact answers. Leave the estimates on the board. The answers are given in the first reading text.

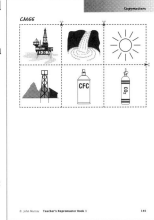

Transcript [CD 4 track 1]
Nous n'avons qu'une seule planète – la Terre. Ce beau globe bleu flotte dans l'espace, loin des autres planètes. Oui, c'est notre petit chez nous – nous vivons ici, mais nous maltraitons la Terre. Par exemple ...

- **Eau:** Chaque habitant de la Terre consomme 120–150 litres d'eau par jour, mais . . . on ne boit que deux litres d'eau!
- **Énergie:** Les habitants des pays du nord utilisent énormément d'énergie. Chacun consomme l'équivalent de 10 tonnes de charbon par an.
- **Forêt:** Au Brésil, on a brûlé plus de 85 500 km² en une année. Chaque année la situation se détériore.
- **CO_2:** Une ville de 24 000 habitants produit 705 tonnes de CO_2 par jour.

Comment tout cela finira-t-il?

1

Students link pictures to figures taken from the text.

Solution
1 10 t; **2** 150 l; **3** 1; **4** 85 500km²; **5** 705 t

Point grammaire: *Chaque, chacun*
This section introduces *chaque* and *chacun*. Stress that *chaque* must be attached to a noun and *chacun* stands alone.

To teach *chaque*, use an OHT of a school timetable. Point out: *Chaque cours dure 50 minutes. Il y a six cours chaque jour. Alors, chaque élève assiste à 30 cours par semaine. Chaque élève passe donc 1 500 minutes en classe chaque semaine.*

To teach *chacun* you could adapt the above ideas or use the following suggestions. You could use a student group to demonstrate on. Give each member a pencil, piece of paper or some other identical item and say. *Bon, voici le groupe numéro 1, qui consiste en 5 membres. Chacun a un ...* Alternatively, use a picture of a rock band: *Voici Music Maestro. Ce groupe consiste en quatre membres. Chacun joue d'un instrument de musique. Alain joue de la guitare,* etc. You could use *vrai/faux* sentences on a demonstration group. *Chacun porte un pull bleu/Chacun porte l'uniforme scolaire/ Chacun est mâle/Chacun a les cheveux courts,* etc. (*Chacun* is *chacune* in the feminine.) To combine the two points you could give students sentences with *chaque* in the question. They use *chacun* in the answer, e.g *Chaque membre du groupe est américain? Non, chacun est britannique.*

2

Students use the phrases given to give a commentary on the pictures of the annual consumption of French consumers. Answers will depend on the choice and ability of the students.

Unité 13 Page 127

This page concentrates on the ecological effects of hamburger production by large multinationals. To give a balanced view, some positive points about multinationals are also given.

Presentation ideas

Start with a simple question/answer session: *Qui aime manger des pizzas? Qui aime manger des hamburgers? Ça coûte combien un hamburger? Combien est-ce que vous en mangez par semaine? Quels en sont les ingrédients? C'est bon pour la santé?*

Then do a re-check: *Qui aime manger des hamburgers?* And note the total. After reading the text, you can ask again and see if the total has gone down.

3

Students match up halves of sentences.

Transcript [CD 4 track 2]
Côté négatif
Numéro 1: Pour avoir un hamburger il faut avoir du bœuf.
Numéro 2: Pour avoir du bœuf il faut avoir des vaches.
Numéro 3: Pour avoir des vaches il faut avoir des champs.
Numéro 4: Pour avoir des champs il faut brûler des forêts.
Numéro 5: Pour brûler des forêts il faut chasser les hommes.
Numéro 6: Pour gagner leur vie, les hommes doivent trouver un emploi.
Numéro 7: Pour trouver un emploi il faut aller en ville.
Numéro 8: Pour vivre en ville il faut acheter de la nourriture.
Si on est pauvre on ne peut pas payer cher . . .

Transcript [CD 4 track 3]
Côté positif
Les grandes sociétés multinationales sont énormément riches. Donc, elles peuvent sponsoriser des événements sportifs comme les Jeux Olympiques.
De plus, ces sociétés plantent des arbres pour remplacer les forêts brûlées.
Aussi, elles produisent des produits qui sont populaires partout dans le monde.
D'ailleurs, certaines sociétés s'occupent de l'éducation des jeunes.
Qui plus est, les multinationales ont beaucoup d'employés y compris dans les pays en voie de développement.
. . . Et ton hamburger, tu l'aimes maintenant?

Point grammaire: Pour + infinitive

This revises the use of *pour* + infinitive. The first part of the above text makes abundant use of this construction. Attention is drawn to the fact that *pourquoi* begins with the same syllable as *pour*.

4 [CD 4 track 4]

Students work out which question produces which answer beginning with *pour*. These are based on the first part of the above text.

Transcript
Question A: Pourquoi est-ce que les hommes doivent trouver un emploi?
Question B: Pourquoi est-ce qu'il faut chasser les gens?
Question C: Pourquoi est-ce qu'il faut acheter de la nourriture?
Question D: Pourquoi est-ce qu'il faut aller en ville?
Question E: Pourquoi est-ce qu'il faut avoir du bœuf?

Solution
A 4; **B** 3; **C** 5; **D** 2; **E** 1

5

Students join sentence halves explaining why people take 'green' measures. Solutions will depend on the choices of the students.

Differentiation opportunity ⬇ ⬆

Students could use ⬆**DW13.1A** or ⬆**DW13.1B** at this point.

- On ⬇**DW13.1A**, students complete gapped sentences choosing words from the box. All sentences involve *pour* (in order to). They then match sentence halves to produce possible solutions to problems. Several answers are possible.
- On ⬆**DW13.1B**, students first match problems to solutions. Several answers are possible. They then formulate sentences (all of which begin with *pour* + infinitive) from the elements of a switchboard. Answers will depend on the choices of the students.

Unité 13 Pages 128–129

These two pages are concerned with the car and the pollution it produces, including that which is caused by its fuel in the raw state.

Presentation idea

You could ask students to tell you what they and their parents use their cars for. This gives further opportunity for using *pour* + infinitive, e.g. *pour aller à la plage; pour faire des excursions; pour venir au collège; pour aller en ville le soir; pour faire du shopping*, etc. You could ask them if they can imagine a world without cars. The following text explains what life would be like.

6   [CD 4 track 5]

Students find the required expressions in the text. Three are examples of the conditional. Students may have been using *on pourrait* for some time. This exercise provides further vocabulary for talking about the environment and pollution.

Transcript

La voiture – amie ou ennemie?

Nous aimons nos voitures – la voiture représente la liberté. Mais les voitures représentent la pollution – elles produisent des gaz toxiques.

Si on n'utilisait pas la voiture:

- on consommerait moins d'essence
- on utiliserait moins d'huile
- on prendrait le bus ou le train
- on ne polluerait plus l'atmosphère
- on respirerait de l'air pur
- on pourrait prendre plus d'exercice
- on serait moins stressé
- on se sentirait mieux

Solution

1 des gaz toxiques
2 moins d'essence
3 l'atmosphère
4 de l'air pur
5 moins stressé
6 on utiliserait
7 on respirerait
8 on pourrait

Point grammaire: The conditional tense

This gives an explanation of the conditional. Students should already be familiar with the imperfect whose endings this tense shares. The explanation stresses the similarity with the future tense. At this point the *si* + imperfect clause is **not** introduced.

Extra idea

Students could take the conditional verbs at the beginning of the sentences in the above text and complete them differently, e.g. *On serait plus stressé! On utiliserait plus de paires de chaussures!* etc.

7

Students choose an appropriate conditional verb from the box to complete the gapped sentences.

Solution

1 On **prendrait** de temps en temps un taxi.
2 On **travaillerait** à la maison.
3 Les bus **coûteraient** moins chers.
4 Les trains **seraient** moins chers.
5 Il y **aurait** moins de voitures dans les rues.

8 [CD 4 track 6]

Students listen to Alain Chasseur reflecting on the advantages and disadvantages of not having a car. They note three advantages and three disadvantages.

Students could be asked to predict what these advantages and disadvantages might be, e.g. *moins de pollution*; *rues tranquilles*, etc. You could write notes on the board. While the students listen to the tape, you could tick off those that they correctly predicted.

Transcript

Alain: Ici Alain Chasseur au micro de Radio Corsaire. Cette semaine c'est la Semaine de l'Environnement et nous allons parler de l'environnement et ses problèmes. La voiture, c'est certainement un de ces problèmes. On en fabrique de plus en plus. Mais où cela finira-t-il? On ne peut pas continuer comme ça. Un jour nous devrons trouver d'autres moyens de transport. Vous pouvez imaginer cela . . . s'il n'y avait pas de voitures? Tout d'abord, on ferait des promenades . . . ce serait agréable. Et il y aurait moins de pollution . . . ce serait aussi très agréable. En plus, les rues seraient très tranquilles. Par contre, ça pourrait être difficile. Il faudrait aller en ville à pied . . . et on ne pourrait pas aller voir ses amis dans une autre ville. Finalement, les villages seraient complètement isolés. Oui, il y aurait des avantages et des inconvénients.

Qu'en pensez-vous? Réflichissez-y, chers auditeurs . . . c'est un sujet de grande importance.

Solution

Some students may be able to give more complete sentences with a conditional, for their replies, but most will be aiming for the following kind of note-taking, with the conditional simply being recognised, not produced.

Avantages	Désavantages
1 Exemple: promenades	1 aller en ville à pied
2 moins de pollution	2 on ne pourrait pas aller voir ses amis
3 rues tranquilles	3 villages isolés

9 [CD 4 track 7]

Presentation idea

Words for 'fuel' are tricky. You may or may not wish to explain the following differences! *Le pétrole* is crude oil, which is also called *le fioul*. This is sometimes spelled *fuel*, and can also mean oil for central heating. The word for fuel is *le combustible*, so oil, petrol and coal are *les combustibles*. Refined oil is *l'huile* and petrol is *l'essence*. A (super)tanker is *un pétrolier (géant)*. The main practical point for students, of course, is not to look for or ask for *le pétrole* instead of *l'essence* at a garage.

Students read the text and decide whether the sentences given are true or false.

Transcript

La marée noire

Le pétrole – c'est noir, et c'est dangereux. Le grand risque? Une «marée noire» sur la côte. En 1999 le pétrolier Erika a perdu sa charge de pétrole près de la côte bretonne. Une énorme marée noire en a été la conséquence. Après plus d'un an on trouvait toujours du pétrole sur les plages!

Des scientifiques anglais ont trouvé une solution à ce problème. C'est une sorte de «gel». Voici leur théorie: si on étendait ce gel sur la surface de la marée noire, il «mangerait» le pétrole. Puis on roulerait le gel comme un «gâteau roulé». Qu'est-ce qu'on ferait après? On ne sait pas encore . . . mais la théorie est bonne!

Solution

1 F; **2** F; **3** V; **4** F; **5** F

Point grammaire: 'Si' sentences

This section introduces the use of *si* + imperfect + conditional.

Presentation idea

Make the pictures from **CM67** into an OHT and cut them up. Place them on the OHP and remove them one by one, saying, e.g. *S'il n'y avait pas de pétrole, il n'y aurait pas de voitures. S'il n'y avait pas de voitures, il n'y aurait pas d'autoroutes. S'il n'y avait pas d'autoroutes, il n'y aurait pas de camions. S'il n'y avait pas de camions, il n'y aurait pas de livraisons. S'il n'y avait pas de livraisons, il n'y aurait pas de supermarchés*, etc.

Various combinations can be used. Write the framework *S'il n'y avait pas de . . ., il n'y aurait pas de . . .* on the board. A student could then rearrange the pictures on the OHT, and others could suggest what to remove, e.g. *S'il n'y avait pas d'autoroutes, il n'y aurait pas de stations-service.* An alternative construction to use would be *Si on n'avait pas de . . . on ne pourrait pas . . .* This would involve the need for an infinitive, e.g. *Si on n'avait pas de voitures, on ne pourrait pas aller au supermarché.*

Tip

This lists some useful expressions involving the conditional. These are:

Qu'est-ce qui se passerait si . . .? What would happen if . . .
Quelles en seraient les conséquences si . . .? What would be the consequence if . . .
Qu'est ce que tu ferais/vous feriez si . . .? What would you do if . . .

10

This exercise gives opportunities for students to use their imagination. They are asked to say what the consequence would be in a number of situations:

Quelles en seraient les conséquences . . .
• *si l'essence coûtait 100€ le litre?*
• *s'il n'y avait pas de pétrole?*
• *si on ne pouvait pas utiliser sa voiture en semaine?*
• *s'il y avait une marée noire sur toute la côte?*
• *si cette marée noire tuait tous les poissons?*

Give them an example or two to indicate how simple or complex you expect the answers to be. Students then try some answers using the expressions given below the exercise. Answers will depend on the choices and abilities of the students.

At this point you could also use ⬇**DW13.2A** and ⬆**DW13.2B**.

■ ⬇**DW13.2A** starts with a vocabulary exercise. Students tick the elements that they would have in their ideal world. They then write sentences using given expressions and the elements that they have chosen. This work could be developed into a display with illustrations by the students of their ideal world and sentences saying what would and what would not exist.

■ ⬆**DW13.2B** Students read a text on the supervolcano under Yellowstone Park. They make predictions as to what would happen if this monster were to erupt. Students then complete sentences involving *si* + imperfect + conditional, choosing the tense as appropriate, and completing the sentences with appropriate content.

Unité 13 Page 130

This page covers floods.

11 📖 [CD 4 track 8]

Students put the pictures in the correct order in accordance with the sequence in the text.

Transcript

Les inondations
Qu'est-ce qui cause les inondations?
Il y a plusieurs causes possibles.
La pluie tombe. La neige fond.
L'eau est emportée par les rivières.
Si elles sont bloquées, les rivières débordent.
Quelles en sont les conséquences?
Les champs sont inondés.
Dans les villes, les rues sont submergées.
Les gens sont forcés de quitter leurs maisons.
Les maisons sont abîmées.
Le paysage est dévasté.

Solution

b, g, d, h, c, f, a, e

Point grammaire: The passive

This covers the present tense of the passive. This form of the verb is for recognition only at this level.

To demonstrate this, use the pictures from **CM68**, cut up into small squares for the OHP. Teach the vocabulary necessary for this: *les inondations, le volcan, le séisme, le tremblement de terre, l'incendie*. Revise the following: *la ville, le village, la ferme, la forêt*. Demonstrate a natural disaster as follows on the OHP. *Les inondations* (move flood from left to right and remove countryside) *dévastent le paysage*. Then invert the positions of these two elements. Place countryside on first. Say *Le paysage est dévasté par les inondations*, and sweep away with flood picture. Write on the board; *Les inondations <u>dévastent</u> le paysage = Le paysage <u>est dévasté par</u> les inondations*.

Continue this process using the following pairs:

Le volcan – la ville.
Le séisme – le village.
L'incendie – la forêt.
Les inondations – la ferme.

Give students a number of sentences, e.g *La ville est dévastée par le volcan*, and ask students to put the slides on the OHT in the correct order.

Differentiation opportunity

⬆ With the OHT slides left on the OHP, more able students could write versions of the sentences.

⬇ Less able students could have a photocopy of **CM68** to cut up. They are then given a series of written sentences such as: *Le village est détruit par le volcan* and *La ville est dévastée par un séisme*. They stick the pictures in two columns labelled *Agent* and *Victime*.

Students of middling ability could have a variety of sentence types, e.g. *Le volcan détruit le village* and *La ville est dévasté par un séisme*. They stick the sentences in two columns labelled *Agent* and *Victime*.

12 📖

In this exercise, students find examples of the passive. Once these have been extracted, you could ask students if they can see why these examples have been picked out. Answer: They are all illustrations of the passive.

Solution

1 sont bloquées
2 sont submergées
3 sont forcés de
4 sont abîmées
5 est dévasté

Differentiation opportunity ⬆ ⬇

⬆ More able students could use these verbs as the 'centre portions' of sentences giving details of disasters. Agreements may need to be changed, e.g.

Les routes sont bloquées; Les maisons sont submergées, etc.

⬇ Less able students could identify the *Agent* and the *Victime* in each sentence.

Unité 13 Page 131

This page covers earthquakes and the use of the perfect tense of the passive.

Presentation idea

Show a brief extract from a video of an earthquake – the Geography department will be a good source for this. With the sound down, give a simple commentary in French, e.g. *La terre tremble, C'est un séisme. Il mesure 6 sur l'échelle de Richter. Les maisons tremblent. Le pont tombe dans la rivière. Il y a beaucoup de victimes. Les villes sont dévastées. Il y a des inondations. Beaucoup de gens sont hospitalisés. Les maisons sont démolies par la force du séisme. Par conséquent, beaucoup de gens sont sans domicile.*

Transcript [CD 4 track 9]

Villes dévastées, des milliers de morts

Les séismes, ou tremblements de terre, sont terrifiants! Saviez-vous qu'en Chine, 650 000 personnes ont été tuées quand la ville de Tangshan a été secouée par un séisme en 1976? Deux décennies plus tard, au Japon, la ville de Kobe a été dévastée par un séisme mesurant 7,2 sur l'échelle de Richter. Plus de 5 000 personnes ont été tuées. Beaucoup de blessés ont été hospitalisés. Des milliers de maisons ont été détruites. Beaucoup de gens ont été brûlés quand des bâtiments ont pris feu.

Plus récemment en Turquie, deux séismes en 1999 ont tué plus de 18 000 personnes et ont blessé 49 000 personnes. Plusieurs milliers ont été laissés sans abri.

En 2001, au Gujarat (en Inde), un séisme a tué plus de 100 000 personnes.

No comprehension questions are set on this text which serves as an introduction to the perfect tense of the passive voice.

Tip

This explains that the passive is used in newspaper, radio and TV reports to explain what happened to people, towns and buildings. Examples are given of the perfect of the passive.

Extra ideas

- Check comprehension of the Kobe passage and the passives that it contains, by means of a question/answer session in which students are challenged to find the evidence in the text to prove the truth of statements you make, e.g. *Il y a eu un séisme énorme a Kobe. Beaucoup de gens sont morts. Beaucoup de maisons sont en ruines,* etc.
- **EGW13 Activity 1** further practises recognition of the passive (see full notes on **EGW13** at the end of this unit).

13 🎧 [CD 4 track 10]

Students listen to a newsflash relating to an earthquake in Indonesia. The report contains examples of the perfect tense of the passive. Students complete the grid with the necessary figures.

Transcript

Alain: Ici Radio Corsaire. Nous avons maintenant un flash . . . En Indonésie, un séisme mesurant 7 sur l'échelle de Richter a dévasté plusieurs villes. Selon les premières informations, 200 personnes ont été tuées, et il y a 3 000 blessés. Plus de 500 personnes ont déjà été hospitalisées par les services de secours. Dans les grandes villes, des incendies se sont déclarés à la suite des tremblements. Dans un immeuble, 36 personnes ont été brûlées lors d'une explosion de gaz. On attend toujours des informations, mais on pense que plus de 5 000 personnes sont sans domicile. Radio Corsaire.

Solution

Tués: 200	Brûlés: 36
Blessés: 3 000	Sans domicile: 5 000 (+)
Hospitalisés: 500 (+)	

Tip

This higher level Tip explains that newspaper headlines are often in the passive and are reduced sentences. An example is given.

14 ✏️ ⬆

Although you are unlikely to be asking students to produce the perfect tense of the passive, this exercise provides an opportunity for them to show full comprehension of headlines by expanding them into full sentences.

Solution

1 La région a été dévastée.
2 Les victimes ont été hospitalisées.
3 L'hôpital Saint-Jean a été détruit.
4 Des milliers ont été blessés.
5 La ville a été inondée.
6 Les gens ont été obligés de nettoyer leurs maisons.
7 Les vieilles maisons ont été démolies.
8 Le gouvernement a été forcé de payer les réparations.

Differentiation opportunity ⬇

For less able students an alternative would be to give them a number of full sentences and ask them to create the headlines by deleting words. This could be done on the board. Each student is allowed to delete one word until the headline is complete, e.g.

- *Paris a été dévasté par les inondations.*
- *Djakarta a été dévasté par un séisme.*
- *Des millions de réfugiés ont été évacués.*
- *Des centaines de maisons ont été démolies.*
- *Les champs ont été submergés par la rivière.*

Unité 13 Page 132

15 📖 [CD 4 track 11]

Students pick out useful expressions from the text.

Transcript

L'effet de serre

C'est quoi, l'effet de serre? C'est simple.
Des gaz toxiques comme les CFC et le CO_2 sont produits par les voitures, les bombes et la consommation des combustibles.
Les gaz montent dans l'atmosphère.
La terre est chauffée par le soleil. La chaleur monte dans l'atmosphère, mais elle est bloquée par les gaz.
La terre devient de plus en plus chaude.
L'effet de serre, c'est un cercle vicieux!

Solution

1 l'effet de serre
2 des gaz toxiques
3 les bombes
4 la consommation des combustibles
5 chauffée par le soleil
6 elle est bloquée
7 de plus en plus chaud(e)
8 un cercle vicieux

16 [CD 4 track 12]

This is perhaps best used as a class-based oral exercise before you go on to task 17.

Students match environmental problems with possible solutions. (See Projet C at the end of this unit for a possible survey on this topic.)

Transcript

L'effet de serre, c'est votre faute? Répondez oui ou non!

1 Vous utilisez un déodorant en bombe?
2 Vous utilisez régulièrement votre voiture?
3 Vous chauffez votre maison au fuel ou au charbon?
4 Vous n'avez pas isolé votre maison?
5 Vous utilisez beaucoup d'électricité?

Alors, vous contribuez sans doute à la création de l'effet de serre.

Solution

1 d; 2 a; 3 e; 4 c; 5 b

17 [CD 4 track 13]

The second reading passage contains some solutions to environmental problems and contains some examples of the subjunctive, although these are not explained at this stage. To support comprehension of the passage, you could write some key words with their English equivalents, all jumbled together, on the board, and ask students to come up and join a French word with its English pair. If you divide the class into two teams and choose people from alternate teams this might liven it up slightly!

Transcript

Mais que faire?
Si on changeait ses habitudes, on pourrait faire des progrès. Si tout le monde isolait la maison, on réduirait la consommation d'énergie. On pourrait utiliser des panneaux solaires pour chauffer sa maison et on pourrait installer un double-vitrage. Il est possible qu'on puisse réduire de 30% la consommation d'énergie de cette façon. Il faut qu'on trouve une solution. Il ne nous reste pas beaucoup de temps! Il est impossible qu'on puisse continuer à augmenter notre consommation de combustibles et d'énergie. Si on continue comme cela, dans cent ans, nous n'aurons plus de combustibles fossiles.

Students take the proposed solutions and place them in a personal order of priority, before working in groups of four to agree a consensus list of priorities.

The following phrases would be useful:

A mon avis . . . Pour moi . . . On doit . . . Il faut . . . Il est essentiel de . . . Il est important de . . . La première priorité c'est de . . .

Homework opportunity

EGW13 Activity 1 further practises *si* sentences with the imperfect and conditional (see full notes on **EGW13** at the end of this unit).

ICT activity

Attention: l'effet de serre.

Aims:

- to revise use of imperatives;
- to reuse the language of the unit in a new context/for a different audience.

1 Teacher refers to the questions and answers of task 16 and shows how they might be used as an exhortation on a poster warning against global warming e.g. *N'utilisez pas . . .*, etc.
2 Students could then create a flyer or poster encouraging people to think more 'greenly'.
3 They should use images to illustrate the warnings.
4 Teachers might ask higher attainers to write in the form of an article for a school magazine.

Unité 13 Page 133

This page concentrates on measures that students and others can take individually to reduce the greenhouse effect and lessen the risk of an environmental disaster.

Students listen to Rachel making a plea to the effect that environmental problems are everyone's fault and everyone's concern.

Transcript [CD 4 track 14]

Plan d'action – Sauver la planète!

La responsabilité est aux autres?
Rachel dit:
En ce qui concerne l'environnement, le problème c'est les autres – les sociétés, les gouvernements, etc. Que font-ils? Ils exportent le pétrole dans des pétroliers énormes. Ils conduisent des voitures partout. Ils brûlent des forêts. Ils vendent tous les produits dans des sacs en plastique. Alors, la responsabilité est aux autres?

Non! La responsabilité est à nous! Qu'est-ce que **nous** pouvons faire, **nous** les jeunes – les adultes de demain?

18 📖🔊

Students propose solutions from the table. This requires some careful selection as some combinations are not solutions at all. Answers will depend on the abilities and choices of the students.

19 📖

Students read and answer the questionnaire. Their answers are held in reserve while they listen to some proposed solutions in the following listening exercise.

20 🎧 [CD 4 track 15]

Students listen to Alain Chasseur interviewing people on the subject of the 'green' measures that they could take.

Transcript

Alain Chasseur: Les questions d'environnement nous concernent tous. Mais qu'est-ce qu'on fait pour sauver la planète? Et qu'est-ce qu'on pourrait faire? Cette semaine, j'ai interviewé plusieurs habitants de Saint-Malo. Monsieur, qu'est-ce que vous pourriez faire pour réduire votre consommation d'énergie?

Numéro 1: Bon . . . ben . . . je prends un bain tous les jours, je pourrais prendre une douche, je suppose.

Alain: Et vous, Madame?

Numéro 2: Moi, je pense que je pourrais installer des panneaux solaires. Comme ça, je consommerais moins d'électricité.

Numéro 3: Chez nous nous avons trois chiens, donc il y a toujours beaucoup de boîtes qu'on jette à la poubelle. On pourrait les recycler, je pense.

Numéro 4: Moi, j'ai une voiture diesel . . . je pourrais la changer, je suppose . . . comme ça, je pourrais utiliser de l'essence sans plomb.

Numéro 5: Ben . . . je prends la voiture tous les jours pour aller au travail, mais ce n'est pas loin. Je pourrais y aller à pied.

Numéro 6: Une autre chose . . . on lit beaucoup de journaux chez nous . . . on pourrait les recycler.

Numéro 7: Alain: Et moi, je pourrais prendre mon vélo, parce que j'utilise toujours ma voiture. Voilà, individuellement, c'est très peu, mais ensemble, on pourrait peut-être sauver la planète.

Solution

1 a; **2** g; **3** c; **4** d; **5** f; **6** e; **7** b

21 🔊✏️↑

Students explain or write down what they could do to reduce pollution and energy consumption.

Unité 13 Pages 134–135

These two pages cover endangered species – including mankind.

Presentation idea

In a class activity, make a list of the names of as many big cats as possible. Most big cats have the same name in French as in English, so this can be a useful exercise in applying a French accent to cognates or near-cognates. The family includes: *le lion, le tigre, le léopard, le panthère, le guépard* (cheetah), *le jaguar, le puma* and *le lynx.* Many students will probably think that the lion is the biggest of the cats, so it may come as a surprise to be introduced to the Siberian tiger. You could also ask where the cats are to be found (*Ils vivent dans quel continent?*). They may be interested to find that the big cats are not confined to Africa, Asia and South America, but that Europe is home to the puma, the lynx and the wildcat (*le chat sauvage*).

The text contains some examples of the subjunctive which are explained in the Point grammaire.

Extra idea

If you want to make use of the text specifically for listening before moving on to do task 22, you could write the following words on the board and ask students to listen out for the **opposite** of them in the text. Some of course are predictable, others require careful listening:

rarement, exactement, petit, laid, médiocre, noire, sud, peu important, pathétique.

Transcript [CD 4 track 16]

Le tigre de Sibérie: Espèce menacée de disparition

Poids: 250–280 kg.

Gestation: 95–111 jours: normalement trois à quatre petits.

Mode de vie: Mâles – solitaires. Femelles – forment des groupes familiaux.

Régime: Mange 9 à 10 kg de viande par jour.

Longévité: Environ 15 ans.

Le plus grand et le plus beau des félins, cet animal superbe est en voie de disparition.

Il est beaucoup plus grand que le tigre de Bengale, et en hiver sa pelure est presque blanche.

Il vit en Sibérie et dans la Chine du nord. Il n'y a dans la nature que 200 individus. Il est donc essentiel qu'on conserve les tigres qui survivent. Heureusement, il y en a encore 200 dans les zoos. Il est très important que nous conservions cet animal magnifique!

22 📖

Students complete a gapped text based on comprehension of the reading passage, choosing words from the box.

Solution

Ce tigre est le plus grand de tous les **chats**. Il **pèse** presque 280 kg. Normalement, la femelle donne naissance à trois ou quatre **jeunes**. Son **habitat** est en Sibérie et en Chine. Normalement, le mâle aime être **seul**, mais la femelle préfère se trouver dans un groupe **social**. Le tigre est un carnivore, et il doit **consommer** entre 9 et 10 kg de viande par jour. Normalement, le tigre **vit** entre douze et quinze ans. Si nous ne faisons pas d'efforts pour le **conserver**, il est possible qu'il puisse disparaître.

Point grammaire: The subjunctive

This introduces the notion of using the subjunctive after expressions of necessity or possibility. With the exception of *puisse*, all the examples in the text, the exercise and the Point Grammaire are recognisable from their indicative forms. The third person singular forms of *avoir, être* and *faire* are given.

23

In this exercise, students are asked to pick out: **a** the expression which triggers the use of the subjunctive; and **b** the subjunctive form of the verb. You could also ask students to identify the infinitive from which these verbs come. There is no need to practise productive use of the subjunctive.

Solution

1 **a** Il est essentiel que **b** fasse
2 **a** Il est possible que **b** disparaissent
3 **a** Il est important que **b** (il y) ait
4 **a** Il faut que **b** conservions
5 **a** Il n'est pas possible que **b** continuiez

Differentiation opportunity⇣

At this point you could give students ⇣**DW13.3**. This is a text about mankind as an endangered species. The structure of the text is similar to the above. The task is to complete a *fiche technique* similar to the text about the Siberian tiger, on the basis of understanding the text. This worksheet would be a good preparation for the text on page 135, in that it would prepare the students for the idea that mankind could actually disappear from the face of the earth.

24

Students prepare a description of an animal, similar to the description given above. They could use *Encarta* (CD ROM in French) to find information, or failing that, *Encyclopædia Britannica* on the Internet (**www.britannica.com**).

ICT activity

Learning objectives

* to use search strategies for an effective search on the Internet;
* to extract details from authentic sources;
* to create a presentation on an endangered species.

1 Teacher discusses with the class what the key words might be for an Internet search. It is hoped they would come up with *animaux/en voie de disparition.*
2 As a class go through **DW13.3** and ensure all headings are clear. Consider additional headings under *qualités*. **DW13.3** could remain as hard copy or could be a word-processed file.
3 Students then research an animal, filling in information under the headings.
4 If pictures are available on-line students should download them to illustrate their presentation.
5 Their written work and presentation could form part of their coursework.

Unité 13 Page 135

This page presents tongue-in-cheek ideas on gloomy prospects for mankind. The first text appears in the form of an obituary, and uses the pluperfect tense.

Presentation idea

Draw a grave marked *L'Homme: Année 3000*. Ask students to predict why mankind disappeared, i.e. what he had done. Note on the board: *L'homme a disparu parce qu'il avait . . .* Give one or two examples and ask for more. Note these down, beginning each with *il avait* + a past participle. After reading the text, check with students to see which reasons correspond in both texts and which are wrong or additional.

25 📖 [CD 4 track 17]

Students find expressions in the text which have the opposite sense to those given in the questions.

Transcript

C'est l'année 3000 – L'homme a disparu de la Terre!

Disparition de l'Homme

Nous avons le vif regret de vous informer de la disparition de l'Homme, ou l'être humain. Cette espèce était en voie d'extinction depuis longtemps.

Pourquoi cet animal intéressant a-t-il disparu? Les raisons en sont multiples:

- Il avait brûlé les forêts qui consommaient le CO_2.
- Il avait pollué l'air, et ne pouvait plus respirer.
- Il avait empoisonné les rivières et les mers. Par conséquent, il n'avait rien à boire.
- Il avait traité la Terre comme une poubelle.
- Il avait trop modifié les plantes et les animaux. Ils ne pouvaient plus se reproduire.
- Il avait enterré des déchets nucléaires. Ces déchets ont empoisonné les champs.
- Il avait détruit toutes les ressources naturelles.
- Il était allé sur la Lune, mais il avait négligé la Terre.
- Il était allé au fond des mers, et il y avait laissé des déchets toxiques.
- Il avait pensé que l'argent était plus important que la Terre.

Aucune famille ne lui survit.

Solution

1 Il avait empoisonné les rivières et les mers.
2 Il avait trop modifié les plantes.
3 Il avait brûlé les forêts.
4 Il avait traité la Terre comme une poubelle.
5 Il était allé dans la Lune, mais il avait négligé la Terre.

Point grammaire: The pluperfect tense

This covers the pluperfect with both *avoir* and *être*.

26 📖

Students make judgements as to what mankind should have done in order to survive. Active use of the conditional perfect is involved. The meaning of *il aurait dû* is glossed as a lexical item rather than a construction.

Differentiation opportunity ⬇ ⬆

⬇ Less able students could add infinitive expressions to the beginnings *il aurait dû/il n'aurait pas dû*, e.g. *conserver l'eau*.

⬆ More able students may be able to use *il aurait dû* actively and add further examples.

Unité 13 Pages 136–137

Checkpoints

Test

The **Test** checks students' skills in the grammatical goals of the unit:

- using *chaque* and *chacun*
- using *si* + imperfect + conditional
- recognising the passive
- using the pluperfect
- recognising verbs in the subjunctive

Solution

1 a Chaque automobiliste utilise 1 500 litres d'essence par an. [1]
  b Chaque Français mange plus de 20 kg de fromage par an. [1]
  c Chaque élève doit lire ses manuels scolaires. [1]
  d Chaque médecin doit travailler dans un hôpital. [1]
  e Chaque écologiste veut sauver la planète. [1]
2 a Oui, chacun peut contribuer au recyclage. [1]
  b Oui, chacune consomme trop d'énergie. [1]
  c Oui, chacun s'occupe des questions d'environnement. [1]
  d Oui, chacune produit des déchets. [1]
  e Oui, chacun risque d'échouer. [1]
3 a oui [1]
  b non [1]
  c oui [1]
  d oui [1]
  e non [1]
4 a Région inondée [1]
  b Villages détruits [1]
  c Gouvernement battu [1]
  d Planète secouée [1]
  e Villageois attaqués [1]
5 a Michel n'a pas pu payer ses achats: il avait perdu son argent. [1]
  b Plusieurs espèces ont disparu au 20e siècle: on avait détruit leur habitat. [1]
  c Il y avait une marée noire: un pétrolier avait échoué. [1]
  d Il n'y avait plus d'essence: les automobilistes avaient tout consommé. [1]
  e Beaucoup d'enfants étaient malades: on ne les avait pas inoculés. [1]
⬆6 a oui [1]
  b non [1]
  c oui [1]
  d non [1]
  e oui [1]
⬆7 a Si nous consommions moins d'énergie, nous ferions des économies. [2]
  b Si on trouvait un autre moyen de propulsion, on pourrait fabriquer moins de voitures. [2]
  c Si les gouvernements faisaient plus d'efforts, ils pourraient résoudre ces problèmes. [2]
  d Nous éviterions ces problèmes, si nous nous occupions de la planète. [2]
  e On ferait des progrès, si tout le monde se mettait d'accord. [2]
  Total [40]

Quiz

The **Quiz** checks students' knowledge acquired in the unit, about:

- pollution: problems and action
- natural disasters: earthquakes and floods
- global warming and climate change
- animals and plants: survival and protection
- action that can be taken to protect the environment

Solution

1	120–150 litres	[1]
2	2 litres d'eau	[1]
3	10 tonnes de charbon	[1]
4	au Brésil	[1]
5	CO_2	[1]
6	Pour avoir des champs pour les vaches	[2]
7 a	Les voitures produisent **des gaz toxiques**.	[1]
b	Ces émissions **polluent l'air**.	[1]
c	Les motos consomment **de l'essence**.	[1]
8	Oil spill, oil slick	[1]
9	Erika	[1]
10	une sorte de gel	[1]
11	any three of the results listed on page 130	[3]
12	échelle de Richter	[1]
13	Kobe	[1]
14	plus de 100 000 personnes sont mortes	[1]
15	l'effet de serre	[1]
16	any three of the suggestions on page 132	[3]
17	oui	[1]
18	400 (200 dans la nature, 200 dans les zoos)	[1]
	Total	[25]

Projets

A Students design a house which can combat the greenhouse effect. They could label and number the parts. A key could give reasons for a particular usage, e.g. 1 *(panneaux solaires): pour réduire la consommation d'électricité.*

B (**ICT opportunity**) Students prepare a presentation on a threatened species of their own choice as an extension/version of the work they have done for task 24 of this unit (see the ICT activity suggestion which follows that exercise). They could use *Encarta* (CD-ROM in French) to find more information, or failing that, *Encyclopædia Britannica* on the Internet (**www.britannica.com**). Students could record an audio or video version of their presentation. They could use the OHP to show pictures (scanned and copied) or they could use Power Point®. Alternatively, a conventional written piece along these lines would be good for coursework purposes.

C For the suggested survey, give students a copy of the *sondage* template **CM8**. As an additional dimension to the survey, students could perhaps invent a scoring system to give their interviewees a mark out of three for each of the multi-choice questions, according to how 'green' they are.

EGW13 teaching notes

Sheet **EGW13** provides extra grammar/homework on recognising the meaning of passive phrases, and on *si* sentences with imperfect and conditional.

Activity 1

This requires students to match headlines to opening sentences of the corresponding articles.

Solution
1 c; **2** a; **3** b; **4** e; **5** d

Activity 2

This practises *si* constructions using imperfect and conditional in an open-ended exercise in which students construct their own sentences, choosing logically from the elements provided.

unité 14
Allons-y! Haïti

Background information on Haiti

Haiti (the name is spelt Haïti in French) shares the island of Hispaniola in the Caribbean with the Dominican Republic (*la République Dominicaine*), which lies to its east. Haiti is the poorest country in the western hemisphere, with an unemployment rate of 70%. The population of about 7 000 000 live in an area of some 27 560 km², making Haiti one of the most densely populated areas in the world.

Haiti depends on its agriculture. A variety of crops are grown including rice, millet, maize, red beans and root crops, such as manioc. The soil is poor, and the island's natural forests have been cut down to make charcoal. Only 1.5% of the island's original forests now remain, although reforestation schemes are under way.

The principal language of Haiti is Creole, that is to say, a natural language that has developed from a pidgin (trading) language. Haitian Creole is a blend of French and African languages. It is of course different from the Creole spoken in Mauritius.

The history of Haiti has been both violent and revolutionary. Hispaniola was originally inhabited by a native tribe known as the Arawaks. The island was colonised by the Spanish who forced the Arawaks to work in their gold mines. French settlers arrived and grew in importance. The island was divided in two in 1697, the French taking the western part of the island known as Haiti ('mountainous land'). The French imported thousands of black African slaves to work the land. By the end of the 18th century there were around 600 000 slaves, living in appalling conditions.

The French Revolution began in 1789, and a black slave by the name of Toussaint Louverture took his cue from the social upheaval in France. The revolution that he led was successful, and Louverture acted as governor until he was captured by Napoleon's forces and transported to France where he died. Haiti became independent in 1804. The next 150 years were a period of instability. The United States attempted to control Haiti between 1915 and 1934. In 1957 François 'Papa Doc' Duvalier seized power and his period as President was particularly bloody – as many as 60 000 people may have died. Duvalier was succeeded by his son Jean-Claude 'Baby Doc' Duvalier who ruled until 1986. Haiti remains a politically troubled state.

The development agency ActionAid is active in Haiti, promoting agriculture, reforestation and water conservation schemes. ActionAid also provides a system of small-scale loans to support local enterprise and income-generating projects. For further information on their valuable work contact:
ActionAid
Chataway House
Leach Road
Chard
Somerset TA20 1 FR
Tel: 01460 23 8000
www.actionaid.org

Unité 14 Pages 138–139

Point d'info [CD 4 track 18]

This shows a map of Haiti, with the Dominican Republic to the east, and a small map to show its position in relation to the Americas and Cuba. The Far West region is also shown, as there are several references to this region in the texts below.

A larger map of Haiti is provided on **CM69**.

Transcript

Haïti est située aux Caraïbes, sur l'île d'Hispaniola, à l'ouest de la République Dominicaine. Haïti est le pays le plus pauvre de l'hémisphère occidental.

Haïti est un petit pays avec une superficie de 27 500 km², comme celle du Pays de Galles, mais il a une population d'environ 7,5 millions! (Comparez: le Pays de Galles – 2,8 millions.)

Les langues officielles sont le français et le créole haïtien. Pourquoi le français? Parce que les Français ont occupé le pays pendant les 18ᵉ et le 19ᵉ siècles. Le créole est une combinaison de français et de langues africaines. Pourquoi africaines? Regardez le texte, *Histoire d'Haïti* ci-dessous.

1  [CD 4 track 19]

Students read the text *Histoire d'Haïti* which was written by a Haitian child and then put the summary at the end into the correct order.

Transcript
Histoire d'Haïti

Haïti a été dominée par les Espagnols et les Français. Voici, en bref, l'histoire du pays, écrite par un écolier âgé de six ans.
J'aime mon pays.
Haïti est le nom de mon pays
Avant il était habité par les Indiens
Les Espagnols sont venus, ils les ont tués
Et les ont remplacés par les noirs d'Afrique.
Il y a un bateau dans la mer qui attaque Haïti.
Ce sont des Espagnols dans leur bateau.
Haïti a peur. Les Indiens se battent avec les Espagnols.
Aujourd'hui, c'est l'Indépendance.

Note: Grammatically, *Haïti* is masculine and the *H* is aspirate. Local usage makes the name feminine and the *H* a mute. This usage has been followed here.

Solution

1 À l'origine, les Indiens habitaient l'île.
2 Les Espagnols ont attaqué les Indiens.
3 Les Espagnols ont tué les Indiens.
4 Les Espagnols ont importé des esclaves africains.
5 Maintenant on est indépendant.

C'est la Révolution!

This text completes the section on the history of Haïti.

2   [CD 4 track 20]

Students read (and listen to) the text and use the letters in the names of Napoléon Bonaparte and Toussaint Louverture to make as many words as possible within a time limit set by you to suit the ability of the students.

Transcript

C'est la Révolution!

En 1791 les esclaves se sont révoltés contre les Blancs. Après cette Révolution, Toussaint Louverture, ancien esclave, est devenu gouverneur d'Haïti. Mais Toussaint voulait l'indépendance. Napoléon Bonaparte, empereur de France, a envoyé une armée de 34 000 soldats. Toussaint a été capturé et exilé en France. Il est mort moins d'un an plus tard.

Extra idea

Using the information on page 138 and the above notes on the history of Haïti, students could draw a time line to show the history of Haïti. They could use the Internet or reference materials to find illustrations of people such as Napoleon, Louverture and Papa Doc Duvalier. The time line could be put up in the classsroom as a visual aid.

3

Students put the events in the day of a young Haitian into order.

Solution

1 f; **2** e; **3** d; **4** j; **5** b; **6** i; **7** h; **8** c

4

Students read five false sentences and find in the text for task 3 the evidence to prove that they are false.

Solution

1 Exemple: L'école finit a midi.
2 Je quitte la maison vers sept heures et demie.
3 Normalement je ne prends pas de petit déjeuner.
4 A seize heures je rends visite à un ami.
5 Je rentre à la maison pour faire mes devoirs.

Extra ideas

At this point you may want to use **CM70**: students complete their own diary page for a Monday, contrasting with the young Haitian's diary page shown on the sheet.

You could also use **CM71**. Students listen to three

young Haitians talking about their hopes for the future.

They tick the relevant boxes on the worksheet according to what is mentioned by each speaker. Help the students with some difficult vocabulary such as *sécheresse, récoltes.*

Transcript [CD 4 track 21]

Zamor Missage: Je voudrais être maçon. Je pense que les maçons auront beaucoup de travail au Far West parce que tout le monde veut une maison. Plus tard, je voudrais aller à l'étranger, surtout en Espagne. Il y a quelques années un de mes cousins est allé aux Bahamas. Il est vendeur là-bas. Mon cousin savait qu'il pouvait gagner plus d'argent dans un autre pays.

Riclaude Datte: Quand j'aurai fini l'école l'année prochaine, j'irai au collège professionnel à Mare Rouge pour apprendre à être mécanicien. Sinon, je serai fermier, comme tout le monde autour d'ici. Mes amis et moi, nous espérons voir un gouvernement fort et courageux. Un tel gouvernement nous donnera de meilleures écoles, de meilleurs emplois, et en plus, notre avenir à nous.

Marc Eldieu: Je réparerai les autobus et les voitures dans une grande ville – je veux être mécanicien. La plupart des gens au Far West essayent de gagner de l'argent dans les champs. Mais ici il y a toujours des sécheresses, des inondations ou des ouragans qui détruisent les récoltes. J'espère qu'on peut faire des préparatifs pour les désastres à l'avenir.

Solution

Espoirs	Zamor Missage	Riclaude Datte	Marc Eldieu
Travail	X	X	X
Voyager	X		
Habiter dans une grande ville		X	X
Écoles		X	
Gouvernement		X	
Faire des préparatifs pour les désastres			X

5

Students match French words to creole words and their illustrations. The partitive articles in French should assist students to match some words to the creole equivalents which begin with the letter D. Saying the creole words aloud may help students to 'hear' the matching French word.

Solution

Mots créoles	Mots français
Bèf	bœuf
Diri	du riz
Diti	du thé
Djondon	champignon
Dlo	de l'eau
Lèt	lait
Lwil	l'huile
Ponmdeté	pomme de terre
Poul	poulet
Sik	sucre

6  [CD 4 track 22]

Students read a text on animals and agriculture in Haïti. As preliminary work, you could revise domestic and wild animals and ask them to predict which animals might live in Haïti or which might be mentioned.

Students classify the six animals mentioned (including fish!) into wild and domesticated types.

Transcript

Les animaux d'Haïti

En Haïti vous verrez beaucoup d'animaux et d'oiseaux. Dans les villages vous trouverez des chèvres et des moutons qu'on vend sur les marchés. Un problème, c'est la santé des animaux, qui est souvent mauvaise.

Si vous visitez le Lac Saumâtre vous y verrez des crocodiles et des flamants roses, de grands oiseaux qui ont de longues pattes.

Haïti fait partie d'une île et donc la pêche est une industrie importante. On pêche près de la côte, mais les bateaux sont en mauvais état et les filets sont souvent déchirés. On vend les poissons sur les marchés. On mange aussi des œufs, et c'est pour cela que beaucoup de familles ont des poulets.

Solution

Animaux sauvages: crocodiles, flamants roses, poissons.
Animaux domestiqués: chèvres, moutons, poulets.

Unité 14 Pages 140–141

7 [CD 4 track 23]

The listening text is largely a list of the crops grown in Haïti. To support the task, ask students to copy the gapped words before listening to the tape. If you feel it's appropriate, pause the tape at the two indicated points (//) to allow students to have a go at completing the words. Alternatively, they could make a start on the more familiar words such as *riz* and *bananes* – using the pictures for reference – before listening.

Transcript

L'agriculture est la principale activité économique du Far West. Les fermiers produisent des bananes et des cacahuètes pour vendre au marché. // Il y a aussi des fermiers qui cultivent le riz qui est un ingrédient important de la cuisine haïtienne. // On peut voir aussi la production de maïs, de petits pois et de haricots rouges. Ce sont des choses que l'on mange normalement à la maison.

Solution

1 d BANANES
2 e CACAHUÈTES
3 b RIZ
4 a MAÏS
5 f PETITS POIS
6 c HARICOTS ROUGES

8  [CD 4 track 24]

Students read a text about the deforestation of Haïti. They then complete the captions for the five pictures, using language from the text.

Transcript

Les forêts en voie de disparition

Marye Charistile habite à Port-au-Prince, la capitale d'Haïti. Une ou deux fois par mois, elle rapporte 20 à 30 gros sacs de charbon de l'ouest de l'île, et elle les vend sur un marché de la capitale. En Haïti, le charbon est la principale source d'énergie.

Le problème, c'est que, pour obtenir ce charbon, il faut couper 15 à 20 millions d'arbres chaque année. L'île n'a maintenant que 1,5% de sa forêt originale. Le paradis se transforme en désert.

Y a-t-il une solution? Oui, il est maintenant illégal d'utiliser du charbon pour faire la cuisine. Les autorités ont commencé à distribuer du gaz en bouteilles.

Solution (variations possible)

1 Marye Charistile **rapporte 20 à 30 gros sacs de charbon** au marché.
2 Elle **vend le charbon** sur le marché.
3 On coupe **15 à 20 millions d'arbres** chaque année.
4 Haïti a perdu **98,5%** de sa forêt originale.
5 On **commence à distribuer du gaz** en bouteilles.

9

Students examine eight sentences and decide if each refers to a problem or solution.

1 They create two lists.
2 They match the solutions to the problems.

Solution

Problèmes

c Les systèmes de crédit n'existent pas.

e L'eau potable est difficile à obtenir.

g Les forêts sont en voie de disparition.

h L'agriculture est en mauvais état.

Solutions

a Il faut créer des systèmes d'eau pour l'usage domestique.

b On doit organiser la reforestation.

d On devrait introduire des plantes qui n'ont pas besoin de beaucoup de pluie.

f Il faut créer des groupes de crédit.

Solution

2 c f; e a; g b; h d

Some work on the Haitian environment would assist students to understand the impact of the poor environment on the lives of the Haitians. The charity ActionAid (see material for the last page of this unit) provides loans for women trading on a small scale and to help local people set up income-generating projects or small businesses such as keeping goats or chickens or setting up market stalls. ActionAid is also helping to set up community shops in the Far West.

 *10* [CD 4 track 25]

Students read a text on natural disasters, in this case, hurricanes.

Transcript

C'est un désastre!

Haïti est un pays tropical et le climat y est donc très chaud. En été il fait presque 30° et en hiver il fait toujours chaud. Le paradis? Peut-être, mais en septembre, il y a souvent des ouragans qui déferlent sur l'île d'Hispaniola. En 1999, l'ouragan Georges a dévasté le pays. Beaucoup de villages ont été inondés et un grand nombre d'Haïtiens sont morts. Qu'est-ce qu'on doit faire si un ouragan approche? Il faut trouver un abri pour sa famille et ses animaux, et attendre la fin de la tempête.

Solution

1 b; **2** a; **3** b; **4** a

11 [CD 4 track 26]

Students read/listen to a text about the work of ActionAid.

Transcript

ActionAid en Haïti

ActionAid est une agence de développement qui travaille dans plus de 30 pays du monde, en Afrique, en Asie, en Amérique Latine, et aux Caraïbes pour aider les enfants, leurs familles et les communautés. On combat la pauvreté et on essaie d'améliorer la qualité de vie des habitants de ces pays pauvres.

ActionAid travaille en Haïti depuis 1996, surtout dans le Far West.

Solution

1 d; **2** a; **3** e; **4** c; **5** b

ICT activity

Learning objective

- to create a high quality presentation illustrating the differences between the two economies.

Using a word processor or DTP package students choose the key differences and import suitable illustrations.

Extra idea

In conjunction with the ICT task, or simply in order to summarise the work done in this unit you could use **CM72** and **CM73**.

CM72 is a gapped table showing details of the UK and Haitian economies. Students fill in the gaps by using the figures below and some logical thought. On the basis of these comparisons, they design a poster to show the differences between the wealth of the UK and the poverty of Haiti. These posters could form part of a display.

CM73 is a differentiated worksheet. The first part invites students of greater ability to summarise their knowledge of agriculture, animals, charcoal, fishing and trade in a short essay of 100–150 words. The second section is a gap-fill exercise which may be tackled by students of lesser ability.

Possible projects/coursework

- If this unit has caught students' interest it is a good springboard for coursework, or you might wish to have a Haitian wall display.
- Students could find articles on the web (including poems) by going to **www.nomade.fr** (search engine) and looking up Haiti. They could write a booklet comparing life in Britain with life in Haiti, with contrasting pages facing each other.
- Alternatively, following the example of the recipe in Unit 10 (Mauritius) they could investigate Haitian cuisine, noting recipes, trying them at home and writing reports. This would give an opportunity for using the perfect and imperfect tenses.

Further information

If you want to find out more about the work done by ActionAid contact the address given above (page 149).

Assessment Tasks: Teacher's Notes

These assessment tasks are provided **on pages 158–88 of the Teacher's Repromaster Book**.

Score Sheets for the Assessment Tasks (one for Foundation, one for Higher level) are provided on pages 162–63 of this Teacher's Guide; they may be copied and completed for each student. Please note that on the scoresheets, the total mark for each group of tasks, and the speaking/writing marks, have been left blank for you to complete because these will depend on your decision about which mark scheme to use for speaking and writing tasks.

Assessment Tasks: Units 1–4 Teacher's Notes

Foundation Listening U1–4 [CD 4 track 27]

When the sheets have been given out, allow students a few moments to read through the questions and make sure they know what to do before you start the recording. The recording should be paused after each speaker (A–G) to allow students to fill in their answers. When all speakers have been heard once, play the recording through once more from the beginning, again pausing after each speaker so that students may make alterations if they wish. With some groups you may feel that a third listening is also appropriate.

Transcript

Announcer: Quels sports aimez-vous?
A: Les sports? Ça ne m'intéresse pas. Moi, j'adore les ordinateurs. J'aime tchatcher sur Internet.
B: Moi, j'adore le foot. C'est mon sport préféré. Je suis membre d'une équipe de foot. On joue le samedi après-midi.
C: J'aime beaucoup le tennis. Je joue tous les mercredis avec ma sœur.
D: Moi, je n'aime pas beaucoup le sport. Je préfère regarder la télé. J'aime surtout les émissions de musique pop.
E: Moi aussi, j'adore la musique pop. Je joue de la guitare. J'aime aussi faire du vélo.
F: Mon passe-temps préféré c'est le basketball. Je vais au centre de sports avec ma copine Fabienne.
G: Pour moi, c'est le karting. Je passe des heures et des heures au parc où on peut faire du karting. C'est super!

Solution

1G; **2**E; **3**F; **4**D; **5**C; **6**B; **7**A
[6 marks, one for each answer except the example.]

To extend the test, you might want to ask students to give one more piece of information for each speaker, or, for example, three extra pieces of information in all.

Higher Listening U1–4 [CD 4 track 28]

When the sheets have been given out, allow students a few moments to read through them to make sure they know what to do before you start the recording. The recording should be paused after each speaker to allow students to fill in their answers. When all speakers have been heard once, play the recording through once more from the beginning, again pausing after each speaker so that students may make alterations if they wish.

Transcript

Announcer: Tu aimes la natation, Sylvie?
Sylvie: Pour moi la natation c'est le sport le plus ennuyeux du monde. Je n'aime pas du tout la natation. Je sais nager, mais aller à la piscine? Non, merci!
Announcer: Et toi, Chantal?
Chantal: Moi non plus, je n'aime pas nager. Moi, je ne suis pas du tout sportive et quand je mets mon maillot de bain – pff, c'est ridicule! De plus, il faut se laver les cheveux après et ça, c'est embêtant. Moi, je préfère la lecture ou regarder les feuilletons à la télé.
Announcer: Aimez-vous la natation, Monsieur Grignot?
M. Grignot: Moi, j'adore la natation. C'est mon sport préféré. Tous les matins je passe une demi-heure à la piscine avant d'aller au bureau.
Announcer: Tous les matins? Ça alors! Et vous, Madame Darcie?
Mme Darcie: Moi, je vais rarement à la piscine, mais j'aime nager dans la mer quand nous sommes en vacances – s'il fait beau!
Announcer: Et toi, Geneviève?
Geneviève: Je ne sais pas nager. Alors, je ne vais jamais à la piscine.
Announcer: Qu'en dites-vous, Monsieur Groubier?
M. Groubier: Moi, j'adore nager dans une piscine privée – à un hôtel par exemple. Je déteste les piscines municipales. Il y a trop d'enfants qui font trop de bruit! Et je ne supporte pas ça!

Solution

1 Geneviève
2 Mme Darcie
3 M. Grignot
4 Mme Darcie
5 M. Groubier
6 Exemple: Sylvie
7 Chantal
8 Chantal
[7 marks, one for each answer except the example.]

To extend the test you might want to ask students to give one more piece of information for each speaker, or, for example, three extra pieces of information in all. Any correct information can be given credit.

Foundation Reading U1–4

Students read the passage and fill in the grid to show whether the statements are true, false or not given in the text.

Solution

1 Exemple: Faux
2 Vrai
3 Vrai
4 Pas dans le texte
5 Faux
6 Pas dans le texte
7 Vrai
8 Faux/pas dans le texte
[7 marks, one for each answer except the example.]

Higher Reading U1–4

Students read the text and write the appropiate names in the boxes next to statements 1–9.

Solution

1 Exemple: Joëlle.
2 Pierre.
3 Pierre.
4 Dani.
5 Dani.
6 Joëlle.
7 Pierre.
8 Dani.
9 Joëlle.
[8 marks, one for each answer except the example.]

Foundation Speaking U1–4 [CD 4 track 29]

Students perform both role-play situations. The 'prompts' are given on the recording, although you may prefer to read them yourself or let a partner read them.

Transcript (Examiner's part)

1 • Quelles matières aimes-tu?
  • Et qu'est-ce que tu n'aimes pas à l'école?
  • Moi, je déteste les repas à l'école. Et toi?
  • J'aime manger des fruits. Et toi?
  • Moi, j'espère travailler comme journaliste. Et toi?
2 • Est-ce que tu aimes jouer au tennis?
  • Tu joues souvent?
  • Tu joues bien?
  • Tu aimes les autres sports?
  • Moi, je n'aime pas le sport. Je préfère regarder la télévision.

Mark Scheme

You may want to use the mark scheme laid down by your GCSE awarding body, or you may use the scheme given here.

For each 'utterance':
2 = communicates without ambiguity
1 = communicates but with some ambiguity
0 = does not communicate
[For each role-play – 5 utterances × 2 = 10 marks maximum.]

Higher Speaking U1–4

Students study the series of pictures and give an account of the events they represent. They may report the events in either the first person or third person but they should use the past tense. The phrases given on the sheet are for guidance only and students should not feel they must include all of them. Conversely, they should be encouraged to be imaginative and to invent details of their own. You should prompt and 'nudge' as necessary in order to keep the account moving and to make it into a conversation rather than a monologue.

Mark Scheme

You may want to use the mark scheme laid down by your GCSE awarding body for this type of exercise or you may use the scheme given here.

Communication – Maximum 15 marks
14–15 Good pace. Communicates well. Expands on given information. Responds to unexpected interjections by examiner.
11–13 Covers all necessary information with little prompting. Gives a little extra information.
8–10 Communicates most of the necessary points. May need a little prompting. Some hesitation.
4–7 Communicates some of the main points with some omissions. Somewhat hesitant. Needs prompting.
0–3 Communicates isolated points only. Hesitant. Unforthcoming.

Quality of Language – Maximum 5 marks
5 Confident. Good pronunciation. Wide variety of vocabulary and structures. Excellent use of tenses. Very fluent.
4 Good pronunciation. Good range of vocabulary and structures. Good command of tenses.
3 Some inaccuracy but with pockets of good French. Adequate range of vocabulary and structures.
2 Frequent errors. Basic range of vocabulary and structures only. Hesitant.
1 Anglicised pronunciation. Very limited range of vocabulary and structures.
[Total for the test – 20 marks.]

Foundation Writing U1–4

1 Students should not feel they need to include the sports illustrated on the sheet – they are included merely to give ideas.
2 Students fill in the form according to the instructions given. They should not reuse the word *français* which is given as an example.

Mark Scheme

1 You may want to use the mark scheme laid down by your GCSE awarding body for this type of exercise or you may use the scheme given here.

  For each of the ten items – 1 mark if communicated clearly (even with inaccurate spelling).
  [Total 10 marks.]

2 See **1** for the mark scheme.

Higher Writing U1–4

You may want to allow students to choose one of these questions or you may want them to attempt both within a given time limit. No mention of the length of students' scripts or of the time allowed is given on the sheets so that you can adapt these to your own requirements. You may, for example, want to ask students to write the number of words laid down by your GCSE awarding body for this type of task.

These stimuli may also be given to students who are preparing coursework assignments under either 'open' or 'controlled' conditions.

Mark Scheme

You should refer to the marking criteria laid down by your awarding body when assessing your students' work on this task.

Assessment Tasks: Units 6–9 Teacher's Notes

Foundation Listening U6–9 [CD 4 track 30]

Allow students a few moments to read the questions and make sure they know what to do before you start the recording. In the column headed 'Other information' they should aim to give one other detail relevant to the speaker. The recording should be paused after each speaker to allow students to write their answers into the grid. When all speakers have been heard once, play the recording through once more from the beginning, again pausing after each speaker so that students may make alterations if they wish.

Transcript

Announcer: Tu vas en vacances, Serge?
Serge: Nous allons en Grande-Bretagne cette année. Nous allons en bateau parce que ma mère n'aime pas le Tunnel sous la Manche. Mes parents adorent Londres. Ils aiment les sites historiques et tout ça.
Announcer: Et toi, Natalie?
Natalie: Nous allons en Espagne. Nous allons faire du camping. Je vais nager dans la mer et me bronzer à la plage. Nous allons en voiture.
Announcer: Tu vas en vacances, Damien?
Damien: Cette année je vais faire le tour de l'Allemagne, en moto.
Announcer: En moto?!
Damien: Oui, c'est ça. Nous allons à Munich pour la Fête de la bière.
Announcer: Que fais-tu, Lucy?
Lucy: Je vais en Thaïlande avec ma famille. Moi, j'adore les vacances exotiques. Nous allons passer deux semaines là-bas. Nous y allons en avion.
Announcer: Et toi, Danielle?
Danielle: Je vais aux États-Unis en avion. Je veux voir les sites célèbres – Hollywood, San Francisco. J'aime aussi les montagnes et les plages.
Announcer: Où vas-tu, Jean-Marc?
Jean-Marc: Moi, je vais en Italie. Je vais avec ma famille, en voiture. On va manger des pizzas et beaucoup de glaces, visiter les sites historiques. C'est magnifique, l'Italie!

Solution

1 Exemple: Serge: Britain – boat.
2 Natalie: Spain – car.
3 Damien: Germany – motorcycle.
4 Lucy: Thailand – aeroplane.
5 Danielle: USA – aeroplane.
6 Jean-Marc: Italy – car.

For 'Other information' accept any other relevant detail (for example, Natalie: going camping/wants to swim in the sea/wants to sunbathe).

[Total 15 marks, 1 for each correctly completed box except the example.]

Higher Listening U6–9 [CD 4 track 31]

Tasks 1 and 2 are based on the same passage. You may want to allow students to work on both exercises at the same time or you may prefer to ask them to complete task 1, and then work on task 2 separately. Allow students a few moments to read through the exercises to make sure they know what to do before you start the recording. The recording should be paused after each speaker to allow students to work through the questions and answers. When all speakers have been heard once, play the recording through one or more times from the beginning, again pausing after each speaker so that students may check their work and make alterations if they wish.

Transcript

Announcer: Quelle marque de voiture avez-vous? Sandrine?

Sandrine: Alors, j'ai mon permis de conduire, depuis deux mois seulement. J'adore conduire mais je n'ai pas de voiture. Je conduis la voiture de mon père. Je veux acheter ma propre voiture – peut-être une Renault Clio. Elles ne sont pas trop chères et, euh, c'est une bonne voiture. Voilà!

Announcer: Et vous, Monsieur Laforge?

M. Laforge: Moi, j'aime le confort. Il est important d'être confortable quand on fait un long voyage. Alors, j'ai acheté une Citroën. J'ai la direction assistée, la climatisation, et bien sûr un lecteur CD. La musique, c'est ma passion – Chopin, Beethoven . . .

Announcer: Que dites-vous, Joëlle?

Joëlle: Moi, j'ai une voiture anglaise – une Ford. Elle est super – petite, jaune et violette. Elle a sa propre personnalité, je crois. Je l'appelle «Bobo». C'est ma meilleure amie.

Announcer: Et vous, Jean-Paul?

Jean-Paul: Moi, je déteste conduire en ville parce qu'il y a trop de circulation. Je préfère prendre le bus ou aller à pied. J'ai une Renault Espace. C'est bon pour les longs voyages en famille. J'ai cinq enfants et deux chiens.

Announcer: Quelle marque de voiture avez-vous, Guy?

Guy: Moi, j'adore les voitures de sport. J'aime conduire vite, de temps en temps très vite! Je déteste les limites de vitesse sur les autoroutes. Elles sont barbantes! Ma voiture, c'est une voiture allemande – une Porsche. Ça, c'est une très bonne marque.

Solution

1   **1** Exemple: Sandrine: Renault Clio – pas chère/bonne voiture.
   2 Monsieur Laforge: Citroën – confortable/direction assistée/climatisation/ lecteur CD.
   3 Joëlle: Ford – aime les couleurs/la personnalité.
   4 Jean-Paul: Renault Espace – grande famille/cinq enfants et deux chiens.
   5 Guy: Porsche – adore les voitures de sport/conduire vite.
   [1 mark for each box in the grid. Total: 8 marks.]
2   **1** h; **2** i; **3** a; **4** e; **5** c; **6** k; **7** m; **8** f
   [7 marks, one for each correct match except the example.]

Foundation Reading U6–9

Students read the passage and fill in the grid to show whether the statements are true, false or not given in the text.

Solution

1 Exemple: information not given
2 No
3 Information not given
4 Yes
5 Yes
6 Information not given
7 Yes
8 Information not given
9 No
[8 marks, 1 for each answer except the example.]

Higher Reading U6–9

Students read the letter extract and answer the questions in English. Full sentences are not required.

Solution

1 Learning to drive. [1]
2 She was frightened/because of the other vehicles. [1]
3 Taking her written test/theory test. [1]
4 a She doesn't have the money. [1]
   b She doesn't understand the technical aspect of cars. [1]
5 She wants to go to Vietnam/the Far East, [1] but Martin wants to go somewhere different/Canada. [1]
6 He wants to:
   go walking [1]
   in the mountains [1]
   and to visit the Great Lakes. [1]
[10 marks, allocated as shown.]

Foundation Speaking U6–9 [CD 4 track 32]

Students perform the two role-play situations. The 'prompts' are given on the recording, although you may prefer to read them yourself or let a partner read them.

Transcript (Examiner's part)

1   • Bonjour, Hôtel Belle Vue.
   • Pour quelle date?
   • Pour combien de personnes?
   • Vous voulez quelle sorte de chambre?
   • C'est pour combien de nuits?
2   • Bonjour. Je peux vous aider?
   • Il y a beaucoup de possibilités.
   • Le prochain train part dans vingt-cinq minutes.
   • Un aller simple pour Strasbourg. C'est ça.
   • Ça fait deux cents francs.
   • Il y a un kiosque ici à gauche.

Mark Scheme

You may want to use the mark scheme laid down by your GCSE awarding body or you may use the scheme given here.

For each 'utterance':
2 = communicates without ambiguity.
1 = communicates but with some ambiguity.
0 = does not communicate.
[For each role-play – 5 utterances × 2 = 10 marks maximum.]

Higher Speaking U6–9 [CD 4 track 33]

Many GCSE awarding bodies require candidates to answer questions on specific topics.

Transcript (Examiner's part)
- Où es-tu allé(e) en vacances l'été dernier?
- Avec qui?
- Tu y es resté(e) combien de temps?
- Comment as-tu voyagé?
- Qu'est-ce que tu as fait? Qu'est-ce que tu as vu?
- Où est-ce que tu as logé?
- Qu'est-ce que tu as mangé? Qu'est-ce que tu as bu?
- Tu as acheté des souvenirs?
- Comment as-tu trouvé ces vacances?
- Où est-ce que tu aimes aller en vacances?
- Pourquoi?
- Qu'est-ce qu'il y a à faire là?
- Quelle sorte de logement préfères-tu?
- Pourquoi?
- Qu'est-ce que tu vas faire cet été?
- Tu vas dormir où?
- Tu vas aller avec qui?
- Par quel moyen de transport?
- Combien de temps vas-tu rester?
- Qu'est-ce qu'il y a pour les jeunes?

Mark Scheme

You may want to use the mark scheme laid down by your GCSE awarding body for this type of exercise or you may prefer to mark on impression giving, say, a maximum of 15 for each of these three categories:

- Communication and content (answering the question adequately, giving extra information, etc.)
- Quality of language (use of tenses, range of vocabulary and idiom, complexity, etc.)
- Accuracy (accent, intonation, verb endings, etc.)

Foundation Writing U6–9

1 and **2** Students should not feel they need to include all – or any – of the items pictured/mentioned on the sheet – they are intended merely to give ideas.

Mark Scheme

1 You may want to use the mark scheme laid down by your GCSE awarding body for this type of exercise or you may use the scheme given here.

For each of the ten items – 1 mark if communicated clearly (even with inaccurate spelling). [Total 10 marks.]

2 For each of the the five 'items' (counting the two activities as two 'items'):
Allow 2 marks for unambiguous communication;
Allow 1 mark if communication is ambiguous;
Allow 0 marks if the item is not communicated.

Ignore errors of spelling and grammar unless they impede communication.
[Total 10 marks.]

Higher Writing U6–9

No mention of length of students' writing is given on the sheet for either of the tasks, so that you can adapt this to your own requirements. You may, for example, want to ask students to write the number of words laid down by your GCSE awarding body for this type of task. These stimuli could also be given to students who are preparing coursework assignments under either 'open' or 'controlled' conditions.

Mark Scheme

You should refer to the marking criteria laid down by your awarding body when assessing your students' work on this task. You may want to ask students to attempt both exercises or you may allow them to choose one of the two.

Assessment Tasks: Units 11–13 Teacher's Notes

Foundation Listening U11–13 [CD 4 track 34]

Allow students a few moments to read the questions and make sure they know what to do before you start the recording. The recording should be paused after each speaker to allow students to write their answers. When all speakers have been heard once, play the recording through once more from the beginning, again pausing after each speaker so that students may make alterations.

Transcript

1 Moi, je préférerais aller au cinéma ce soir.
2 J'aimerais monter à la Tour Eiffel demain.
3 Pour aller au marché, Monsieur, il faut prendre la deuxième rue à droite.
4 Moi, je vais en ville. J'aimerais acheter une nouvelle robe.
5 Mon plat préféré, c'est une glace au chocolat.
6 Moi, j'adore manger les légumes – toutes sortes de légumes.
7 Quand j'étais jeune j'habitais au bord de la mer.
8 Tu veux visiter le château? C'est à, euh, dix minutes d'ici.
9 Ce soir j'aimerais danser dans une boîte de nuit. Tu viens, chéri?
10 Monsieur, j'ai perdu mon chapeau. C'est un grand chapeau de paille.
11 Ça suffit, merci. J'ai déjà mangé assez de jambon.

Solution

1 Exemple: B; **2** C; **3** B; **4** C; **5** A; **6** A; **7** B; **8** B; **9** A; **10** C; **11** A
[10 marks, 1 for each answer except the example.]

Higher Listening U11–13 [CD 4 track 35]

Allow students a few moments to read through the exercises to make sure they know what to do before you start the recording. The recording should be paused where indicated to allow students to write down their answers. When the entire passage has been heard once, play the recording through one or more times from the beginning, pausing as before so that students may check their work and make alterations if they wish.

Transcript

Announcer: Ça serait comment, le monde idéal? Qu'en dis-tu, Gérard?
Gérard: Pour moi, le plus grand problème de ce monde est la guerre. Dans un monde idéal il n'y aurait pas de guerre. Dans une guerre c'est toujours les enfants qui souffrent le plus. Dans un monde idéal il y aurait assez de nourriture pour tous, il n'y aurait pas d'enfants qui meurent de faim. Les problèmes sociaux sont parmi les plus grands problèmes aussi – le racisme, les aggressions et tout ça. Moi, je préférerais un monde où chaque individu puisse vivre en sécurité. Ça, c'est très important.

Announcer: Et toi, Véronique? Qu'en dis-tu?
Véronique: Moi, j'aimerais un monde où on consommerait moins d'essence et moins de pétrole, où on prendrait le bus ou le train, et où on ne polluerait plus l'atmosphère. Pour moi, le plus grand problème, c'est l'effet de serre. Moi, je préférerais respirer l'air pur et me sentir mieux. Il est important de penser à nos enfants et au monde de demain. On risque de détruire les forêts et de polluer les océans.
Announcer: Quelle est ton opinion, Sylvie?
Sylvie: Moi, je préférerais un monde dans lequel tout le monde serait moins stressé. Dans le monde idéal on prendrait plus d'exercice et il n'y aurait pas de gaz toxiques dans l'atmosphère. Ce sont les plus grands problèmes du monde actuel, à mon avis.

Solution

1 Exemple: Gérard
2 Sylvie
3 Véronique
4 Véronique
5 Véronique
6 Gérard
7 Gérard
[6 marks, 1 for each answer except the example.]

Foundation Reading U11–13

Pupils choose A, B or C in each case, as in the example.

Solution

1 B; **2** A; **3** B; **4** C; **5** A; **6** B; **7** C; **8** A; **9** C; **10** B; **11** A
[10 marks, 1 for each answer except the example.]

Higher Reading U11–13

Students read the extract from a tourist brochure and tick the statements which are true, according to the extract. You may want to penalise students who tick more than four statements – subtract one mark for each tick above four.

Solution

2, 3, 6, 8
[Total 8 marks, two for each correctly identified answer.]

Foundation Speaking U11–13 [CD 4 track 36]

Students perform the four role-play situations, selecting one of the options each time a choice is given. Where the rubric indicates 'Answer the question' they should respond in any way which is appropriate.

The 'prompts' are given on the recording, although you may prefer to read them yourself or let a partner read them.

Transcript (Examiner's part)

1 • Alors, qu'est-ce qu'on va faire?
 • Bonne idée.
 • Oui. Quelle sorte de films aimes-tu?
 • Moi aussi.
 • À vingt heures.

2 • Bonjour. Vous désirez?
  • Très bien. Vous voulez manger quelque chose?
  • Je regrette. Nous n'en avons plus. Vous voulez autre chose?
  • Pas de problème.
  • Ça fait 15 francs. Merci.

3 • Oui, je peux vous aider?
  • La première rue à gauche et puis tout droit.
  • Ce n'est pas loin. Vous y allez comment?
  • Et vous passez combien de temps ici?
  • Alors, bon séjour!

4 • Où veux-tu aller cet après-midi?
  • Bonne idée.
  • À trois heures. Et où?
  • Très bien. Et qu'est-ce qu'on va faire après?

Mark Scheme

You may want to use the mark scheme laid down by your GCSE awarding body or you may use the scheme given here.

For each 'utterance':
2 = communicates without ambiguity.
1 = communicates but with some ambiguity.
0 = does not communicate.
[For each role-play: 2 × 4 utterances = 8 marks maximum.]

Higher Speaking U11–13

Students study the series of pictures and give an account of the events they represent. They may report the events in either the first person or third person but they should use the past tense.

The phrases given on the sheet are for guidance only and students should not feel they must include all of them.

You should prompt and 'nudge' as necessary in order to keep the account moving and to make it into a conversation rather than a monologue.

Mark Scheme

You may want to use the mark scheme laid down by your GCSE awarding body for this type of exercise or you may use the scheme given here.

Communication – Maximum 15 marks
14–15 Good pace. Communicates well. Expands on given information. Responds to unexpected interjections by examiner.
11–13 Covers all necessary information with little prompting. Gives a little extra information.
8–10 Communicates most of the necessary points. May need a little prompting. Some hesitation.
4–7 Communicates some of the main points with some omissions. Somewhat hesitant. Needs prompting.
0–3 Communicates isolated points only. Hesitant. Unforthcoming.

Quality of Language – Maximum 5 marks
5 Confident. Good pronunciation. Wide variety of vocabulary and structures. Excellent use of tenses. Very fluent.

4 Good pronunciation. Good range of vocabulary and structures. Good command of tenses.
3 Some inaccuracy but with pockets of good French. Adequate range of vocabulary and structures.
2 Frequent errors. Basic range of vocabulary and structures only. Hesitant.
1 Anglicised pronunciation. Very limited range of vocabulary and structures.
[Total for the test – 20 marks.]

Foundation Writing U11–13

1a and **1b** Students should not feel they need to include the items pictured on the sheet – they are intended merely to give ideas.
2 This type of grammar-based activity features on the specifications of some awarding bodies.

Mark Scheme

1a and **1b** You may want to use the mark scheme laid down by your GCSE awarding body for this type of exercise or you may use the scheme given here.

For each of the five items – 1 mark if communicated clearly (even with inaccurate spelling).
[Totals: **1** – 5 marks; **2** – 5 marks.]

2 You may want to use the mark scheme laid down by your GCSE awarding body for this type of exercise or you may use a more flexible scheme depending on the ability of your students. You may, for example, be tolerant of poor spelling depending on the ability of the students. For example, merely copying an infinitive should not be rewarded but you may want to reward a 'near miss' at a verb ending. With more able learners, however, you may want to insist on absolute accuracy if a mark is to be awarded.
[Allow 1 mark per 'gap' – total 15.]

Higher Writing U11–13

You may want to give students the choice between the two questions or you may want to ask them to attempt both. No mention of length of students' writing is given on the sheet so that you can adapt this to your own requirements. You may, for example, want to ask students to write the number of words laid down by your GCSE awarding body for this type of task.

Mark Scheme

You should refer to the marking criteria laid down by your awarding body when assessing your students' work on this task. Since it would be possible to produce responses to these stimuli which use only the present tense, you might want to encourage students to look for ways of incorporating other tenses so as to gain higher marks. Task 2, in particular, lends itself to practice of the conditional.

These stimuli may also be given to students who are preparing coursework assignments under either 'open' or 'controlled' conditions.

Synoptic Assessment Tasks: Teacher's Notes

Foundation Listening (synoptic) [CD 4 track 37]

1 Allow students a few moments to read the questions and make sure they know what to do before you start the recording. The recording should be paused after each question to allow students to write their answers. When all extracts have been heard once, play the recording through once more from the beginning, again pausing after each extract so that students may make alterations if they wish.

Transcript

1 – Bonjour, Monsieur. Vous désirez?
– Je voudrais l'assiette de fruits de mer, s'il vous plaît.
2 – Excusez-moi. Vous pouvez m'aider? Je cherche la gare.
3 – Où as-tu mal, Sylvie?
– J'ai mal à la tête. Aïe!
4 – Bonjour, Madame. Je voudrais ces cartes postales s'il vous plaît. Ça fait combien?
5 – Moi, je ne mange jamais de chocolat, mais j'adore les fruits, surtout les oranges.
6 – Où est-ce qu'on va se retrouver ce soir?
– Devant l'hôtel de la Plage?
– Bon, ça va.
7 – Marie et moi, nous sommes allées en Haïti – en mars, en avion.
8 – J'ai passé mes vacances en Grande-Bretagne. Nous avons eu de la pluie – pendant quinze jours! Brr!
9 – Et qu'est-ce tu veux faire quand tu quitteras l'école, Martin?
– Je ne sais pas. Je veux voyager, passer un an en Amérique du Sud ou en Afrique peut-être.

Solution

1 **1** d; **2** f; **3** h; **4** e; **5** i; **6** c; **7** g; **8** b; **9** a
[9 marks, one for each answer except the example.]

2 Allow students a few moments to read the questions and make sure they know what to do before you start the recording. When the passage has been heard once play the recording through once more from the beginning so that students may make alterations if they wish.

Transcript

Je m'appelle Grégoire. J'ai 15 ans et j'habite à l'île Maurice. Je parle anglais et français, l'un et l'autre, et je voudrais voyager. J'ai déjà visité les États-Unis mais je ne suis jamais allé en Europe. Je veux faire mes études en France. Je voudrais être médecin. Mon père, lui aussi, est médecin. Il travaille ici à l'hôpital. J'aime ce pays. Les gens sont très aimables, mais beaucoup de gens sont très pauvres. Il fait souvent beau, mais nous avons des orages énormes! Je voudrais visiter l'Angleterre, mais on m'a dit qu'il fait souvent très froid là-bas et qu'il y a trop de brouillard. C'est vrai? Je ne sais pas. Je l'ai vue à la télévision et au cinéma, mais je n'y suis jamais allé.

Solution

1 Mauritius [1]
2 America [1]
3 they are friendly [1]; many are poor [1]
4 often warm [1]; enormous storms [1]
5 from television/cinema [1]

[7 marks.]

Higher Listening (synoptic) [CD 4 track 38]

Allow students a few moments to read the questions and make sure they know what to do before you start the recording. The recording may be paused in the places indicated to allow students to write their answers. When the passage has been heard once, play the recording through once more from the beginning, again pausing as indicated so that students may make alterations if they wish.

Transcript

– Dis-moi, Thierry, qu'est-ce que tu aimes à l'école?
– Euh, c'est difficile parce que moi, j'aime toutes les matières. J'aime surtout les sciences – la physique, la biologie.
– Et l'informatique?
– Hmm, ça va, mais je n'aime pas beaucoup surfer sur Internet. C'est ennuyeux parce que je trouve difficile de trouver l'information que je cherche et ça prend trop de temps . . .
– Et qu'est-ce que tu aimerais faire quand tu quitteras l'école?
– Euh, après le bac je veux aller à l'université. Et après, je vais travailler comme, euh, je sais pas, comme ingénieur, technicien, quoi.
– Tu n'as pas de projets pour l'avenir, alors?
– Non. L'important pour moi, c'est de gagner beaucoup d'argent.
– Tu veux te marier?
– Je ne sais pas. Peut-être quand j'aurai trente ans ou plus.
– Et des enfants? Tu veux avoir des enfants?
– Pff! Quelle question! Je ne sais pas. Euh, oui, pourquoi pas? Un garçon et une fille, pourquoi pas? Mais pour moi le plus important c'est d'avoir une bonne voiture. Moi, je veux mon permis de conduire aussitôt que possible et acheter une Porsche ou une BMW.
– Oh là là! Est-ce que tu penses à l'environnement? Une grande voiture, ça pose des problèmes pour l'environnement, n'est-ce pas? Ça te concerne?
– Pas du tout. J'ai entendu parler des forêts qu'on détruit en Amérique du Sud et le trou dans la couche d'ozone par exemple, mais ça ne me concerne pas du tout. Pas de problème.
– Est-ce que tu as beaucoup voyagé? Tu es allé à l'étranger par exemple?
– J'ai fait un échange avec un élève anglais qui venait de Southampton, mais il était un peu arrogant et très sarcastique et, pff, j'ai trouvé l'Angleterre . . . très ennuyeuse. La nourriture, pff! La sauce à la menthe, pfff! Je n'ai aucune envie de visiter d'autres pays étrangers.
– Hmm, tu regardes beaucoup la télévision, Thierry?
– Je regarde beaucoup la télévision, au moins quatre heures par jour. C'est intéressant. Les feuilletons, ce sont mes émissions préférées.

Solution
1 Exemple: oui
2 Oui
3 Pas dans le texte
4 Oui
5 Oui
6 Pas dans le texte
7 Pas dans le texte
8 Non
9 Non
10 Non
11 Pas dans le texte
12 Non
13 Non
14 Non
[13 marks, one for each answer except the example.]

Foundation Reading (synoptic)

Students choose the picture which fits the printed extracts and write the appropriate number.

Solution
1 Exemple: a; 2 d; 3 e; 4 m; 5 f; 6 k; 7 b; 8 l; 9 j;
10 i; 11 c
[10 marks, one for each answer except the example.]

Higher Reading (synoptic)

Students read the printed text and the gapped sentences underneath. They choose words from the box at the bottom of the page to fill the gaps. The box contains more words than they will need.

Solution
1 Exemple: Pendant leur temps de libre beaucoup de Français **aiment** nager.
2 Les femmes et les hommes aiment **faire** de la natation.
3 Beaucoup de gens aiment regarder les courses de **vélo**.
4 Les sports d'**équipe** comme le rugby sont moins aimés que le cyclisme.
5 Très **peu** de gens jouent régulièrement au rugby.
6 Selon le **sondage**, faire la cuisine est une des activités les plus populaires.
7 Beaucoup de personnes aiment **travailler** dans le jardin.
8 Après avoir **mangé** les Français aiment se reposer.
9 Beaucoup de gens aiment **dormir** après le déjeuner du dimanche.
[8 marks, one for each answer except the example.]

Foundation Speaking (synoptic) [CD 4 track 39]

Students perform the three role-play situations. In number 3 they select one of the options each time a choice is given. Where the rubric indicates 'Answer the question' they should respond in any way which is appropriate.

The 'prompts' are given on the recording, although you may prefer to read them yourself or let a partner read them.

Transcript (Examiner's part)
1 • Bonjour, vous désirez?
 • Qu'est-ce que vous voulez pour commencer?
 • Et puis?
 • Je regrette. Nous n'en avons plus. Vous voulez autre chose?
 • Vous voulez quelque chose à boire?
 • Voilà.
2 • Bonjour. Je peux vous aider?
 • Voilà.
 • Deux euros, s'il vous plaît.
 • Il y une banque sur la place du marché.
 • Au café «Soleil». Vous êtes en vacances ici? Vous venez d'où?
3 • Bon, des chambres . . . C'est pour combien de personnes?
 • Et vous restez combien de temps?
 • C'est bon.
 • Ici à gauche.
 • À huit heures. Qu'est-ce que vous allez faire demain?
4 • Tu reçois combien d'argent de poche?
 • Qu'est-ce que tu fais avec ton argent de poche?
 • Quels sont tes passe-temps préférés?
 • Ça coûte combien?
 • Tu as un petit job? Tu travailles pour ton argent?
 • Tu fais des économies? Pourquoi?
 • Tu achètes des cadeaux pour tes amis et ta famille? Qu'est-ce que tu achètes par exemple?
 • Tu vas en ville pour faire du shopping. Qu'est-ce que tu aimes acheter?
 • Tu vas avec qui?
 • Tu vas en vacances. Qu'est-ce que tu aimes acheter?
 • Où as-tu passé les vacances l'année dernière?

Mark Scheme
You may want to use the mark scheme laid down by your GCSE awarding body or you may use the scheme given here.

For each 'utterance':
2 = communicates without ambiguity.
1 = communicates but with some ambiguity.
0 = does not communicate.
[For each role-play: 2 × 4 utterances = 8 marks maximum.]

Higher Speaking (synoptic) [CD 4 track 40]

Students should be given the opportunity to speak at some length on the topics given. You might want to set a target of, say, two minutes per topic. They could use the prompts on the sheet in order to keep going. If you want to avoid a monologue on the student's part you may want to interject with the prompts on the sheet, or other similar ones. The phrases given on the sheet are for guidance only and students should not feel they must include all of them. Conversely, you may want to include other, more unexpected ones in order to challenge more able students.

Transcript (Examiner's prompts)

1 Parle-moi de ton école.
- C'est quelle sorte d'école?
- C'est une école mixte?
- Quelles sont tes matières préférées?
- Parle-moi de ta routine scolaire.
- Parle-moi de tes professeurs.
- Et tes camarades de classe?
- Tu as beaucoup de devoirs?
- Tu fais du sport à l'école?
- Et la musique, et le théâtre?
- Il y a une cantine?
- Tu portes un uniforme?

2 Parle-moi de ta famille et de tes ami(e)s.
- Ils s'appellent comment?
- Comment ça s'écrit?
- Ils ont quel âge?
- Et ses cheveux? Ses yeux? Son caractère?
- Quels sont ses passe-temps préférés?
- Qu'est-ce qu'il ou elle fait comme métier?
- Tu as des animaux domestiques?

3 Parle-moi de la région où tu habites.
- La région s'appelle comment?
- Elle se trouve où?
- C'est une région industrielle?
- C'est une région touristique?
- Qu'est-ce qu'il y a à voir ici?
- Et qu'est-ce qu'il y a à faire?
- Qu'est-ce qu'il y a pour les jeunes?

4 Parle-moi de ta maison ou de ton appartement.
- C'est où?
- C'est quelle sorte de maison ou d'appartement?
- Combien de chambres y a-t-il?
- Tu as ta propre chambre?
- Tu as un jardin? Qu'est-ce qu'il y a dans le jardin?
- C'est calme ici ou c'est bruyant?
- Il y a des magasins tout près?
- Tu aimes habiter ici ou non? Pourquoi ou pourquoi pas?

5 Parle-moi de ton temps libre.
- Quels sont tes passe-temps préférés?
- Tu aimes quelle sorte de musique?
- Tu aimes quels sports?
- Tu le fais avec qui et où?
- Ça coûte combien?
- Qu'est-ce que tu aimes regarder à la télévision?
- Qu'est-ce que tu aimes quand tu vas au cinéma?
- Qu'est-ce que tu as fait le week-end dernier?
- Qu'est-ce que tu as fait pendant les vacances dernières?
- Qu'est-ce que tu vas faire le week-end prochain?

6 Quels sont tes projets pour l'avenir?
- Qu'est-ce que tu vas faire après les examens de GCSE?
- Quelles matières espères-tu étudier et pourquoi?
- Tu espères aller à l'université?
- Tu as choisi quelle profession et pourquoi?
- Tu veux te marier et avoir des enfants?
- Tu veux acheter une voiture?
- Tu veux habiter où? Dans quelle sorte de maison?
- Tu veux voyager? Avec qui?

Mark Scheme

You may want to use the mark scheme laid down by your GCSE awarding body for this type of exercise or you may use the scheme given here.

Communication – Maximum 15 marks
14–15 Good pace. Communicates well. Expands on given information. Responds to unexpected interjections by examiner.
11–13 Covers all necessary information with little prompting. Gives a little extra information.
8–10 Communicates most of the necessary points. May need a little prompting. Some hesitation.
4–7 Communicates some of the main points with some omissions. Somewhat hesitant. Needs prompting.
0–3 Communicates isolated points only. Hesitant. Unforthcoming.

Quality of Language – Maximum 5 marks
5 Confident. Good pronunciation. Wide variety of vocabulary and structures. Excellent use of tenses. Very fluent.
4 Good pronunciation. Good range of vocabulary and structures. Good command of tenses.
3 Some inaccuracy but with pockets of good French. Adequate range of vocabulary and structures.
2 Frequent errors. Basic range of vocabulary and structures only. Hesitant.
1 Anglicised pronunciation. Very limited range of vocabulary and structures.
[Total for the test – 20 marks.]

Foundation Writing (synoptic)
Mark scheme
You may want to use the mark scheme laid down by your GCSE awarding body for this type of exercise or you may use the scheme given here.

1 For each of the five items in each list – 1 mark if communicated clearly (even with inaccurate spelling). Maximum: 5 per list, 40 in all.
2 For each of the the four 'items':
Allow 2 marks for unambiguous communication.
Allow 1 mark if communication is ambiguous.
Allow 0 marks if the item is not communicated.
Ignore errors of spelling and grammar unless they impede communication.   [Total: 8 marks.]

Higher Writing (synoptic)
You may want to give students the choice between the two questions or you may want to ask them to attempt both. No mention of length of students' writing is given on the sheet so that you can adapt this to your own requirements. You may, for example, want to ask students to write the number of words laid down by your GCSE awarding body for this type of task.

Mark Scheme
You should refer to the marking criteria laid down by your awarding body when assessing your students' work on this task. These stimuli may also be given to students who are preparing coursework assignments under either 'open' or 'controlled' conditions.

Name: _____ **Class:** _____ **Date:** _____

Assessment Tasks Score Sheet (Foundation)

	Maximum mark	Score
Assessment Tasks: Units 1–4		
Foundation Listening	6	
Foundation Reading	7	
Foundation Speaking		
Foundation Writing		
Total for Units 1–4		
Assessment Tasks: Units 6–9		
Foundation Listening	15	
Foundation Reading	8	
Foundation Speaking		
Foundation Writing		
Total for Units 6–9		
Assessment Tasks: Units 11–13		
Foundation Listening	10	
Foundation Reading	10	
Foundation Speaking		
Foundation Writing		
Total for Units 11–13		
Course Assessment Tasks		
Foundation Listening 1	8	
Foundation Listening 2	7	
Foundation Reading	10	
Foundation Speaking		
Foundation Writing		
Total for Course Assessment		

Name: _____ **Class:** _____ **Date:** _____

Assessment Tasks Score Sheet (Higher)

	Maximum mark	Score
Assessment Tasks: Units 1–4		
Higher Listening	7	
Higher Reading	8	
Higher Speaking		
Higher Writing		
Total for Units 1–4		
Assessment Tasks: Units 6–9		
Higher Listening 1	8	
Higher Listening 2	7	
Higher Reading	10	
Higher Speaking		
Higher Writing		
Total for Units 6–9		
Assessment Tasks: Units 11–13		
Higher Listening	6	
Higher Reading	8	
Higher Speaking		
Higher Writing		
Total for Units 11–13		
Course Assessment Tasks		
Higher Listening	13	
Higher Reading	8	
Higher Speaking		
Higher Writing		
Total for Course Assessment		